# World Dialogue on Alcohol
# and Drug Dependence

# World Dialogue on Alcohol and Drug Dependence

# World Dialogue on Alcohol and Drug Dependence

edited by

Elizabeth D. Whitney

**Beacon Press   Boston**

Copyright © 1970 by Elizabeth D. Whitney
Library of Congress catalog card number: 76–101329
International Standard Book Number: 0–8070–2776–6
Beacon Press books are published under the auspices
of the Unitarian Universalist Association
Published simultaneously in Canada by Saunders of Toronto, Ltd.
Printed in the United States of America
9    8    7    6    5    4    3    2

## Acknowledgments

With deep appreciation I make acknowledgment to the authors of this book for their valuable contributions of experience, time, and patience, in the face of extremely busy schedules. They have been kind and understanding as we worked together, often under pressure, to fulfill our obligation to bring this volume before the public.

Special thanks go to my husband, James Otis Post, who has worked closely with me, giving technical assistance, and continual encouragement.

Appreciation goes also to the many friends, whose work in the field have fueled the fires of action to bring problems of alcoholism and drug addictions to solution, and who have offered invaluable suggestions and criticism.

Special thanks are due Dr. John B. Jewell of Ayerst Laboratories whose encouragement and support over the years have sparked my spirit through many dark days.

# Contents

Introduction  ix

PART ONE · THE WORLD MEETS THE CHALLENGE OF
ALCOHOLISM · xiii

ARCHER TONGUE, *The Past and Present Status of Alcoholism, an
Overview*  1

LEON FLECK, *The Twelve-Year Struggle Against Alcoholism in
France*  20

THROBJORN KJOLSTAD, M.D., *Alcoholism in Scandinavia*  41

RODNEY SEABORN, M.D., and A. P. DIEHM, *Alcoholism in
Australia*  66

JAROSLAV SKALA, M.D., *Czechoslovakia's Response to
Alcoholism*  90

GIUSEPPE MASTRANGELO, M.D., *Recent Developments in the
Struggle Against Alcoholism in Italy*  116

SELDEN BACON, PH.D., *Meeting the Problems of Alcoholism in the
United States*  134

ELIZABETH D. WHITNEY, *Voluntary Agencies, Their Past and
Future Roles*  146

PART TWO · METHODS OF ATTACKING
ADDICTIONS · 153

JOHN NORRIS, M.D., *Alcoholics Anonymous*  155

RUTH FOX, M.D., and BARRY LEACH, M.A., *Office Treatment of the
Alcoholic by the Private Physician*  173

REV. JOSEPH L. KELLERMANN, *The Minister's Role in Recovery from Alcoholism* 199

HARRISON TRICE, PH.D., *Alcoholism and the Work World: Prevention in a New Light* 221

EBBE CURTIS HOFF, PH.D., M.D., *The Use of Pharmacological Adjuncts in the Comprehensive Therapy of Alcoholics* 240

◂ DAVID J. PITTMAN, PH.D., *Jamming the Revolving Door: New Approaches to the Public Drunkenness Offenders* 263

DAVID J. MYERSON, M.D., *Assessment and Treatment of Youthful Drug Users* 277

H. DAVID ARCHIBALD, *A Response to the Drug Age* 296

*PART THREE · NEW DIMENSIONS · 309*

M. M. GLATT, M.D., *Alcoholism and Drug Dependence—Under One Umbrella?* 311

❧ JORGE MARDONES, M.D., *Predisposition to Alcoholism* 367

• ELIZABETH D. WHITNEY, *Issues and Trends* 384

*Appendix* 389

*Index* 391

# Introduction

On a September morning in 1968, my husband and I made our way into the big, rambling lobby of the Shoreham Hotel in Washington, D.C., to attend the 28th International Congress on Alcohol and Drug Addictions. We entered an atmosphere buzzing with the activity of many of the two thousand experts gathered from around the world to discuss problems of alcohol and drug addictions.

At the registration desk stood nervous latecomers, signing for hotel accommodations, then picking up programs, bulletins, and tickets, moving on to peer at badges and greet friends. Some from other lands, a bit lost in the uproar, milled about searching for familiar faces or sat in oversize armchairs arranging papers. Chairmen for the day's activities were rounding up their speakers, or issuing last-minute instructions to their assistants, while members of the press were being briefed on the chief participants. Slowly the assembly gathered in the main hall for the opening session.

Many of these friends had worked for years with me toward the same goal of advancing knowledge of alcoholism and drug dependence. Thinking of the difficulties we had had in obtaining sound and practical material for our work, an idea came to me that I determined to try out, right here at this congress. I would attempt to assemble a group of eminent experts in the field to write articles on many of the aspects of alcoholism and drug dependence in a kind of dialogue that could benefit all workers in the field, and indeed could be understood and used by anyone interested.

Valuable as they are, professional journals seldom contain informal discussions by experts that might deal with the practical clinical approach to a health problem. They are more likely to feature theoretical studies presented in technical language, which, while extremely important from a pure-research point of view, limits interest to researchers and the scientific community. My conception would hope to reach students, agency workers, and even the general public.

In my years as executive director of a large voluntary agency specializing in problems of alcoholism, I had known at first hand the desperate need of doctors, lawyers, teachers, librarians, institutional directors, clergymen, employers, and educated laymen for concise and reliable information on this major health problem. From time to time all professionals have sought help along these lines, and there is little to offer them except fragments gleaned from medical or scientific papers, or from speeches presented at public conferences, most of which are hastily prepared and hardly intended for immediate use by workers in the field.

With my growing conviction that an urgent need existed for simply written material for practical application, I began to seek reactions to the idea from a number of the world-renowned authorities at the congress. From the beginning, the response was enthusiastic. I began asking for contributions to a compendium of articles which would launch the idea I had inaugurated. Of the fifteen authorities present at the congress who were selected for the volume, not one declined. On the contrary, all offered full cooperation in getting the project under way, not only promising to contribute articles themselves, but introducing me to their colleagues from other countries with the recommendation that they, too, join the group. As a result, after the congress new contributors from Europe, South America, and Australia were soon added to our list of authors.

Inspired by the proof of genuine interest, work began in earnest on the book entitled *World Dialogue on Alcohol and Drug Dependence*. Extensive correspondence led to several meetings among the authors, in the United States in early 1969, and later at the June International Conference in Budapest. This exchange of communication among the contributors developed international understanding of what people were accomplishing in various aspects of the work. It is not possible for a first volume of this sort to be comprehensive; but it does present a selection which represents a number of nations administering active health programs, and a great variety of disciplines. From such a broad spectrum information which in some instances had not been previously available, even to the most knowledgeable, can be understood and studied by any interested reader.

The usual crop of difficulties grew as the work progressed, emphasized by the international character of the book which presented language problems and a few misunderstandings. These were, in time, weeded out, so that ultimately the harvest was fruitful. Unavoidable delays which forced postponement of the original publishing date may have mellowed and improved the book.

I share the hope of the contributing authors that the knowledge and experience accumulated over long years of intensive work and represented by the articles in this volume may be put to immediate practical use, whether in education, research, or on the firing line in the battle against alcohol and drug addictions.

All around the world attitudes toward the great health problems are going through a period of transition. Discussion among the experts, as presented here, can smooth out much misunderstanding and the difficulties which obstruct progress. If through participation by such a broad group of experienced professionals a door is opened to greater knowledge and understanding, this book will have served a useful purpose.

ELIZABETH D. WHITNEY

# Part One

# The World Meets the Challenge of Alcoholism

# The past and present status of alcoholism: an overview

## ARCHER TONGUE

Archer Tongue, executive director of the International Council on Alcohol and Addictions, has organized fifteen successive annual International Institutes on the Prevention and Treatment of Alcoholism. He is ICAA representative to the U.N. Commission on Narcotic Drugs and to the WHO Expert Committee on Drug Dependence, and associate editor of the journal *Alcoholism*. His survey article is an introduction to the more specialized pieces which follow.

In September 1968, nearly 2,000 persons attended an International Congress on the subject of alcoholism in Washington, D.C. In an era when international meetings on every conceivable subject are commonplace, it received only passing notice in the press reports of the day.

At some future date, however, historians of alcoholism may see this event as marking a turning point in the international recognition of alcoholism as a health problem, one worthy of the attention of experts in many disciplines. In the largest congress on alcoholism the world has yet seen, physicians, sociologists, biochemists, jurists, economists, health administrators, clergy, social workers, and others mingled in sessions with many persons who themselves had recovered from the disease and who make a contribution in cooperation with scientific and professional workers in dealing with the medicosocial problem alcoholism represents.

The first scientific congress on alcoholism was held in 1878 in Paris. Has it taken ninety years to get alcoholism recognized and to achieve cooperation among the disciplines? Scientific and public acceptance of alcoholism as a medicosocial problem—indeed as a problem at all—has been slow and uneven. It is true that from the earliest period of recorded history alcoholic beverages have been produced and consumed, and it is equally true that society throughout history has tried to deal with problems arising from their use. In the last two centuries, however, supposed shortcuts to a solution have prevented an understanding of the problem as essentially one of public health. Legislative devices to prohibit or restrict consumption or to control production and distribution in specific ways have been given priority and have hindered the approach which has now brought together many disciplines in a concerted program of research, education, and treatment. This, then, would seem to be the international achievement marked by the Washington Congress.

## EARLY APPROACHES IN COMBATING ALCOHOLISM

It is not surprising that socially conscious citizens in Northern Europe and North America, in the face of widespread drunkenness in the nineteenth and early twentieth centuries, promoted moralistic, persuasive, and later legislative programs to combat alcoholism. Even though certain pioneering physicians in the nineteenth century saw alcohol abuse as a medical problem, the times were not propitious for general acceptance of this concept. It was perhaps inevitable that an extreme frontal attack on alcoholism—total prohibition—had to be tried before society was ready to accept the so-called drunkard as an alcoholic, someone to be helped and rehabilitated through individual and public initiative. This does not minimize the importance and indeed the imperative need of prevention programs, but highlights the need to condition social attitudes toward those persons who, in a society where the use of alcoholic beverages is part of the social fabric, develop into compulsive drinkers.

In the 1920s, League of Nations proposals to recognize alcoholism as a health problem were largely abortive. Neither governments nor individuals had grasped the concept of alcoholism as more than an individual weakness which could be controlled by persuasion or legislative measures. In some of the wine-producing countries a laissez faire attitude prevailed. There were virtually no restrictions, and concern about alcoholism was viewed as a threat to vital economic interests.

## NEW APPROACHES

In the mid-thirties new approaches began to emerge. Alcohol-dependence was more widely seen as a compulsive condition needing treatment in a health setting. This coincided with the notion that alcoholics could help rehabilitate one another on the basis of their own experience and insights.

These developments were particularly marked in North America, which had experienced extreme legislative policies in regard to alcohol. In many European countries the acceptance of the new ideas did not represent a complete break with the past, since there had been a certain continuity of cooperation and even identification between those who favored legislative measures and those involved in treating alcoholic patients. Acceptance of the new ideas was probably more difficult in those countries which had neither a strong moralistic or legalistic movement against alcohol, nor much scientific or medical interest in the problem. In these nations the use of alcoholic beverages was often an integral part of the daily diet and had no connotation of deviance from accepted moral, religious, or social standards. In France, for example, the idea that alcohol is a dependence-producing drug did not easily meet popular acceptance.

When the World Health Organization (WHO) came into being at the end of World War II, there was a new climate of opinion on alcoholism in many of the member states. Alcohol was considered an area of public-health activity and a valid concern of the organization. The impetus given to the concept of alcoholism as an illness by WHO in the 1950s led to the establishment of public and voluntary organizations on all continents to aid the alcoholic and inform the public. Nearly all the states and provinces of the United States and Canada organized official services for alcoholism treatment, either through special commissions or foundations integrated in state or provincial health departments.

The year 1954 is particularly noteworthy in that two nations— France and the Soviet Union—reversed previous practice and recognized alcoholism as a national health problem. The French set up a Special Committee for the Study and Publicity of Alcoholism, directly responsible to the Prime Minister; and the Soviet Union initiated a nationwide program of education and treatment in which all medical personnel and institutions were expected to cooperate. Since 1954, country after country has entered the field, establishing services that reflect the structure of health administration and the characteristics of the problem in their own areas. Even countries such as Spain and Italy, where the problem was formerly thought to be minimal, have been obliged to provide services to cope with the growing incidence of alcoholism.

A very wide spectrum of arrangements, procedures, and services to aid the treatment and rehabilitation of alcoholics is now in operation throughout the world. In addition to using existing general mental and industrial health services, a large number of distinctive services specially adapted to the needs of the alcoholic have been instituted, based on experience obtained in the field over the past twenty-five years. These services include information centers and consultation bureaus, sobering-up stations, hangover clinics, halfway houses, hostels, alcoholics' clubs, rehabilitation farms and villages, day hospitals, mobile rural units, telephone-therapy services, and even centers for specific professional groups, such as treatment homes for alcoholic clergy. Dedicated persons, medical and lay, are found all over the world, and in the most varied systems, initiating, implementing, and improving the facilities at national, provincial, municipal, and individual levels.

There is much discussion about whether most alcoholics need prolonged hospital treatment or can be successfully treated in outpatient facilities. A British investigation concluded that treatment services should include all types of facilities, comprising both inpatient and outpatient, long-term and short-term components, if every type of alcoholic is to be helped.

## A NEED FOR EVALUATION

In the immediate future, there is a real need for increased impartial evaluation of existing services. Budget and personnel are limited everywhere, and it is urgent that program efficiency be appraised so that each community may have the services best suited to its needs.

The World Health Organization, which by means of special subcommittees and seminars in the 1950s guided governments on a broad range of topics related to alcoholism and its treatment, has in recent years, through its Expert Committee, specifically concerned itself with advising member states on services needed for prevention and treatment of alcohol dependence at the present time. Particular attention will now be given to evaluating existing programs, and the results will help countries improve services, and encourage developing countries to set up new services on a sound basis. This is important, because in many areas, for example the newly independent African states, alcoholism represents a significant health problem. Critical evaluation has already started in North America through various studies of programs and their problems. If progress already made in getting health authorities to accept and underwrite needed programs is maintained, realistic evaluation of program achievement and potential must be undertaken without delay.

## MOTIVATION FOR TREATMENT

Perhaps the major task facing those who desire to improve effectiveness in helping the alcoholic recover is that of motivating the client or patient to treatment. This is indispensable if the alcoholism rate in any community is to be kept within bounds. Various community agencies can and do play a vital role in this area. Assuming that a majority of alcoholics are employed somewhere, it is clear that early detection and encouragement to seek advice and possible treatment can be facilitated with the cooperation of employers. In some countries, for example France, industry began to be interested in this question through research which indicated that alcohol abuse caused industrial accidents. A further step was to recognize that it might be in the interest of both management and labor to seek to reduce accidents and absenteeism, not by dismissing the employee, but by helping him overcome his disability.

The concern of industry, business management, and trade unions varies greatly from country to country. In some nations industrial health programs are actively dealing with alcoholism; and specialized programs have even been set up to counsel employees. In other nations virtually nothing is done. An excellent program of early detection is used in one of the regions of the French State Railways. In an annual medical examination of every employee—manual, clerical, or administrative—testing for incipient alcoholism is a standard procedure. The early detection of alcoholism in industry, and the role of the different cadres (management, foremen, fellow employees, industrial doctors, etc.) is receiving considerable attention at the present time. Experience and research will show how the various components of a modern business or industry can best work together to help the prospective alcoholic employee, and in this way the enterprise as a whole.

There is also the need to motivate to seek treatment people suffering from alcoholism who do not go out to work, or are self-employed, or employed in small industrial or business units. The family doctor and clergyman, who visit homes and are often consulted about problems at an early stage, can make a special contribution. Mobilizing doctors and the clergy to encourage early consultation and treatment is highly desirable. More and more it is recognized that these professional people, as well as many others, should receive during their training up-to-date information about alcohol dependence and how it may be treated. The World Health Organization has recommended that all medical students be given adequate information on this problem, as indeed should clergy, social workers, probation officers, and members of similar professions. Some alcoholism programs provide training to community professional people. To combat alcoholism effectively, community health and religious institutions should be equipped to counsel those who need help with drinking problems.

Many countries are debating compulsory treatment measures. It has often been held that successful treatment of alcoholism depends on one's seeking help voluntarily and taking an active interest in the process of rehabilitation. Certain countries have, however, foreseen the possibility of compulsory treatment in their legislation, empowering authorities to insist on treatment if the alcoholic is a danger to himself or to others. This seems to be a reasonable provision to protect an alcoholic's family, but it should be used only as an ultimate resort. It has been shown, however, that treatment under compulsion can be effective and enduring. In fact, some kind of compulsion exercised by employers or family often occurs in cases of voluntary motivation. The paternal attitude to cover up for an alcoholic, sometimes characteristic of employers or colleagues, does no real service to the individual concerned. In various areas of public health, authorities have certain compulsory powers in the interest of individual and community health. Used sparingly, there would seem to be no valid reason why such powers cannot be effective in the field of alcoholism.

## LEGAL ACCEPTANCE OF THE DISEASE CONCEPT

Widespread use of the disease concept of alcoholism has naturally had repercussions in the judicial field. There is inevitably a time lag between the enunciation of medical definitions and their acceptance by legal authorities, who must necessarily exercise prudence in evaluating new ideas. Recognizing alcoholism as a disease for sickness insurance benefit is a case in point. Acceptance is gaining ground in many countries, but there are many aspects of this particular problem which need discussion and elucidation. The question of estimating the working capacity of the alcoholic after treatment, the degree of invalidity, and associated problems are under study in different countries.

A question which has stirred public opinion recently is whether it is just to criminally prosecute a drunkenness-offender who has committed no offense other than being drunk in public. If alcoholism is an illness and the alcoholic is a sick person, it follows that his arrest and criminal prosecution solely for exhibiting a symptom of his illness is as arbitrary and as much a denial of human rights as would be the arrest of a diabetic who collapses and causes a stir in a public place because of insulin imbalance.

In drawing this question to the attention of the United Nations Commission on Human Rights recently, the International Council on Alcohol and Addictions expressed the view that all alcoholics taken into custody solely because of public intoxication should be subject to separate treatment appropriate to their status as unconvicted persons, as stated in the international covenant on civil and political rights. It is felt that it may be necessary at times to take an intoxicated alcoholic into custody to prevent him from doing damage to himself or to others. The authority, however, should be based on medical rather than criminal grounds. Just as an injured or incapacitated ill person may be removed from public streets or buildings by the police and taken to a hospital without being arrested, so should an intoxicated alcoholic be treated. Should it become necessary for the state to exercise control over the liberty of an individual, a separate type of non-prosecutory proceeding before a judge on the advice and recommendation of a doctor should be held before the individual can be detained. This is in line with respect for the inherent dignity of the human person and protects him from degrading treatment.

In many large metropolitan areas today, the problem of public drunkenness is a time-consuming and expensive operation for police and judicial authorities. The central sobering-up station, like those operating in cities of Poland and other countries of Eastern Europe, represents a practical attempt to improve the present situation. The operation of sobering-up centers, under the joint administration of police and health authorities, where drunken persons found in public streets can be taken, receive necessary medical attention, sleep off the effects of their abuse, be advised and directed to treatment if they return repeatedly, and where they pay for lodging and attention without the stigma of incarceration in a police cell, has proved a great advantage. This system has been put into practice in some American cities, modified in accord with local conditions. The prefect of the Paris police has for some years operated a service for the counseling and rehabilitation of alcoholics, as well as for members of his own force who may have drinking problems. Such action is in line with a trend to involve police and judicial authorities in the therapeutic procedure, thus stimulating interdisciplinary concern with the alcoholic in the interest of public health. Moreover, for those alcoholics who commit offenses calling for prison sentences, there should be opportunity in prison for treatment and rehabilitation. Prison programs to help alcoholics are operating in the United States, Czechoslovakia, and elsewhere.

The dilemma authorities face everywhere, when courts refer alcoholics who are drunkenness-offenders for medical treatment, is that rehabilitation facilities are often not available; and existing services are stretched to the limit of their intake capacity. While courts and detention authorities welcome easing their burden in confining drunken persons, treatment facilities almost everywhere need to be expanded.

## ALCOHOL AS A SOCIAL PROBLEM

As mentioned earlier, in some countries—notably in North America—the prohibition experiment resulted in neglect of the problems of alcohol in society, as distinct from those of alcoholism. Since there was widespread revulsion against criticism of drinking, it was appropriate to accept the concept of alcoholism as an illness and the possibility of successful treatment and at the same time declare that such action was in no way related to social drinking. In fact, it was pointed out that only a certain proportion of those who drank socially became alcoholics. Programs in alcoholism education in the immediate prewar years and after did not want to be associated with efforts to restrict social drinking through legislation. It was understandable therefore that the emphasis should have been placed on alcoholism and not on alcohol problems.

The general public's attitude toward organizations concerned with alcoholism is crucial in many countries, and it is interesting to note that the problem of obtaining public understanding of desirable goals in the matter of alcoholism as a public health problem is hindered by semantic difficulties. For example, in Latin and Slavic languages it is difficult to avoid the preposition *against* even when no prohibitory sense is intended. English is fortunate in that the preposition *on* can easily be used in relation to activities dealing with alcoholism in a way that is not appropriate in many other languages. The importance of this question is not always realized, but the notion that anyone dealing with the problem of alcoholism is somehow concerned with prohibition or restriction is not easily dispelled. The illness concept has been of great service in changing negative reactions to public and private discussion of alcoholism problems.

It has become increasingly clear that in the last five years more and more bodies hitherto exclusively concerned with the illness concept of alcoholism and with treatment services have begun to realize that the problems of alcoholism and the problems of alcohol cannot be separated. In other words, drinking and traffic accidents; education on the effects of alcohol; legislation on the production, distribution, sale, pricing, and taxation of beverages; liquor advertising; and prevailing drinking customs are all interrelated in the total problem we call alcoholism. In fact, the word *alcoholism* in French and other continental languages signifies the whole complex of problems associated with man's use of beverage alcohol, and is not simply a disease concept.

The subject with perhaps the greatest impact in the public mind, since it touches everyone very closely, is traffic safety. Scientific investigation has clearly shown that the use of alcohol is related to traffic accidents; and many countries have laws dealing with this problem. One of the main issues bearing on this question today is the need for legislative coordination concerning blood–alcohol concentration deemed dangerous for a driver and subject to penalty by law. For example, a truck driver traveling from Norway to Italy might pass through four or five different regulatory systems, varying from strict legislative control in Norway to no specific restrictions in Italy.

Other forms of transport face alcohol problems. Railroads in most countries have for many years enforced regulations concerning alcohol use by employees. Nearly all public aviation companies have precise provisions concerning alcohol consumption to which pilots must adhere. More attention must be given to the relation between alcohol consumption and flying safety in private aviation. In the area of marine transport WHO indicated in 1968 that an analysis of illnesses and accidents affecting seafarers showed that the underlying cause is often alcohol masked under another name. In a study of deaths on Swedish ships, for example, an outstanding number of accidents with all sorts of designations were found on closer scrutiny to be attributed to intoxication. It is also interesting to note that the forthcoming Fifth International Conference on Alcohol and Traffic will include problems of alcohol and space travel.

In some countries, enforcement of legislation concerning drink and driving has no connection with health authorities concerned with alcoholism treatment. On the other hand, in areas where road accidents involving alcohol are reported to health authorities, it has been possible to discover and to help persons suffering from alcoholism who were either unaware of their condition or had not sought appropriate treatment. This is one instance of valuable interagency cooperation.

From a world viewpoint, there is a growing tendency everywhere for governments to see the problem of the drinking driver in a most serious light. A particular example in recent years has been Great Britain. Although driving under the influence of drink had been an offense since 1925, no compulsory tests for blood-alcohol concentration had been required by law until recently. Such proposals were met by the firmly held view that they would interfere with the liberty of the individual. Strong legislation has now been introduced whereby any driver can be asked to take the first stage of an alcohol test on being stopped by the police for cautioning, for some minor traffic infringement, or when involved in an accident whether at fault or not; in fact, any driver the police suspect has been drinking can be forced to take the test. Although finding these restrictive measures irksome, the public has gradually accepted their validity and remolded social patterns of drinking to conform to the requirements of the law. The government's advisory leaflet in Britain advises "if you are going to a party, decide beforehand who is going to do the drinking and who is going to do the driving."

Although transport accidents involving alcohol receive much more prominence, there are other areas in which drinking in-

volves hazards. In some countries considerable research has been
done on the relation of alcohol to industrial accidents. In France,
for example, where drinking in some circles may start early in the
day and continue with and without meals throughout the day—
even though drunkenness is rare—it has been found that drinking habits have a significant bearing on the industrial accident
rate.

The World Health Organization has drawn attention to an
area in which little research has been done, the relation between
home accidents and alcohol consumption. This is a problem quite
distinct from that of the alcoholic's treatment of his family which
has received considerable attention. While newspapers often carry
stories about individuals falling or setting fire to the home where
one would suspect alcohol to be involved, there are no statistics
on this subject. It would seem that the relationship between drinking habits and accident-proneness deserves scientific study.

The foregoing observations indicate some of the issues which
persons concerned with alcohol and alcoholism problems are
facing throughout the world today. Basically, however, the most
tantalizing problem of all is to know how to frame a program
of education and information which will give people a sound understanding of the subject without evoking hostility, disbelief,
resentment, skepticism, ridicule, apathy, or indifference—reactions occurring around the world today when alcoholism problems are raised.

The variety of forms in which alcohol may be consumed as a
beverage is matched by the astonishing variety of attitudes, beliefs, prejudices, traditions, and misunderstandings which accompany its use and misuse. Anthropological research has shown that
even in primitive societies alcohol consumption played a special
role, such as providing relief from tension on particular occasions,
for example, after the harvest. Such community drinking occasions were strictly controlled by tribal leaders.

The use of alcoholic beverages in religious ritual, social hospitality, ceremonial functions, and festive occasions has given
the alcoholic beverage a symbolic function in social life today.
The places where alcoholic beverages are sold—the French bistro,

the English pub, or the ubiquitous bar—all play an important social role in the life of a community. Thus few people can escape making judgments on alcoholic beverages; that is to say, whether or not they wish to drink them, how much they wish to drink, how much is good for them, etc. Such judgments will usually be couched in some such term as "moderation," but there is no very precise indication of just what this implies. Most people are aware that alcohol abuse does exist and that certain persons become addicted to alcohol, but the attitude toward excessive consumption is ambivalent, often a combination of amused tolerance and condemnation of the addict for his so-called "vice" and inability to control his drinking.

## EDUCATION AND PREVENTION PROGRAMS

In the 1920s and 30s there were a variety of attitudes toward beverage alcohol use and control. In the United States and in Finland total prohibition of alcoholic beverages was applied. In Britain and elsewhere a complicated licensing system governing sale and consumption was considered the most effective means of keeping alcoholism in check. In Germany, the view of alcohol as a racial poison was emphasized, and experiments were conducted to attempt to show direct genetic influences of alcohol consumption. In the Soviet Union, alcoholism was viewed as a product of capitalist society which would be eliminated by nationalization of production and sale, and by individual self-restraint.

Today the different philosophies underlying information and teaching programs may be summarized under five categories:

*1.* Education to encourage abstinence or strict moderation. In Finland, Sweden, and Norway the state subsidizes temperance organizations engaged in alcohol education.

*2.* Education to show that alcoholism is an illness and that the alcoholic needs treatment.

*3.* Education aimed at limiting consumption. Advice to the population to reduce drinking; setting a maximum daily consumption level, as in France; or urging general moderation, as in Poland.

   4. Inclusion of the subject in a general program of health education, as in Czechoslovakia.

   5. Education to show what are good and bad drinking habits.

Of course, in any program one may find a combination of approaches, and the emphasis depends to a large extent on prevailing traditions, attitudes, and drinking patterns. In France, where the third and fifth approaches are emphasized, alcoholism is considered a nutritional problem. In fact, a national congress on alcoholism in France was held under the title: "Alcoholism —a Nutritional Error."

More and more it is being recognized that, to be effective, educational effort needs to be directed at specific sectors of the population. In Switzerland, the State Federal Commission Against Alcoholism has prepared a handbook for all medical practitioners. Material has also been prepared for migrant workers, in their own languages. Workers in the building trades, for example, are particularly vulnerable to alcoholism. To stimulate an informed awareness of the problem among professional groups—especially doctors, nurses, health administrators, social workers, and police —the Group of Studies on Alcoholism was established a few years ago in French Switzerland. This body regularly organizes training conferences for professional people. In some European countries there are medical societies on alcoholism, such as the Doctors' Study Group on Alcoholism in France, the British Medical Council on Alcoholism, and organizations of physicians interested in alcoholism in Scandinavia. We can now discern a real effort to reach other professions. In Sweden, conferences have been arranged for journalists, and material has been prepared for the army. Such specialized approaches have succeeded in securing cooperation of professions on a national or regional basis.

   Alcoholism is primarily a disorder of the middle aged, but nevertheless has its roots in youth and young adulthood. The younger generation therefore must have a particular place in any prevention program. While some legal regulation of consumption, including taxation and pricing, has its place, attitude influence should be the main aim of alcoholism education. Young people should be aware of harmful ways of drinking and understand that drunkenness is undesirable in social life today. Instruction in school should be reinforced by parents and other adults when youth begins experimenting with drinking. In many communities young people use alcohol as early as age thirteen or fourteen, often at home in the presence of their family, modeling their behavior on adult patterns and regarding drinking as a sign of maturity.

There has been considerable discussion in different countries recently about the desirability of teaching young people how to drink. The argument has been made that normal drinking habits, especially with meals, can serve as protection against alcoholism. This viewpoint tends to find support in countries where drinking outside meals is customary. Two comments should be made about this view. First, the possibility of successfully transferring specific drinking habits from one culture to another is problematical; instead of replacement, the result may be reinforcement and extension of existing drinking habits. Secondly, countries often cited as having correct drinking habits, such as Italy and Spain, now face considerable alcoholism problems themselves. At the recent international Institute on Alcoholism held in Milan, Italian specialists reported that with growing urbanization it had become impossible to maintain traditional drinking habits, and health authorities were obliged to deal with the problem. Even in the south of Italy, in Naples, the subject was sufficiently serious to warrant holding a medical symposium on alcoholism in December 1968. Government-sponsored alcoholism-prevention programs in such wine-growing countries as France, Hungary, and Bulgaria definitely advise against early alcohol-beverage consumption by youth, even with meals in a family setting.

A Canadian alcoholism program reveals that in a typical decade about 25 percent of the alcoholics either die or make a recovery. From decade to decade, however, total incidence of alcoholism increases about 15 percent so that each decade about 40 percent (just under 4 percent a year) is being added to the total. Thus the task of the prevention program is to reduce from 4,000 to 2,000 or less the total of new alcoholics each year. The problem will decrease slowly if this can be accomplished.

One suspects that comparable situations exist in many other areas. Clearly, any effective treatment program must bear in mind the need to develop preventive techniques. It should be recognized that the distinction between prevention and treatment is rather artificial, since both activities are part of one complex action, to limit alcoholism and its effects.

## A COMPREHENSIVE APPROACH TO ALCOHOL AND DRUGS

Associating alcohol with other drugs in a prevention, treatment, and research program has been a recent development. This approach was endorsed by the fourteenth report of the WHO Expert Committee on Mental Health issued in 1967. Its subject was "Services for the Prevention and Treatment of Dependence on Alcohol and Other Drugs." To support this approach it was pointed out that there were many similarities in causes and treatment. Moreover, transfer from one drug to another and the combined use of drugs are increasingly observed. In many countries the changing pattern of drug abuse by adolescents is significant and poses many problems. Much has been achieved in recent years in removing the stigma from alcoholism. Public and official attitudes have moved from a condemnatory to a therapeutic concept with recognition of alcoholism as an illness. This has not happened to the same degree with drug abuse, and a similar change in attitude toward drugs should be encouraged.

The recommendation of the WHO report will possibly have considerable influence in stimulating a comprehensive approach to these questions on the part of many governments and local authorities. In certain countries legislatures are already dealing jointly with the two problems. In general, however, the two subjects have been separated, particularly in prevention and law enforcement. Moreover, in a number of European countries the problem of drug addiction did not until recently (and in some countries still does not) represent an acute problem. However, it is becoming clear that increased use and abuse of psychotropic drugs is of growing concern to governments and the public in many countries.

Organizations already engaged in both areas include the Alcoholism and Drug Addiction Research Foundation, Ontario, Canada; the Office for the Prevention and Treatment of Alcoholism and Drug Addiction of Quebec, Canada; the National Federation of Consultation Bureaus and Institutions for the Treatment of Alcoholics and Other Addicts, Belgium; the Foundation for Research and Treatment of Alcoholism and Drug Dependence of New South Wales, Australia; the Central Office Against Addiction Dangers, Federal Republic of Germany; and the Addiction Research Unit, Maudsley Hospital, London, United Kingdom. The North American Association of Alcoholism Programs is also including information on drug dependence in services it offers to members, some of which have adopted the comprehensive approach.

In the area of international agreement and law-enforcement, alcohol, "the domesticated drug," as Jellinek termed it, is in a quite different category from other drugs. The United Nations Narcotics Commission in 1968 stated that the abuse of alcohol was not within the terms of the commission.

The comprehensive approach is being applied at a different pace and in a different way, according to local conditions. What is important is to gain acceptance of the fact that the drug (whether alcohol or another substance), the user, and the environment are interacting factors which must be taken into account in developing an overall program to deal with abuse.

## NATIONAL AND INTERDISCIPLINARY COOPERATION

It is with some satisfaction that one can record growing cooperation among the many organizations trying to deal with alcoholism problems in any one country. For many years in the Scandinavian countries, for example, it has been common to speak of a national alcohol policy (*Alkoholpolitik*). All elements in treatment, prevention, and research, as well as those involved in production, distribution and sale, in fiscal measures, and legislation, are to some extent in contact, so that there is some coordination in framing national policy on alcohol questions. In Poland national cooperation was felt to be of such importance that in 1957 an interministerial Commission on Alcoholism was appointed, composed of the vice-ministers of nine ministries and chaired by the Minister of Labor and Social Services. As one of its tasks, the commission had to work out a national plan, which led to the enactment of comprehensive legislation on alcoholism, taxation, sale, and consumption regulations. Directives to implement legislation were drawn up by various ministries—Health, Labor, Communications, Marine, etc.

Finland, Hungary, and Norway have also passed omnibus legislation, and it is becoming recognized that the complex of problems associated with alcohol consumption and alcoholism cannot be separated. The establishment of national research institutes or foundations in Norway, Finland, Chile, the Netherlands, and the United States, as well as regional research foundations in Canada and elsewhere, demonstrates a trend in interdisciplinary cooperation which will facilitate a total approach to the problem.

A national alcoholism policy will exploit the use of the mass media to reach every segment of the population. The World Health Organization has already contributed much in focusing the attention of governments and health authorities on alcoholism questions. Other United Nations agencies concerned with social and cultural affairs can be utilized. Regional governmental bodies, such as the Council of Europe and the League of Arab States, both of which have been represented at recent meetings of the International Council on Alcohol and Addictions, have various aspects of these problems under consideration. Furthermore, there are a variety of nongovernmental, international bodies covering many areas of human activity—medical, social, educational, and religious—whose points of reference relate in some way to alcohol problems. It is imperative to mobilize such resources in creating informed world opinion. Alcoholic beverages are consumed almost everywhere, but alcoholism or alcohol misuse is by no means everywhere understood.

After ninety years of international cooperation, some headway has been made in fostering a constructive, humanitarian attitude toward those human beings who directly or indirectly are exposed to suffering through almost unavoidable deviant use of a socially accepted and widespread drug. In this age of international sharing of knowledge and resources, there is a potential in the field of alcoholism for international exchange of experience among scientific and professional workers, as well as recovered alcoholics, which gives grounds for believing that the problems of living with alcohol in modern society may not be insuperable.

# The twelve-year struggle against alcoholism in France

## LEON FLECK

The wine-producing nations encounter special difficulty in that both tradition and economic interests prevent them from even acknowledging the existence of alcoholism, much less recognizing it as a serious disease. Leon Fleck ably describes the twelve-year struggle in France, first to win acceptance of alcoholism as a health problem, and then to begin a program to control it. He is presently secretary general of the High Committee on Study and Information on Alcoholism, attached to the staff of the Prime Minister.

## THE PROBLEM OF ALCOHOLISM IN FRANCE

Alcoholism is a common scourge throughout the entire world in both industrialized and developing nations, but it has certain characteristics peculiar to each country and region. In France, for example, it produces both economic and social results which deserve mention here.

### Economic aspects

Alcohol plays an important role in the French economy in terms of both production and trade. Everyone knows that France is the world's largest producer of wine; but, more important, wine growing constitutes the single or main form of income in several of the *départements* (the four *départements* of Languedoc-Roussillon, the Bordeaux region, the Loire country, Bourgogne, and Alsace). It is estimated that wine growing involves about one million people. The total production of wine, varying from year to year, averages about 60 million hectoliters* (1.5 billion gallons) and often reached 75 million hectoliters (1.9 billion gallons) when Algeria was part of France.

*Table 1*

DECLARED PRODUCTION OF WINE
(in thousands of hectoliters)

| YEAR | France | France & Algeria |
|------|--------|------------------|
| | | QUANTITY |
| 1955 | 60,065.6 | 74,464.3 |
| 1956 | 50,450.0 | 69,080.9 |
| 1957 | 32,499.9 | 47,785.5 |
| 1958 | 46,144.9 | 59,971.6 |
| 1959 | 58,276.4 | 76,877.0 |
| 1960 | 61,192.7 | 77,043.5 |
| 1961 | 46,714.8 | 62,346.7 |
| 1962 | 73,478.0 | |
| 1963 | 56,083.0 | |
| 1964 | 60,563.0 | |
| 1965 | 66,568.0 | |
| 1966 | 60,935.0 | |
| 1967 | 60,992.9 | |
| 1968 | 65,120.2 | |

Beer production is nearly 20 million hl., while cider fluctuates between 10 and 18 million hl. from year to year.

Finally, the production of distilled spirits is equally important, but our discussion will be limited to the production of those spirits which are regulated by or named after their place of origin (cognacs, armagnacs, mirabell, kirsch, etc.) and which directly concern the producers and private distillers.

The advantage of the private distiller lies in the potential for the producers of wine or distilled fruit to have personal accounts without paying the corresponding taxes within the yearly 10-liter limit of pure alcohol, a privilege which has been exploited in the

---

* 1 hectoliter = 26.4 gallons [translator's note].

past. In 1960, for example, there were 3,110,081 registered distillers; only 2 million actually did any distilling.

The figures on consumption of alcoholic beverages are perhaps even more striking than production figures as shown for the year 1960:

> about 59 million hl. of wine
> about 16 million hl. of beer
> about 11 million hl. of cider

In addition, the consumption of distilled alcohol (aperitifs, liqueurs) rose to nearly 500,000 hl. of pure alcohol in this same year.

The total consumption of alcoholic beverages of all kinds (beer, wine, aperitifs, liqueurs, etc.) represents 8,380,000 hl. of pure alcohol.

If we compare the various totals of consumption with the adult population, we obtain the following volume per adult, still for the year 1960:

> 189.4 liters* of wine
> 35.4 liters of beer
> 27.2 liters of pure alcohol (all spirits included)

In terms of spending, the consumption of alcoholic beverages (both domestic and imported) represents about 12 percent of household expenses for the year 1960. Let us point out further, in order to emphasize the economic import of this problem, that in France there are 238,302 cafes and 143,910 liquor stores.

### Social aspects

The outstanding importance of alcohol in the French economy exercises a considerable influence—or more precisely, a pressure —on the social behavior of the French people. Alcohol, in all its forms, is part of the French social life. Wine, the most popular national drink, and the customary aperitif (liqueur to a lesser degree) are commonplace in all social classes, including the most

* 1 liter = 1.057 quarts.

*Table 2*

TOTAL CONSUMPTION OF WINE

(A.O.C., V.D.Q.S., V.C.C.)*** (in hectoliters)

| YEARS | TAXED TRADE V.D.Q.S., V.C.C. | TAXED TRADE A.O.C. | TOTAL TAX-FREE TRADE* | TOTAL |
|---|---|---|---|---|
| *1956/1957* | 46,052,660 | 3,764,700 | 10,473,000 | 60,290,360 |
| *1957/1958* | 45,141,004 | 3,168,293 | 7,523,630 | 55,832,927 |
| *1958/1959* | 41,842,563 | 3,014,933 | 11,526,607 | 56,384,103 |
| *1959/1960* | 42,891,492 | 3,526,954 | 11,867,943 | 58,286,389 |
| *1960/1961* | 42,226,197 | 3,756,959 | 13,188,090 | 59,171,246 |
| *1961/1962* | 42,755,352 | 3,975,287 | 9,706,357 | 56,436,996 |
| *1962/1963* | 42,692,362 | 4,564,886 | 12,565,660 | 59,822,022 |
| *1963/1964* | 43,360,216 | 4,918,463 | 11,297,240 | 59,575,919 |
| *1964/1965* | 43,156,443 | 5,080,747 | 9,997,994 | 58,235,184 |
| *1965/1966* | 43,064,909 | 5,242,453 | 10,194,919 | 58,502,281 |
| *1966/1967* | 42,457,000 | 5,357,000 | 10,801,932 | 58,615,945 |
| *1967/1968* ** | 41,615,000 | 5,310,000 | 9,595,000 | 56,520,000 |

* Tax-free trade = domestic consumption by the producers
  1. Tax-free trade at the A.O.C. represents a very small volume (on the average of 600,000 to 700,000 hl. per year).
  2. The actual amount of tax-free trade should be decreased by the loss caused by evaporation during the process of condensation—a quantity which varies accordingly with each year.
** Compared with the preceding years, we record a total decrease of:
  0.8% for the A.O.C.
  1.9% for the other wines
*** A.O.C. = Vin d'appellation d'origine controlée (excellent quality)
  V.D.Q.S. = Vin delimite de qualite superieur    (superior quality)
  V.C.C. = Vin de consommation courant          (table wine)

modest. In the villages the peasants love to "have a nip" from their own products, especially in the morning, in or with their coffee.

But France is also the country of good living and of moderation. Both these characteristics are reflected even in consumption of alcohol. Drinking is heavy, but regular, so that alcoholism assumes forms that are not always easily detected. This phenome-

*Table 3*

## TOTAL CONSUMPTION OF PURE ALCOHOL CONTAINED IN ALL TYPES OF ALCOHOLIC DRINKS

Wine, cider, beer, aperitifs [whiskey included], pure natural wines, brandy, and liqueurs (in thousands of hectoliters)

| YEAR | NUMBER |
|------|--------|
| 1951 | 7,810 |
| 1952 | 8,140 |
| 1953 | 8,290 |
| 1954 | 8,410 |
| 1955 | 8,570 |
| 1956 | 8,670 |
| 1957 | 8,560 |
| 1958 | 8,390 |
| 1959 | 8,300 |
| 1960 | 8,380 |
| 1961 | 8,490 |
| 1962 | 8,510 |
| 1963 | 8,660 |
| 1964 | 8,940 |
| 1965 | 9,010 |
| 1966 | 8,970 |

SOURCE: I.N.S.E.E.

non has been recognized by all observers, particularly Jellinek. Thus, if the number of excessive drinkers, in France can be placed at 2 million, as stated in a study by Dr. May, 1959, or 13 percent of the active male population between 20 and 55 years of age (according to a controlled study by Dr. LeGo in 1967), the number of exceptionally heavy drinkers is minimal.

Similarly, alcoholism in France, caused generally by excessive consumption of wine, is usually not the primary type which is based on psychological need, but rather the secondary type based on habit. This type is much less obvious (no signs of drunkenness), but its long-term effects are more harmful because more deceiving. This peculiar nature of alcoholism in France undoubtedly explains why alcoholic cirrhosis is more frequent than elsewhere, and why French doctors attribute cirrhosis of the liver to the excessive consumption of alcoholic beverages.

Caused essentially by habitual drinking, French alcoholism is due as well to ignorance fostered more or less by those concerned. Actually, since the signs of drunkenness are generally absent, the drinker is not aware of the long-term effects, and when they become manifest—often after several years—it is obviously too late.

Thus, we have isolated the two main causes of alcoholism in France, and if we are to conquer the enemy, action must be taken on these two fronts, namely:

> —the socioeconomic pressure exerted by alcohol, and its political implications
> —the social habits based on ignorance


## THE CREATION OF THE SPECIAL COMMITTEE

Alcoholism, which caused a severe problem in France before World War II, had, by the same token, practically disappeared during the war because the production and consequently the consumption of alcoholic beverages fell to almost nothing. But after the war, the scourge returned and spread by leaps and bounds. Between 1946 and 1955, deaths caused by alcoholism soared from 2,700 to 13,000; and the number admitted to psychiatric hospitals for alcoholism increased from 800 to 11,000.

The government then decided to take up the fight and intensify the battle against alcoholism which, until then, had been staged sporadically and with very limited funds by private organizations. In 1954 it created a special organization linked directly to the Prime Ministry and called the Special Committee for the Study and Publicity of Alcoholism to which it entrusted a threefold mission:

> —to study the problems of alcohol and alcoholism
> —to recommend to the government all measures capable of reducing alcoholism

—to distribute information to the public in conjunction with concerned groups, both public and private.

Armed with the information made available through scientific study, the special committee was charged with battling the two main causes of alcoholism—socioeconomic necessity and public ignorance.

We will limit this report to an account of the warfare that was waged, on one front by legislative and procedural measures; and on the other, by publicity campaigns. And we will try to evaluate the gains and losses of this twofold operation.

*Legislative and procedural measures*

The production and sale of alcohol have been regulated in France for a very long time, but until World War II it can be said that the business of fighting alcoholism remained virtually unknown to legislative powers. The laws and regulations were, for the most part, aimed at either quality control of the products (especially wine), at the fiscal management and state monopoly of these products, or at maintaining public order (control over cafes, a check on public drunkenness).

The Vichy Government took the first moves specifically designed to curb alcoholism, but most of them were abandoned after the Liberation and it was only at the beginning of 1953 that the resolution to control alcoholism was reintroduced into the law.

Historically, there were two sets of bills—the first between 1953–1955, the second between 1959–1960. The first group of enactments, made possible by the regulatory law passed on July 11, 1953, concerned the private distillers and the distilling industry, the sale of alcoholic beverages, and cafes. The decrees on November 13, 1954, deprived owners who were not qualified as agriculturists the private distillers' privilege, clamped down on professional distillers, put a limit on the number of stills, raised the purchase tax on alcohol, and forbade the legal transfer of certain cafes. A decree of November 22, 1954, raised the tax on cafe licenses, and the rulings from February 1 to May 20 modified the different aspects of control of these establishments.

We should also mention here the law of April 15, 1954, concerning the harmful effects of alcohol.

Throughout this first phase, the special committee proposed another modest but generally coherent program concerning the production and trade of alcoholic beverages, encouraging the production and consumption of fruit juices and the compulsory distribution of nonalcoholic beverages in businesses. But this plan fell into oblivion following a change of government.

A forceful ordinance of January 7, 1959, and a decree of the same date greatly increased the penalty for infraction of the laws governing cafes, and forbade any publicity supporting strong alcoholic beverages such as anisette or whiskey. But it was during the second half of 1960 that more numerous and important measures were taken—for example, the law of July 30, 1960, commissioning the government to issue orders to combat alcoholism.

These orders, dated August 30 and November 29, 1960, were issued to:

> —completely suppress the advantage held by private distillers (including growers) but only after the death of the concerned party;
> —close down cafes located near certain hospital zones (sanitoriums, psychiatric clinics, rest homes) and to limit the number of them in highly populated or industrial areas;
> —forbid the advertisement of alcoholic beverages in sports arenas or to youthful audiences;
> —forbid the sale of alcoholic beverages on credit or on business premises.

By raising certain taxes on alcoholic beverages, people were likewise inclined to cut down their consumption.

LEGISLATION TO CONTROL DRUNKEN DRIVING. We will reserve a special section for this aspect of the legislative program, because it concerns neither the fight against the socioeconomic pressures of alcohol, nor the direct struggle against alcoholic illnesses, but rather the assured safety of travelers on the road.

According to Article 1 of the French traffic code, to drive an automobile in a drunken condition or under the influence of alcohol is punishable as a misdemeanor. Before the law of May 18, 1965, the code even made a distinction between the two states, actual drunkenness and simply being under the influence of alcohol, yet made them equally punishable. Since the May 18 law, there is but one interpretation of what constitutes an offense: driving under the influence of alcohol even in the absence of overt signs of drunkenness.

But even now the alcoholic state is not consistently defined. Unlike most other industrial nations, in France there is no legal measurement of the amount of blood–alcohol concentration to establish if a person is driving under the influence of alcohol. It should be emphasized that, until just recently, magistrates and members of the police force were formally opposed to the establishment of such a standard. They felt that due to the variation in individual tolerance levels, and in order to safeguard the integrity of the one making the judgment, the degree of drunkenness should be evaluated on an individual basis, in particular on one's own behavior, and not by a purely mechanical criterion such as the blood test.

Unfortunately, this position taken by the police and the magistrates resulted in very contradictory practices and in conflicting court cases, in subjective appraisals, and even in unfair and rather ineffective restraints.

As demonstrated by many serious studies, a large number of traffic accidents are caused by drinkers, and the risk increases sharply with the rise in blood–alcohol concentration. Thus, it is evident that proper prevention requires, first, that drivers not operate a car if they have surpassed a certain alcohol level, and, second, that offenders be given objective treatment and a standard penalty.

Thus opinion in France was slowly swayed toward the adoption of an established legal blood–alcohol ratio. Two important major steps have already been approved:

The May 18 law permitted alcoholic detection by the breathylator, thus giving the police an objective means of detection by which to screen suspects before giving a blood test. But the breathylator was never considered to be absolute proof of the alcoholic level—only a blood test could offer this proof.

After the resolution of the European conference of Ministers of Transportation in Hamburg, recommending all member states to uphold a legal level of 0.80 percent alcohol in the blood, and following the spectacular decrease of accidents in Great Britain after its adoption of this standard in 1967, the magistrates themselves were won over to the support of the measure. For the moment, the Minister of Justice had to be content with issuing memoranda to the public prosecutor in order to initiate action against drivers operating under an alcoholic level of at least 1 percent.

The Special Committee for the Study and Publicity of Alcoholism, in order to conform to the recommendations of the Conference of Hamburg, and to the methods practiced by other countries, asked that disciplinary action be taken when the alcohol level reached a reading of over 0.80 percent.

This done, the special committee also envisions a third stage now in preparation. Its objective is to obtain a legal assessment of the threshold of alcohol in the blood above which the driving of an automobile would constitute a misdemeanor. The Minister of Social Affairs, Maurice Schumann, in collaboration with the special committee, proposed a legal project with this in mind. Only recent political events have prevented this project from being submitted to Parliament.

### Publicity and educational action

Alfred Sauvy could write: "Alcoholism is a form of underdevelopment, an anachronic illness whose remedy lies in culture." As we pointed out in the beginning, alcoholism, particularly in France, is a type of cultural underdevelopment whose prevention, at least, can be overcome through publicity and education. Its cure still remains clearly in the medical realm.

Because of social habits and the economic importance of wine in France, it is absolutely unthinkable that alcoholism could be prevented by advocating abstinence. Besides, it is not necessary to become totally abstinent in order to avoid alcoholism; it is sufficient to drink in moderation, that is, to refrain from exceeding a certain alcoholic level.

This limit of moderation has been determined by computing both the ability of the human body to burn alcohol and the medical findings from a number of French hospitals. The studies made in these institutions actually showed that cirrhosis of the liver is practically nonexistent among those persons who consume less than 1 liter of wine a day; that it is, however, found among those who exceed this limit; and that it is quite frequent among those who consume over 2 liters.

It was by reason of these two findings that the Academy of Medicine recommended keeping below the following limits:

> —never more than 1 liter of 10 percent wine a day for a manual laborer
> —never more than .75 liter for a sedentary
> —never more than .50 liter (or its equivalent in alcohol) for a woman
> —no alcoholic beverages for children

The special committee adopted this doctrine and based its publicity and education programs on it, proposing, of course, the above quantities as maximum limits and not as recommended rations. This doctrine was popularized in two ways:

> —by publicity through the advertising media
> —by in-depth educational articles

PUBLICITY THROUGH ADVERTISING. The advertising campaigns were designed to bring to the attention of the public the dangers of excessive alcohol consumption, without going into the reasons. Like sales publicity, they used slogans such as "Vitality–Sobriety" or "Safety–Sobriety," which were broadcast and exhibited according to standard procedures:

—on billboards along the highways, in public transportation vehicles, in stadiums, in public places (town halls, police stations, Social Security offices, etc.)

—in "shorts" shown at theaters between films or inserted into the reels themselves

—on radio and television; television spots, shown regularly, were an effective agent

IN-DEPTH EDUCATIONAL PUBLICITY. To accomplish the educational goal, the special committee employed four media: the press, the schools, informative brochures, and full-length television films.

Information in the press consisted of articles on one or more aspects of alcoholism in some of the daily or weekly publications; the presentation and wording concealed the publicity angle. Articles in dailies were generally addressed to a large public, while those in magazines sought to reach more specialized *milieux* (woman, children, etc.).

The effort in the schools was certainly the most interesting and most effective part of the special committee's plan. They furnished teachers with documented pamphlets and tried to interest children by distributing blotters which acclaimed, directly or indirectly, the virtues of sobriety (for example, the "Lives to Follow" series). Children were often taught and quizzed by means of special pictures, and they entered national contests richly endowed with prizes; these are still considered an important success.

The special committee tried both to combat alcoholism among women, and to make them guardian of their husband's and children's health, and protectress of family unity.

Some groups, because of their social responsibility, were informed in great detail. Teachers and professors were given a specially edited brochure containing all the necessary facts. Another brochure, drafted by a company doctor, was intended for medical workers, but could also be used profitably by social workers or by responsible trade unions.

Certain aspects of alcoholism have been the object of particularly intense campaigns, three of which deserve mention here. The first sought to distribute nonalcoholic beverages in business establishments, with very encouraging results. The second reported—and still does—on the dangers of drunken driving and is coordinated with the project for instituting a legal blood–alcohol threshold. The third is directed toward making the public and responsible groups aware of the tremendous economic toll of alcoholism.

*Results achieved*

In assessing the results after twelve years of struggle, two questions must be posed. Our original hypothesis was that alcoholism is based on a lack of knowledge and that to combat it we must educate the public. We must necessarily ask: Did the information distributed actually reach the public? Did the information result in lowering the incidence of alcoholism?

The comparison of results obtained from two public surveys in 1958 and in 1965 serves to measure the drastic improvement in publicity. It can be confirmed that the French were made aware of the campaigns to combat alcoholism, realized the danger of alcoholism, and knew the recommended limits of consumption. The specific campaigns fulfilled their aims.

FRENCH AWARENESS OF ANTI-ALCOHOL CAMPAIGNS. In 1958, only 47 percent of all persons asked responded spontaneously that they had noticed the campaigns to combat alcoholism. By 1965, this percentage rose to 97 (82 percent of the men; 77 percent of the women). The degree of perception varies according to socioprofessional status (90 percent among employers, 66 percent among agricultural workers); according to geographical region (90 percent in the Rhone region, 89 percent in the Paris area, 62 percent in the south); and according to the population of a given locality:

—71 percent in areas of less than 2,000 inhabitants
—75 percent in towns of 2,000–10,000 inhabitants
—77 percent in towns of 10,000–100,000 inhabitants
—88 percent in cities of more than 100,000 inhabitants

The advertisements most noticed were those in the Metro in Paris (75 percent) and along the highways (48 percent). The articles were noticed by 33 percent, and television commercials by 23 percent.

AWARENESS OF THREAT TO SOCIETY, TO THE FAMILY, AND TO THE INDIVIDUAL. In 1965, 94.5 percent of all persons interviewed considered alcoholism a scourge to society (75 percent in 1958). The percentage was approximately the same (93–95 percent) regardless of age, profession, sex, or regional background. Of all persons interviewed 27 percent felt that the most harmful consequences of alcoholism are those that affect the family, while 26 percent felt that these are hereditary traits. Among the illnesses associated with alcoholism, 68 percent mentioned diseases of the liver, 48 percent mental illness, and 40 percent tuberculosis and other disorders. Concerning the dangers of alcohol to children's health, 72 percent maintained that they never gave alcoholic drinks to children under 14 years of age.

AWARENESS OF CONSUMPTION LIMITS. To the question "Do you know the recommended maximum daily limits of wine consumption?" the answers were as follows:

| QUANTITY | 0 LITER | ¼ LITER | ½ LITER | 1 LITER | 1½ LITERS | 2 LITERS |
|---|---|---|---|---|---|---|
| *For a manual laborer* | — | — | 5% | 48% | 18% | 21% |
| *For a sedentary worker* | — | 10% | 52% | 30% | 4% | — |
| *For a woman* | 1% | 40% | 40% | 8% | — | — |
| *For a youth between 14 and 20* | 13% | 44% | 28% | 5% | — | — |

One can see that 53 percent estimated that a manual laborer should not have more than 1 liter of wine per day (compared with 22 percent in 1958); 81 percent thought a woman should not have more than ½ liter; and 57 percent felt that youths from 14 to 20 should not consume more than ¼ liter. But the increase in understanding is most evident if we compare the average admitted consumption during the time the surveys were conducted in 1948, 1953, 1955, and 1965.

| YEAR | FOR A MANUAL LABORER | FOR A SEDENTARY WORKER | FOR A WOMAN |
|------|------------|---------|-------------|
| 1948 | 1.7 litres | 1.0 litre | 0.5 litre |
| 1953 | 1.6 litres | 0.9 litre | 0.5 litre |
| 1955 | 1.8 litres | 0.8 litre | 0.6 litre |
| 1965 | 1.3 litres | 0.6 litre | 0.4 litre |

The figures for the year 1965 are very close to the actual recommendations made by the Academy of Medicine and by the Special Committee for the Study and Publicity of Alcoholism.

COMPREHENSIVE COVERAGE IN THE CAMPAIGN. Researchers found that the anti-alcohol campaign made an impact in the following key areas:

*Traffic accidents:* 52.5 percent credited accidents to alcohol abuse; 30 percent said they did not drink before driving; but 44 percent did not know about either the breathylator test or the legal level of alcohol in the blood.

*Youth:* 60 percent knew that alcohol produces liver ailments; 70 percent knew that people could become alcoholics without ever being drunk. Their knowledge about alcoholic drink was often better than the adults' (92 percent knew about liqueurs, 84 percent about wine, and 49 percent about beer). 62 percent of this group held that wine is not required for adult health, and 83 percent knew that only the manual laborer should be allowed to consume more than 1 liter of wine per day. 46 percent said they had drunk beer, wine, or cider once in a great while, but 35 percent said they drank watered-down wine quite regularly. (Only 20 percent of the adults admitted giving diluted wine to their children.)

*Women:* 25 percent of the women tried to reduce the wine consumption in their households; 55 percent did not feel obliged to give alcoholic drinks to messengers and mailmen; but 82 percent felt it necessary to serve an aperitif to dinner guests.

*Teachers:* Of the total French population, teachers are, according to the evidence, the best informed on the problem of alcoholism, and the most aware of its dangers—comforting hope for the future. 97 percent of them considered alcoholism a social evil; 56 percent attributed traffic accidents to alcohol abuse; 76 percent had never given alcohol to children under 14. 90 percent agreed that a person can become an alcoholic without realizing it.

On the average, teachers allow the following daily wine consumption rates: 0.25 liter for adolescents between 14 and 20; 0.4 liter for women; 0.5 liter for sedentary males; and 1.1 liters for manual laborers.

Of the teachers 55 percent said that their students are interested in the problem of alcoholism.

### Has alcoholism decreased in France?

There were never any precise statistics determining the number of alcoholic cases in France, and the estimates made by Dr. May in 1959, despite their inaccuracy, were never revised. Therefore it is not possible to measure directly the decrease (or the possible upsurge) of alcoholism. But we can draw one empirical conclusion, and point out some indirect results.

Everyone agrees that young people under the age of twenty-five drink much more alcohol than preceding generations did at the same age. This finding, which has been documented not only by doctors but also by bartenders and army officers, is confirmed by statistical studies on death due to alcoholism in a cross section of age groups.

The indirect results belong to two classes, shown by mortality figures, on the one hand, and by consumption statistics, on the other.

CHANGES IN THE NUMBER OF DEATHS AND CASES OF CIRRHOSIS OF THE LIVER ATTRIBUTED TO ALCOHOLISM. As indicated in Table 4, death caused by cirrhosis increased greatly between 1955 and 1957 with two periods of decline, in 1957–58 and in 1964. The number reached in 1967 (17,463) was clearly above the peak attained in 1956 (14,176). Nonetheless, statistics from the first eleven months in 1968 (see Table 6) show a slight drop compared with 1967.

*Table 4*

DEATHS DUE TO ALCOHOLISM
AND CIRRHOSIS OF THE LIVER

| | ALCOHOLISM | | CIRRHOSIS | | TOTAL |
| YEAR | *Number of deaths* | *For every 100,000 inhabitants* | *Number of deaths* | *For every 100,000 inhabitants* | *For both causes of death* |
|---|---|---|---|---|---|
| *1955* | 4,595 | 10.6 | 13,101 | 30.3 | 17,696 |
| *1956* | 6,103 | 14.0 | 14,176 | 32.5 | 20,279 |
| *1957* | 5,916 | 13.4 | 13,468 | 30.6 | 19,384 |
| *1958* | 4,291 | 9.6 | 11,490 | 25.8 | 15,781 |
| *1959* | 4,707 | 10.4 | 12,038 | 26.7 | 16,745 |
| *1960* | 5,074 | 11.1 | 13,401 | 29.4 | 18,475 |
| *1961* | 4,976 | 10.8 | 13,840 | 30.1 | 18,816 |
| *1962* | 5,482 | 12.0 | 14,660 | 31.0 | 20,142 |
| *1963* | 5,702 | 12.0 | 15,684 | 33.0 | 21,386 |
| *1964* | 5,209 | 10.8 | 15,370 | 32.0 | 20,579 |
| *1965* | 5,816 | 11.9 | 16,749 | 34.0 | 22,565 |
| *1966* | 5,635 | 11.4 | 17,178 | 34.8 | 22,813 |
| *1967* | 5,465 | 11.0 | 17,463 | 34.8 | 22,928 |

The change in the death rate caused by alcoholism is, properly speaking, quite another story. It, too, reached a peak in 1956 (6,103), diminished in 1957 and 1958 (4,291), then soared again until 1963, but never reached the record set in 1956. Since 1965, death due to alcoholism fell regularly (5,465 in 1967). This drop-off was already noticeable in 1968, as the numbers compiled for the first eleven months show a decrease of about 20 percent from the preceding year (see Table 6). Particularly important is the decrease in the *percentage* of deaths, which fell from 14 out of 100,000 citizens in 1956 to 11 out of 100,000 in

*Table 5*

## TOTAL NUMBER OF DEATHS AND COMMITMENTS
## TO PSYCHIATRIC HOSPITALS FROM 1946 TO 1967

| | DEATH FROM CIRRHOSIS OF THE LIVER | DEATH FROM ALCOHOLISM | TOTAL DEATHS | ADMISSIONS TO PSYCHIATRIC HOSPITALS* |
|---|---|---|---|---|
| 1946 | 2,763 | 481 | 3,244 | — |
| 1947 | 3,199 | 743 | 3,942 | — |
| 1948 | 4,530 | 1,330 | 5,860 | — |
| 1949 | 5,710 | 1,564 | 7,274 | — |
| 1950 | 6,843 | 2,362 | 9,205 | — |
| 1951 | 8,359 | 2,653 | 11,012 | — |
| 1952 | 9,727 | 2,838 | 12,565 | 6,704 |
| 1953 | 11,897 | 3,905 | 15,802 | 8,178 |
| 1954 | 12,071 | 4,106 | 16,177 | 11,051 |
| 1955 | 13,101 | 4,595 | 17,696 | 11,425 |
| 1956 | 14,176 | 6,103 | 20,279 | 14,870 |
| 1957 | 13,471 | 5,916 | 19,387 | 14,327 |
| 1958 | 11,490 | 4,291 | 15,781 | 11,575 |
| 1959 | 12,038 | 4,707 | 16,745 | 13,316 |
| 1960 | 13,004 | 4,866 | 17,870 | 14,810 |
| 1961 | 13,379 | 4,749 | 18,128 | 15,622 |
| 1962 | 14,194 | 5,238 | 19,432 | 18,711 |
| 1963 | 15,684 | 5,702 | 21,386 | 21,898 |
| 1964 | 15,370 | 5,209 | 20,579 | 21,665 |
| 1965 | 16,749 | 5,816 | 22,565 | 25,334 |
| 1966 | 17,178 | 5,636 | 22,814 | 25,937 |
| 1967 | 17,463 | 5,465 | 22,928 | |

* The rise in the number of admissions into psychiatric hospitals (for chronic alcoholism and alcoholic psychoses) is due to the development of special services for the care and cure of these cases during recent years.

1967, and which will probably drop to 9 out of 100,000 in 1968 (statistics not complete at printing*).

In other respects, the study of the mortality rate on a cross section of age groups stressed an upward trend toward the older

* Translator's note.

*Table 6*

## COMPARATIVE MONTHLY STATISTICS OF DEATH FROM ALCOHOLISM AND CIRRHOSIS OF THE LIVER
1967 AND 1968 (first 11 months)

| | ALCOHOLISM | | CIRRHOSIS OF THE LIVER | |
|---|---|---|---|---|
| MONTH | *1967* | *1968* | *1967* | *1968* |
| January | 525 | 484 | 1,486 | 1,432 |
| February | 471 | 415 | 1,382 | 1,470 |
| March | 481 | 378 | 1,503 | 1,423 |
| April | 424 | 278 | 1,428 | 1,380 |
| May | 444 | 309 | 1,426 | 1,411 |
| June | 406 | 303 | 1,367 | 1,305 |
| July | 509 | 359 | 1,383 | 1,364 |
| August | 420 | 365 | 1,549 | 1,366 |
| September | 446 | 340 | 1,423 | 1,409 |
| October | 404 | 362 | 1,462 | 1,503 |
| November | 443 | 320 | 1,488 | 1,561 |
| Total for the first 11 months | 4,973 | 3,913 | 15,897 | 15,624 |
| December (*projected*) | 492 | | 1,566 | |

persons. In 1956, the highest rate was found among those persons between 50 and 60 years of age; at present, it rests among those between 65 and 70. Finally, the comparison between successive generations shows that at any given age the mortality rate is declining progressively.

Current studies will perhaps enable scientists to determine the reasons for the discrepancy between the death rate for cirrhosis and the rate for so-called alcoholism, but even now we can observe a decline in the death rate from alcoholism; and also we see the first signs of a reversal in the number of deaths attributed to cirrhosis.

The number of persons admitted to psychiatric hospitals has not been tallied here, since the total was not considered significant.

*The consumption of alcoholic beverages*

WINE. The consumption of wine, the national drink, saw an appreciable decrease: 60,290,360 hl. in 1956–57 as compared to 56,520,000 hl. in 1967–68. The average consumption per person fell from 201 liters a year to 178.5 liters (a drop of 20 percent).

CIDER. The consumption of cider was cut almost in half between 1955 and 1967.

BEER. By contrast, beer drinking went up by nearly 40 percent.

SPIRITS. The consumption of distilled liquor showed a peculiar change. For example, the consumption of whiskey and anisette rose considerably, while rum fell sharply, and wine aperitifs first fell then rose.

Altogether, the known consumption of liquor rose: 546,000 hl. of pure alcohol in 1956 to 861,000 hl. in 1967.

TOTAL. The total known consumption of alcohol seems to have risen slightly (8,670,000 hl. of pure alcohol in 1956 to 8,970,000 hl. in 1966) but individual consumption has slightly fallen off (28.9 liters in 1956 as compared to 27.9 liters in 1966).

*The consumption of non-alcoholic beverages*
The consumption of these drinks has risen in considerable proportion, moving from a low of 100 in 1950 to 341 in 1963. Most spectacular was the increase in fruit juices, which went from 279,000 hl. in 1958 to 1,156,950 hl. in 1967.

*Additional findings*
We must mention, in conclusion, the following facts:
    In 1960, before the law of August 30 suppressing, little by little, the advantage of the private distiller, the number of people claiming this privilege rose to 3,110,081. Out of those, only 1,-912,171 actually ran distilleries during the campaign of 1960–61. For the campaign of 1966–67, those showing a profit from this

license numbered only 2,691,195 (418,886 had disappeared) and only 1,464,630 among them actually ran distilleries.

In an undertaking involving more than 50,000 paid workers, the medical services detected 700 new alcoholics during the year 1955, but only 18 during 1965.

## CONCLUSION

It is much too early to draw any definitive conclusions from this report on the twelve-year fight against alcoholism. Moreover, we have always contended that it takes an entire generation for the effects of such a struggle to become truly apparent. Yet, while we admit that alcoholism remains a particularly serious problem in France, we are able to cite some significant steps which could point the way to a reversal in the trend, and which, if maintained for several years, could well be the beginning of a total victory. In any case, France now seems to be the only country in which alcoholism is declining, a fact which makes the major point: that both publicity and the continuing education of the young are effective weapons against alcoholism. From then on, with a lot of will power, and a few financial backers, the battle may be won.

# Alcoholism in Scandinavia

*THROBJORN KJOLSTAD, M.D.*

From a tradition of heavy drinking, Scandinavia inherited an alcoholism problem that in the last fifty years was boldly attacked in a variety of ways. When prohibition failed and centralized control proved ineffective, responsibility was given to local agencies which now capably handle the problem. Dr. Throbjorn Kjolstad is medical director of alcoholism treatment in Norway and serves as medical expert on the advisory board of the International Council on Alcohol and Addictions. He is also co-editor of the journal *Alcoholism* Zagreb/Lausanne.

## HISTORICAL BACKGROUND

In the Nordic sagas alcohol as an intoxicant played an important role. Intoxication was a cause of both ridicule and concern. The attitude toward intoxication was rather ambivalent. It was considered proper for a man to be "high," but he was expected to "hold his beer." It was regarded as a test of manhood to be able to drink a lot of "mjød" and still sit at the table. To "pass out" was looked on as feebleness. For women it was supposed to be immoral to get drunk. Parties were mostly drinking sessions, and follies committed during these were not considered incriminating. A small king who drowned in an enormous "mjød" tank was thus immortalized by the ever-present "skald." The Nordic gods, Odin and his household, every evening drank and fought, but recovered next morning by pork and "mjød."

Occasionally men got furious in drinking sessions, and went "berserk." In this state they slaughtered friend and foe alike, and often were slain in the end. If not, they were not held responsible for their deeds as "berserkers." It is not sure if this state was a "pathological intoxication" by alcohol alone or if muscarine from fly agaric were added to the brew.

The national brew, "mjød," was quite a powerful intoxicant, and probably held up to 10–12 percent alcohol. At the end of the Viking age, wine was rather rare in Scandinavia, but with increasing commerce from France and other wine-producing countries, wine gradually got a foothold. Wine became the drink of the higher classes, and "mjød" was reduced to be the drink of the lower classes.

In the sagas, it doesn't seem that "mjød" was considered as food; but when wine was introduced, this was regarded both as valuable food and as medicine. The belief in alcohol as a healing substance seems to be imported, but "mjød" certainly held high esteem as a roborant.

The drinking patterns of the Middle Ages in Scandinavia are not well known, but probably Christendom did ameliorate the raw customs of the Viking age. Heavy drinking did occur, however, and about 1200 the Norwegian King Sverre gave a speech of warning against the uncontrolled use of wine.

The somewhat idyllic picture of the Middle Ages came to an end when distillation was introduced in the seventeenth century. Soon "brennevin," that is, distilled spirits, were produced everywhere; and as it was held to be of high nutritive value and a preventive to almost any illness, the use of spirits leapt to enormous quantities. Literally every medical prescription of the age contained alcohol in some amount, and the effect of the medicine certainly was largely due to the alcohol.

Some control of distillation was due more to financial difficulties in royal circles than to consideration of the detrimental effect of alcohol abuse. The crown put taxes on distillation, but at the same time encouraged distillation as a sound way of dealing with potato and grain surplus.

In the middle of the nineteenth century alcohol abuse made

quite a number of responsible citizens concerned, and in Norway an attempt was made to establish a moderation movement. What was advocated as moderation, or temperance, however, was so liberal that the movement very soon disappeared. Partly on religious grounds, partly on a humanitarian basis, there came forward at this time an abstinence movement, later improperly named temperance movement. This movement soon got a big following in Norway, and a fair one in Sweden, but was not to be popular in Denmark. The abstinence movement declared war on all kinds of alcohol, and all use was labeled abuse. The slogan "alcohol is a poison, and every use of poison is abuse" was widely accepted, and the movement did a lot to make people think. On the other hand, the movement engaged a strong opposition, and its aim, prohibition, was denounced as a serious impingement of personal freedom. Many moderate drinkers sided with the abusers rather than with the "temperance" people. Another slogan of the abstinence movement was that all use of alcohol will lead to abuse and to alcoholism.

As mentioned, the movement for abstinence flourished in Norway, and during World War I prohibition was established after a plebiscite that gave some 55 percent majority for prohibition. The immediate effect was a decrease in the number of arrests due to public intoxication; and patients with delirium tremens almost vanished from the hospitals. However, these striking results did not persevere, and after two to three years, both arrests and delirium tremens were on the increase again. The prohibition also was relaxed for commercial reasons. Norway had to import Spanish wines in return for the export of dried fish. Illegal distilling and smuggling also took over production and distribution, and in the middle twenties the smugglers became "heroes," and no one would bear witness against a "home-brewer." It soon became obvious that the majority of the nation opposed prohibition, and in 1926, after a new plebiscite, it was abolished.

Since then, the production of spirits is monopolized by the state in Norway, and there are restrictions on sale and serving of alcohol. Further, a policy of making alcohol rather expensive has worked the price steadily upward. Whether these restrictions and the price policy have had an effect on consumption, and on abuse, is very difficult to say. Few things can raise a more heated discussion in Norway than the "alcohol question."

In Sweden, prohibition never was established, but a rationing system was introduced about 1920 which gave all adults the right to buy a certain amount of spirits monthly. The rations were rather liberal, and after much discussion the system was dropped in 1955. This resulted in a national "orgy" that lasted about two years, but in the early sixties consumption rates and alcohol psychosis were again down to the figures of 1953–54.

In Denmark, no rationing or prohibition was tried, but a price policy seems to have worked to some effect. In 1917, prices were increased 500 percent on spirits; and the rate of arrests and alcohol psychosis fell to almost zero in some months. Then it slowly increased, and after four or five years was at the 1917 level. This shows that a price "shock" will have a time-limited effect on consumption and related complications, but gradually the shock will be overcome. The slow, steady increase in costs of spirits will not have this kind of effect, but will probably influence the consumption of moderate drinkers who, unlike the abusers and alcoholics, will find spirits too expensive.

In Finland, alcohol abuse was very widespread, and this led to a strong prohibition movement. Prohibition was enforced after a plebiscite, but the results obtained were exactly the same as in Norway, and prohibition was dropped in the late twenties.

## DRINKING PATTERNS IN SCANDINAVIA

The attitude toward alcohol in Scandinavia today is fairly rational. Very few, if any, regard alcohol as a nutriment, and unlike France, wine is not considered necessary for the worker. Alcohol as medicine has lost its role since the advance of the effective antibiotics, although still quite a few believe alcohol can prevent or cure a heavy cold. The belief in alcohol as a source of warmth is still widespread, and every winter there will occur fatalities as some believe they can survive in the open by use of great quantities of alcohol. It is very difficult to root out this superstition, and at sports events during the winter it is customary to bring a pocket flask of spirits to hold up temperature and fighting spirit.

If we look at the consumption rates in the Scandinavian countries, expressed as amount per adult yearly, we find the rates generally low compared to other countries, for instance, France, Italy, and Greece. Rates differ among the countries in Scandinavia, too, with Finland and Norway at the bottom. In these countries consumption is about 4 liters of pure alcohol per adult yearly; in Sweden some 5 liters; and in Denmark 5 to 6 liters. The figures are generally on the increase, but rather slowly.

However, these figures don't tell much, if anything, about the drinking patterns, unless they are scrutinized closely. For instance in Norway, the 4 liters of alcohol officially consumed certainly must be augmented with 2 to 2½ liters of illegally produced spirits, which brings the rate on a par with the Danish figures. Further, these figures are established by dividing the entire consumption by all adults above 15 years of age, which in some countries results in misleading figures concerning drinking patterns. Keeping to Norwegian figures, we know that about one third of the adult population is abstinent, and of the two thirds that use alcohol, women, still one third, drink very moderately. This means that the estimated amount of legal and illegal alcohol is consumed by one third of the adult population, which gives a figure of 15 to 18 liters of alcohol annually per capita. In Denmark, the use of alcohol is much more common, and there are very few abstainers, which means that the official figures correspond more closely to actual drinking patterns. In Sweden and Finland the circumstances are similar to those in Norway.

If we go to another source of information, arrests for public drunkenness, we find the figures in Norway, Finland, and Sweden much higher than in Denmark. This could be due to differences in the police approach to the problem, but that will hardly explain the substantial difference. Furthermore, legislation has been almost identical up to 1966. In consequence, we must assume that the drinking pattern is "harder" in Sweden, Finland, and Norway than in Denmark, and that this difference is rooted in other things than official control on sales of alcohol or police interference.

In all four countries, prices of alcohol are high, and the average income fairly equal. The restrictions on sales are more severe in Finland, Sweden, and Norway than in Denmark. It is true that there have been fluctuations in drinking patterns, as revealed by complications, arrests, and delirium tremens. During World War II, for instance, alcohol was hardly available for some years in Norway; and in 1964 there was a strike in Sweden that actually stopped distribution of spirits. On both occasions arrests and delirium tremens decreased dramatically, but very soon reached "normal" levels as the alcohol became available again.

How should we then explain the difference? It might be that one of the answers is given by a Dane, who said: "You Norwegians drink to forget, but we Danes drink to have fun." In general, it is true that Danes are more easygoing than Swedes and Norwegians, and certainly the Danes will show less aggression when intoxicated than Norwegians. In my opinion, however, it is the attitude toward the intoxicated state that is most decisive. In Norway one will find, especially in the middle-size and larger towns, milieus where it is considered *normal* to be drunk at least once a week. To grow up in this kind of milieu means that young men are expected to drink heavily, and this occurs mostly at the age of 16–17. The young man is not ashamed at having been drunk. On the contrary, he will boast of it, and very often exaggerate both the consumed amount and the intoxication. Sometimes he even brags about having "passed out."

A fairly true picture of drinking patterns in Scandinavia shows, in my opinion, that in Denmark the use of alcohol is very common; abuse isn't rare, but is more controlled, and leads to lesser complications socially than in the other countries. In these, total abstinence is not regarded as peculiar, and from 20 to 30 percent of the population hardly touch alcohol. Then there is half of the population that drink very moderately; while the rest will abuse alcohol to a high degree with heavy consequences to their health and social status.

Among the alcoholics of Sweden, Finland, and Norway one will also find a much higher proportion of neurotics and psychopaths than in Denmark. Correspondingly, guilt feelings are more pronounced in alcoholics of the former countries. If we compare the etiological background of alcoholics, we find that the majority of Danish alcoholics have started out as "social drinkers," but Norwegian and Swedish alcoholics are "problem drinkers" from the beginning.

## DRINKING AND DRIVING

With the enormous increase in automobile traffic and speed on the roads after World War I, it was very soon clear to authorities that driving and intoxication didn't match very well. Accordingly, about 1930 the Scandinavian countries enacted laws that made it illegal to drive when intoxicated. In Norwegian law it was regarded as *proven* that the driver was intoxicated if he had an amount of alcohol in his blood that exceeded 0.05 percent; and this called for an obligatory prison sentence of some three weeks. Further, the driving license was withdrawn for at least two years. The law was considered very strict, but the relatively low number of accidents caused by drunken drivers indicates that the law has had a general preventive effect. The other Scandinavian countries have similar laws, but the blood–alcohol percentage range is higher; in Denmark 0.1 percent; in Sweden, 0.08 percent; and in Finland, 0.1 percent. There are plans, however, to make the Scandinavian laws concerning driving identical. The number of drivers sentenced for driving "under the influence of alcohol" in Norway is some 2,500 annually. Of these, less than 3 percent have a blood–alcohol concentration between 0.05 and 0.1 percent; the rest have above 0.1 percent. The law may be too strict in some cases, but it is generally accepted by the population as fair.

## PREVENTIVE MEASURES AND EDUCATION

The belief that availability of alcohol is a decisive factor in the consumption rate has been the reason for introducing a system of restrictions on sales and serving of alcohol. When prohibition was dropped in Finland and Norway, one of the conditions was that the state should establish a monopoly of production and distribution of all distilled spirits; and the sale of wines also should go through the government's shops. These shops have very restricted hours, and are not allowed to advertise. The prices are under the surveillance of parliament. Beer is produced without direct control of the state, but is not allowed to contain more than 7 percent alcohol.

Further, there are restrictions on where alcohol can be sold and served. The state stores may be opened only in towns with more than 4,000 inhabitants, and only after approval in a local plebiscite. Thus rural towns and villages have no spirits and wine shops.

Beer sale and serving is also under the control of local authorities, and there are many areas which are "dry." A citizen living in a "dry" place, may order beer directly from the nearest brewery, but redistribution is not allowed. The restrictions are certainly circumvented, and the effects are debatable.

In Sweden, the rationing system, "Brattske systemet," has been in operation for nearly thirty years. After a prolonged debate, it was abolished by the parliament in 1955, and since then restrictions in Sweden are similar to those in Finland and Norway. In Denmark, there are no restrictions on production and sale; wines, spirits, and beer can be bought anywhere and at all times when shops are open.

It is very difficult to evaluate the effect of restrictions, but the experiment in Sweden in 1955 shows that a letdown of restrictions certainly will lead to a temporary increase in the abuse of alcohol and its consequences. It has been postulated that restrictions lead to abuse "as forbidden fruit tastes best," but this is more than doubtful. It is probable that the attitude toward drunkenness is a far more decisive factor than any restrictions, unless these are really "watertight" and supported by 90–95 percent of the population.

In Norway and Sweden education and information on alcohol until 1950 were influenced to a high degree by the pamphleteering of the abstinence movement. One may look askance at the rather unbalanced views in these pamphlets, but it is more than probable that they gave a certain counterbalance to the "laissez faire" attitude of the community. On the other hand, cooperation with moderate drinkers was impossible, and toward the end of the 1940s rather strong opposition developed. The view of alcoholism as an illness began to get a foothold, with more emphasis on the medical problem than on moral aspects. As the rise of the A.A. movement threatened to break all ties to established institutions, the medical profession became more interested in alcoholism. A period followed when the moral problem in alcoholism was almost forgotten; it was purely a medical question. This attitude prevailed for some years, but since the middle 50s, a more balanced viewpoint has been advocated in education and propaganda. In Norwegian and Swedish schools, curriculum education on alcohol problems is obligatory.

In Finland, education is also well balanced, but in Denmark there is little concern with the alcohol problem in schools and other educational institutions.

## TREATMENT OF ALCOHOLICS

Trends in the therapeutic approach to alcoholism have differed, according to the extent of the problem, the attitude toward drunkenness, and, last but not least, geography. In Denmark, with a relatively concentrated population, an outpatient service may serve nearly every area; in Norway, on the other hand, it is impossible to cover the scattered population that way. In such circumstances, institutions for inpatient treatment are the answer. Since developments in Norway may serve as a prototype of the Scandinavian approach, we will take a closer look at conditions there. First, we must consider how the general attitude toward alcoholism has influenced treatment efforts.

A century ago there was no distinction between alcohol abuse and alcoholism. The indigent drinker was looked down upon but the well-off drinker was usually "exported," and forgotten by the family. In this way, the upper classes could claim that alcohol was no problem for them. Indigent drinkers, on the other hand, couldn't get away at all and became dependent on society, which was considered shameful. As the social complications of alcoholism further accelerated their social downfall, it was inevitable that these alcoholics were despised by everybody. Their behavior was regarded as proof that alcoholics were amoral and completely unreliable. The only possible conclusion to be drawn was that moral failure caused alcoholism, thus confusing the symptoms with the cause, which so often happens in medicine.

The first attempts at treating alcoholics were initiated in 1909. It was thought that since alcoholism was moral depravity, more or less forced abstinence combined with moralistic indoctrination would in time change the alcoholic's attitude toward drinking. The moralizing and time were regarded as the most important factors, but also regular work hours and an atmosphere of tolerance were considered important. A pioneer in the work was the "Blue Cross," which opened its treatment home that year. It was supposed that one year was the minimum time required for a change. Much emphasis was laid on creating a *home* for the patients, and institutions that joined in the Blue Cross program were all named "homes." Patients were cared for on a voluntary basis, and there was no possibility of retaining a patient if he changed his mind after a month or two. The first institution, the "Blue Cross Home," still exists, but its program has been modernized.

In 1910, the Norwegian Medical Association opened a new treatment home which was supposed to give a more medically oriented treatment, but in reality it did not differ much from the system in the Blue Cross Home. After some years the medical association found it impossible to continue, and the institution was taken over by the state. In 1926, the state opened a new institution, intended for both voluntary patients and alcoholics sentenced under the act of vagrancy, begging, and drunkenness. This new institution was run on more strict lines, and very soon became a disciplinary institution. The treatment, however, didn't differ from that of other institutions, although more emphasis was put on work.

In the years following World War I, social conditions became ever more desperate for the underprivileged classes, and with the belief that alcoholism was a social as well as a moral problem, more thought was given to the task of improving the alcoholic's living standards. To a certain degree this was accomplished by the general improvement of living standards during the later thirties, but in the meantime, much money and energy were spent in unsuccessful treatment approaches. In 1932, a law was passed that established committees in each town and each country district (the "sobriety committees") which had various functions. They were expected to carry out education on alcohol problems and to intervene in individual cases where necessary. Generally, the committees called in the patient and gave him advice and later, if necessary, a warning. If this were not sufficient, the committee could arrange for institutional treatment. In cases where the patient was a danger to himself and his family but would not accept treatment of his own free will, the committee had power to order compulsory treatment for a period of up to twelve months. In these cases the committee sat together with the local judge and followed strict rules of procedure. The law however, did not do much to improve treatment facilities, and it is noteworthy that up to 1950 all treatment was administered by nonmedical personnel, with one psychiatrist employed as supervisor, but only on a part-time basis.

When the A.A. movement was introduced in Norway in 1947–48, the slogan "alcoholism is an illness" was readily accepted by all alcoholics and abusers of alcohol, but society in general was rather skeptical, as were, with few exceptions, the physicians. When Antabuse was developed, a wave of optimism accelerated medical acceptance of alcoholism as an illness; and medical treatment was advocated, especially by A.A., which boasted that it would take over the treatment completely.

Still, very few people had a clear concept of what kind of illness alcoholism is, and what was meant by medical treatment. Even if the A.A.'s and some physicians were rather enthusiastic (and a bit prophetic), it was very soon obvious, that, apart from a small percentage, the initial success of the treatment could not give lasting results. Many began to doubt the slogan, and a certain pessimism entered the field, together with a more or less open conflict between the moralists and the A.A. members.

In the late fifties, however, the waters calmed, and now alcoholism is regarded as an illness which has symptoms and consequences in moral, social, and medical areas.

In 1957 alcoholism was accepted by insurance companies as a treatable illness. This has been an enormous advantage, and the expansion in treatment facilities available for the alcoholic has been significant.

All experience in alcohol treatment so far indicates that we need specialized institutions, and that within the institutions we also need further differentiation. There are many variables in alcoholism, and it is important that we make clear in what sense we use the terms *alcoholism* and *alcoholic*.

I think it would be best if we accepted Jellinek's criteria. The loss of control over the extent of intoxication is certainly one symptom among others, but in my experience, it is the symptom which leads to disaster, and is most difficult to make the patient recognize in himself. What functional or organic change is behind this loss of control we do not know at this time, but we do know that nothing can be done about it. The change seems to be irreversible; with few exceptions, most specialists in the field agree on this point.

In Norway, the gamma form of alcoholism is predominant, as in Sweden and Finland. In Denmark, we find a far greater percentage of delta drinkers. In both groups we find the disease in different stages, and therapy must be applied accordingly. In Norway, a system of therapeutic facilities has been developed gradually. We don't believe this is *the* answer to these problems, but we hope it is of interest to other workers in the field to see how a small country with a scattered population approaches the therapy challenge.

In the following scheme, alcoholics are divided into groups according to the development of the illness, and treatment facilities are indicated in the squares. The arrows indicate what we think is the proper method of treatment. When the shaft of the arrow is a dotted line, we find the approach is doubtful.

The patients in Group I are hardly "suffering" from alcoholism at all, and we often hear it said, "They aren't in need of treatment; they *can* stop drinking." Usually this kind of patient only needs information about risks and, after a failure or two to drink "socially," will leave alcohol. He is easy to handle, often grateful, and gives a good prognosis. But then he is only in the top layer, 3–5 percent of all alcoholics to be treated. (When a country wants to begin a treatment scheme, it should begin with this kind of patient. He is a good risk and nothing succeeds like success in alcoholism treatment.)

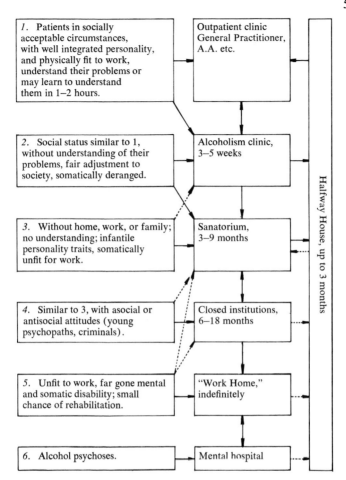

| | |
|---|---|
| *1.* Patients in socially acceptable circumstances, with well integrated personality, and physically fit to work, understand their problems or may learn to understand them in 1–2 hours. | Outpatient clinic General Practitioner, A.A. etc. |
| *2.* Social status similar to 1, without understanding of their problems, fair adjustment to society, somatically deranged. | Alcoholism clinic, 3–5 weeks |
| *3.* Without home, work, or family; no understanding; infantile personality traits, somatically unfit for work. | Sanatorium, 3–9 months |
| *4.* Similar to 3, with asocial or antisocial attitudes (young psychopaths, criminals). | Closed institutions, 6–18 months |
| *5.* Unfit to work, far gone mental and somatic disability; small chance of rehabilitation. | "Work Home," indefinitely |
| *6.* Alcohol psychoses. | Mental hospital |

Halfway House, up to 3 months

Group 2 patients are less cooperative in some ways, as they lack insight, but their physical condition usually makes them more amenable. The prognosis in this group is also fairly good, if treatment involves psychotherapy and is followed up with outpatient care.

Group 3 comprises the majority of gamma alcoholics in Norway. They are worn down mentally and physically and need long treatment. Prognosis isn't too good, though far better than in Group 4, which constitutes the most difficult problem in all treatment efforts.

Group 5 patients are no problem as treatment subjects, but they are in bad need of charity, not only in the economic sense.

The treatment institutions hardly need description, but we would like to emphasize that *all* the indicated institutions are necessary if one wants to come to grips with *all* alcoholics in need of treatment. It is perhaps best to begin with an outpatient clinic. How to build the institutions isn't very important. What brings results is the ability of the staff to give *and take* in therapy, and this can be done in a shack as well as in a palace.

The question of voluntary or compulsory treatment must also be considered. There is no *right* answer to this; prevailing conditions very often will determine what is possible or necessary.

In Norway, the overwhelming majority of patients come voluntarily to the sanatoria, and compulsion is rarely exercised. (It is, however, evident that if there were no authority to compel treatment, some patients who now come voluntarily would not do so.) It should be mentioned also that patients can be sent to a sanatorium by sentence of the courts; one of the state's sanatoria is run on rather stricter lines (though still a fully open institution), and it is to this sanatorium that such patients are admitted.

The situation of the voluntary patient is rather curious. He signs a statement indicating his willingness to accept treatment for a stated period, usually twelve months (though it is in fact rare that the treatment lasts so long). Once admitted to the sanatorium, however, the patient is not free to discharge himself, until the period he himself has agreed to is up. This provision holds in spite of the legal axiom that a man cannot sign away his own freedom. The decision that the time has come for discharge rests solely with the medical director for the care of alcoholics. The patient is thus, in this regard, in exactly the same situation as the patient who was committed under compulsion.

In practice, a patient will not be refused discharge when there seems, according to qualified opinion, a good chance of success. But when necessary, the patient can be held until he has sufficient insight, or until work has been found for him, or until his social circumstances in other ways are satisfactorily arranged.

Patients discharged before their agreed time is up are in many cases asked to sign a "probation agreement." Under these terms, the patient accepts a small degree of supervision by his local sobriety committee and agrees to immediate readmission in the event of a relapse, for a further period of twelve months. The probationary period is usually one year. Other patients are discharged as "unfit for further treatment," though in such cases we prefer to add "for the time being" in order to leave the door at least ajar. Such a diagnosis is rarely made before several admissions have taken place without improvement (or without cooperation on the patient's part).

Readmission is, of course, no rarity. Two periods in sanatoria seem to be necessary in about one third of the cases, and after a second admission the outlook may be quite good. Patients who require three admissions, however, have definitely a worse prognosis, and if four are necessary, the chance of success is poor.

What constitutes therapy in alcoholism? In our view, it must include medical attention, social readjustment, and moral rebuilding. If we drop one or two of these factors, we are only treating a part of the problem. The physical care in social readjustment does not need further explanation, but the mental and moral aspects deserve close attention.

If we agree that loss of control is the leading symptom, the answer to the problem is simple enough: an alcoholic must never drink alcohol again. When a patient is allergic to raspberries or lobster, we find it very easy to persuade him never to touch the stuff again. Why cannot the alcoholic accept it the same way? There are many reasons, and I think it is very important to keep them in mind when we try to help the alcoholic. The most important motives for drinking can be divided into primary and secondary impulses.

In the first group, the expectation of euphoria through intoxication is probably the most important motive for drinking. The euphoria in itself is a temptation, and as a change in the daily life routine it is highly valued. Further, *loosening of inhibitions* is a motive for people who are introverted and anxious in company with others. Persons with a low *frustration threshold* will often turn to the bottle for consolation, and *depressed* minds think they can gain a higher spirit with alcohol beverages. Social drinking mores are of great importance, and the higher the tolerance to intoxicated people, the more alcoholics we find in a society. In many places the shame is not in being drunk, but in not being able to drink.

Alcohol is a habit-forming drug as well as an addictive drug, and the habit, if indulged, is a motive that can be said to lie between the primary and secondary motives. We know from many other situations of daily life how much we rely on habits and should not be surprised to see that alcoholic habits too have great importance. It is common to hear both abusers and alcoholics talking about drinking as something they just *do,* without really thinking of what they are doing. It somehow just happens to them that they are drinking again.

The secondary motives are above all escape mechanisms. The abuse brings a lot of personal and social difficulties, and intoxication is the easiest way to get rid of guilt and remorse. Early in the drinking career euphoria is most pronounced, but later on euphoria disappears and only oblivion remains as an escape. That does not stop alcoholics from dreaming of euphoria, and they always hope they will be able to enjoy intoxication again. Sometimes they do have a very short spell of euphoria which provides a new impulse to try again. In the alcoholic's mind, the secondary motives are the real reasons for drinking, and he thinks that if all his difficulties were done away with, he could stop drinking, or at least excessive drinking.

Therapy, therefore, must have an aim that reaches far beyond sobering up a patient and telling him not to be naughty again. It must try to get to the bottom of his problems, both the actual ones and those which inevitably will be reactivated, and help the patient to find a new way to a tolerable existence. Just as we cannot "heal" the allergic patient, we are not able to guarantee to the alcoholic that he will not relapse. On the contrary, we must warn him that a relapse is certain if he makes another attempt at drinking. Re-education is needed, and that can only happen if the patient cooperates.

How does psychotherapy come into this? Obviously there is no demand for psychotherapy in the cases that can be arrested with information and warning, assuming that the concept of psychotherapy is not extended to imply all kinds of personal guidance. For intractable cases, psychotherapy is very restricted, and in most of them probably a waste of time and money.

In Group 2 cases we can do something with psychotherapy. We must, however, not make the error of thinking that psychotherapy alone can work wonders. It is only as an integrated part of a full rehabilitation program that we can gain full value from psychotherapy. The social, physical, and moral rehabilitation of the patient is the aim of therapy, and psychotherapy must conform to these aims; it must not become an aim in itself. If we just dig conflicts and complexes out of the past and present, and look on them only, we are making the same error as the physician who gives electric treatment for polyneuritis without considering the diet fault behind that illness.

Most psychiatrists are well aware of this, but I think there is some danger in the overemphasis on psychotherapy, and many patients believe that treatment—that is, psychotherapy—can work miracles without their cooperation. We very often meet a patient who says: "I would quit drinking, if it weren't for my nerves," which means that the doctor is expected to "fix" his "nerves."

I think this danger exists also because the concept of illness has been stressed too much in discussion of alcoholism. Most people think that every illness has its penicillin, which implies that of course alcoholism also must have a special drug. We must be very careful in treating the alcoholic, because he is inclined to put all responsibility on the therapist, a position which is certainly flattering; but it won't work.

In all forms of psychotherapy the therapist will have to deal with difficulties springing from the patient's ignorance of his own reactions and motives, as well as unconscious (and conscious) resistance based on fear. The unconscious resistance has perhaps been overemphasized at the cost of conscious resistance. The patient's fear of "losing face" is very real. It is not only toward the therapist that he has this fear. Very often his "subjective status" in the family and at work will suffer by admission of helplessness in mental problems.

This is even more pronounced when we deal with alcoholics. They exhibit all the general symptoms of neurosis, which may be of preaddictive or postaddictive origin. The postaddictive neurotic reactions may be caused by the addiction, or only be concomitant to the addiction, caused by other factors. This must be cleared up in early treatment, as procedure must be adjusted to the different variations.

Some patterns of neurotic reactions are almost specific for alcoholism, or at least vastly exaggerated in alcoholism. They are caused by alcohol directly or indirectly but do not disappear with abstinence and are very often the cause of relapse in abuse.

SOCIAL ISOLATION. Perhaps the most obvious of these symptoms is social isolation, which is very often looked upon as an objective difficulty, not as a neurotic reaction. In fact it is both. The alcoholic will, during his many attempts at abstinence, undermine the faith his family and friends may have in him, and after a number of failures they will turn their backs on him. His approaches will be neglected or rebuffed, and he will stop his approaches for contact. In time he will react with fear and aggression against anyone who tries to help him; he will anticipate moral indoctrination and eventual rejection. In this way the alcoholic reinforces his isolation, and this will lead to further isolation.

MENTAL ISOLATION. The alcoholic is, in his opinion, shut off from everyone but those with whom he drinks. He doesn't feel he *belongs* to these "companions," but still they represent his only contact with other persons, and this contact will continue only as long as he continues his abuse. The alcoholic will lose interest in everything but alcohol, until his existence becomes extremely drab, intoxicated or not. He will dread reality, because this means facing an enormous load of guilt and responsibility. The mechanisms used to avoid reality are mostly simple negation, or substitution. The alcoholic will let every conscious moment be filled with trifles, and he is always on the lookout for such things. If there aren't any, he will invent some and can be very ingenious at that. Just to stop abuse doesn't break this habit; the alcoholic will need long training to face reality again.

Further, the alcoholic is mentally isolated in time. He lives in the moment, and will draw the blinds to the past as well as the future. By limiting his outlook to 12–16 hours, he escapes all kinds of planning which make memory as well as anticipation necessary. The maximum effort of planning will be limited to the next day's supply of alcohol, and even this planning will be done in a very direct and often primitive way.

The alcoholic will often see himself as the victim of unfortunate circumstances, and thus escapes responsibility for his abuse. This in time makes him demanding toward his therapist, and society in general. He dwells in the center of his vicious circle where all his social and personal shortcomings are motives for continued abuse, and he can't see outside this circle.

To complicate the situation further, the alcoholic will use alcohol as the way out of all difficulties. Alcohol is his medicine against depression, anxiety, fear, and restlessness. It is his armor against a hostile world, his shield from guilt and remorse. Without it, he feels naked and exposed to a reality he can't face. Over months and years he gets used to this, and withdrawal from alcohol will not help him right away. On the contrary, he will often be worse off in most ways without alcohol, and accordingly it is no surprise that forced abstinence in itself doesn't cure an alcoholic. To function socially, one has to be experienced. The alcoholic hasn't had this experience for years, and fails hopelessly in attempts to live rationally.

All the escape mechanisms in alcoholism also bar the alcoholic from knowledge about his own condition. Most alcoholics who come for treatment feel they need help but don't know *what* they need help for or from or how the help can be given.

They will either want relief from all secondary difficulties, a relief they believe will cure everything, or they expect a miracle treatment that will do away with their craving forever. They lack understanding of their own condition, and believe very often that they only have to *decide* to stop their abuse. After an hour or two with the therapist they will say: "Now I understand that I must quit alcohol, and will do that." To the therapist's question whether this hasn't been "decided" ten or a hundred times before, the answer is a frank: "That is true, but this time I really mean it." They are honest enough, as they have been in all other moments of "decision," but they don't realize that it takes more than a decision to quit the habit.

How do we cope with these patients? Obviously the answer is that they need psychotherapy. They need help to get real insights about their condition, their reactions, and attitudes. They must be taught that their symptoms are changeable, that their standard answer—"I am that way"—will not be accepted as an explanation for all relapses.

We are accustomed to look at individual therapy as the most expedient way to help our patients. The trust in the therapist is easily gained in the direct relationship, without rivals. The feeling of security in knowing that what is said is between the two makes it easier to break off treatment when reality begins to threaten too much. It is the patient's security valve. He will be more than happy to have the therapist all to himself, and will try to enclose himself with the therapist in a relationship that is sealed off from reality. Instead of being alone in his mental "shell box" he will have the therapist as a companion, with whom to share his difficulties, to empathize, and to indulge in fantasies. He will harp on opinions about everything, and when the therapist tries to put some reality into the sessions, he will be told: "Now listen, you haven't really understood my problems, now I will explain,——" and the alcoholic starts all over again to "explain."

The alcoholic will simply abuse the therapist as long as possible. He very often takes advantage of the therapist's not being an alcoholic, saying: "Of course, you can't understand this at all. According to the A.A. slogan: 'Only an alcoholic can understand an alcoholic.' " If these difficulties are overcome by tactful handling and tolerance, the treatment may seem to proceed successfully for some time. The patient will discuss his reactions, and eventually take a more realistic view of himself. The patient and the therapist both become optimistic until the moment arrives when the alcoholic must try out his insight in society. Usually this will end in a relapse. The patient hasn't broken out of his isolation; he can't face reality on the outside. Only in the sanctuary of the therapist's consultation room is he able to play with reality.

How many therapists have felt terrible frustration after endless hours of seemingly successful therapy, we don't know. But we do know that many of them have dropped their alcoholic patients because of such experience. Of course, they ought to have anticipated this failure. The alcoholic is socially sick, and must be treated as such. He has to be trained to function socially again.

How do we overcome this difficulty? The answer is simple enough. We create a small controlled society for the patient's training. This society must to a certain extent be sheltered, so that at least for a while the demands on the patient aren't too overwhelming. At the same time it must be demanding enough so that the patient can't continue to play hide-and-seek with himself. The best answer is, in my opinion, a group of patients with a realistic leader.

In *group therapy* the patient must not be allowed to "pair off" with the therapist or another group member during sessions. If he does, he is maintaining his isolation. The striving to do this is very marked in opening sessions. The alcoholic will need much more time to become a positive member than the average neurotic patient, and he will turn back to the security of isolation as soon as he feels threatened in some way, which is often. Setbacks in group progress are common in the treatment of alcoholics and should not disappoint the therapist too much.

Alcoholics will often protest that they cannot divulge their secrets in the company of other patients, because they fear others won't keep them. This may be a real fear, but usually it is only a way to avoid facing reality, or to withhold information from the therapist. Outside the group they very often talk freely to other patients about things they try to hide in sessions. Afterwards, they even complain that because of group therapy they can't have any secrets. The truth is that they reject their own "confessions," because they may be too painful to cope with. And they have more to hide from the therapists than from other patients, who will "know" anyway.

Because he has lost contact with reality, the alcoholic will often tell stories that are a long way from the truth. This doesn't mean that he is consciously lying. He may be honest, but his memory is twisted by wishful thinking. He will be terribly hurt when told that he is lying, and the therapist must be careful in correcting him, explaining his inability to see the truth at the moment. A trained therapist will know that beginning a new group and getting it going takes more work on his part than is usual in group therapy with "ordinary" neurotics. The passive resistance in an alcoholic group is formidable, and the technique of keeping a "loaded" silence will not work. Alcoholics will just "wander" off in fantasies of their own, and can sit for an hour or more without feeling pressure or anxiety. Only the therapist will become panicky.

The best way to get an alcoholic group going is to give information on alcoholism in a general way. It must not be a moralistic approach; the therapist must have a thorough knowledge about alcohol, its effects, and alcoholism in general. If his information is incomplete or wrong, he will only be the laughing stock of the group. When the information is digested, i.e., when the group has a clear understanding of what alcoholism is, the next step is to make the members realize that they are alcoholics. This is a crucial point. If patients start discussing their symptoms right away, we are lucky. In most groups we must ask a lot of leading questions of each patient, and here thorough knowledge of each patient's *historia morbi* is essential. Otherwise the patient will suppress the truth, and give only a superficial account. In this phase other patients will work as a corrective to an individual member, and can pin him down when necessary. The risk is that the group members deal too gently with each other, which at times forces the therapist to be very provocative.

When the symptoms have been worked through, and the group intellectually admits to alcoholism, the next step is to gain an emotional acceptance. This can be done only by working on the patients' attitudes toward themselves and society. They have to learn that their emotional life is much more important than the reasoning which gives them ready-made "solutions" to all difficulties. In analyzing their emotional motives, they can come to grips with the powerful factors that rule their lives. It is a painful process, and resistance is high in this phase of treatment.

When emotional acceptance is achieved, the group proceeds to make members work on their reaction habits. This will come very naturally if the previous step is accomplished well. The patients now feel that something "really important" is happening to them, and they often become overoptimistic. They must be warned, however, to recognize that this attitude is wrong, and must be changed, and that there is still a long way to go. The therapist will have a hard time keeping the group proceeding in a meaningful way. Sometimes it is inevitable that one or more group members have a relapse before they understand that it takes training to control one's reactions. They will return less optimistic, but more realistic; and therapy can go on in a more down-to-earth atmosphere.

I find no reason to go into all the pitfalls for the therapist dealing with alcoholics. They include all the difficulties we know from therapy in general, and in addition, coping with our own attitude toward the alcoholic, which usually isn't too tolerant. It is rather difficult not to feel pharisaic when confronted with countless relapses. The temptation to wash our hands of responsibility and say they *are* hopeless is great. No wonder that many therapists give up in despair and turn to more rewarding cases. Since much has been written about hypnotic therapy with alcoholics, I would like to say that this certainly is a fast way to spectacular, but short-lived, success. In our experience we find that dependence on the therapist becomes so extreme that the alcoholic only substitutes the therapist for alcohol. As soon as the contact is cut off, a relapse is sure to follow.

Psychoanalysis may help some alcoholics, especially those who are extremely neurotic before becoming addicted. The neurosis is the cause of addiction, not the result. Addiction in itself responds poorly to analytic approaches.

The role of prescription drugs in alcoholic therapy is rather complicated, and can be controversial as well as paradoxical. One is inclined to say that for alcoholics all drugs should be banned; the aim of therapy is to get rid of dependence on alcohol. There are at least two fallacies in this reasoning: The drug isn't specified; and we can't be sure the alcoholic is able to live without alcohol. If we go further, however, we soon find that there is some truth in the slogan: no drugs. There is a tendency to move to other drugs which the alcoholic may believe are less dangerous. In this he will be disappointed; drugs that give him relief are always dangerous.

Still, there are phases in therapy when drugs are necessary. The intoxicated alcoholic brought into the hospital may be rather a nuisance. He is often boisterous, demanding this and that, and above all, wants to be given more alcohol. Sometimes he is on the border of a delirium or fit. To sedate a person in this condition is always wise, and one must take into consideration what kind, and what amount, of alcohol the patient has consumed.

In treating alcoholics the deterrent drugs, disulfiram and calciumcarbamide, have an important role as a means of keeping the patient sober temporarily. They are of high value during initial phases of treatment, and on occasions when there are special difficulties or temptations to cope with. One must always keep in mind, however, that these drugs don't do anything to the *motives* to drink. They don't take away the craving for alcohol, and only a patient bent on sobriety can be helped by them. To believe that a month's or a year's abstinence based only on disulfiram can alter the patient's attitude is pure superstition.

The *aversion* therapy has been highly recommended by several treatment centers. We have also tried it, but with little success. We think this treatment may work where the motive to drink is chiefly social, i.e., outside the patient.

In conclusion, I would like to emphasize that although therapy with alcoholics gives little reward in many, or perhaps most cases, there is still much we can do for these patients. We must not aim too high, always keeping in mind that our efforts must be realistic, adjusted to the patient's real needs and possibilities. Everyone must have his chance in therapy whether the outlook is grim or not. We are surprised at the relapse of many patients we regard as good prospects, but sometimes we also find that cases we have written off as hopeless suddenly turn round and are resocialized. We don't know enough to give the correct prognosis in most cases, and factors unknown to us are always at work. Above all, we should remember that we are dealing with complicated conditions, and so far there is no "right" approach that covers all the difficulties in treatment of alcoholism.

## REFERENCES

1. G. D. Banks, "The Treatment of Alcoholics in Norway," *British Journal of Addictions,* Vol. 59, No. 2.

2. Th. Kjolstad, "Psychotherapy of Alcoholics," *British Journal of Addictions,* Vol. 61, pp. 35–49.

3. ———, "Gruppentherapie bei Alkoholikern," *Wiener Med. Woch. Schr.,* 1965, No. 5, pp. 146–158.

4. ———, "Psychotherapy in the Treatment of the Alcoholic," *Alcoholism,* Zagreb: 1966, Vol. 1, pp. 75–84.

5. ———, "Alcoholism and Its Treatment in Norway," *Alcoholism,* Zagreb: 1966, Vol. 51, pp. 1–12.

6. ———, "Die Aufgaben der spez. Anstalt für Alkoholkranke," *Symposium über den Alkoholismus,* Vienna: 1968.

7. ———, "Psychotherapy, Group Therapy, and Drugs in the Treatment of Addicts," *International Congress on Group Psychotherapy,* Vienna: September 1968.

# Alcoholism in Australia

*RODNEY SEABORN, M.D., and A. P. DIEHM*

A small organization known as the Langton Clinic in Sydney became the first voluntary treatment center for alcoholism and drug dependence in Australia. From a modest beginning grew an active, nationwide campaign to battle these twin health problems. Constantly in the center of the action, Dr. Rodney Seaborn and his associate, Peter Diehm, worked together, culminating their efforts in 1969 as chairman and executive director, respectively, of the 29th International Congress on Alcoholism and Drug Dependence. The story of the development of the Australian program indicates how effective determined work by a few individuals can be.

When the history of systematic research and data collection in relation to addictions in Australia is written, it is certain that the point of departure will be September 1966, when it was agreed by the International Council on Alcohol and Addictions that the Foundation for Research and Treatment of Alcoholism and Drug Dependence of N.S.W. (hereafter called "FRATADD" *) would be the host foundation in Sydney to the 29th International Congress on Alcoholism and Drug Dependence.

The decade 1956 to 1966 had seen very substantial development of treatment resources in every state of Australia and the expenditure of vast sums of governmental and private money on

* Before 1966, FRATADD was "FRATA"—the Foundation for Research and Treatment of Alcoholism of N.S.W.

the establishment and maintenance of hospital facilities. This development has been accelerated appreciably throughout September 1966, to the present time, in both government and voluntary programs and, indeed, in private hospitals. But the necessity for data retrieval and communication is only now coming to be generally recognized, and this present awareness is in very large measure attributable to the stimulus provided by preparations and planning for the 29th Congress.

Alcoholism as a substantial public health problem probably dates from the arrival in 1788 of the First Fleet, which sailed into a beautiful harbor (Sydney Harbour) and founded the first Australian settlement, later to become the city of Sydney.

The Fleet of eleven ships carried a cargo consisting for the most part of convicts sent out from England. In the early days of New South Wales, rum was extensively and, for a short time, universally used as currency, with official approval. The present Sydney Hospital, the first in Australia, was originally called the "Rum Hospital" because the currency used to build it was virtually in the form of rum. Also, in the early days of our nation, the abuse of rum, associated with the politics of the day, resulted in the famous "Rum Rebellion." The unhappy convict life of many of our original settlers, together with the use of rum as barter and for favors, probably resulted in considerable alcoholism. The treatment then, no doubt, would have been exclusively punitive.

The first legislation for compulsory treatment of "inebriates" was the "Inebriates Act," which became law in the state of New South Wales in 1912. Comparable legislation was introduced in other mainland states between 1912 and 1927 and has, with but minor revisions, remained operative in New South Wales until the present time. In other states, new legislation has been quite recently introduced to incorporate compulsory treatment for drug addiction as well as alcoholism (for example, the "Alcohol and Drug Addicts [Treatment] Act" of South Australia).

Although there had been some experimentation in private hospitals for the treatment of alcoholism before the introduction of the first inebriates legislation, the first offenders committed under the legislation were confined in the State Penitentiary. Very shortly, however, this practice was abandoned except in the case of notoriously violent patients; instead of going to the State Penitentiary persons committed were confined in state psychiatric institutions for periods ranging from three to twelve months. There is evidence to support the view that motivation for this change from prison to psychiatric institutions was practical expedience rather than humanitarian concern or any intention to provide adequate treatment. The treatment afforded was essentially custodial care and segregation from the temptation and opportunity to drink.

The introduction of Alcoholics Anonymous to this country in 1946 provided considerable stimulus for the development of hospital treatment services; and the initiative in this direction was taken by private hospitals—the first and perhaps the best known of which was started on the initiative of a psychiatrist, Dr. Silvester Minogue, himself a recovered alcoholic. Dr. Minogue was primarily responsible for introducing Alcoholics Anonymous to Australia. He has done and is still doing much in the treatment of the alcoholic.

Through the missionary zeal of the pioneering members of Alcoholics Anonymous, it was not long before A.A. groups were established within the psychiatric institutions to which alcoholics were committed under the Inebriates Act. The impact of these groups, and the enthusiastic official support accorded them, did much to modify the "custodial" nature of the treatment. The present emphasis on therapeutic programs within these institutions is in large measure attributable to A.A. institutional groups in the decade 1946 to 1956.

Alcoholics Anonymous performed two vital functions which, more than any other factors, have been responsible for the rapid extension of treatment resources throughout the Commonwealth of Australia over the past decade. First, A.A. members provided incontrovertible evidence that alcoholism can be successfully treated. This encouraged an increasing number of persons to seek assistance and highlighted deficiencies of our hospital treatment resources. Second, responsible A.A. members by their restraint, perseverance, and example, challenged officials, professional bodies, and the community at large to reconsider the hostile attitude toward alcoholism as moral deviance. From this ferment of reappraisal it became clear that the incidence of alcoholism, at least in the metropolitan community, was far greater than had been recognized and that "something must be done."

It was quickly established that Alcoholics Anonymous was effectively precluded by "tradition" from being involved in the complex task of pressuring governments, organizations, and the community to provide the substantial funds needed for development of an adequate treatment program for alcoholism. It seemed that the only persons aware of what needed to be done were those who, within the restrictions of membership in Alcoholics Anonymous, were effectively restrained from doing it.

This problem was resolved in 1956 by the establishment of a voluntary organization in the city of Sydney, N.S.W., namely, FRATADD of N.S.W. FRATADD had, as its primary objective, the development of resources for the treatment of alcoholism and the modification of hostile popular and official attitudes toward alcoholism and alcoholics. Since the establishment of FRATADD, organizations having substantially similar objectives have emerged in every state of the Commonwealth; some, voluntary organizations registered as nonprofit companies, and others with government sponsorship. Virtually all of the very large number of treatment facilities, public and private, now operating throughout the Commonwealth have been established or substantially extended because of the work of voluntary organizations.

FRATADD made great strides in its early efforts to promote popular acceptance of alcoholism as a medical disability that can be treated successfully, but was seriously embarrassed by the glaring inadequacy in treatment resources available to the many persons encouraged by FRATADD's educational activities to seek voluntary treatment. Psychiatric hospitals were at this time under very serious pressure for admission of psychiatric patients, and quite unable to meet the demand for voluntary admission of alcoholics. Almost all available accommodations for alcoholic patients were filled by those forced to get treatment under the Inebriates Legislation. To further complicate an already serious situation, increasing numbers of alcoholics were seeking assistance at a much earlier stage in their drinking careers than was heretofore the case, but they were understandably quite unwilling to accept the stigma of admission to a psychiatric institution.

Happily, FRATADD was able at this time (1959) to acquire a small but ideally located hospital to provide voluntary treatment for many alcoholic patients. It was the foundation's intention to provide voluntary hospitalization for that large group of patients now coming forward who were unable to afford substantial fees for private hospital treatment. Lacking financial resources to enable it to maintain such a hospital, FRATADD, through negotiation with the government of N.S.W., was successful in having the hospital incorporated as a public facility. Thus the Langton Clinic became the first public hospital in the Commonwealth of Australia to be devoted exclusively to the treatment of alcoholism on a voluntary, general hospital basis. So successful was this institution that very quickly it became necessary to extend the inpatient accommodations and substantially enlarge outpatient services.

At the outset two conditions were imposed as matters of general policy: first, only voluntary patients could be accepted; and second, a person's ability to pay must not be taken into account. These two principles have been religiously observed to the present day.

The clinic is an incorporated public hospital, governed and administered by an elected Board of Directors. The original twelve-man board included some six members of long standing of Alcoholics Anonymous, but the majority at present are nonalcoholics.

The clinic is bound by the same by-laws and rules that apply to every other public general hospital in the state, and its administrative structure and both medical and nursing services are in every way comparable to those of a general medical hospital. The orientation is medical, but to a great extent therapy is psychotherapeutic. Individual psychotherapy plays a prominent part, as well as daily group therapy and exposure to Alcoholics Anonymous and Narcotics Anonymous. The clinic now has an inpatient department of fifty beds, and a fairly extensive outpatient service operating throughout the day and early evening.

Medical services are provided by a full-time medical superintendent (physician), three part-time physicians, a part-time psychiatrist, a pathologist, and a clinical chemist. Also available on request are four consultant physicians and two consultant psychiatrists. The medical staff is assisted by a full-time clinical psychologist and three part-time psychologists, upon whom the group therapy program substantially depends. A medical social worker for inpatients and a full staff of general trained nurses completes the staff.

Two points about the medical staff are worthy of note. First, the nonpsychiatric members have acquired a high degree of competence in the use of psychotropic drugs. Second, the psychiatrists generally see only those patients referred by the physicians and do not routinely see patients on admission.

We do not suggest that this is an ideal arrangement, for we are acutely conscious of the deficiencies in our psychiatric service and are trying at the moment to provide for at least one full-time psychiatrist. However, the circumstances under which the clinic has functioned for the past nine years lend considerable emphasis to the role of the physician in treating addictions, an area once seen as the exclusive domain of the psychiatrist. The operation of the clinic during this period provides sound evidence of the value of the general hospital approach to the treatment of addictions for an identifiable group of patients.

The duration of inpatient treatment is about three weeks, with an outpatient follow-up of weekly visits for an indefinite period, for either personal counseling, group psychotherapy, or both. Membership in Alcoholics Anonymous or Narcotics Anonymous is encouraged.

It is recognized that, at present, not all addicts could benefit from the treatment provided by the Langton Clinic; ours is but one of several alternatives that should exist in every community. However, the demand for the clinic's services has been more than sufficient to indicate that, in the future, there must be a greater emphasis on this type of treatment facility. Because of the demand for voluntary hospitalization, it has been both possible and necessary for the clinic to be selective in its admission policy.

The basic criteria for admission are: motivation (not always easy to assess), capacity to benefit from treatment which is largely verbal, and absence of chronic psychotic disturbance. Our rejection of the retarded, under-socialized, and skid-row alcoholic does not imply that he is regarded as untreatable, or not worth treating, but simply that he is unlikely to benefit from the clinic's regimen, which is properly seen as but one of several possibilities. We feel that the range of alternatives and variations must constantly be extended. In fact, there are other agencies in Sydney exclusively concerned with this important group of patients.

The clinic admits about one thousand patients annually. Some 80 percent are referred by local general practitioners. Social welfare agencies, churches, Alcoholics Anonymous, and AL Anon send another 10 percent. Others come as a result of publicity relating to the clinic, self-referrals, and the recommendation of former patients.

The success of a voluntary public hospital for the treatment of addictions depends largely on its ability to attract patients who are reluctant to admit the necessity for seeking treatment. For this reason, we would say without qualification that the success of our clinic has depended largely on the educational activities of FRATADD.

Another important consideration is the hospital's reputation and the public confidence it inspires. In this area more than most, "nothing succeeds like success." The range of services, medical and para-medical, both at inpatient and outpatient levels, and the supportive rehabilitation services must be adequate. In this connection we should mention that the clinic operates Langton House, a residential rehabilitation center which admits selected patients on discharge from the clinic. These patients are selected by a panel comprising the medical superintendent, the clinical psychologist, and the social worker, and each must be able to pay minimum board and lodging charges. Langton House has accommodation for fourteen men and is financially self-supporting from board and lodging charges.

Patients at Langton House follow their usual occupations by day, attend the clinic as outpatients on one or two evenings weekly, and are encouraged to join local Alcoholics Anonymous and Narcotics Anonymous groups. The success rate at Langton

House measured in terms of long-term sobriety, social adjustment, and employment stability is quite impressive.

The clinic also has the capacity and willingness to treat the spouse and, where necessary, the whole family of the addict. The full range of outpatient services is available to the families of the addict, and every encouragement is given them to attend regularly.

Although a voluntary hospital for the treatment of addictions cannot expect to undertake total patient care, it does have a responsibility to investigate, diagnose, and arrange for the treatment of concomitant physical ailments so commonly found in addicts.

In New South Wales a study of all hospital services is being undertaken on the basis of long-term regional planning. One consideration is the relationship of the special hospital for treatment of addictions to other hospitals and welfare services of the region, and its integration with all the other agencies in any way concerned with the treatment of addictions. The clinic now also provides referral service for other hospitals in the city.

Whether it wishes or not, the voluntary public hospital for the treatment of addictions must accept a substantial responsibility for teaching and research. FRATADD discharges this responsibility largely through Langton Clinic.

Over the past ten years, one in every five patients admitted to Langton Clinic for treatment of alcoholism has been a female, but there are no rehabilitation services for female addicts in the state. Impressed by the success of the Langton House center for male patients, FRATADD has sought to establish a similar facility for female addicts. This has so far proven beyond the foundation's financial resources; but a ladies' "Silver Lining Committee" was established three years ago to raise funds, and we expect the first residential rehabilitation center in Australia for female addicts to be opened in 1970 in Sydney.

An indication of the effective working relationship between FRATADD and the State Health Department is the fact that the foundation's advice was sought on the establishment of the Health Department's first special unit for treatment of alcoholism. In 1962, the Health Department established a special unit within the Lidcombe State Hospital for treatment of alcoholics on a voluntary basis, and named the unit FRATA House in recognition of the work of the foundation. FRATA House provides services for inpatient and outpatient treatment of alcoholics comparable to the services of the Langton Clinic, though inpatient treatment is usually for a longer period.

Australia now has some 45 hospital units and outpatient counseling centers established exclusively for treatment of addictions. The development of services in each state has been undertaken independently, but it was not long before the need was felt to provide some formal means of communication, between organizations in each state concerned with alcoholism programs and between professional workers in the field. The first objective has now been accomplished by the establishment of the Foundation for the Research and Treatment of Alcoholism of Australia (FRATA of Australia), a voluntary organization to which FRATADD of N.S.W. and the voluntary foundations of the other states are affiliated, and on which most governmental agencies are now represented either by members or observers. This body meets quarterly in different states in rotation, and all offices within the organization also rotate between states. The second objective, communication between professional workers, has been substantially accomplished by the annual Summer Schools of Alcohol Studies conducted by Melbourne University and the Alcoholism Foundation of Victoria.

By 1966, the structure of a substantial alcoholism program, extending throughout the Commonwealth, had been established. At this time there was little awareness that Australia could be facing a serious problem from the misuse of drugs other than alcohol, and it was not until a series of seminars was convened by the Institute of Criminology in Sydney that any serious attention was focused in this direction. Following the consideration of material contributed to these closed seminars and the investigations of its own Research Council, the Foundation for Research and Treatment of Alcoholism of New South Wales decided that it must extend its concerns to incorporate problems of drug dependence; and in 1966, this foundation became the Foundation for Research and Treatment of Alcoholism and Drug Dependence of New South Wales (FRATADD)—the first voluntary organization in this country to be concerned with the problems of drug dependence.

To return to the problem of alcoholism, we should note that, other than FRATADD's establishment of Langton Clinic, Langton House, and Frata House as already mentioned, the development of hospital services for the treatment of alcoholism in Australia has not proceeded according to any predetermined program, but rather, each hospital, or each alcoholism unit within a hospital, was established to meet a particular crisis. This more or less haphazard development has in some ways been valuable, because it has led to extensive experimentation with the institutional environment in which treatment is offered, and with the nature of the treatment. Of the great number of treatment centers now functioning, no two are directly comparable, each having important unique features.

Quite fortuitously, the placing of alcoholism treatment resources in the metropolitan communities seemed to have proceeded on the assumption (which can now be reasonably justified) that the alcoholic population can be divided into at least six distinct groups (which will not be described here), with further refinement and subgroupings emerging from the more detailed investigation of patients applying for treatment. It is of interest, and of considerable practical import, to understand that each of the treatment and rehabilitation centers has designed its intake and treatment procedures to meet the needs of a specific group of patients, and that none has claimed that its resources are adequate to treat all comers.

However, it has proven extremely difficult to evaluate the outcome of treatment in any of these institutions because of the tremendous problems yet to be resolved before adequate follow-up studies can be attempted. Nevertheless, some studies, possibly too restricted in scope and hampered by many recognized deficiencies in design, were attempted and formed the basis of papers presented to particular sections of the 29th International Congress. Should these attempts and evaluations accomplish nothing other than to focus attention on deficiencies, they will have served an invaluable purpose.

In short, after twenty years of work on the development of

treatment resources for alcoholics, we had by mid-1966 achieved substantial and diversified treatment capability, the beginnings of a rehabilitation service, no established research capacity, and a dawning awareness of an embryonic but viable drug problem in our midst. It was at this stage of development that we were faced with planning for the 29th Congress. Initially, the responsibility for organization of the congress rested jointly with the International Council on Alcohol and Addictions and FRATADD of N.S.W., and immediately we in Sydney were confronted with the necessity to develop simultaneously two structures—executive and scientific—and to extend each of these to embrace all states of the Commonwealth.

The effort in creating these parallel structures produced substantial benefit and has important long-term implications. Having only very recently become involved with problems of drug dependence, it was necessary for FRATADD of New South Wales to build a complex scientific organization that would include representatives of every scientific discipline and every state and voluntary agency having a substantial involvement in the problem of addictions. At an initial meeting the major areas of concern were listed as:

1. Medicine
2. Psychiatry
3. Law and implementation (medicolegal)
4. The social and behavioral sciences
5. Education
6. Social welfare
7. Traffic safety

This provided a frame of reference for planning the congress. Specialist committees, having widely representative membership, were set up to examine addictions from each of these standpoints, and to produce a congress program appropriate to the interests of the professional groups involved in each of these areas. Because the accomplishments of each of these committees will have significance well beyond the congress, we feel it would be of interest to describe the work of some of them.

## MEDICOLEGAL

The coincidence of FRATADD's new concern with problems of addictions, the initiative of the Institute of Criminology in convening a series of interdisciplinary seminars on drug dependence, the passage of new drug control legislation, the emergence of the Australia Academy of Forensic Sciences, and the granting of an International Congress on Alcoholism and Drug Dependence to be held in Sydney was truly remarkable, even providential, and underscores the significance of 1966 in the history of treatment of addictions in this country. Out of this ferment emerged guidelines and terms of reference for a critical examination of the medicolegal aspects of addictions per se, and the infinitely broader concept envisaged for the International Congress, at which it was intended from the outset to examine addictions from many standpoints.

In 1966, the consensus of informed opinion was that drug abuse had certainly not reached any serious dimensions in Australia. However, from a consideration of trends in other countries it was recognized that preventive measures should be initiated to circumvent the emergence of a serious drug problem. The initiative in beginning this first major review of drug abuse and of the legal and the social sanctions against addiction was taken by the Institute of Criminology in Sydney under the direction of the Chief Justice of New South Wales, the Honorable Sir Leslie Herron, and the Dean of the Faculty of Law at the University of Sydney, Professor K. O. Shatwell. In a series of closed meetings extending over a period of several months in the latter half of 1966 reports were considered by representatives from the Police Drug Squad, the judiciary, the magistracy, customs officials, Health Department officials, prominent academics, pharmaceutical manufactures, psychiatrists, and physicians in private practice as well as members of the Justice Department, Child Welfare Department, the Department of Corrections, FRATADD of N.S.W., and executives of other voluntary health and welfare agencies.

A comprehensive, carefully documented report resulting from

these meetings was made available to legislators of the Common-wealth and of the state of New South Wales. This method of initiating serious inquiry into matters of public concern and the participation and unstinting cooperation of government depart-ments is probably peculiar to Australia and focuses attention on the role and responsibility of nongovernmental agencies in the formulation of public policies in this country.

From one of these seminars, and out of the meetings of the judiciary which followed, emerged the nucleus of the medico-legal committee of the 29th International Congress on Alcoholism and Drug Dependence. Almost every member of this committee had been involved in the Institute of Criminology meetings and many were in fact members of the institute. Represented on the medicolegal committee are FRATADD of N.S.W., the Institute of Criminology, the Australian Academy of Forensic Sciences, the Sydney Metropolitan Board of Magistrates, the judiciary, the New South Wales government departments of health, justice, child and social welfare, and police, the Commonwealth depart-ments of customs, the Adult Probation Service, the university department of law and sociology, and the major hospitals con-cerned in the treatment of addicts.

Although the Institute of Criminology seminars sparked an initial penetrating look at the problem of addictions in Sydney and made some interesting projections about probable future development, it was beyond the scope of this body to provide for periodic review or to initiate a continuing program of sys-tematic investigation.

Though the primary function of the medicolegal committee was to plan a program for its section of the congress, the paucity of information available forced the committee to embark on a program of systematic inquiry into vital medicolegal aspects of addiction which had hitherto received no serious consideration.

Until this time each of the agencies represented on the com-mittee had worked in splendid isolation, seeing the problem of addictions only from the narrowly circumscribed perspectives of its own immediate practical involvement. For example, the Drug Squad Officers were familiar with the circumstances of an arrest but had little opportunity to discover what became of an addict until he was arrested a second time. Similarly, the physician was familiar with the addict in the hospital but knew little about his past or in most cases what became of him after discharge. Magistrates, willing to adopt a therapeutic rather than punitive approach, were handicapped by inadequate information and had virtually no opportunity to seek medical evidence on which to base assessment. Further, though each of the agencies concerned with addicts maintained some records designed to meet its own administrative need, there was no basis on which these records could be compared or interrelated; and certainly no adequate attention had been paid by anyone to the crucial question of methodical data collection and retrieval.

An interesting illustration of immediate practical benefits from the work of the medicolegal committee is the "Langton Project" as reported on at the Congress. As previously mentioned, the Langton Clinic is a public hospital established by FRATADD of N.S.W. in 1959 for the treatment of alcoholism. Following the Institute of Criminology seminars, the deficiencies of treatment resources for addicts met severe criticism. The Board of Directors of the Langton Clinic offered to make available a small part of the resources of the clinic for a controlled experiment to assess the value of short-term inpatient treatment of addicts, followed by extended outpatient follow-up under appropriate supervision.

An invitation to participate in this study was extended to a research group, including a senior representative of the Police Drug Squad, a magistrate, a senior officer of the Adult Probation Service, a representative of the Commonwealth Employment Service, the Prison Medical Service, the medical superintendent and the clinical psychologist of the Langton Clinic, which was asked to design and carry out a study to compare the effectiveness of this form of treatment with treatment of longer duration in other institutions. It is not our concern either to describe the study or to anticipate its conclusions, which have been discussed at the congress. But we are concerned to emphasize that great practical value has already accrued to each of the agencies participating in this study through improved communication and through new insights into the problem of addictions. There is little doubt that the perspective of each of the participants has broadened considerably and that new opportunities for mutual assistance are constantly emerging. From this small-scale study could well emerge a substantial coordination of resources in prevention, rehabilitation, and treatment.

It is quite fascinating to see how improved communication has already been extended to day-to-day work on matters not directly related to the project. This is important because the first introduction most addicts have to treatment is at the time of arrest or conviction for drug offenses. The deliberate use of the law enforcement services to get addicts to treatment is developing in a most commendable way. It is our hope that the excellent degree of cooperation and coordination achieved on a small scale by the participants in this project will ultimately lead to a similar degree of cooperation between all departments and agencies.

The committee is also involved in the first attempts at statistical and demographic research undertaken in this city relating to alcoholism and the abuse of other drugs. Much of the exceedingly difficult groundwork has been laid and many of the obstacles removed from the path of future research workers, who will find an acceptable basis already established for the launching of more sophisticated projects.

Of incalculable practical significance is a most interesting study under the medicolegal committee's direction of the attitudes of the many groups having official or professional responsibility in relation to the treatment of addicts, and the correlation (if any) between these attitudes and the outcome of treatment. But perhaps the most encouraging development is the virtually continuous review of the drug legislation in the state of New South Wales. The philosophy of the law and the specific provisions of the legislation and its practical administration and implementation are being subjected to constant, painstaking scrutiny by eminent jurists, legislators, health services administrators, and their professional advisors. It is fair, therefore, to say that these groups and projects are influencing the law and the manner of its implementation to meet a developing drug problem.

We are deliberately exploiting the opportunities afforded us through the 29th Congress, and invite the attention of other countries to the very real and enduring benefits (as well as the burdens) of being host to international meetings of this kind.

## TRAFFIC SAFETY

The emphasis of the Australian contribution to the 29th Congress was focused on major areas of immediate practical concern in this country. We feel this is quite legitimate because the areas of importance to us are of equal concern to all those countries trying, with limited resources, to come to grips with the complex of problems only now emerging in serious dimensions. One such area of major and immediate practical concern is that of traffic safety. In the year 1968–1969, traffic accidents attributable directly to drunkenness have increased 22 percent, deaths by 44 percent, and injuries by 23 percent compared with the preceding year.

The correlation between alcohol and drug abuse and traffic accidents is well documented, and has prompted revised or new legislation related to drinking and driving in all Australian states within the past two years. In New South Wales, the breathalyser has been in constant use in the metropolitan area and in the densely populated industrial cities of the central coastal area. Experience with the breathalyser and statistical evidence related to its use was documented in reports to the congress. But so great is the concern over the steadily increasing rate of road accidents and with the number of drivers convicted in N.S.W. with blood–alcohol levels in excess of the legal 0.08 that, in conjunction with the Road Safety Council of New South Wales, FRATADD organized a three-day symposium under the presidency of Sir William Hudson on the subject of alcohol, drugs, and traffic safety. Considerable research was undertaken in preparation for the symposium, including a study of the effects of varying blood–alcohol levels on the driving of a group of skilled racing drivers, whose performance was compared with that of a group of average motorists under stringently controlled circumstances.

Studies such as this have brought into effective working liaison police traffic experts, police breathalyser experts, the staff of the

School of Applied Psychology of the University of New South Wales, experts from the Confederation of Australian Motor Sport and other motoring organizations, as well as the professional staff of the Langton Clinic—all of whom have a common concern with motoring safety.

Much work has been done in many countries on the correlation between alcohol and driving performance, and, therefore, in the 29th Congress Alcohol, Drugs, and Traffic Safety Symposium, a special effort was made to give a more prominent role to drugs other than alcohol, and their effects on driving performance. However, of even greater significance than the considerable volume of valuable research stimulated by the congress was the working liaison effected among many agencies heretofore working in comparative isolation. The symposium has prompted a critical examination of legislation relating to alcohol and other drugs and driving and its effectiveness in reducing road accidents. It has also stimulated an inquiry into the scientific basis of the various "legal" blood–alcohol levels applying in different states of the Commonwealth. The permissible blood–alcohol level question is vexing, but in the interest of motorists traveling interstate, as well as in the interest of greater road safety, it is important that the experience of the different states having varying "permissible blood–alcohol levels" be compared and the question of uniformity among states be raised.

*EDUCATION*

Prevention programs related to either alcoholism or other drugs are not as yet effectively established in this country, although considerable experimentation is being carried out in some states, notably Queensland. Until very recently the only program operative in state schools in N.S.W. consisted of occasional lectures advocating, for the most part, "total abstinence." But even these lectures, out of time with prevalent community attitudes to social drinking, have been discontinued. For some years FRATADD has by invitation given lectures on alcoholism and recently on drug abuse to a number of private schools. The invitations to give these lectures have been irregular and unpredictable. In the past year a number of voluntary organizations have sprung up concerned with preventive education in relation to drugs other than alcohol. These organizations have become involved more or less haphazardly in some senior schools and in community education. The overall result has been ineffectual because of the irregular and haphazard nature of the lectures and the wide variations and contradictions in content.

Nevertheless, over the past two years officials have become more aware of the necessity for education about alcohol, drug, and tobacco abuse within the context of the health education curriculum for senior students (15–18 years). In fact, time has now been allocated in the health education program of all secondary schools for instruction on these topics. This has focused attention on the urgent need for research to determine the content and methods of instruction on these subjects, and for the development of effective teaching aids.

An invaluable stimulus to progress in this area has come through the Education Committee of the 29th Congress. Membership of this committee includes senior representatives of the Education Department, academics from the Faculty of Education of Sydney University, representatives of teacher training institutions and the Centre for the Advancement of Teaching of the Macquarie University, and members of the Health Education Division of the Health Department.

The committee has defined its concerns in relation to preventive education programs in three major areas: for schools, for the professions, and for the community. These three areas figured conspicuously in the program of the congress. We were most anxious to take advantage of opportunities afforded us by the congress to discuss with educators from other countries what methods they have used and which proved most effective. In this regard, Dr. G. R. Meyer, Director of the Centre for the Advancement of Teaching, is establishing a permanent collection of program reports, instructional material, and teaching aids as resource material for those involved in planning Australia's education programs.

In November 1964, the Commonwealth of Australia appointed a Senate Select Committee of Enquiry into drug usage in this country, and called on experts attending the 29th International Congress to assist the enquiry. One of the specific aims of the select committee was to investigate the present programs of preventive education. We can confidently anticipate that the full resources of the Commonwealth and all state governments, as well as of such nongovernmental organizations as FRATADD, will be concentrated on this urgent task.

The state government of N.S.W. convened a meeting of all state and voluntary agencies at present involved in drug education in Sydney to discuss a study of resources and to formulate some uniformity in the approach to preventive education. The Commonwealth government planned a two-week residential conference of health educators from all states to be held throughout the two weeks immediately following the congress for the immediate preparation and introduction of systematic preventive education related to the misuse of drugs, on a Commonwealth-wide scale.

Such dramatic development was not envisaged when it was decided two years ago that preventive education should be one of the major areas to be covered in the program of the congress. The further involvement of the Commonwealth government, which will necessarily lead to the involvement of all state governments and of every voluntary organization concerned with prevention, research, or treatment of alcoholism and drug dependence, underscores very heavily the practical value the Congress has already had in this country. It indicates, too, the tremendous potential for long-term development.

## SOCIAL AND BEHAVIORAL SCIENCES

Although in N.S.W. in 1966, one or two psychologists were employed full time in the treatment of alcoholism, it would be more than misleading to suggest that there was at that time any substantial involvement of the social and behavioral sciences in either treatment or research relating to addictions. The positive contribution of the congress in this area has been, first, to prompt a tentative exploration of the contribution the social and behavioral sciences have to make to a multidisciplinary prevention, research, and treatment program; and second, to map out the areas in which the participation of these disciplines is vital to the formulation of a comprehensive program. Here too, the harsh necessity of preparing contributions for the congress program led to the initiation of some worthwhile basic research studies that otherwise would not have been attempted. It also brought social scientists into an intimate working relationship with representatives of the several other disciplines who have a concern with alcoholism and drug dependence.

Although research has been difficult because of inadequate financial support, a considerable research potential has now been established through the surprisingly willing involvement of the Departments of Sociology and Applied Psychology of the University of N.S.W., the School of Behavioural Sciences at Macquarie University, and other established research institutions.

We are conscious of the limitations of our own resources and have been aware for some time of the real benefits we could derive through closer communication and cooperation with research institutions and individual research workers in other countries. We are certain that these considerations apply with even greater force to many other countries in this geographical region. An opportunity was taken at the 29th Congress to discuss with the International Council on Alcohol and Addictions and other experts the mechanisms necessary to provide for a more effective and formalized system of communication between research workers of all countries, and more adequate international reporting and documentation of current research studies. Should an effective system of communication emerge from this, then another achievement of practical worth will have been accomplished through the 29th Congress.

## RESULTS OF THE CONGRESS

The 29th International Congress provided the greatest opportunity we are likely to have in this country for coordination and development of treatment and research activities, and for the development of the potential that has been latent in our state. We are acutely conscious of the inherent weakness of this rapid development, and are well aware that the structure we have built could disintegrate even more quickly than it was established.

The quite remarkable degree of communication and cooperation among a disparate group of departments, institutions, and agencies, as well as individuals, that was accomplished in the course of preparation for the congress provided a dramatic demonstration of the role of the voluntary agency as a catalyst. It has also been shown that any one of the agencies involved in the congress organization, acting in isolation, can accomplish little. Acting within the structure of a completely voluntary yet disciplined association with other agencies, the potential of each agency is vastly enhanced, and the capacity of the entire group becomes formidable indeed.

The various professional committees composed of individuals who are leaders in their specialties, originally gathered together by FRATADD for the multidisciplinary approach to planning the 29th International Congress, have seen the importance of close communication among themselves. The various member committees are eager to remain intact and to extend the scope of their investigations. They are willing to form the nucleus of a research institute, to be established by FRATADD. The potential from such a beginning is enormous and has received tremendous support from the Board of FRATADD. In this planning, FRATADD has also received most encouraging support from the government of New South Wales, and it is most likely that the institute will emerge as an effective working synthesis of governmental and voluntary resources.

The title "Addiction Research Institute" possibly implies more than is presently intended. Stringent financial limitations preclude establishing such an institute as the deservedly renowned Karolinska Institute in Sweden, nor can we expect in the immediate future to match the resources of foundations such as the Alcoholism and Drug Addiction Research Foundation of Ontario. Our immediate concern is to preserve intact the structure already established, and to provide the accommodation and the immediate funds necessary to enable it to undertake and carry out the systematic extension of those functions for which it is well equipped in terms of professional skills and resources.

Urgently needed basic research within the scope of the proposed addiction research institute would fall into the following four categories:

*1. Epidemiological studies*

(a) Extent of drug abuse in circumscribed areas.

(b) Variations in types of drug abuse, within and between circumscribed areas, cultures, and subcultures.

(c) Determination of high- and low-risk individuals and populations in regard to drug dependence and abuse, including comparative studies on causative factors.

(d) Drug abuse among adolescents.

(e) The role of drugs in causing accidents.

(f) Relationship between the different types of drug dependence and delinquent behavior.

*2. Sociological studies*

(a) Distinctions made between use and abuse of drugs in various cultures and subcultures.

(b) Characteristics of deviant drug-using subcultures.

(c) Comparison of legislative and other measures (for the control of drugs and the treatment of drug-dependent persons), including their enforcement, their possible effects on extent and pattern of drug abuse.

*3. Clinical studies*

(a) Longitudinal studies of drug-dependent individuals, such as the origin and development of dependence; replacement or addition of different drugs in the course of dependence or replacement of dependence by another mental disorder; relation between personality structure and choice of drugs and response to treatment.

(b) Evaluation of different methods and programs of treatment.

(c) Identification of types of drug-dependent personalities.

(d) Development of more precise diagnostic tools.

(e) Evaluation of the dependence liability of new drugs.

*4. Studies related to education and training*

(a) Attitude surveys.

(b) Determination of groups at risk.

(c) Methods of developing social sanctions against drug abuse.

(d) Effects of training on the handling of patients.

Should it appear that these areas conform very closely with those recommended in the annexure to the 14th report of the WHO Expert Committee on Mental Health, this is not by coincidence but rather by deliberate design; we feel this report has laid the pattern for basic research which could very well be adopted internationally.

Should the perpetuation of the various committees established for the planning of the 29th International Congress be successfully accomplished through the creation of an addiction research institute, then it can truly be said that the history of systematic research into addictions of this country will date from 1966, when the approval of the International Council on Alcohol and Addictions was granted for an International Congress to be held in Sydney.

## SUMMARY AND CONCLUSION

FRATADD's objectives are the furtherance of treatment, education, and research concerning alcoholism and drug dependence. We have tried to indicate the influence that this voluntary organization, in implementing its objectives, has exerted on a community. Although our organization is driven by a need to grapple with the problems of alcoholism and drug dependence, it is not motivated by any emotionalism or preconceived prejudices.

We have tried to give historical perspective to the origins and development of efforts to deal with alcoholism and drug dependence in Australia. We have mentioned some early clumsy attempts in our country to deal with these problems, attempts that were often merely custodial or punitive. We have touched on the difficulties facing legislators, law enforcement bodies, and therapists, lacking knowledge and facilities. We have stressed the need for coordination of effort, and improved communication among the various disciplines. We have briefly sketched how and why the foundation established the Langton Clinic, FRATA House;

and how and why it intends to establish a female hostel. We have also indicated the foundation's involvement in education and research.

Finally, we have highlighted FRATADD's activities as host foundation to the 29th International Congress on Alcoholism and Drug Dependence. This honor and responsibility served as a catalyst to speed up our own activities, improve communication, and strengthen coordination among all interested agencies. We have described the congress planning committees, the nucleus of a proposed Addiction Research Institute which we feel will fill an important role in an overall program to combat the growing problems of alcoholism and drug dependence.

Although our purpose has been to describe the role and some of the activities and influences of a voluntary organization, we must emphasize that FRATADD does not want to operate in competition with governmental agencies, but rather to use its resources to complement the services of the state.

# Czechoslovakia's response to alcoholism

## JAROSLAV SKÁLA, M.D.

Alcoholism began to be recognized as a major health problem in Czechoslovakia at about the same time that the battle was joined against it in America, yet the methods of attacking the disease differed widely. Dr. Jaroslav Skála's description of the progress from the first detoxification center in Prague to the centralized program of today makes an interesting comparative study. Since 1953, Dr. Skála has been expert advisor on alcohol problems to the Ministry of Health in Czechoslovakia, and also to the Mental Health Section of WHO.

## PRODUCTION, CONSUMPTION, AND COST

It is generally known that alcohol has never been, and will never be, consumed evenly by the population, as perhaps economists think when they show statistics of the average consumption per annum. Alcohol has a different value to different individuals; though people may drink the same kind of alcohol, their nervous and psychic systems differ, and the same substance may affect them differently.

Obviously, alcohol does not appeal to everyone equally. People to whom it has a specific subjective appeal will want it again; they will want it ever more frequently, and in time they will require an increasing dose to attain the same effect, whether their interest in it is for euphoria, or sedation. Thus, in due course, some people who started drinking at the same rate as others will gradually begin to differ from the others, both in the amounts they require for their desired needs, and in the frequency of their intake.

How does this come about? Alcohol has a specific effect on the nervous system. Simplified, this may be expressed in one sentence—it rapidly and remarkably changes mood. If it is true that alcohol affects different people in different ways, then those are in greater danger to whom it gives the most. It lessens unpleasant tension and the feeling of insecurity, suppresses a sense of disappointment and failure, and creates in the dreary emptiness of everyday life intervals of elevated mood.

It has been estimated that if 100 people start drinking a daily half liter, about 20 will within a few years begin to drink excessively; of these 20, five to seven will, after some further years, lose control over their drinking. It is hard to predict who will fall into which category.

On the basis of investigations in Poland, Holland, and the United States, we know that there is a minority which consumes a large proportion of alcoholic beverages; we may assume in Czechoslovakia, too, alcoholics and regular excessive drinkers constitute something less than one tenth of the total population. Yet they drink up to fifty percent of the total alcohol consumed. Table 1 shows this situation.

*Table 1*

| PERCENTAGE OF POPULATION | PERCENTAGE OF CONSUMED ALCOHOL | PERCENTAGE OF DAMAGE CAUSED |
|---|---|---|
| *10* <br> *regular excessive drinkers and alcoholics* | 50 | 100 |
| *90* <br> *consumers and occasional drinkers* | 50 | 0 |

Czechoslovakia, unlike some other countries, e.g., Finland, Sweden, and the United States, has practically no abstinents among the adult population. Thus there is no counterweight on public opinion. "A good example to the young" is lacking, because the adult who does not take at least beer is looked upon as being as abnormal as the alcoholic. The golden mean is considered not the occasional consumer but rather the drinker.

To describe the stages of alcoholism, we have used to advantage the developmental phases according to Jellinek.* It appears that to a certain extent and with certain modifications, these phases could be applied to large groups and to whole nations respectively. I should describe the present situation in our country as symptoms of the second phase, characterized by a growing tolerance to alcohol and rationalization, i.e., a system of reasons and alibis for the abuse of alcohol.

I very much fear that we still do not appreciate the danger signs of this phase, and that probably we shall have to go on to the next phase, which will be alarming enough to compel us to put preventive measures in first place against the struggle of alcoholism.

### Table 2

| YEAR | 1953 | 1956 | 1959 | 1962 | 1965 | 1967 |
|---|---|---|---|---|---|---|
| *100% spirit consumption per capita per annum in liters* | 3.8 | 4.3 | 5.2 | 5.7 | 6.9 | 7.6 |
| *Percentage of beer* | 50 | 50 | 56 | 64 | 64 | 59 |
| *Percentage of wine* | 18 | 15 | 26 | 16 | 20 | 24 |
| *Percentage of spirits* | 32 | 35 | 18 | 20 | 16 | 17 |
| *Index of consumption of 100% spirit per capita per annum* | 100 | 114 | 137 | 150 | 181 | 200 |

If we want to describe alcoholism in Czechoslovakia, we must admit the fact that people have sufficient financial means to buy alcohol.

The annual per capita expenditures on alcohol have soared since 1946, partly due to the increased price of wine and spirits, but also due to increased per capita consumption of beer.

The rise in expenditure was primarily due to increased alcohol consumption, especially beer; and only secondarily to the in-

* See E. M. Jellinek, *Disease Concept of Alcoholism* (New Brunswick: Publications Division, Rutgers University, 1960), Chapter II.

creased price of wine and spirits. This is shown by the steady growth of annual average consumption per capita, expressed in the amount of spirit beverage, the annual average of which rose from 3.24 liters in 1938 to 6.97 liters in 1967.

It is obvious that alcohol consumption is increasing on a national scale.

The foregoing table reveals:

—That the proportion of beer increased between 1953 and 1962 from 50 percent to 64 percent.

—In the proportion of wine there were certain deviations both ways in the course of 14 years.

—The proportion of spirits dropped from 35 percent to 17 percent between 1956 and 1967; i.e., to less than one half. Particularly marked is the drop between 1956 and 1959, due to the substantial price increase of concentrated alcohol in 1958.

The development of beer alcoholism in this country is supported by the long tradition of our brewing industry, in accord with the slogan "Die Brauerei und Teich macht die Herren reich" (Breweries and ponds make the masters rich). This has been intensified in recent years by improved techniques and working efficiency.

Since 1936 consumption of beer has more than doubled, with a high in 1966 of 132 liters per capita, as compared to 51.8 liters per capita in 1936. Annual per capita consumption of wine in 1936 was 7.2 liters per capita, and fell to 6.1 liters per capita in 1950. It rose steadily to 1967, with a high of 18.6 liters per capita.

In 1966 and 1968 Czechoslovakia held top place in beer consumption in the western world.

The consumption of alcohol is characterized by a drop in the use of spirits following the increase in price in 1958. The growing consumption not only of beer but also of wine, demonstrated how a price policy can influence the consumer. Table 3 shows a comparison of prices for 1937 and 1963.

*Table 3*

| BEVERAGE | PRICE IN KORUNY | |
| | *1937* | *1963* |
| --- | --- | --- |
| *1 liter beer 10°* | 2.60 | 2.60 |
| *1 liter wine* | 12.— | 19.— |
| *1 liter 40% rum* | 19.— | 80.— |

If we calculate how much we should pay for 1 liter 100 percent spirit purchased in the form of beer, wine, or strong drink, we arrive at figures that reveal taxation of alcohol in these beverages (see Table 4).

*Table 4*

| PRICE IN CROWNS FOR 1 LITER 100% SPIRIT | *1937* | *1965* |
| --- | --- | --- |
| *Beer* | 85.— | 85.— |
| *Wine* | 108.— | 170.— |
| *Spirits* | 48.— | 200.— |

The difference in taxes and thus in the price of individual kinds of alcohol in 1963 and in 1937 appears to be acceptable in the sense that the more concentrated the beverage, the higher the tax.

The enormous consumption of beer and the high tax for other beverages may be one of the principal reasons why the population spends a greater percentage of the national income on alcohol than does any other nation. This has been disclosed in an international survey of alcohol consumption expressed in the quantity of 100 percent spirit in liters per capita per annum for various western countries for 1963 and the percentage of expenditure from national income spent by the populace on alcoholic drinks (see Table 5).

From the tabulated surveys the following facts emerge:

1. In CSSR, expenditure on alcohol amounts in 1968 to 11 milliard Kcs, which is not to be interpreted as a sign of a high living standard, but as an expense which necessarily lowers the living standard.

Table 5

| | 100% SPIRIT IN LITERS PER CAPITA IN 1963 | PERCENT OF THE NATIONAL INCOME EXPENDED ON ALCOHOLIC DRINKS |
|---|---|---|
| 1. France | 20 | 5.5 |
| 2. Italy | 13 | 5 |
| 3. Switzerland | 10 | 4 |
| 4. Germany | 9 | 6 |
| 5. Belgium | 7 | 4 |
| 6. England | 6 | 5 |
| 7. U.S.A. | 6 | 2.7 |
| 8. Czechoslovakia | 5.8 | 7 |
| 9. Denmark | 5 | 4.5 |
| 10. Sweden | 4 | 4 |
| 11. Finland | 3 | 3 |
| 12. Norway | 3 | 3.5 |
| 13. Holland | 3 | 2.8 |

2. The state draws substantial revenue from alcohol, which can be expressed in exact figures, and this apparently makes quite an impression on our economists.

3. On the other hand, there are losses and damages that can be expressed in figures, and in even more deplorable results which cannot as yet be expressed in economic terms. To name a few examples:

   a. In 1961–1966 every sixth divorce in this country was caused by alcoholism of one of the parties.

   b. In the years 1958–1966, 20 percent of criminal offenses were directly due to the abuse of alcohol, and 33 percent indirectly.

   c. Within the period of five years (1960–64) 12 percent of all male suicides had some relation to alcohol abuse; in the age group 30–50 years, it amounted to 25 percent. In 1964, which recorded a drop in the suicide rate, the contribution of alcohol in suicides increased by a full 50 percent.

   d. In the beginning of 1969 the number of people registered for alcoholism in anti-alcoholic centers was 100,000. On the basis of the Prague records, however, their actual number is estimated at 250,000.

e. The number of alcoholic psychoses dropped markedly in the era of spreading beer alcoholism, especially in the Czech lands (Bohemia).

*LEGISLATIVE ACTION: Excerpts from Act 120 of 1962 Concerning the Struggle against Alcoholism*

*Preamble*

Alcoholism impedes the establishment and development of the rules of socialist life; causes social, economic, ethical, and health damage and might disturb the building up of a developed socialist society.

In order that all state agencies and all social, economic, and other bodies develop a uniform effort in the struggle against alcoholism, the National Assembly of the Czechoslovak Social Republic passes the following act:

Section 1

*Introductory statement*

1. The struggle against alcoholism is focused predominantly against excess consumption of alcoholic beverages, consumption of these in noxious products or under unsuitable circumstances, e.g., before going to work or starting other activities, during work hours, in illness and pregnancy, as well as against consumption of alcoholic beverages by children and adolescents.

2. According to the present act the following beverages are considered alcoholic: spirits, beer, and wine and other beverages containing more than 0.75 percent [vol.] alcohol.

Section 3

*Central Anti-alcoholism Body*

1. The struggle against alcoholism is coordinated and methodically controlled by the Central Anti-alcoholism Body of the Ministry of Health.

2. The members of this body are representatives of min-

istries and other central organs and social organizations, as well as other persons. They are appointed and replaced by the minister of health according to the suggestion of the competent authorities of the ministry of health. The minister of health also appoints the Chairman.

3. The Central Anti-alcoholism Body submits initiative suggestions for developing and intensifying the struggle against alcoholism and follows or controls all measures against alcoholism.

4. The statute of the Central Anti-alcoholism Body is accredited by the Government.

## Section 5

*Anti-alcoholism bodies of national committees*

1. For the coordination and securing of the tasks of the struggle against alcoholism regional, district, or local (municipal) anti-alcoholism bodies are established by the national committees.

2. The chairman of the anti-alcoholism body is a member of the council of the national committee, usually the chairman of the Health Commission or of the Cultural and Educational Commission.

3. Regional anti-alcoholism bodies are methodically controlled by the Central Anti-alcoholism Body, district anti-alcoholism bodies by the Regional Anti-alcoholism Body; local (municipal) anti-alcoholism bodies by the District Anti-alcoholism Body.

4. Statutes of the anti-alcoholism bodies are accredited by the competent national committees.

## Section 9

*Preventive means*

1. It is not allowed to:
    a. sell or serve alcoholic beverages, not even in sealed packages, to persons under 18 years, to persons who in case of doubt are unable to prove by their identity cards that they are older than 18 years, to persons hospitalized in health institutions, to flushed or intoxicated persons, nor to offer to, or arrange for, or otherwise enable these persons to consume such beverages,

b. serve alcoholic beverages or make possible their consumption to anybody at dance entertainments, public meetings, or sport and cultural events, with the exception of:

aa. beer and wine in case of dance entertainments and public meetings,

bb. beer with the maximum contents 10 decigrams (of alcohol) in case of sport events,

c. serve alcoholic beverages, with the exception of beer with the maximum content 8 decigrams (of alcohol) in works canteens,

d. distil alcohol in households,

e. admit persons under 15 years to public places where alcoholic beverages are served after 8 o'clock P.M., unless accompanied by adult persons legally in charge of them.

2. Prohibition concerning sale of alcoholic beverages (item 1a) does not include sale of beer to persons under 18 years if they carry it away from the place of business.

3. The national committee can limit or prohibit

a. sale and serving of alcoholic beverages on certain days or under certain conditions in restaurants and similar places, retail shops, or other places freely accessible to the public,

b. displaying of alcoholic beverages in show windows or show cases inside places of business or other places freely accessible to the public, as well as advertising the consumption of alcoholic beverages.

Section 10

1. Persons engaged in occupations usually connected with danger to man's life, health, or property are not allowed to drink alcoholic beverages while so engaged, immediately before engaging in it, or even at other times, if these persons might find themselves under the influence of alcohol due to the previous consumption.

2. Persons mentioned under item 1 must—on summons by the state health administration or public security organs—un-

dergo a medical examination, so that it can be determined whether they are influenced by alcohol or not.

### Section 12

1. A person who, due to consumption of alcoholic beverages, arrives in a state calling forth public scandal or in a state in which he endangers himself, his family, environment, or property, must undergo treatment in an anti-alcoholism institution established for this purpose—the sobering-up station—until he completely sobers up. The anti-alcoholism institution can require such person to attend lectures held at the anti-alcoholism institution. Public security bodies are to cooperate if necessary in transportation of such persons to the institutions.

### Section 13

1. A person who, due to consuming alcoholic beverages repeatedly, arrives in a state calling forth scandal or unfavorably influencing his family or work performance or who repeatedly arrives in a state otherwise damaging to the public interest, or who by such consumption causes health damage (further only alcoholic) must undergo, according to the decision of the anti-alcoholism institution, a dispensary treatment; he must specifically

    a. undergo an examination of the state of his health.

    b. undergo outpatient treatment.

Appeals against the above decision, if not fully granted by the director of the Institute of National Health, are to be decided by the national committee, within the competence of which the respective institute of national health is administered.

2. If the alcoholic does not undergo treatment, or if the outpatient treatment does not prove sufficient, and the alcoholic refuses to undergo voluntary inpatient treatment, a compulsory clinical treatment can be imposed upon the alcoholic by the district national committee acting at the suggestion of the health institution.

### Section 14

*Payment of alcoholic's salary*

If other educational means proved insufficient, and if by paying the salary to the alcoholic the interest of his children and other dependents were impaired, the respective trade union body can appoint (in cooperation with the anti-alcoholism institution and after agreement with the local national committee in charge as determined by the alcoholic's residence) a person who will draw down the alcoholic's salary in whole or in part; in case of members of uniform farmers' cooperatives, the decision can be made by the local national committee in cooperation with the anti-alcoholism institution. The recipient of the salary or part salary must use it only for the benefit of the alcoholic, his children, and other dependents.

## TREATMENT AND REHABILITATION

The first inpatient treatment center operated in the present republic from 1909 to 1913; the next, from 1924 to 1939. Both centers were administered by an ex-priest. The first outpatient clinic was founded in 1928. Until the beginning of World War II, there were only three such clinics established by the Czechoslovak Union of Abstinents.

At present there are three types of anti-alcoholism institutions in our country, viz.

1. Sobering-up stations: intoxicated persons who endanger themselves or others are taken to these stations, mainly by the police. There are 53 sobering-up stations at present, with over 400 beds. During the past ten years they have treated 250,000 persons.

2. Outpatient clinics: over 200 clinics register at present 100,-000 persons (95 percent of them men). Outpatient clinics have been established in all districts and form a part of psychiatric treatment.

3. Inpatient clinics: three specialize in treating alcoholism within the framework of psychiatric clinics and psychiatric hospitals.

At the end of the year the Ministry of Health receives statistical data from all these institutions and, after analyzing the data, determines methods and organizational measures concerning alcoholism prevention and therapy which in our country forms an integral part of psychiatric treatment.

Act 120 of 1962 (a second amendment of the original 1922 act against alcoholism) puts emphasis on alcoholism as mainly a political, social, and economic problem. The medical aspect is mentioned fourth. Paragraphs 12, 13, and 14 of the act provide for the treatment and rehabilitation of alcoholics. They also establish compulsory treatment, as ordered on the recommendation of the alcoholism outpatient clinic of the health department of the national committee. The duration of compulsory treatment is up to twelve months. This form of treatment must be distinguished from so-called detention treatment ordered by the court. Treatment ordered by health institutions, as well as detention treatment, also occurs in health institutions, and alcoholism clinics forming part of psychiatric institutions. So far, differentiation of departments according to the type of alcoholic patient exists only in Prague where there are special departments for voluntary treatment, compulsory treatment, and the treatment of criminal alcoholics.

There are altogether 20 clinical wards with about 700 beds in our country. If we had a capacity and differentiation, similar to that in Prague, the total bed count would reach the necessary capacity of 2,000. In addition, the essential duration of hospitalization could be maintained: for voluntary patients, 3 months; for voluntary recidivists 4–6 months; for patients under compulsory treatment 6–12 months. In the future we hope to establish a department of the so-called D-type, for curable alcoholics requiring 1–3 years' rehabilitation (see Table 6, pp. 104–105).

## ALCOHOLISM CLINIC IN APOLINÁŘSKÁ AT PRAGUE

The development of treatment and rehabilitation facilities for alcoholics is a challenging task, requiring long-term, systematic effort. The following is a chronological survey of the development of individual institutions and activities in Prague and especially in our alcoholism clinic in Apolinářská:

1. first outpatient clinic at Prague                              1946
2. aversion treatment (emetin, apomorphine) at the university psychiatric clinic          1947
3. social-therapeutic club                                        1948
4. specialized alcoholism clinic as inpatient department of psychiatric clinic in Apolinářská (originally 20 beds; since 1952, 50 beds)          1948
5. sobering-up station (detoxication center) in Apolinářská          1951
6. inpatient department at the psychiatric hospital for treatment of cases sent by court order (70 beds)          1952
7. a network of 10 district outpatient clinics and the founding of a regional clinic serving as their methodological center          1953
8. a special outpatient clinic for adolescent drinkers and alcoholics (18 years and under)          1957
9. rehabilitation center (inpatient department) for compulsory treatment ordered by health institutions (32 beds) as a part of alcoholism clinic in Apolinářská          1958
10. patients with other drug dependencies admitted in Apolinářská          1961
11. summer tent camps (14-day stay) for acutely treated alcoholics and ex-alcoholics from Apolinářská          1962
12. patients' Sunday social club (in alcohol-free restaurant)          1963
13. intensive group psychotherapy for marital partners of patients          1964
14. day-hospital (in the last weeks of inpatient treatment) and night hospital for repeated recidivists          1965
15. youth center: adolescent drinkers and alcoholics, and alcoholics' children          1967
16. small department for inpatient treatment of women alcoholics and drug dependents (6 beds)          1967
17. detention treatment of criminal alcoholics in the course of imprisonments—cooperation of the Apolinářská with the Penological Institute (experiment)          1968–1969

18. laboratory for research on alcoholism and drug dependencies                                        1968

*Adversion treatment*

In 1946, the author first became acquainted with the methods of conditioned aversion described by Thimann. Since 1947, this form of therapy has been applied to nearly 6,000 patients at the alcoholism clinic in Apolinářská, the first 2,000 treated in groups of eight. Later, various modifications of the technique were systematically explored (e.g., frequency of sessions, choice of emetic). In 1958, some 161 patients were selected at random for either a full therapeutic program including aversion therapy or a similar regimen without aversion therapy. Twelve months after treatment 56.5 percent of the former and 46.7 percent of the latter group were total abstinents.

It is the general conclusion of the author that aversion therapy should be regarded as a kind of "larval" form of group psychotherapy. In the past, many investigators considered aversion therapy a kind of "diaper" which alcoholism treatment has now outgrown. However, after some 22 years of application, the author views it more as a kind of morning exercise, an introduction to the overall therapeutic program.

*Apolinářská regimen*

In psychiatry, the institutional regimen can be understood in various ways. In my opinion, however, it must essentially be an instrument for the psychotherapist and his work. It is clear that all regimens reflect the theories and value systems of those who devise them, that is, the members of the therapeutic team and particularly the head therapist. There can thus be no one scheme for the development and application of regimen. This program will be successful only if it reflects the opinions and work of the therapeutic team; the members play their part in it naturally and spontaneously.

The Apolinářská regimen (A-regimen) has been developing for many years; it is centered on alcoholism. In relation to the development of alcoholism, Jellinek and others stress the importance

TABLE
SUGGESTED DIFFERENTIATED INPATIENT

| | TYPE A | TYPE B |
|---|---|---|
| *Duration of treatment* | 3–4 months | 4–11 months |
| *Disease symptoms* | abuse with habitual toxicomania; some alcoholic psychoses (delirium tremens, hallucinosis) | oligophrenia with IQ under 70; some alcoholic psychoses (Korsakov); alcoholic dentia; incipient hepatic cirrhosis; nonalcoholic toxicomania |
| *Character of treatment* | 1) voluntary treatment 2) first stay | 1) voluntary treatment* 2) assessment of district national committee |
| *Attitude of patient to treatment* | willing and able to cooperate | willing and able to cooperate in this institution within the framework of its therapeutic program |
| *State of alcoholism as a disease and its social consequences* | character of treatment and patient's attitude toward it are decisive | 1) index of voluntary treatment is decisive 2) refused voluntary treatment 3) alcoholism complicated by asocial manifestations |
| *Components of treatment program:* | | |
| *1) Drug therapy* | light | light |
| *2) Psychotherapy* | heavy | heavy |
| *3) Therapeutic regimen* | light | medium |
| *4) Work* | 4 hours daily | 4–5 hours daily |
| *Financial arrangements* | health insurance | health insurance |

(In cases of willful violation of treatment, cost of
[*Bulletin of the Ministry of Health*, 1967, Instruction

# 6

## TREATMENT OF ALCOHOLICS

| TYPE C | TYPE D |
|---|---|
| usually 6 months, or longer | usually one year or more |
| psychopathia and secondary character alterations, advanced alcoholic dementia | psychopathia and secondary character alterations, with aggressive features |
| 3) detention of treatment according to Section 72 of criminal law<br>* *Type C:* repeated several times | 1) repeated assessment of district national committee<br>2) detention treatment according to Section 72 of criminal law |
| 1) negative attitude to treatment<br>2) insufficient cooperation, due to decrease of intellect | intensity of the disease is decisive |
| 1) asocial manifestations of nonaggressive type<br>2) character and intellectual decay of the patient's personality | 1) asocial manifestations of aggressive type<br>2) unmanageable in a C-type institution |
| light<br>medium<br>heavy | none<br>light<br>medium |
| 5 hours daily | 6–7 hours daily |
| health insurance, invalid's pension, or social security | financial subsidy (on an individual basis); possibility of obtaining payment for work performed |

treatment per day must be paid by patient or his family
No. 4])

of psychological characteristics in future alcoholics, on which alcohol, as a central psychotropic substance, evidently acts more intensively and rapidly than in nonalcoholics. This entails the longing for and repeated use of alcohol under tension and anxiety, or to overcome frustration.

A sparing and forbearing regimen is unsuitable for the treatment of alcoholics; a consistent, demanding, and, of course, effective regimen is required. Solving varied individual conflicts in the presence of the whole group evokes the interests of others and their participation and cooperation. The fact that the whole group, i.e., the therapeutic community, is kept continually informed of what is going on contributes to the formation of desirable interpersonal relations between patients and increases the feeling of responsibility of the individual toward the group, and at the same time, that of the group to the problems of the individual patient.

Since the A-regimen not only keeps the patients adequately employed but also cooperatively involved in the operation and management of the department, we can speak of it as activating and humanizing. From morning to evening, for weeks and months, patients carry out a whole series of tasks, take part in diverse activities, fill various functions, form new interests, learn new things, receive only what they deserve, and cooperate with others. They gradually acquire self-confidence and a sense of responsibility.

A certain atmosphere develops in every department, either spontaneously on the part of the patients, or intentionally on the part of the therapeutic team. Both the level and the continuity of the psychotherapeutic atmosphere is, of course, a very difficult matter. Experience with A-regimen has shown that it requires from each member of the team, especially the leader, at least ten hours a week with the whole group.

*Criminal alcoholics*

A group of seven therapists from Prague alcoholism clinics attended two courses of a 5-month treatment for sentenced alcoholics (each course consisting of a group of 20 alcoholics); the treatment was performed during imprisonment. The members of the therapeutic group were two psychiatrists, two social workers, three nurses, and two laymen-therapists—ex-alcoholics. The program (three three-hour sessions per week) consisted of lectures and psychotherapy in small groups of five members, as well as the whole group. Psychodrama and sociometry were included. All patients also wrote in a diary three times a week. It was a closed group which started treatment together; four, five, or even six months later the individual members finished their sentences and went home. A report was forwarded to the respective outpatient clinics about their treatment with a request to complete the treatment and also administer disulfiram for the period of one year. Many patients began a temporary stay at the specialized alcoholism clinic in Apolinářská after their release from prison, in order to adapt themselves in the form of night nursing to a life of freedom.

At present, the results of the experiment are being processed with a suggestion to the ministries of justice and health to carry out in the future detention treatment during imprisonment throughout the whole country.

The essential preconditions of the treatment are:

1. that patients are concentrated in special abodes, preferably in special small departments.
2. that the program is held 2–3 times a week for 3 hours.
3. that therapists from the nearby alcoholism inpatient clinics attend the treatment.
4. that the ratio of therapists to patients be no less than 1 to 4.

In Czechoslovakia 12,000–20,000 persons were imprisoned in recent years; at least 20 percent of these committed a crime under the influence of alcohol. Detention alcoholism treatment was ordered in one quarter to one half of these cases. If the treatment were performed during imprisonment, it would save time for the prisoners and beds for the health institutions.

*Social clubs*
We have had very good experience with the therapeutical social club. The author has directed the therapeutically oriented discus-

sions in the club since 1948 (1,000 discussions in all). The discharged and already abstinent patients meet in a department lecture hall. Meetings at the club are animated and enriched by the presence of patients who participate regularly and have continued their abstinence from three to twenty years. It is not easy to attain gradual identification of beginners with the seniors. The therapist acts as a catalyst in this process by means of appropriately selected discussions.

Our experiences during the past seven years with summer tent camps were also very good. In each of the twenty tents there is one patient who has been abstinent for at least three years and one patient who has just begun treatment. The identification process is far more rapid and intense under such conditions and beneficial for both the patient groups. For the already abstinent patient antialcoholic work is the best way to maintain his abstinence.

Regular activity in such a club, where he sees abstinent and relapsing cases as well, prevents the therapist from both overestimating his success and also from becoming frustrated and quitting. He is kept down to earth, close to his patients who need his help; and his endurance during the hard first ten years is facilitated, until he is able to earn in the following decades the gratification that comes from his work.

### Results of the treatment in Apolinářská

Since 1948, well over 5,000 persons have started voluntary basic treatment at the inpatient alcoholism clinic in Apolinářská, yet very many of these have not finished it. The following table gives a detailed picture of the situation from 1964 to 1967.

*Table 7*

| YEAR: | 1964 | 1965 | 1966 | 1967 | 1964–1967 |
|---|---|---|---|---|---|
| *No. of persons applying for the basic treatment* | 245 | 250 | 258 | 230 | 983 |
| *No. of those who actually started the treatment after several weeks' waiting, or in case of free beds, were hospitalized immediately, without waiting* | 171 | 180 | 190 | 182 | 723 |

*Table 7 (Continued)*

| YEAR: | 1964 | 1965 | 1966 | 1967 | 1964–1967 |
|---|---|---|---|---|---|
| Left within the first days of stay (within 2 weeks) | 37 | 20 | 22 | 22 | 101 |
| Left in the later course of the treatment | 30 | 30 | 34 | 28 | 122 |
| Left because of disease, injury (transferred to other clinics) | 3 | 9 | 7 | 5 | 24 |
| Suspended because of serious violation of the regulations or insufficient cooperation | 12 | 26 | 20 | 18 | 76 |
| Total patients who did not finish the treatment | 82 | 85 | 83 | 73 | 323 |
| Total patients who finished the treatment | 89 | 95 | 107 | 109 | 400 |

The treatment results are evaluated only for patients who finished the voluntary, approximately 3-months program:

*Table 8*

| YEAR: | 1962 | 1963 | 1964 | 1965 | 1966 | 1962–1966 |
|---|---|---|---|---|---|---|
| percentage of one-year abstinence | 61 | 55 | 60 | 60 | 62 | 57.5 |
| percentage of unimproved one year later | 12 | 30 | 19 | 11 | 19 | 18 |

Relapses occurred in nearly one half of the cases within the first three months after finishing the treatment. Thirty to thirty-five percent of the patients succeeded in maintaining a 5-years uninterrupted abstinence.

## SOBERING-UP STATION (DETOXIFICATION CENTER) AND EPIDEMIOLOGY OF ALCOHOLISM IN PRAGUE

The specialized alcoholism clinic in Prague had functioned for about one year when I began to feel the necessity of establishing a health facility which would take care of intoxicated persons. I contemplated a night outpatient clinic where intoxicated persons could be escorted and hospitalized instead of spending long hours on the bunk at the police station or in prison. My primary attention was focused on the difficult handling of intoxicated persons by the law. In less than two years my idea was realized, first in the form of a night and soon afterwards also a day sobering-up station. The station has twenty-two beds in the same building with the alcoholism clinic. Both health institutions form part of the Psychiatric Clinic (Medical Faculty, Charles University) and have a common head physician.

The sobering-up station operates as follows:

1. The intoxicated person is brought in by an ambulance or public security emergency van.

2. The person and his property are handed over to the care of health personnel and the crew of the ambulance or emergency van leaves.

3. The detained person takes off his clothes (or his clothes are taken off) and is put in bed; if necessary the person is cleaned, examined, and treated by the physician, and a blood specimen withdrawn for analysis.

4. In the course of the eight- to twelve-hour stay, detained persons are taken care of by 2–3 members of the sanitary personnel (men and women alike), 4 patients on duty who are presently under treatment, one physician-psychiatrist, and during the day by a social worker.

The sobering-up station in Prague has been functioning for eighteen years and is generally considered a lesser evil, saving patients from potential complications.

The aims and procedure of the sobering-up station are the following:

1. The intoxicated person is detained for a period necessary for sobering up (8–12 hours; in cases of serious intoxication even longer). The essential examination and treatment are carried out either by a physician together with the sanitary personnel of the station or by a consultant on call. In emergency cases the patient

is transferred to another department of the hospital. In the period
1951–1969 more than 60,000 persons were treated at the station.

2. Upon leaving, the sober visitor is handed a paying-in slip
by the nurse, or the administrative clerk withholds 118 crowns
from him (corresponding roughly to earnings for 8–12 hours
work); persons detained for the first time (who are Prague residents) are handed an invitation to the so-called "school," held
once a month. During 1957–1968, 42,690 persons were detained;
of these 16,591 or approximately 40 percent were first-detained
Prague residents. Of these 9,017, or 54 percent of those invited,
attended our school.

3. A copy of the admission form is forwarded to the outpatient
clinic nearest to the patient's residence. By the beginning of 1969,
ten Prague outpatient clinics had treated 20,000 persons; according to a modest estimate, at least two-thirds of these had entered
on the basis of a report sent by the sobering-up station. In the
period of 1957–1966 the total increment in the outpatient clinics
amounted to 17,962; of these 10,623, or nearly 60 percent of the
detained, had been entered in the files of the outpatient clinics,
whereas in 1957 the percentage was only 35 percent. At present
the percentage is much higher. The systematic activity of the
sobering-up station initiated and intensified the activity of further
antialcoholism institutions; the sobering-up station is therefore a
very important component for prevention.

4. The statistically evaluated data recorded on detained persons serve as a source of information about the epidemiology of
alcoholism among the million residents in our capital city.

I consider other results of the statistical analysis interesting
and informative about aspects of alcoholism among the urban
population of Prague.

1. In the period 1956–1964 the frequency of detentions
showed a constant increase from Monday to Saturday; Sunday
had the least number. After the introduction of free Saturdays, in
1965, Friday has been the most frequent, closely followed by
Thursday; Saturday dropping to third place. Two hypotheses can
be deduced: that the frequency of alcohol abuse increases along

with increasing fatigue or tension and the advancing work week in general; that the abuse does not take place so much with drinkers at home as it does with drinkers from the place of work.

2. As far as the time distribution of detentions is concerned, in 1958–1968 nearly always the most frequent time was between 10 P.M. and 4 A.M. Within these 6 hours 53 percent were detained; before 12 noon only 4 percent were detained. In 1968, a shift of the most frequent detentions was observed toward earlier hours, i.e., until 10 P.M.

3. An analysis of persons according to profession shows a somewhat lower percentage of manual workers than the total recorded for the whole Prague population, throughout the whole period of the activity of the station. The decreasing number of persons from the household and persons in retirement is conspicuous. Whereas the former decreases in the whole population of Prague, due to rising employment, the latter increases but the unchanged pensions of retired persons do not allow them to purchase such luxury goods as alcohol and "visits" to the sobering-up station.

4. The percentage of women detained (about 10,000 persons were detained per year), in the course of five years amounted to 8.5 percent, 5.9 percent, 5.4 percent, 4.0 percent, and 5.7 percent. The percentage probably for the following reasons: evidently the number of prostitutes of the old type, who were repeatedly detained, decreased; alcohol abuse in women is psychogenic, not sociogenic as in men (i.e., connected with frequent sitting in pubs over a glass of beer), and the public attitude toward a drunken woman is still very uncompromising. Thus the percentage of women recorded at the sobering-up station and Prague outpatient clinics amounts to 6 percent.

5. The most important finding from the sobering-up station's statistics is the fact that the male population escorted to the station, as compared with the total male population in Prague, in the course of years took an alarming shift toward younger age groups. This can be best seen in the following table:

We found that most of our patients at the inpatient clinic started excessive drinking before attaining 20 years of age; if in the 60s the number of young men brought in to us in acute alcoholic intoxication increased, in five to fifteen years a certain number of them will become alcoholics. This suggests an increasing wave of alcoholics reaching a peak around 1975–1980. Let us hope the wave will be followed by a decrease in later years.

A report on adolescents to 18 years detained at the Prague sobering-up station was presented by Mečíř, based on a study of several hundred at a special adolescent outpatient clinic. For 17

*Table 9*

PERCENTAGE OF MEN FROM 15 TO 70 YEARS

| AGE CATEGORY: | 1955 | | 1964 | |
|---|---|---|---|---|
| | *in Prague* | *at the SS* | *in Prague* | *at the SS* |
| 15–20 | 6.2 | 5.9 | *12.8* | *17.5* |
| 21–25 | 7.5 | 8.4 | *9.5* | *17.6* |
| 26–30 | 9.9 | 16.1 | 6.8 | 12.9 |
| 31–35 | 11.7 | 17.3 | 8.2 | 12.5 |
| 36–40 | 7.3 | 9.3 | 9.9 | 10.9 |
| 41–45 | 11.9 | 14.4 | 10.8 | 10.7 |
| 46–50 | 13.5 | 12.8 | 6.5 | 4.9 |
| 51–60 | 21.1 | 12.6 | 22.2 | 10.6 |
| 61–70 | 10.9 | 3.2 | 14.1 | 2.4 |

N = 329981  N = 3547  N = 365165  N = 2842

percent it was an incidental abuse; 74 percent were in the initial and prodromal phase according to Jellinek; 9 percent were in the crucial and terminal phases. In the group with incidental abuse personality defects were found in less than 5 percent and a poor educational environment was found in 25 percent. On the other hand, in adolescents under 18 years old who arrived at the terminal phase, personality problems were found in 76 percent and poor educational environment in 57 percent.

6. The alarming data of the Prague sobering-up station prompted a nationwide investigation into the drinking habits of soldiers on compulsory military duty in the Czechoslovak army. Of the 2,115 questionnaires received the following conclusions could

be drawn about young men aged 19–21 (who had been treated in the sobering-up station:

| | |
|---|---|
| Complete abstinence for more than 3 years | 0.8% |
| Abstinence 1–3 years | 0.6% |
| Consume alcoholic drinks in doses not calling forth euphoria | 4.4% |
| Consume alcoholic drinks in euphorizing doses | 79.0% |
| Markedly excessive drinkers consuming at least twice a week and more often alcoholic beverages containing more than 100 g. absolute alcohol | 14.3% |
| Alcoholics according to own evaluation, after being acquainted with the definition of Act 120/1962 | 0.9% |

The investigation was also confirmed by the Ministry of Consuming Goods Industry study which showed 30 percent of young men to 24 years drinking more than 2 liters of beer a day, i.e., more than the physiological need of liquids.

7. Three investigations conducted by the Prague sobering-up station with the cooperation of the alcoholism outpatient clinics revealed the percentage of patients with more or less incidental intoxication, as compared with those whose systematic abuse caused a permanent problem.

*Table 10*

| YEAR OF DETENTION | YEAR OF INVESTI-GATION | NO. OF PERSONS INVESTI-GATED | NO. OF ANSWERS | OF THESE *alcoh.* % | *nonalcoh.* % |
|---|---|---|---|---|---|
| 1951 | 1952 | 500 | 300 | 80 | 20 |
| 1955 | 1957 | 1200 | 869 | 64 | 36 |
| 1951/66 | 1967 | 120 | 84 | 64 | 36 |

Thus of three detained persons one had an incidental abuse, whereas the other two had a lasting problem resulting from their abuse and required care and help from antialcoholism institutions.

8. The percentage of those detained for the first time during the years 1957–1969 varied between 57 and 61 percent; the per-

centage of those twice detained varied from 14 to 16 percent; and the percentage of those repeatedly detained varied between 22 and 26 percent. This implies that even with such high numbers and the detaining of intoxicated persons, a high degree of homeostasis exists.

# Recent developments in the struggle against alcoholism in Italy

### GIUSEPPE MASTRANGELO, M.D.

When a nation produces wines which are of great importance to its economy, it does not readily admit the danger of these products to the national health. Consequently, the battle to control the incidence of alcoholism (one of the highest in the world) in Italy has been extremely difficult. Dr. Giuseppe Mastrangelo is director of the Service for the Prevention and Treatment of Alcoholism in Milan, and has at last made his fellow countrymen realize that they do indeed face a major problem. His article should inspire many who find their own struggle against the disease difficult.

## RECOGNIZING THE PROBLEM

Before discussing recent developments in the struggle against alcoholism in our country, it is necessary to determine whether alcoholism exists as a social problem in Italy; and, if so, to estimate the extent of the phenomenon.

In Italy, public opinion as a whole considers that there can be individual alcoholics, but that alcoholism does not exist as a national problem. This same belief is shared in other parts of the world by many persons who, in good faith, consider Italians as an example of a sober people, whose general habit of drinking wine in preference to spirits does not lead them to alcoholism.

It must now be stated that this belief is without foundation, and that common opinion on the subject does not correspond to the facts. Let us take this occasion to demonstrate, on the basis of incontestable evidence, how matters really stand.

From September 22 to 28, 1913, the XIV International Congress Against Alcoholism took place in Milan. From the records of that Congress, now a bibliographical rarity, we know that all the countries of Europe, many from North and South America, Australia, Russia, and China were represented, all on the official invitation of the Italian government. From this we can conclude that the problem of alcoholism existed in Italy, and that its importance was recognized both by the Italian government and the people.

Many representatives of the intellectual and active life of the country, many temperance organizations, and distinguished political and civic personalities accepted the invitation of the General National Committee. Opening the Congress, Senator Marchiafava, the most prominent Italian clinician of his times said:

> We see the increasing numbers of intoxicated men . . . we see the damage caused by this poison that eats away the best gifts of life . . . this deceiving drink that, protected by the desire for profits, disperses all noble ideals. . . . We read statistics which show a continuous increase of alcoholism in our towns and villages. . . . Would to God your condemnation of this woeful abuse, whose fellows are sorrow, crime, and death, could wipe away the ignorance, the mistakes, the prejudices that hinder the sound knowledge of what is good and bad for the preservation of health, for the feelings of human dignity, and for the improvement of the race. If only alcohol abuse could be controlled, as we all fervently hope, not a small piece of desolation and evil would disappear. . . .

But the tragedy of World War I followed; and in 1924 scientists and public authorities realized that the situation had worsened. In the meantime, Fascism took over, and soon wiped away a number of free democratic organizations that were fighting for temperance, sobriety, and moderation. Italy, that had given hospitality to the International Congress Against Alcoholism in 1913, had to give up its membership in the Bureau International contre l'Alcoholism and resign from all other societies of this kind. The demagogic nationalism imposed by Fascism could not admit that among a people "of navigators, of saints, and of heroes" there could also be immoderate drinkers. The devastating consequences of this psychological warping of national thought still live today in an infinite number of ways which influence a social climate that is complex and full of deep contradictions. And so, whereas small nations like the Netherlands and Switzerland boast of highly developed social programs against alcoholism, official Italy (53 million people, greatest producer of wine in the world) always systematically absents herself from the world struggle against alcoholism.

Italian legislation has completely ignored any modern approach to the problem, and has allowed old laws to fall into disrepute. Meanwhile, the manufacturers of alcoholic beverages, who have at their command all information media, influence their customers to consume more and more, and establish their names as part of the national pride, almost as sacred as the flag.

A huge literature celebrates Bacchic rites and traditions, with triumphant intolerance of every possible restriction. Public opinion and its political representatives are conditioned by skillful publicists who urge them to believe that alcoholic drinks are not only completely harmless, but even necessary to good health. The beverage industry, although admittedly one of the pillars of the national economy, is shown by this biased propaganda as the support, directly or indirectly, of at least five million Italians.

In Italy for such reasons, alcoholism and its damaging effects are ignored as if they did not exist; and responsible Italian authorities, when questioned on the subject by the concerned branches of the United Nations, have always declared, no doubt in good faith, that alcoholism remains an insignificant phenomenon in our country. This false belief has been shared by a number of foreign researchers, such as Sadon, Lolli, and Silvermann, all of whom have been disproved by Perrin.

Facts and figures are now in order. Italy is the greatest producer of wine in the world, with 75 million hectoliters in 1967, a figure that is bound to grow with the progress in cultivation techniques, and with the increase in industrialization. France ranked second with 60 million hectoliters.

Consumption is also acknowledged to be very high, but remarkable disagreement exists among the various statistical studies. According to the Bulletin Hebdomadaire de Statistique, for example, the annual consumption of anhydrous alcohol totaled 24 liters per capita per year from 1953 to 1965. Lower estimates from other statistical sources set the minimum annual consumption from 1965 to 1967 at 13.8 liters per capita, as compared to 6 liters in the United States, 5.7 liters in England, and 4.8 liters in Sweden.

As this enormous quantity of alcohol, predominantly in the form of wine, is mostly drunk by adult males in the north of Italy, it is obvious that alcoholism is more serious in the northern districts like Lombardy, Liguria, Piedmont, and Venetia.

We shall examine testimony on the continuous increase in illness and mortality due to cirrhosis of the liver, the increase in hospitalization of younger persons, and in the number hospitalized in mental institutions—all unquestionable signs of a corresponding growth of alcoholism, as Jellinek has shown.

As a matter of fact, tradition and custom establish drinking as part of the daily nourishment of Italian people. Through domestic initiation to drinking from infancy on, an unquenchable need for alcohol is developed, which eventually develops into toxicosis. In accordance with the critical analyses by Wendell and Kellar, we must calculate at least one alcoholic for every one hundred people, that is 530,000 individuals chronically subject to intoxication, needing immediate treatment and rehabilitation. Actually, in the northern districts the percentage of alcoholics will run substantially higher, with peaks in the villages of Venetia reaching 15 to 18 percent.

It has been estimated that each individual alcoholic costs society two to four million lira per year, directly or indirectly, the amount varying with his status. Translated into dollars, alcoholism costs Italy at least three billion dollars a year, a tremendous amount in relation to the Italian budget, and a sum equivalent to the total cost of alcoholism to the United States and France. Yet in the United States, in France, in Canada, and in many other countries modern facilities are organized in the struggle against alcoholism, whereas in Italy nothing similar for the purpose exists. It seems certain that alcoholism, the cause of this invisible but constant waste of lives, energy, and money, must also be considered a cause of the political, social, and economic distortions that have so often afflicted our contradictory country, so loved, and so abused.

The late Umberto De Giacomo, a great Italian psychiatrist who died in 1967, certainly a reliable source, used to say of himself:

> I am not one of those fanatics of the Anti-alcohol League who pester the whole of mankind with boring speeches. [But in 1959, during a lecture on the problems of alcohol in Italy for the World Day of Mental Health, he remarked:]
> The World Health Organization has pointed out that if a physical disease reaches the proportions of some of the psycho-social diseases of our time, such as alcoholism and other toxicomanias . . . , a state of emergency would soon be declared, and strong counter measures immediately taken.

Increasing mental illness, from which highly civilized people generally suffer more because of their restless way of life, is to a certain extent counterbalanced by the continuous improvement in the prevention and treatment of a good number of psychic troubles, owing to a better knowledge of their origin, development, and action. But the light of this knowledge must not be hidden in the ivory towers of scientific institutions. On the contrary, it must shine from them so that it can enlighten and direct public opinion, and especially guide those who are responsible for the progress and welfare of the people.

The social and hygienic problem of alcoholism has been known and attacked from ancient times. Spartans used to make the Ilots drunk to infuse the youth with disgust for wine. In Athens, according to Dracon's laws, which were said to have been written in blood, drunken men could be sentenced to death. Julius Caesar wrote that in Germany the Suebi refused to import wine for the same reason that Hector refused the cup that Hecuba handed to him, which was that he feared wine would lessen his strength. Shakespeare gives us a perfect gerontologic prescription when he says, "Though I look old, yet I am strong and lusty, for in my youth I never did apply hot and rebellious liquors to the blood."

In more recent times, French realistic literature, especially in some of Zola's work, has left gloomy pictures of typical social consequences of alcoholism.

In Italy in 1907, Seppilli, who had been commissioned by the Italian Psychiatric Society to make an inquiry into alcoholism, at the end of his report expressed the hope that our country, too, following the example of other civilized European nations, would begin to prepare for the fight against alcoholism, which he considered a "terrible social evil." But in spite of his plea, and of a number of strong pronouncements by psychiatrists which appeared seventeen years later in 1924 on the occasion of a new Congress of the society, the same proposals had to be made again, as very few practical results had followed the first occasion.

After the end of World War II, one of my colleagues, Giovanni Bonfiglio, restated the whole question, publishing in 1954 a statistical study on the growth of alcoholic psychoses, covering the whole country for the six-year period 1947–1952. Other studies on the subject were published at the same time, covering single districts such as Vercelli (Dogliani), Sassari (Romerio), Como (Bedini), Siena (Stefanacci), Arezzo (Parigi), Salento (Di Sansebastiano), and Bologna (Carloni).

The conclusions drawn by all these scientists were similar to those of Bonfiglio, showing a progressive increase in hospitalization of alcoholics, which was singled out as one of the causes of overcrowding of mental hospitals. In Italy in the six years from 1947 to 1952, alcoholics hospitalized for the first time totaled 7,973; during the four years from 1953 to 1956, 6,540; with an increase of the annual rate of the hospitalized from 1,330 a year for the first six years, to 1,610 a year in the following four years. From 1947 to 1956 registered cases totaled 14,513.

This palpable increase of alcoholic psychosis follows a continuous, almost regularly ascending curve, showing that the increase from 900 first-hospitalized cases in 1947 to 1,600 in 1952, and to 1,900 in 1956, was a proportionately greater increase than either the growth of population or the number of persons hospitalized for other kinds of psychoses. The percentage of alcoholic psychoses to all types of psychoses was 4.58 percent in 1947, reached 6.55 percent in 1952, and rose to 7.03 percent in 1956.

Moreover, all these statistics refer only to first hospitalizations, although it is well known that relapsing alcoholics return frequently, shuttling from mental hospitals to bars, and vice versa. It can therefore be assumed that the number of alcoholics in Italy (and in France) reaches approximately 11 percent of the total amount of those hospitalized in mental institutions.

Finally, these statistics, concerned only with first-time or relapsing alcoholics, do not reflect the responsibility that alcohol must bear in the increase of many other psychoses of different sorts to which drinking contributes heavily. Nor does it consider the consequences, often very serious, to the physical and mental health, and to the moral reactions, of the children of alcoholics. Epilepsy frequently results, and is, for example, widespread in the district of Salento.

The frequency of alcoholic psychoses is not the same in all Italian provinces. It is well above the average in the north, about up to average in central Italy, and below the average in the south. This is probably due to the higher standard of living of the working classes of the northern regions, where industry is often better developed than agriculture. Statistics indicate that for every four alcoholic farmers there are six alcoholic industrial workers.

Also, in northern Italy the larger number of entertainment establishments make the use of alcohol easier. The consumption of spirits is widespread, especially brandy, which is even more toxic than vodka or whiskey due to its higher content of methyl alcohol.

In July, as is typical in all summer months, the graph of alcohol psychosis reaches its highest peaks. Consumption decreases progressively in autumn, spring, and winter, in that order, which shows beyond doubt that alcoholics drink more to offset warm weather than cold.

Many alcoholics who perform hard physical work drink to find relief from thirst and fatigue. Other workers are induced to drink by the nature of their work, among them barmen and porters, who are often offered drinks; wholesalers and middlemen, who do business with a toast; farmers, who like to sample the products of their vineyards.

The maximum frequency of alcoholic psychosis is found in men of 45 to 50. As the old saying goes, men in their fifties give up women and take to drinking. But the male climacteric is only one of the causes of alcoholism. Many shy young men drink wine and spirits hoping to assert themselves, to overcome their inferiority complexes, or to solve other emotional conflicts. Other individuals drink because they are influenced by their friends, or because they are slaves to imitation. Rare cases of dipsomania (as psychiatrists call the pathological impulse) lead to a temporary but irresistible compulsion to drink too much alcohol. Finally, there exists a large number of hedonists, often with psychopathic or abnormal personalities, who drink only for pleasure. They enjoy aperitifs and sweet liqueurs, and give snobbish parties at which large quantities of strong drinks, cocktails, and champagne are served. This road leads from use to misuse, and from misuse to addiction.

Obviously, we cannot remain unconcerned when a medical and social problem like alcoholism is shown to be the cause of 24 percent of the highway accidents (according to recent world statistics); or of 35 percent of crimes (according to the French Ministry of Justice); or of 16 percent (according to Deshais) or of 22 percent (according to Heuyer) of births of deficient children; or of 11 percent of hospitalizing in mental institutions (according to our own experience). Psychiatrists are obligated at this point not only to point out the seriousness of this situation, but also to propose remedial action to political and medical authorities that could at least hold this major health problem in check, if not indeed eliminate it.

## A CALL TO ACTION

The following basic preventive measures against alcoholism should be set up in Italy: the number of licenses to sell spirits and the hours of opening for the vendors must be limited. Sales of liquor to minors must be prohibited. A dry regimen in schools, boarding schools, and colleges should be maintained. When equally strict measures were recently relaxed in Sweden, the incidence of alcoholic psychosis immediately rose.

Second, hygienic campaigns against alcoholism must be intensified, not only with school children, but also among adults, making use of the modern media for propaganda—television, cinema, and radio—and of special educational films, which could be produced by the Italian League for Mental Hygiene and Prophylaxis.

Third, the government, following the example of what has been accomplished through legislative action in France, should develop a financial policy that encourages exportation and restrains importation of wine products. Also it should promote the production of soft drinks, curb unlicensed distillers, and limit the methyl alcohol content of spiritous liquors, which contain this poison in amounts sometimes up to 3 percent. Methyl alcohol can be eliminated during industrial processing by removing the pectin from which it derives, or by other methods of de-methylization.

Another important approach could be made through a social policy that would promote the intellectual and moral development of the people, particularly of the poor. Entertainment for all ages (such as television) should be made less expensive, so that it could be enjoyed at home, rather than in taverns and bars. Housing should be improved, to make home more attractive for workers and pensioners.

An Italian center for scientific, social, and legal research on alcohol and its problems, similar to the School of Alcohol Studies at Rutgers University (formerly at Yale) in the United States, could be most useful. Facilities should be set up to educate those who, because of their work, social position, or way of life are likely to become alcoholics. For those who have descended into alcoholism, detoxification units should be set up in special hospitals, which would include regular follow-up treatment routines (psychotherapeutic as well as medicinal) for the prevention of relapse.

In summary, the problem of alcoholism, together with other critical sociomedical problems such as geriatrics and epilepsy, must not be overlooked in the coming reform legislation of the medical codes of the country. On the contrary, alcoholism should be established as one of the main concerns of mental hospitals and mental hygiene and prophylaxis centers.

In February 1965, the Italian Institute of Social Medicine organized a successful meeting on "Current Problems of Alcoholism in Italy" in which a remarkable number of highly specialized researchers took part. The records of the meeting demonstrate the essential agreement of all participants on the seriousness of the problem in Italy. We quote the following passage from Mario Corsini, social worker, enumerating the social and cultural inducements toward alcoholism:

1. Growing pressures of economic and social demands.

2. Disintegration of family life due to ability of finding personal satisfaction outside the home.

3. Increase of competition within the family, as women become workers with increasing frequency.

4. Slackening of social control over individual behavior.

5. Replacement of former models of moderation and conformity with the model of individual success.

6. Slackening of emotional ties and solidarity between members of the family and members of social groups.

7. Isolation caused by forced separations among families due to migration. In a society such as ours, man is more and more alone. Strains and failures, immaturity, and the sense of inferiority can easily lead weaker personalities to seek escape in alcohol whenever troubles occur.

At the same meeting, Ferdinando Antoniotti noted that consumption of wine in Italy had grown from 109.6 liters per capita in 1950, to 143.4 in 1962; the consumption of beer from 27.8 liters to 81.1 liters in the same period; and the consumption of spirits from 1.3 to 1.6 liters. He concluded that in recent years there had been an increase of alcoholic psychoses, alcoholism, and cirrhosis of the liver which could be directly traced to the growing consumption of alcoholic drinks.

Giacomo Perico, S.J., in a lucid report on alcoholism published in the review *Aggiornamente Sociali* (April 1967), wrote:

In Italy the consumption of anhydrous alcohol was 11 liters per capita in 1938, 18 liters in 1950, and 24 liters in 1963. Considering that in Italy anhydrous alcohol is 96 percent consumed in wine, for 1963 it can be determined that Italians drank 180 liters of wine per capita, or about half a liter per day for every person. Since the alcohol consumers are for the most part male adults, the figure must have been considerably higher for them.

Official statistical data for 1964 and 1965 confirm the preceding indications. In 1964, 53,559,000 hectoliters of wine were consumed in Italy, together with 4,297,000 hectoliters of beer; in 1965, 55,964,-000 hectoliters of wine, and 4,590,000 of beer.

According to the same official data, in 1964 Italians spent the equivalent of $1,500,000,000 on alcoholic drinks, $1,100,000,000 on tobacco, and $855,000,000 on education and entertainment. In 1965 the total spent on alcohol rose to $1,600,000,000.

During a symposium organized by the Italian Automobile Club (ACI) at Salsomaggiore in May 1963, I presented a report, "Alcohol and Neuropsychiatric Diseases, and Their Connection with the Human Factor in Traffic Problems," which analyzed contributions by eminent scientists like Father Gemelli, Tiziano, Ancona, Meschieri, Grasso Biondi, Di Macco, Mitolo, Cecchetto, Sacchi, Sotgiu, Mangili, Fiamberti, Zanaldi, Mascherpa, Campanacci, Cattabeni, and Acchiapatti.

I particularly stressed a persuasive study by the last author on the inadequacy of Italian legislation and the lack of official statistics concerning the relation of alcohol to car accidents.

During the same symposium in Salsomaggiore, Giovanni Bonfiglio read a report on "The Seriousness of Alcoholism in Italy," from which I will quote a most interesting passage:

In Italy the cost and danger of alcoholism is still underrated, both by public opinion, and by doctors, administrators, and legislators. In view of the importance of the problem, legislation on alcoholism and its relation to traffic is urgently needed.

Common belief still holds that alcoholism in Italy is negligible. Some even think that, because of the improvement in the standard of living and of the change in social habits, the use and misuse of alcoholic drinks has been reduced. Many people, in support of this mistaken opinion, mention the fact that drunken men are very rarely seen, and that nowadays taverns are patronized by only a few customers, usually of the older generation. But these persons do not consider that the intoxicated man who, thirty years ago, dragged himself home, walking unsteadily, now drives a car or a motorcycle, thus escaping people's notice. Those who maintain that taverns are patronized by only a few older customers, forget that in recent years members of the younger generation in constantly increasing numbers meet in nightclubs and bars, where spirits are readily available.

Unfortunately, figures on consumption of alcohol in recent years demonstrate beyond doubt the error of believing that alcoholism in Italy is not a problem, or that it is gradually decreasing. Many readers will be astonished by the unbelievable size of these figures, which reflect the fact that consumption in Italy is greater than in most of the other nations. In Europe, for instance, we are second only to France; but in France, the problem is known, studied, and fought against, while in Italy public opinion deceives itself into believing that alcoholism is not an outstanding social or medical problem.

In 1941, 63 liters of wine per capita were consumed, and this figure has gradually climbed to 120 liters in 1961. The increase in consumption of beer has been even greater, and that of spirits really is terrifying. Consumption per capita of spirits in 1941 was 0.3 liters, which by 1961 had grown to 1.5 liters. In twenty-one years consumption of wine has doubled, beer has tripled, and spirits has quintupled.

Some authors, American especially, have pointed out that the increase in consumption of alcoholic drinks is not always accompanied by a corresponding increase of diseases caused by alcohol; but these authors were dealing with very small increases of from 3 percent to 10 percent, whereas in Italy the increase has been so enormous that it inevitably has brought along an increase in all diseases connected with alcoholism. Actually, psychiatrists in mental hospitals report a continuous increase in recent years of the various kinds of alcoholic psychoses.

National statistics show that those hospitalized for alcoholic psychoses totaled about 900 in 1947, and 2,700 in 1962. This 200 percent increase was not due to a tendency to hospitalize patients more easily, nor to improved hospital facilities, nor to a change for the better in the public attitude toward mental hospitals. Actually, all these circumstances favor hospitalization for all kinds of psychoses; but hospitalization for alcoholic psychoses amounted to 4.4 percent of those admitted in 1947, and 12 percent of all those admitted in 1962. Likewise, in 1947 alcoholic admittances came to 1.9 percent per hundred thousand people, but rose to 7 percent in 1962. This relation between the number of original hospitalizations for alcoholism and the general population continues to grow, an alarming development, especially when compared to figures for other nations.

Without dwelling on statistics, I will note that in the United States, a country whose problem of alcoholism is known to be serious, the rate is only 4.2 percent per hundred thousand people. The difference between this percentage and that found in Italy becomes even more relevant if we consider that American statistics exclude those younger than 15, whereas Italian statistics include the entire population.

Alcoholic psychoses affect with continually growing frequency inhabitants of towns, especially industrial centers, rather than those who live in the country. Female alcoholism has also especially increased in industrial areas, where women are now more frequently employed.

Yet alcoholic psychoses along do not give a complete picture of the increase of alcoholism and its diversified somatic and psychic consequences. Considering the alarming increase of such psychoses evident in Italy since World War II, we recognize that other diseases caused by alcoholism have certainly grown at similar rates, as, for example, in the case of cirrhosis of the liver, which has increased at a rate which parallels that of alcoholism. The increase in cirrhosis cases noted both in Italy and in France serves to demonstrate how groundless is the old belief, widely held in both countries, that wine is by far less dangerous than spirits.

Actually, in both countries, where wine is the staple beverage, cirrhosis of the liver caused by alcohol is more common than in other countries, such as the United States, where consumption is mainly in the form of spirits. Cirrhosis caused by alcoholism runs 65 percent in Italy, 80 percent in France, but drops to 50 percent in the United States.

An interesting question arises of whether alcohol, consumed regularly in small quantities at many times during each day, as in France and Italy, is more harmful than if consumed in occasional large quantities, as in the United States. One answer lies in the per capita usage, which, while no complete or detailed statistics are available, does indicate that consumption of alcohol is greater in the wine producing countries.

According to an American author (Sharfenberger), the daily use of small quantities of alcohol is more dangerous than the occasional ingestion of large quantities; and the damage caused by alcoholism is more nearly related to frequency of ingestion than to large quantities occasionally introduced into the body.

What is difficult to ascertain is the total quantity of alcohol consumed by both types of drinkers over a long period. Information on this point, although difficult to obtain, could be of considerable importance because it would indicate the less dangerous way of drinking alcohol. In Italy, where along with alcoholism by wine, alcoholism by spirits is now beginning to spread, we now have the opportunity of studying this question which could add useful elements to our knowledge of alcoholism and its pathology, although of course some years will be needed before it will be possible to evaluate the damage caused by protracted use of strong drink, as Italy has only recently begun to use spirits on a broad scale.

Some research seems to indicate that the pathological consequences, both physical and psychical, are more serious from alcoholism due to wine than if caused by spirits. Indeed, while the consumption of strong drink has been increasing in recent years in Italy, almost all the alcoholic psychoses to date have been caused by wine. In further support of this, we find that signs of cardiovascular damage, alteration of hepatic functions, and cases of gastrectomy are very much more frequent in subjects intoxicated by wine than in subjects intoxicated by spirits.

Wine drinking has many allies in the traditional beliefs, cultural prejudices, and above all in economic interests, whose importance we can easily appreciate if we remember that in 1959 Italians spent more than one billion dollars on alcoholic drinks. All these obstacles must induce us not to relax our efforts, since, when the facts on alcoholism are understood, it will be possible to move forward in Italy as it has been in many other nations.

During a recent symposium on "Alcohol and the Doctor" (Udine, March 22, 1969), Luigi Massignan synthesized his thought thus:

> Alcoholism is a social disease that more than any other (apart from its medical aspects) involves the individual personality, the family, social structures, and work, imposing itself as a political and moral problem.
>
> The growth of this individual and social phenomenon is with one consent considered more and more alarming.
>
> Excessive use of alcohol drinks implies an individual inclination on the nature of which scientists do not yet agree, but which is certainly encouraged and made easier by customs, traditions, prejudices, and economic interests, for which our society is evidently responsible, especially because this same society always intervenes too late, and then only to punish or reject the alcoholic.

There are, of course, exceptions to this general situation; but they are due to the local action of individuals, which has not, until now, succeeded in developing on a national scale with any effectiveness.

The great majority of the medical profession remains thoroughly indifferent to the problem of alcoholism and seems hardly conscious of it, sharing in this the traditional approach of the country. Outstanding physicians preside over various groups of the "Friends of Wine" and periodically celebrate the virtues of the grape.

A small minority of doctors, however, perhaps one of every thousand, works on the problem and issues scientific papers of varying importance. Unfortunately, this production is not always supported by real interest in the problem. For many it originates from the chance necessities of a career, such as required professorship examinations. Such superficial interest explains in part the nature of the crisis facing the Italian university which has not yet been resolved. Such pseudoscientific production is rarely interdisciplinary, and usually confined to the lesser and seldom-read reviews.

Notwithstanding some reservations, and the objections stated above, it must be recognized that a small segment of the medical fraternity does work seriously on the problems of alcoholism and is seeking to cooperate, as witness the considerable number of meetings organized in recent years, some of which should be mentioned here:

June 12, 1960, at Siena: Prophylaxis and Outpatient Treatment of Alcoholics.

May 24–25, 1963, at Salsomaggiore: Alcoholism in Road Accidents.

February 27, 1965, in Rome: Topical Problems of Alcoholism in Italy.

June 15, 1965, in Turin, during "Medical Days": Psychiatric and Social Aspects of Alcoholism.

June 27–29, 1965, in Milan: Italian Society and Alcoholism.

March 23, 1969, at Udine: Alcoholism and the Doctor.

June 7–8, 1969, in Venice: Liver and Alcohol.

June 14, 1969, at Miradolo Terme: Alcoholic Heptopathy.

Other symposia treating various aspects of the problem of alcoholism have been held in Bari, Montecatini, Abano, Rome, Naples, Milan, Florence, and several other Italian centers. In Stresa every September the Italian Automobile Club holds its important Conference on Road Traffic, and has often discussed alcoholism in relation to road accidents. At the 1967 Conference, a resolution was adopted recommending legalizing breath tests for drivers who had been drinking.

Only Milan, of all the 92 Italian districts, has had in operation a service for the Prevention and Treatment of Pathological Alcoholism which is a result of thirty-two years of effort on my part, ever since, as a young psychiatrist, I began to realize the importance of the medical and social aspects of alcoholism. Many difficulties have been overcome, and many more have yet to be surmounted, but the service can be recognized as the first official attempt to deal with the problem in all its aspects, from prophylaxis and therapy to rehabilitation.

Under our plan, every district hospital is provided with a department for alcoholics, now totaling 1,350 beds, a number still far short of the need. Discharged patients are followed up by consulting centers, hampered by insufficient staff and facilities. In the near future, we hope to be able to organize, within the Alcoholism Service, a Center of Alcohol Studies, to research various aspects of the disease, mainly epidemiology, motivations for drinking, and preventive methods.

The establishment of this service in the Milan district represents progress in comparison with the other Italian districts, but it has also brought into prominence the enormous problems that will have to be solved, such as the need for specialized personnel, for detoxification centers, and for rehabilitation centers.

Probably the only way to deal with the problem of prevention is to make use, on a national scale, of the multidisciplinary approach. To accomplish this, a national association of all those interested has been formed, entitled the Italian Society for the Study of Problems of Alcohol and Alcoholism (SISPAA), for which I serve as General Secretary. Incorporated in 1966, the society is divided into four research departments: biological, psychological, pharmacological, and social. Unfortunately, after a promising start, so many of the difficulties arose that have been described in the preceding pages that many of our efforts have been nullified. We do, however, have hopes for a more promising future.

This survey can be concluded on an optimistic note with the mention of one effort that has proved a great success in this difficult struggle, and that is the 14th International Institute on the Prevention and Treatment of Alcoholism, held in Milan, June

10–15, 1968, under the auspices of the International Council on Alcohol and Addictions.

All sorts of difficulties threatened the organization of this institute, but were overcome at last. Because of the hundreds of participants from Europe, the United States, Canada, Australia, and other parts of the world; because of the number, the variety, and the high quality of its reports; and because of its interdisciplinary discussions, the congress met with a large measure of success.

The nation, the district, and the City of Milan cooperated to give full support to the meeting. The press followed with hundreds of articles, which helped reach our most important aim in Italy, the education of the public concerning alcoholism. Pope Paul VI, in a lengthy special message to the congress, for the first time officially recognized the importance and seriousness of alcoholism, and urged a campaign of prevention, a message that will certainly be of great value for the faithful of any denomination.

## CONCLUSION

Wide scientific documentation proves beyond doubt that in Italy alcoholism constitutes a most imposing social problem. The seriousness is worsened by lack of public understanding, which can even refuse to recognize what has been scientifically demonstrated. Almost all the authorities reflect the popular point of view, offering little more than a formal acknowledgment of the existence of alcoholism. Legislative reform of outdated laws, and strong enforcement action are most urgently needed.

Under the complex social and cultural conditions obtaining in Italy, informative and educational campaigns will be necessary to convince not only the responsible authorities but also the general public of the existence of the disease of alcoholism, and the urgency of preventing and controlling this serious menace to the health and welfare of the nation.

# Meeting the problems of alcoholism in the United States

SELDEN D. BACON, Ph.D.

To separate the study and treatment of alcoholism from concern with liquor traffic, temperance, and prohibition has been a difficult task. For many years, propaganda and confusion about the nature of the problem have obscured the truth. Dr. Selden D. Bacon has spent many years of ardent work, researching and disseminating the facts on alcoholism and alcohol-related problems in the United States. He is director of the Center of Alcohol Studies at Rutgers, the State University, New Jersey.

This presentation will propose a sociohistorical view of reactions to the problems of alcohol in the United States over the past twenty-five years. To some extent these developments are reflected in Canada; and perhaps the same forces, though probably in different garb and with varying strength, are to be found in other societies around the world.

No historical period can be effectively described without discussing its roots in the preceding years. I will briefly scan two previous periods in the national history of planned and unplanned responses to the problems of alcohol. The first, the period of the *classical American temperance movement,* I will place between 1825 and 1925, and will recall only the features of special relevance for understanding most recent developments.

First, all problems associated with alcohol were held in essence to be one and the same thing: whether the disapproved occurrences involved accidents or political graft or rowdyism or alcoholism or sexual misadventures or indolence or waste of resources, alcohol was the name of the problem.

Second, by simple extension of idea and strategy, any use of beverage alcohol, no matter what its form or quantity or purpose, became, ipso facto, "a problem."

Third, alcohol was held to be intrinsically a moral and spiritual evil, a characterization more basic than any other for this movement.

Fourth, attack upon the alcohol problem was primarily to be a legislative affair, with national prohibition as the final tactical goal; secondarily, the attack was to be launched through indoctrination about the evil of alcohol, with dramatic use of illustrations and threats, this program to be directed above all toward children and youth.

The classic temperance movement in the United States was magnificently organized and, in its earlier years, enjoyed leadership of the highest quality. To the surprise of many, it was one of the most liberal of American reform movements, espousing such causes as the rights of labor, international peace, woman's suffrage, and free, universal education. It was also a jealous movement in relation to the subject of alcohol: It was to be the sole arbiter of information, understanding, policy, and action in this field—whether the subject was law or medicine or religion or politics or education or science or anything else: either a person was *for* the Movement or was *for* its enemies, the Wets. Major institutional support was gained from the Protestant churches. On occasion, extensive abstinence campaigns of Catholic, especially Irish Catholic, origin served as an allied force.

From about 1875 on, one can see from the vantage point of history that changes were taking place which would eventually weaken this movement. However, the period of its greatest manifest power was yet to come. Three times between 1840 and 1915 more than half the country was controlled by Prohibition, and finally the goal of national legislation was achieved in 1919. But the changes weakening the movement were visible by 1900. I will list six of these developments.

First, the society itself was moving from the status of a frontier, rural, and small-town nation, largely of northwest European origins, and clearly of an extractive economic nature, to an urban, polyglot society of an industrial nature, one marked by an almost fantastic degree of individual mobility.

Second, the forms of drinking customs were undergoing major changes, switching from use of distilled spirits to use of beer; the act of drinking moving from commercial outlets to families, clubs, and organizations; the proportion of women users markedly increasing; the purposes of drinking shifting from that of getting drunk to that of enhancing other social purposes.

Third, formal education and mass communication media increased enormously in scope, with a gradual rise in the level of sophistication which made the simplistic messages of the classic movement decreasingly attractive and increasingly suspect.

Fourth, the rise of the scientific method, especially as this came to be applied successfully to various diseases.

Fifth, the new modes of recognizing, attacking, and (in many cases with marked success), controlling what are called social problems, again with special emphasis on certain diseases.

Sixth, a development within the movement itself—namely, both a rigidity in structure, idea, and action setting in at the close of the nineteenth century which resulted in its becoming a stereotype of old reform movements; and also a wide swing in its position in American society, a change more in the society than in the movement, resulting in its characterization as an extreme conservative rather than advanced liberal group.

In large part because of the monolithic power of the classic movement, these developments resulted not in new ideas, new organization, and new action, but, quite the contrary, in evasion, self-imposed ignorance, avoidance, ridicule, and denial.

The second historical period I call *limbo*. Extending from perhaps 1925 to 1940 or 1943, only the sensitive historian, gifted with the hindsight of 1955 or 1960, could find anything positive, innovative, or constructive for meeting what we can see so clearly today as truly massive problems related to alcohol and its use which continued, perhaps even increased, during that time. The direct problems such as the so-called "accidents" associated with excessive use, the related diseases, the broken lives of alcoholics —all these continued. The indirect problems, those associated with programs of alleviation and control which manifestly failed and which bred deep alienation from and distrust of basic social institutions—government, religion, education, and health services —became an ever-increasing sore—perhaps more damaging to the total society than the direct problems from which they sprang. Parents and community leaders were fearful and uncertain.

And what did people in the society do? To those who were to mount the new attacks following 1940–1944, it seemed as if there were a gigantic conspiracy by government, by industry, by the foundations, by educators, by the health and welfare professions, by researchers, and by the mass media, a conspiracy to avoid recognition, responsibility, or action. No meaningful records were kept, no relevant training conducted, no research supported, and, of course, no service provided. And, to top it off, avoidance, ridicule, and belittlement were visited on those attempting change. Yet there was in fact no conspiracy in the usual meaning of the word. Rather, it was massive social avoidance, an avoidance enhanced by the distasteful image of the old Wet-Dry conflict. Individual cases, when they could no longer be hidden, resulted in punitive actions, sometimes official in terms of jailing or repeated short-term confinement in mental institutions, sometimes in terms of social ostracism and discharge from employment, but always actions of great social cost to communities, groups, and society, of deep pain to families and individuals, and of no visible help or hope to anyone. And the immediate problems were matched by the institutional problems: education on alcohol was archaic and futile or carefully avoided; laws were unenforced, avoided, and ridiculed, the courts and jails were bogged down with old ritual, disgust, and inefficiency; the churches were in conflict. The list is long; the atmosphere suffused with hopelessness. I have named the period "limbo"; and limbo is hard to describe.

And so, following the near-century of the magnificent movement and the following fifteen to twenty years of limbo, we come to the past quarter century. I will suggest the following descriptive words to characterize this last period: Recognition, Action (including study), Fractionalization, Turmoil, and Hope. These five terms should at the least suggest a basic change from the preceding period. But even as I make this assertion, I must add that even today the impact of the two preceding periods is still strong, can still dominate thinking, opinion, and action in this locality, in that organization, and in various situations. Hopelessness, punitive responses, ignorance, and avoidance have not disappeared. The turmoil is not only within the new and changing scene, but responses from the archaic and older periods are still raucous, even still violent, and merge with more rational— at least more current—disagreements; and these enhance prejudice and prolong that fractionalization which appears to me as the major weakness of current developments in the alcohol problems field in this nation.

But the outstanding characteristic of the past twenty-five years has been *recognition*. It is a recognition of greater scope, greater discrimination, and greater intellectual maturity than that of the classic temperance movement and represents the opposite of the evasion and denial of the period of limbo. The nineteenth century recognition was indiscriminate, simplistic, and couched entirely in terms of evil. The more modern viewpoint recognizes, first, that there is widespread, customary use of alcohol beverages, use which does not constitute a social problem (except for the classic temperance view). Second, there are very real, extensive, and deeply painful problems immediately associated with deviant use. Third, these alcohol problems are problems of quite different natures, e.g., highway use problems, cirrhosis, a variety of alcoholisms, and entirely different sorts of problems, e.g., misdemeanors, family disruption, and suicide, can be associated with and sometimes enhanced by alcohol use; consequent to this understanding it follows that different controls will be required for the different problems. Fourth, it is increasingly recognized that a major set of problems related to alcohol are *not* of an immediate relationship to alcohol use, in fact, require no use of alcohol at all, but rather are problems stemming from a long-lived series of attempts at control of the direct problems through education, law, religious activity, taxation—attemps which not only failed but which elicited deep-seated social antagonisms as well as a history of evasion, denial, and ignorance.

This recognition, with weaknesses to be described in a moment, has encompassed particularly such direct problem areas as problem drinking in business and industry, the chronic drunkenness offender in the police-court-jail network, the alcohol-affected highway crash, and the alcoholisms. Perhaps even more basically it is to be seen in the searching review of their philosophies by leading Protestant denominations, by sociological and anthropological studies of the custom of drinking, and by a revival of mature and clearly more sophisticated interest in the goals, problems, and quality of education for youth about drinking. I would not wish to confuse you with the word recognition. It refers to open, symbolic communication which consists of observations or beliefs that there are such problems, communications coming from recognized leaders in a wide variety of fields. It is a major change. But it does *not* mean that action which might rationally be expected to follow has in fact occurred. The United States government through its most powerful representatives in the legislative, judicial, and executive branches has at long last recognized these problems and called for extensive national effort; but it is also to be noted that the budget for the federal effort of this nation of over 200,000,000 people is less than the alcohol program budget of one Canadian province with a population of slightly more than 7,000,000 and generally estimated to have less extensive alcohol problems. Similarly, the American medical profession may have formally and repeatedly recognized the extraordinary size, severity, and complexity of the alcoholisms, but this does *not* mean that the subject matter is part of the curriculum of medical schools or that hospitals generally give equal admission and quality service to alcoholics or that physicians generally accept such patients. Recognition is of cardinal importance for change, but the step from recognition to rational action can be a long, long journey indeed.

But *action* and also research have occurred over this 25-year period. The tremendous growth and extraordinary impact of Alcoholics Anonymous following 1942; the rise since 1944 of state alcoholism bureaus, small in budget as they are; the summer schools of alcohol studies, starting at Yale in 1943, now found the country over, with a record of perhaps 25,000 having attended; the report of the Cooperative Commission and the very existence of the National Alcoholism Center; the experiments with halfway houses and detoxification centers; the rise of the National Council, of the North American Association, of the Smithers Foundation; the development of the *Classified Abstract Archive of Alcohol Literature* and the *International Bibliography of Studies on Alcohol*; the extensive sociological studies on alcohol, unknown before 1943. There has been national action since 1943 on a scale incomparably greater than anything in the previous half century. Clinical and biochemical studies and clinical services have multiplied many, many times.

There has been action and there has been study. In terms of the magnitude and extraordinary diversity of direct and related problems they remain rather small, even pathetically so in the eyes of those trying to cope; but compared to the previous half century, which admittedly produced little beyond conflict and avoidance, it has been a promising start, both in service and in research. Service is chiefly clinical and is of the nature of repairs, not control and prevention. However, this sort of repairing approach can lead to, and in other problem areas in the past has led to, greater control, even prevention. Recognition, action, and study have proceeded these past twenty-five years in this country.

Perhaps the universal and monopolistic character of the classic temperance movement and, in opposing fashion, the broad scope and emotional strength of avoidance in the period of limbo were to guarantee what I select as the greatest weakness of current developments in the United States to meet the problems of alcohol with rational programs. I call this *fractionalization*. It is fractionalization in recognition, fractionalization in action or service programs, and fractionalization in research.

The classic movement had called all alcohol problems one and the same thing and had viewed what was to them a single phenomenon—namely, "Drink" or "Alcohol"—as an expression of Evil. In the rejection of this philosophy and program, there was an equally simplistic conception—namely, the philosophy and program of total Evil and total Prohibition are wrong, and the less said about it the better. In the face of this somewhat ambiguous and clearly aggressive cast of mind, it is hardly surprising that renewed recognition of alcohol problems should succeed only if bits and pieces of alcohol problems were proposed. Any suggestion that there were many problems and that they were inextricably interwoven immediately resurrected the idea of total Evil and the program of total Prohibition.

Alcoholism was selected, partly by force of circumstances and partly as a quite conscious policy, as the wheelhorse of change in the alcohol problems field. Between 1940 and 1955 it was separated out from the other alcohol problems. Alcoholics Anonymous, the local voluntary committees on alcoholism, and the emerging state divisions on alcoholism all publicly stated, almost as a basic credo, that alcoholism had nothing to do with other alcohol problems, that they proposed no program and held no group concern for those other problems. They also denied the role of evil and called alcoholism a disease. Not only did they adopt this position in order to get away from classic temperance viewpoints, but also in order to move toward respectable, professional status and even grasp at the positive values of a glamorized medical science. They had no interest, at times even an antipathy, toward groups concerned with alcohol education, sales controls, the highway traffic problem, or, perhaps above all, the ethics and aspects of morality of uses of alcohol in society. Their dedication and effectiveness was such, that many concerned with other alcohol problems began to interpret those other problems as being in fact *alcoholism;* schools brought A.A. members into classrooms on alcohol education; churches and temperance groups allowed, even rushed to incorporate, alcoholism as their dominant target; courts and jails and parents became concerned about alcohol*ism.*

But the other problems, once the program to help alcoholics had opened the door, now began to gain recognition *on their own.* And they too showed all the signs of independence, even isolation, both from each other and also from the alcoholism control programs. The alcohol highway safety group lived in a world apart from the alcoholism control groups. Those concerned with chronic drunkenness offenders, the Skid Row problem, more and more divorced themselves from the alcoholism programs which insisted that these particular sufferers were at best but 5 percent of the alcoholic population, often were not really alcoholics anyway, and, worst of all, carried in dramatic fashion that image, so devastating to alcoholism programs, that all alcoholics were drunken bums. In fact, the recent federal and city interest and expressed intent to mount a major program for meeting the police-court-jail problem of drunkenness has met with outspoken suspicion and even antagonism from many in the anti-alcoholism field. The new alcohol-education-for-youth groups, after a decade or more of uneasy alliance with the anti-alcoholism groups, have begun to show increasing separation. Completely aloof from all these groups have been the alcohol beverage control boards of the fifty states. The isolation of these different organizations would be laughable if the problems were not so extensive and so serious.

But all this is fractionalization only in the world of action and service. What about the worlds of conception, question, and research? Unfortunately, the same characterization seems almost more prevalent, if this is possible. Not only does this stem, as in the action world, from the experience of the monolithic and limbo periods, but also from the very history of scientific and arts research itself, which has proliferated into so many specialties, each with its private language, departments, associations, expertise careers, professions, journals, and conferences, that the Tower of Babel seems a small structure indeed. That each may have a contribution to make to this most complex human-social problem is hardly to be doubted. But that each—or that any one —holds a golden key to resolve the problems becomes ever more ridiculous as their numbers increase.

I have written elsewhere of the major models of thinking, emoting, and planning in the sphere of alcohol problems in this country: the medical or disease model, the youth malleability model, the legal-legislative-punitive model, the older "evil" model, the economic control model, the public health model. For an understanding of the fractionalization of thinking about alcohol problems in the arts and sciences of this country, it is important to realize, first, that each of these models is subdivided into specialized schools and theories, resulting in perhaps twenty groups in all; second, that the differences between the major and the minor groups are extreme, both in understanding and in policy; and, third, that these differences are displayed in a social setting in which avoidance, ignorance, and general distaste for the subject of alcohol problems is still widespread.

This leads to the subject of *turmoil*. There are leaders in the field of just the alcoholisms who are convinced that a biochemical breakthrough is the real answer, or that A.A. is the real answer, or that moving care and protection and responsibility out of the legal network is the real answer, or that better general mental health is the real answer, or that changes in public attitudes about drinking are the real answer, or that a reorganization of medical services through community structures with a comprehensive health goal is the real answer, and so on and so on. These groups are in very real conflict, one that is enhanced by a gamesmanship ritual in the area of grants for research and by political games-manship in both service and research areas. And, even in this one area of the alcoholisms, there is an almost magical belief in the sufficiency of the word "disease" to explain the phenomenon and to determine the appropriate structure and leadership for both research and service.

The same sort of turmoil can be seen in the field—or I should more properly say fields—of law. Those concerned with civil rights and legal procedures in the area of public drunkenness seem utterly *un*concerned with legal problems dealing with con-trols over sales. Yet a third group is concerned with law and law enforcement in the area of driving and drinking, and they may soon find themselves in direct conflict not only with the civil rights group but also with the whole structure of alcoholism re-habilitation services.

Again, those concerned with alcohol education for youth find themselves in a most uncomfortable situation, experiencing far more powerful impact of the classic temperance and limbo periods than do those in the medical or legal fields and at the same time showing all the strain imposed by the general external criticisms and internal self-doubts so manifest in the American educational world this past twenty years. Their dilemma is well illustrated by observation of the disagreements expressed by some about *what* should be taught in *what* classes while others are questioning whether the school should have a major role *at all* in this specific area of both personal and social behavior, an area rendered doubly disturbing because of laws about age restrictions which are quite generally violated, certainly in spirit and extensively in fact, with quite general equanimity by all concerned.

There is fractionalization and turmoil within each of the different action spheres and research spheres and between these different spheres. The outstanding manifestation, perhaps, is the utter absence of any national policy on the problems of alcohol.

And yet, despite the lack of any comprehensive national philosophy or program, and despite the fractionalized turmoil in study and service, and despite the continuing manifestation both of the old simplistic warfare of Wets and Drys and also of the avoiding, evading responses of the 1920s and 30s, despite these liabilities, I would say with real conviction that the major characterization of the present day is one of *hope*.

It is an old saying in this country that "While there is life there is hope." The big difference vis-à-vis movements to combat alcohol problems between 1938 and 1968 is the matter of "life." Where before there was monolithic hostility, a hostility carrying massive evasion and avoidance as its major consequence, there has been a following history of growing awareness, increased service, and increased study. True, this has been fractionalized, has been replete with isolated, narrow, and often warring factions with rigidly held, almost arrogantly held, beliefs, with an obvious lack of coherent philosophy and national policy. But it is a living, active, and growing field. And there are signs of a more mature, more comprehensive, and more discriminating approach: The Report of the Cooperative Commission; the movement toward collaboration between the largest of the alcoholism control programs; the renewed, constructive, and serious concern with temperance, this time with a small rather than a capital "T," this time in concert with, rather than up in arms against, other structures and forces in the society; the holding of international congresses; of special note is the *Classified Abstract Archive of the*

*Alcohol Literature,* now being used more and more widely, with its broad scope of subject matter, its extensive cross-referencing to all arts and sciences, and its continuity in scientific reporting —this last characteristic manifesting a major change from what may be called the fractionalization in time and history which has so plagued the research field. The current appearance of the *International Bibliography of Alcohol Studies* is yet another step in the same direction. Such developments, and there are others, indicate that the awareness and recognition of the past twenty-five years are leading to something beyond fractionalization and turmoil, are leading to a more dignified, comprehensive, rational, and effective program, one geared to other facets and forces in our national life, one which will increasingly control and finally in large measure prevent these extensive, intertwined, and, in large measure, unnecessary problems of our society.

# Voluntary agencies, their past and future roles

## ELIZABETH D. WHITNEY

Twenty-five years constitute a short span of time and activity, when compared to centuries of interest in alcohol and drugs. However, more research, education, and rehabilitation concerning alcohol and drug addiction have been accomplished in the last quarter century than in the one hundred years preceding.

At the opening session of the Yale School of Alcohol Studies in 1943, Dr. Jellinek stated: "Problems of alcohol will be solved by the people," and this assertion has been proved valid by the voluntary groups, the associations, and the councils on alcoholism, direct descendants of that same school.

The first students were called together and asked to suggest a name and the future functions of the new school. The Yale Plan of Alcohol Studies evolved first, and was soon followed by the Yale Center of Alcohol Studies which eventually transferred to New Jersey, and there became the Center of Alcohol Studies, at Rutgers, the State University, in New Brunswick. In December 1963 the school dedicated its own modern building, Smithers Hall, named to commemorate the Smithers family, long staunch supporters of the fight against alcoholism.

From the first, workers in the field of alcoholism have given their full support to the center, have contributed ideas, hard work, and money, and in return have received information, training, and materials for studies in an organized professional school. The center also provides a summer school of intensive review and refresher courses for field workers; it maintains a research library of technical information, papers, and books on alcoholism; and it publishes the *Quarterly Journal of Studies on Alcohol* to bring current information to professionals in the field. Finally, the center operates its own research laboratories in Smithers Hall.

In keeping with modern demands, the Rutgers Center has restructured its curriculum. Formerly students from the widely varied fields of law, religion, medicine, business, social service, and community organizations all studied together in the same lecture and seminar rooms; today special courses are given for individual interests, with only a few general courses planned for the entire group.

Aside from the summer students, interested individuals from around the world attend the regular university sessions from September to June, living and eating in the college facilities, but concentrating in the field of alcoholism.

The Rutgers School has grown from fewer than one hundred original applicants to thousands, both in the summer school and the standard courses. Other universities, following the Rutgers summer school pattern, offer similar opportunities in the western, southern, and southwestern sections of the United States. Still others have broadened their curricula to include such specialized courses as work on industrial or medical alcoholism.

Dr. Jellinek, the first Director of the Yale School, moved on to other areas of the United States, then to sixteen other countries in various parts of the world, stimulating group interest in alcohol studies and research. He had, however, sparked the formation in 1944 of the National Council on Alcoholism, founded by Mrs. Marty Mann, staffed by officers of the Yale School, and financed by that university until 1950. Mrs. Mann, its director, energetically promoted the National Council which soon developed into a general information center on alcoholism, collecting and distributing literature, publishing many expert papers on many aspects of the subject from research, and establishing citizens groups in local communities. Most of the latter became affiliates of the N.C.A., with autonomous programs and financing, but adhering to the policy and tenets set up by the national organization.

The Greater Boston Council on Alcoholism became the first voluntary citizens group to affiliate itself with the National Council on Alcoholism, holding its initial organizational meeting in December 1944, and opening for operation in July 1945. Within a year three similar groups had followed the example of the Greater Boston Council, and were dispensing information, and counseling alcoholics and their families. These were the first community nonprofit organizations specializing in problems of alcoholism in the United States. Soon others, stimulated by the success of these initial councils, began to open information centers for public education and to promote better facilities for the treatment of alcoholics. At the end of ten years, 52 such committees were in operation, and by 1966, the N.C.A. listed 83 affiliated Councils in the United States, and 10 abroad.

Of the foreign countries, the Union of South Africa first associated with the National Council on Alcoholism in the United States in the late forties, and later established its own National Council. In 1963 a National Council similar to the N.C.A. was put into operation in England, and was soon expanded to include Ireland and Scotland. Canada also was well along with its national program of research and education, and had initiated its National Council on Alcoholism. Finally, Australia, determined to arouse public interest and to sway public opinion, has turned to voluntary agencies. Once such citizen groups get under way with a sound program, change is imminent.

When voluntary groups with professional memberships enter the fight, they relieve the citizen groups of much of the responsibility for the more technical aspects of combating a disease such as alcoholism. The American Medical Association entered the lists in 1956, and broadened its activities with a more comprehensive program in 1966. The North American Association of Alcoholism Programs, established in 1948, has been foremost in stimulating and influencing sound alcoholism legislation in the United States, leading to the passage of federal laws which now provide funds for research, education, and rehabilitation on alcoholism and drug abuse.

Only recently, alcoholism care and control received special attention in Washington. The House Subcommittee on Health Appropriations restored $4 million to the Federal 1969–70 budget to provide for community facilities and services under PL 90–574. Senator Harold E. Hughes (D.–Iowa) of the Alcoholism and Narcotics Subcommittee then focused wide attention on the subject, and in three days of extensive hearings declared, "The time is ripe to launch an unprecedented, all-out campaign against alcoholism, on the massive, realistic scale that is needed." Declaring that groups working in the field must close ranks and "speak a common language on the subject of alcoholism," the Senator added that the "aura of hopelessness around our attitude toward the treatment of alcoholism needs to be exploded right now."

At the same hearing, NAAAP Executive Secretary, Augustus H. Hewlett, termed alcoholism "the most pervasive and destructive medicosocial problem in American society today." He continued, "Although first on the moon, America remains one of the last among the major countries in either the Communist or the Free World to develop and promote a comprehensive national attack on this problem." Pointing out that the deleterious effects of alcoholism are complicating factors in the treatment and cure of other diseases, Mr. Hewlett told the subcommittee that "we cannot develop a policy covering this disease of alcoholism without considering other alcohol-related problems."

As Executive Secretary of the NAAAP, Mr. Hewlett represents one of the most active and influential societies working in the field of alcoholism and drug dependence in America today, concerning itself with modern research, treatment, and rehabilitation, as well as legislation. Recently the NAAAP has been considering broadening its base to include drug addiction, a trend evident among many voluntary agencies.

For twenty-five years, Towns Hospital, a private institution in New York, has been treating both alcoholism and drug addiction and receiving little or no publicity for its efforts by agencies on alcoholism or in the public media. This is not an isolated case, but holds true for a number of competent private hospitals and clinics which effectively treat alcoholism and drug addictions.

Until recently, only a few public hospitals concerned themselves with heavy drug addiction (heroin and the like), an outstanding example being the Kentucky State Hospital, probably the leader in the country. Since Federal money has now become available for the treatment of drug addicts, more hospitals are handling such patients, e.g., the Boston State Hospital has a program for young people which Dr. Myerson discusses in this volume. In other parts of the United States, we can find many state hospitals that have been conducting research and treatment projects in the past five years. Dr. Vernelle Fox, at the Georgian Clinic in Atlanta, has interested herself in such patients, along with alcoholics, for a number of years, as has Dr. Ebbe Hoff, at the Medical College of Virginia at Richmond. These are but a few examples of many scattered throughout the country.

Voluntary programs on drug addiction are particularly scarce, partially because drug traffic is illegal, and all use or possession is subject to criminal action, making the handling of a drug problem quite different from that of alcohol which is legally permitted and promoted. Few drug victims will allow newspaper stories, magazine articles, or television interviews for fear of prosecution, in contrast to the alcoholic who often does not hesitate to share his troubles with a sympathetic audience. Much less, therefore, is known by the general public about the drug problem, and consequently less voluntary effort is expended in its solution. Alcoholism has been publicized widely in the United States and around the world since 1943; it is a well known problem and has opened the door for public education on other drug problems.

One promising approach to the drug victim is through group therapy, widely used in state and private mental health institutions. An outstanding voluntary group, following the model of A.A., calls itself Synanon and, after ten years of trial chiefly on the West Coast, is rapidly expanding its effective rehabilitation of drug addicts, especially among youth, where most of the drug problem is found.

Alcoholics Anonymous has inspired many other health and rehabilitation programs by its success in alcoholism. Workers in the therapeutic field understand that nothing is more natural than for one sufferer to relate to another experiencing similar trouble. In the little-known addiction problems, intuition and understanding play a positive role in the therapy. Chuck Dederich, founder of Synanon, makes himself a natural "fit" for the "misfits." A maverick among mavericks, he has been termed by Sally O'Quin, writing about him in *Life* Magazine, a "madman with delusions of grandeur, a saint, an opportunist, a brilliant executive, a latter-day Socrates, an arrogant egotist, a herd of one elephant."

Mr. Dederich states, "Our purpose is to help all people," and Synanon makes the perfect medium for his particular genius, which has helped thousands of desperate people, not only drug addicts but people with varied personal problems, discover a way out through group therapy.

No one person, group, or organization ever can or will meet the needs of all people. There are, for example, quiet, respectable, and unpretentious persons who are addicted to both alcohol and drugs, about whom no one ever hears. Protected by friends and relatives, and by money, they can remain as private as they choose, and would not fit into any type of group. Their only salvation, if such exists, will come on a strictly private basis, and not through an A.A. or a Synanon.

We have outlined above the functions of various voluntary agencies currently in operation: The Yale School, now the Rutgers Center for Alcohol Studies; the National Council on Alcoholism and its local affiliates; the American Medical Association; the North American Association of Alcoholism Programs; the private hospitals and clinics; Alcoholics Anonymous and Synanon. The list is imposing, but by no means complete.

As public departments of the government increasingly take over the physical responsibility for treating the alcoholic and the drug dependent, the functions of the private organizations face inevitable change. Some will lose importance, some increase in strength; but certainly the vital work of the private agency will continue, adapted to the times and the needs of the future.

# Part Two

# Methods of
# Attacking Addictions

# Alcoholics Anonymous

*JOHN NORRIS, M.D.*

From an idea explored by two desperate people thirty-five years ago, Alcoholics Anonymous has grown into a vast network of groups, practicing perhaps the most effective therapy for recovery from alcoholism yet developed. The spectacular story of A.A. has been told and retold, but as related here by Dr. John Norris, chairman of the Board of Trustees of the General Service Board of Alcoholics Anonymous, it falls into perspective as seen by a man who has worked with the founder of A.A. almost from the beginning.

## ORIGIN AND GROWTH

Alcoholics Anonymous is a fellowship of men and women who share their experience, strength and hope with each other that they may solve their common problem and help others to recover from alcoholism.

The only requirement for membership is a desire to stop drinking. There are no dues or fees for A.A. membership; we are self-supporting through our own contributions. A.A. is not allied with any sect, denomination, politics, organization or institution; does not wish to engage in any controversy, neither endorses nor opposes any causes. Our primary purpose is to stay sober and help other alcoholics to achieve sobriety.

This is the definition of Alcoholics Anonymous which is printed in every copy of the *A.A. Grapevine* (monthly magazine of the fellowship) and many of the official publications. It is read at many meetings. It is prominently displayed in many meeting rooms. It bears careful study, for there are no wasted words yet the significant parts of the story are included.

A.A. developed in the vacuum left by the professional caretakers of society at a time when alcoholics, caught in the morass of the fixed biases of the wet-dry controversy, were almost universally rejected. Physicians, psychiatrists, hospitals, social workers, and clergymen either refused to care for them, called the problem by another name, or turned them over to the tender mercies of penal institutions. Professionals further clouded the situation by disagreeing, at times violently, on the nature of the problem. Religionists, seeing only the broken homes, broken promises, irresponsible living, warped lives of children in families where one or both parents drank heavily, spoke only of the moral aspects of excessive use of alcohol. Physicians, those few who would care for any people in trouble with alcohol, saw some of their patients who were able, adjusted, constructive, lovable people when they weren't drinking, change completely while they were drinking. They saw patients stop, then begin to drink again with no apparent reason and knowing full well that they were always in trouble when they drank. These physicians were aware of nutritional deficiencies and other physical factors and felt, even as far back as Benjamin Rush, that physiological factors must play a part in the continued irrational drinking of alcoholic beverages by some people. Psychiatrists, trained to look for emotional, mental, and situational factors, found emotional and personal and situational problems in all alcoholics. They believed that these factors were causative and that, if these causes were removed, people could continue to find the solace that they needed in alcohol without losing control. Social workers, most of them psychiatrically oriented by training, followed this lead. They failed to recognize alcohol as a major cause in the troubled families in their case lists, believing rather that people needed the comfort of alcohol to endure their life circumstances. Almost everyone believed that there was no help for these people, that any time spent trying to salvage them was wasted.

This was the vacuum that existed in 1935 when a New York stockbroker, repeatedly hospitalized for acute alcoholic intoxication in Towns Sanitarium in New York City, dramatically lost his obsession for alcohol after being told by his physician that he couldn't survive many more episodes of acute intoxication and that there was nothing more that medicine could do for him. This coincided with some contacts with the thinking of the Oxford Group, through an old school drinking companion who had stopped drinking at the time. There were then some months of total abstinence, during which time he had talked with numerous other men in serious trouble with alcohol, trying unsuccessfully to pass on to them what had happened to him. Then, discouraged because of a business failure and alone in Akron, Ohio, he felt the need to talk with another alcoholic so that he could stay away from drinking (up until then, talking with other alcoholics had kept him sober). He was introduced to a surgeon who had been trying unsuccessfully to stay away from alcohol through participating in the Oxford Group in Akron. After several weeks of close contact and one bad slip on the part of the physician, they decided that it was time to see if their experience applied to anyone else. A nurse in the Akron City Hospital, with whom the doctor had worked on occasion, told him that there was a patient who had been treated many times for alcoholism, whom they could visit. This man became A.A. number three.

From this beginning in June of 1935, A.A. has grown to its present stature. Growth at first was very slow. New candidates were people known by those who had been able to stop drinking after meeting with the original three. After some months in Akron the New Yorker returned to New York and, one at a time, formed a group of previously thought hopeless alcoholics. They stayed totally abstinent by accepting in depth the following ideas: [1] that it was impossible for them to drink and stay alive (this was explained by the allergy of the body and obsession of the mind concept that had been given to the New York broker by Dr. William D. Silkworth at Towns Hospital); [2] that they needed help to overcome the obsession; [3] that they must get honest with themselves and others; [4] that they make amends or restitution for wrongs that they had committed; and [5] that they should try to help others who were in trouble with alcohol stay sober by passing on to them their own experience of recovery.

Gradually, very gradually at first, the tiny groups in Akron and New York grew. People were staying sober; for months, and then years! Some of these people moved to other communities and started groups there. To the amazement of those who had worked with and suffered at their hands, these alcoholics were staying sober, with a quality of living which was almost beyond reproach. They were paying up old debts which had been thought uncollectible. They were making amends for wrongs done, some of them in the distant past. They were thankfully willing to help someone else in trouble with alcohol, with no thought of cost or effort, even for complete strangers. Families which had been in turmoil and breaking up or broken up, became what families can be at their best. A warden at one of New York State's prisons could say that the atmosphere of the whole prison had changed since the A.A. group had been started there. And some of us who were fortunate enough to be invited to an open meeting were startled when speakers would say in apparently complete sincerity, "Thank God I'm an alcoholic." Something had happened to them. They were changed, and the change was all for the better. Friends and associates began to talk about it. This was news. And in September 1939, *Liberty* magazine carried an article "Alcoholics and God," written by Morris Markey. About 800 telephoned and written requests for help came to the address mentioned in the article. Each one was answered personally.

A.A. began to grow rapidly in both New York and the Akron-Cleveland areas. Along with growth came troubles and dreams. There was a need for money to support those who were spending all their time and resources in helping more and more alcoholics, to pay rent, telephone, and mailing expenses. There was a need for literature that would record the thinking and experience of those who had found their way out of slavery to alcohol so that a wider audience could be reached and, perhaps more important, there would be less chance of misinterpretation and misunderstandings. There were personality clashes and struggles for positions of leadership as people recovered physical health and energy.

Recoveries in increasing numbers and duration raised dreams of hospitals, rest homes, rehabilitation facilities the world over, all built and supported by Alcoholics Anonymous. Large amounts of money would be needed, and the New Yorkers turned to the Rockefeller family as a most likely resource. Mr. John D. Rockefeller, Jr., was interested and hosted a meeting attended by several influential men, where the ideas, experiences, and dreams of this group of recovering alcoholics were presented. At this meeting Mr. Rockefeller urged that the group give up its dreams of property and institutions since, in his opinion, these things would destroy what he believed could be a significant movement of volunteers. Some dreams were shattered, but the wisdom of his advice was accepted and has remained one of the working principles of the Fellowship, as it is seen in the definition of Alcoholics Anonymous with which this article begins. A most unusual experience for some of us on the Board of Trustees has been to refuse to accept substantial gifts or legacies. "A.A. is self-supporting." No member of A.A. can contribute to the support of the New York office more than $200 in any one year, even in their will!

In the meantime, the thinking and experience of about one hundred of the early members was made articulate in the Twelve Steps which they felt were the basic principles responsible for their recovery. From the beginning, however, these were presented as suggestions, not as law.

*The twelve steps*

     1. We admitted we were powerless over alcohol . . . that our lives had become unmanageable.

     2. Came to believe that a Power greater than ourselves could restore us to sanity.

     3. Made a decision to turn our will and our lives over to the care of God *as we understood Him.*

     4. Made a searching and fearless moral inventory of ourselves.

     5. Admitted to God, to ourselves, and to another human being the exact nature of our wrongs.

6. Were entirely ready to have God remove all these defects of character.

7. Humbly asked Him to remove our shortcomings.

8. Made a list of all persons we had harmed and became willing to make amends to them all.

9. Made direct amends to such people wherever possible, except when to do so would injure them or others.

10. Continued to take personal inventory and when we were wrong promptly admitted it.

11. Sought through prayer and meditation to improve our conscious contact with God *as we understood Him,* praying only for knowledge of His will for us and the power to carry that out.

12. Having had a spiritual awakening as the result of these Steps, we tried to carry this message to alcoholics, and to practice these principles in all our affairs.

As years went by, groups sprang up all over the continent. Each group was independent, and each shaped to some degree by the personalities of the strongest members in it. Groups were often torn by personality conflicts and struggles for power as these alcoholics fought their way back to normal living. The earliest members, founders of a group, would, after some months of leadership, become possessive and domineering. New people coming in would develop strength and influence. The older member, dethroned, might start another group, sulk on the sidelines, and become known as a "bleeding deacon," or get drunk and drop out of sight. Fortunately there was surprisingly little of the latter. All these things were, individually and collectively, growing pains, and it became evident to the founders that guidelines for group relationships were needed. So the traditions grew out of experience, observed and recorded by the two men who started all of this. Here again the method of presentation is as recorded experience, not as law.

*The twelve traditions*

1. Our common welfare should come first; personal recovery depends upon AA unity.

2. For our group purpose there is but one ultimate author-

ity . . . a loving God as He may express Himself in our group conscience. Our leaders are but trusted servants . . . they do not govern.

3. The only requirement for AA membership is a desire to stop drinking.

4. Each group should be autonomous except in matters affecting other groups or AA as a whole.

5. Each group has but one primary purpose . . . to carry its message to the alcoholic who still suffers.

6. An AA group ought never endorse, finance or lend the AA name to any related facility or outside enterprise, lest problems of money, property and prestige divert us from our primary purpose.

7. Every AA group ought to be fully self-supporting, declining outside contributions.

8. Alcoholics Anonymous should remain forever non-professional, but our service centers may employ special workers.

9. AA, as such, ought never be organized; but we may create service boards or committees directly responsible to those they serve.

10. Alcoholics Anonymous has no opinion on outside issues; hence the AA name ought never be drawn into public controversy.

11. Our public relations policy is based on attraction rather than promotion; we need always maintain personal anonymity at the level of press, radio and films.

12. Anonymity is the spiritual foundation of all our Traditions, ever reminding us to place principles before personalities.

## MEETINGS AND ORGANIZATIONS

Two types of meetings have developed: the open meeting at which anyone is welcome, especially those who are looking for help for themselves or some member of their family. There are usually two or three speakers who will tell of their experiences while drinking and since becoming active in A.A. The closed meeting is attended only by active members and may take several forms. It is usually a discussion in which everyone takes part. It may concern one of the steps, a tradition, an article from A.A.'s monthly publication, *The Grapevine,* or some current problem of a member.

It is in the closed meetings, in my judgment, that the real growth toward maturity takes place, that members gather the strength and understanding to carry out the hard work of recovery. Groups have a chairman who usually serves only six months at a time, and a secretary who may—but usually doesn't—serve for a longer period. Most groups meet once each week in a rented room or hall, or in rooms made available by churches or other community facilities. In such cases contributions are made toward heat, light, and janitor services. Some groups meet more often. Many members will attend meetings of several groups, at times traveling long distances to attend meetings of new groups or groups in small communities that need moral support. They will also go out of their way to answer a call for help from someone in trouble, or to introduce a new friend to a group nearer his home. All this, of course, is in addition to answering the individual calls for help which are known as "twelfth step" calls. These can come at any time of day or night. In larger communities where there are several groups they may join forces to establish a central office, with a paid staff. Such offices coordinate the activities of the groups in the area, answer calls for help, maintain a supply of A.A. literature, and provide speakers for A.A. meetings, schools, P.T.A. meetings, church groups, or other groups interested in learning about A.A. If there is a program in a local hospital or penal institution which depends on A.A. for help, volunteers are recruited through this office. It is sometimes a meeting place where members, new and old, drop in for a cup of coffee and conversation. Telephone numbers of these centers of activity are listed in regular telephone directories, and someone is available to answer throughout the day and most of the night.

Each group elects a member, almost always one of the older members, who serves for two years as general service representative. This person receives all communications from the General Service Office in New York City and is expected to pass this on to the current chairman and secretary of the group. Once each month the G.S.R.s in a district will discuss problems and plans. Each year they select a committeeman, usually a member who has had more years in the fellowship, and a better understanding of A.A. as a whole. He will know more about how problems have been solved in other parts of the country and help the groups in their relations with each other and the larger community. Districts vary in size, depending primarily on the number of groups in a city or state. A state may have one committeeman or several. Committeemen from a region meet periodically to work out regional plans and programs, stimulate the development of services to hospitals and prisons, inform the public about A.A. so that people still in trouble may find their way to help, and once in two years elect a delegate to the General Service Conference made up of 90 delegates from all over North America. The General Service Conference meets for six days each April in New York to learn what is happening in A.A. over the world, to share experiences and find solutions to problems, to discuss finances, and to consider the need for new or different literature. The conference also considers general policies regarding relationships with other organizations (for those who are interested, these policies are described in some detail in the pamphlet "Cooperation But Not Affiliation," and more briefly in "Alcoholics Anonymous in Your Community"; both are available from Box 459, Grand Central Post Office, New York City 10017), to elect trustees for the General Service Board and approve, or disapprove, of the nominations for the officers of this board, and, in general, to consider, discuss, and act on any matter thought by any of the groups to be important to A.A. as a whole.

The Board of Trustees is made up of both alcoholics and non-alcoholics. When it was first formed, no member of A.A. had had more than three years of sobriety. At that time it was felt that there should be a majority of non-alcoholics on the board. In 1967 this was changed, and the present plan is that there will be seven non-alcoholics and fourteen alcoholics. Seven of the alcoholics come from various parts of North America, nominated by states in a region and elected by delegates and others, primarily from that region, at the General Service Conference. Other alcoholics are selected because of some special skill, such as business, publishing, or law, in addition to their dedication to A.A. Four of them come from the New York area in order that they may be available frequently to help out at the General Service Office. The other three, also selected because of some expertise, are chosen from other parts of the United States and Canada. Alcoholic trustees serve for four years and cannot succeed themselves. The board meets four times a year, along with its functioning committees: Finance, Public Relations, Literature, Policy, International, and Nominating. In addition, it receives reports on its two operating divisions: A.A. World Services, Inc., and the A.A. Grapevine, Inc.

Morris Markey's 1939 article in *Liberty* magazine stimulated considerable growth in A.A., but the real spurt came in 1942 when *The Saturday Evening Post* published an article about A.A. by Jack Alexander. This brought a flood of calls for help from all over North America. Again, each letter or telephone call was answered individually. In each case an attempt was made to establish personal contact. New groups were rapidly formed. At first they were widely scattered. When a call for help was received in New York, word went out to the nearest group, requesting that they make contact. Often members would travel many miles to answer these calls. Sometimes a new member would start a group in his own community among his friends. Thus A.A. has grown with increasing speed as more people have come to know about it, as the communications media have written and talked about it, as general public interest and involvement have developed through the activities of the National Council on Alcoholism, the North American Association of Alcoholism Programs, and the Rutgers (formerly Yale) Center for Alcohol Studies. For the last several years new groups have been formed and registered with the New York Office at the rate of about one thousand each year. In April 1967, there were more than 14,000 groups with which the office was in communication to some degree. There were 830 groups in prisons and more than 600 in hospitals. All of these, of course, had the approval of the administration of the institution. There are groups registered in 90 countries, most of these started by a person who first found his way into the fellowship in North America.

## HOW DOES A.A. WORK?

How does it work? This question is often asked and never answered to anyone's complete satisfaction, perhaps because we so often try to answer the question "why" at the same time. The mechanics of the process are simple: one or two people who have found an answer to their alcoholic problem go out of their way without thought of payment to talk with and help another person, who also has a problem with alcohol. They help him to understand that nothing improves so long as he drinks, but that it will inevitably get worse. They also show him that there is a way to live happily without alcohol. They give the new · prospect the formula for recovery and invite him to join a group of people who accept him without reservation and share with him their "experience, strength, and hope." The effectiveness of this becomes understandable when we realize how much people who have been in real trouble with alcohol have suffered from their rejection by society. It is ironic that they may be more rejected by fellow drinkers than by total abstainers. "Why don't you drink like I do?" "Why can't you drink like a man?" they are asked. They are no longer welcome among their former associates, to say nothing of society in general. And they themselves often have accepted society's judgment. They have no hope that they can ever get out of the squirrel cage in which they find themselves. At this low point in their lives they are welcomed as equals into a group of friendly, happy people. They are no longer outcasts. They are told that it is physically impossible for them to be controlled drinkers. This part of the situation is not weakness of will, but rather a structural difference, comparable to an allergy. They are told that they must get their lives in order, are given a formula or schedule to accomplish this, and are assured that they will have lots of help along the way. After they have begun to take some real responsibility for themselves, they are urged to take some other responsibility. This can be for other people who are in trouble, through direct personal contact or by taking part in some group maintenance activity.

It is here, in my judgment and experience, that one finds the key to happy sobriety. A.A. members find meaning and purpose for their lives in helping to meet another's needs, and find it in a way open to few other people. As the Vienna psychiatrist Viktor Frankl says, it is the finding of meaning in life which most deeply inspires mankind. At the 30th Anniversary Convention in Toronto in July 1965, the more than ten thousand people assembled there accepted the following declaration: "When anyone, anywhere reaches out for help, I want the hand of A.A. always to be there. And for that: I am responsible." It was the high point in the convention.

One day I was talking with a man who had been sent over to my office because he was in trouble on the job because of his drinking. He said he had accepted the idea that he couldn't drink without getting into trouble and agreed that he should not drink any more. He also agreed to talk to an A.A. friend of mine. When the three of us got together, he said, "I can handle it myself. I'll do it my own way." My A.A. friend grinned as he said: "I'm not saying that you can't, but if you do it our way it will be fun." This, I believe, is another key to long sobriety. It must be happy sobriety or it is likely not to last. A consistent impression that one gets in A.A. groups is that these people are happy. They have a sort of serenity that seems to me rather rare in these hectic days.

A mistake that we professionals have made rather frequently in the past has been to expect A.A. members to clean up all the mess, including the problems with the rest of the family, while we wash our hands of the whole affair. We reject not only the person and family presently in trouble, but also A.A. One of the more mature members of A.A. in New York was speaking to a group of physicians and social workers about A.A. several months ago. His opening gambit was to ask: "How many of you have heard of A.A.?" Almost everyone had. "How many of you have been to an A.A. meeting?" No one had. "How many of you have read any A.A. literature?" No hands went up. "Is this the way you would write a prescription?" He was, of course, pointing out the importance of coming to know at first hand how to use this resource which has demonstrated its effectiveness.

Attendance at several meetings is important, as the first one or two may give only a limited picture. An added value obtained from attending meetings is that misunderstandings can be corrected, and one will come to know people on whom he may depend for help. Professionals and A.A. members working together can help many who could not be reached by either alone. Unless we do make the effort to understand each other, both A.A. members and professionals are likely to know only of the others' failures and so perpetuate the rejection.

In some parts of the world, and in some cultures, A.A. has been accepted slowly. The difficulty of translating North American colloquialisms into other languages and even into the English spoken in other countries has been a deterrent to the kind of understanding at depth that is necessary for acceptance. Cultural differences and patterns of alcohol use also produce differences in attitude toward people whose drinking is out of control. This affects the sense of guilt and worthlessness that is the emotional matrix in which A.A. developed. The resistance to and resentment of authority, so large a part of North American culture, evidenced by A.A.'s determination to be self-supporting, has not been understood in many countries where people have customarily looked to government or "superiors" for answers and support. In countries where religious taboos against alcohol strongly dominate the culture A.A. must be so anonymous that it is almost impossible to find a group when one is started. So some different adaptations of the basic idea of A.A. have developed in other countries, for example, Golden Key in France and Ring-I-Ring in Denmark. So far, at least, these have been limited in extent.

## HOW EFFECTIVE IS A.A.?

Rarely, since A.A. has become generally known, has a criticism of A.A. or serious doubt about its validity been raised publicly. Almost always it is mentioned favorably as a treatment resource in articles published about alcoholism. Professionals, however, frequently raise questions in private. Just how effective is it? How many have stopped drinking in and through A.A.? How long have they remained sober? Aren't they just changing one obsession for another? Do they become potentially more destructive without alcohol than they were with it? How can a group of untrained nonprofessionals be as effective as they say they are? Isn't this just another bunch of religious nuts?

The fifth chapter of the book *Alcoholics Anonymous* begins with the words: "Rarely have we seen a person fail who has thoroughly followed our path." Some members have estimated that half of those who come to A.A. succeed in staying sober with the first contact, that half of the rest recover at some later time, and that only one quarter of those who try A.A. fail completely. This has been questioned, since many of us have known several who have rejected A.A. and its program after a meeting or two, while others flatly refused to consider it. What facts are there? Two or three limited surveys have been done in the past: one in Texas which traced the experience of the members of one group, another—more elaborate—survey was conducted among members of groups in New York City, and another in England. None of these gave us quite the assurance of the impact and long-range effectiveness of the movement that we wanted and believed the facts would justify. We knew that more than six hundred thousand copies of the book *Alcoholics Anonymous* had been sold. We believed that, since these books cost $4.50 apiece, the overwhelming majority of these purchases meant considerable interest on the part of a person. We knew that many copies have been read by more than one person. We also knew that many, sober in A.A., have never owned or read the book. We knew that other books and pamphlet literature were being bought at the rate of well over half a million copies each year. We knew that *The Grapevine* has had a monthly circulation of about fifty thousand copies for the last couple of years. We knew that there was a substantial demand for translations of much of this literature into French and Spanish, and a developing demand for translations into several other languages. We knew how many groups had registered and the rate at which new groups were forming. We knew that the average delegate at the General Service Conference had been an active member, totally abstinent, for eleven years, and that this had been true for at least five years.

But how many members are in A.A. and for how long have they been sober? Is it effective with women in sufficient numbers to be significant? We were certain that we could not devise a survey that would give us any reasonably accurate estimate of the number of people who attended a meeting or two and didn't like it. Nor could we find the people who have come, achieved sobriety, and returned to normal life in society, but no longer attend meetings.

What reasonably accurate data could be developed? In order to answer this question and to see whether we could find some of our weaknesses, the Board of Trustees of A.A. employed a psychologist in New York City who had had broad experience in devising questionnaires and evaluating the results statistically. Six questions were prepared which we felt could be answered quickly, which would have little chance of misunderstanding, and which would give us some of the information that we wanted. To determine the feasibility of any questionnaire—would A.A. groups cooperate?—and specifically this one, it was tried out in five widely separated areas of North America, asking only those present at the meeting where the form was distributed to fill it out.

There was no attempt to increase attendance and no attempt to contact any of the regulars who might not have been at that meeting. This questionnaire was accepted in the five areas without any resistance. The results were surprisingly consistent in all regions of the continent. On the basis of the response we felt that a comprehensive survey could be made, using in general the same questions: age, sex, length of time since the last drink, what or who had stimulated them to attend their first meeting, length of time between their first contact with A.A. and their last drink, and the frequency of attendance at meetings. The delegates at the General Service Conference in New York in April 1968 agreed to distribute a kit of questionnaires to about five percent of the groups in their home area, picking average groups. Nearly five hundred kits went out to the delegates in June of that year. Instructions going with the questionnaire urged that no one fill out more than one if he happened to attend two meetings where they were distributed. By the end of July nearly 466 kits had been returned, filled out by 11,355 people! 8,549 were men, 2,542 were women. On 264 of the forms no sex was recorded.

*Between the ages of fifteen and nineteen* 90
*Between twenty and twenty-nine* 718
*Between thirty and forty-nine* 6,481
*Between fifty and sixty-four* 3,407
*Over sixty-five* 449
*Age not recorded* 210

Length of sobriety—time since the last drink
*Less than one year* 4,320
*One to five years* 3,962
*Six to ten years* 1,513
*Eleven to fifteen years* 740
*Fifteen to twenty years* 417
*Over twenty years* 229
*Don't know* 9
*No answer* 165

Length of time between first contact with A.A. and the last drink
*No difference in time* 4,654
*One year or less* 2,604
*Two to five years* 2,096
*Five to ten years* 931
*Ten to fifteen years* 458
*Fifteen to twenty years* 293
*More than twenty years* 106
*No answer* 204
*Incomplete information* 9

Frequency of attendance at A.A. meetings
*Every day* 444
*Three to six times a week* 5,202
*Once or twice a week* 5,080
*Two to three times a month* 183
*Once a month* 59

*Four to five times a year* 46
*Two to three times a year* 85
*Once a year* 21
*Less than once a year* 56
*No answer* 179

Factors most responsible for attendance at first meeting
*A.A. member* 6,225
*Family* 3,865
*Physician* 1,840
*A.A. literature* 780
*Clergyman* 740
*Employer* 623
*Newspaper* 556
*Magazine* 482
*Friend* 462
*Counseling agency* 445
*Hospital* 215
*National Council on Alcoholism* 182
*Television* 173
*Clubs, Social organization* 138
*Radio* 120
*Psychologist* 108
*Social Worker* 43
*Army Officer* 23
*No answer* 600 (Many respondents named more than
one factor.)

These results were first reported at the 28th International Congress on Alcohol and Alcoholism in Washington, on Thursday, September 19, 1968.

Several figures in this survey are interesting and significant. The response was unusually high and adds to its validity. The number of women, in the ratio roughly of one woman to three men, suggests a trend. (The usual figure given in the past for alcoholics has been one woman to five men.) The unexpectedly large number of people under twenty years of age, and the high proportion of those under fifty years of age as compared to those over fifty, suggests that people are recognizing trouble and seeking help in their twenties, thirties, and forties rather than in their fifties. The figures on length of sobriety are harder to interpret, and should be viewed in relation to the length of time A.A. has been in existence. The numbers sober more than five years are impressive, as I see no reason to doubt the honesty of those who filled out the questionnaire. The length of time between the first contact with A.A. and the last drink are interesting and to some degree reassuring in that the effort made in establishing the first contact may not be wasted. One's interpretation of the frequency of attendance figures will reflect one's bias. The final table indicates that the growth of A.A. still depends largely on one alcoholic seeking out another, although pressure by the family is a major factor. Physicians, in spite of many misunderstandings and considerable critical comment on both sides, are a major source of referral to A.A. The communications media are also important. It is surprising and disappointing that social workers are so far down the list, in that they must see many families in trouble where alcohol is a factor.

It is important, as these figures are considered, that no extrapolations or interpretations are made that the method and circumstances do not justify. There has been no attempt to say that, since about five percent of the groups in North America were given the questionnaires, the active membership is twenty times the figures given. Certainly there should be no attempt to guess from these figures the number of people who have found sobriety in A.A., have become reintegrated into society, and are no longer attending meetings. Taken at face value they represent a significant impact on a condition which most of the "caretakers" of society have considered hopeless, and which we must admit is one of the major killers of our day.

# Office treatment of the alcoholic by the private physician

*RUTH FOX, M.D., and BARRY LEACH, M.A.*

Effective treatment of the alcoholic presents so many difficulties that many doctors avoid this area of medicine. Patients seem more difficult to work with, and the cure is often questionable. That office treatment can be effective and rewarding, however, is amply demonstrated by the results that Dr. Ruth Fox and her associate, Barry Leach, have obtained. Dr. Fox, for many years medical director of the National Council on Alcoholism, is a practicing psychiatrist specializing in alcoholism problems. She is president of the American Medical Society on Alcoholism and author of *Alcoholism, Its Scope and Treatment*. Barry Leach is a psychologist who has worked closely with Dr. Fox and conducts many of her group therapy lectures. He has contributed much to a system of rehabilitation available to the entire medical profession.

Nearly 4,000 alcoholics have been treated in the office of the senior author since 1948 with remarkably encouraging results. It is her conviction that alcoholics are among the most rewarding patients any physician could hope to help, and Dr. Fox's previous experiences as a laboratory research director, as an internist, as a pediatrician, and as a psychiatrist and psychoanalyst do afford her some basis for comparing the satisfactions in several fields of medical work.

Since the near future will see more physicians treating alcoholics than ever before, this article begins with a description of the current treatment being given in Dr. Fox's office. Summarizing more than two and a half decades of experience—both successes and failures—this article will attempt, therefore, clearly to delineate at least one way in which almost any physician can treat alcoholics in his office with good results.

In addition, we shall outline some of the steps which led to the present treatment methods. And finally, we shall also offer some comments on selected developments in the alcoholism treatment field. These last are mostly specialized treatments for particular segments of the alcoholic population, at specific points in the illness, as observed and studied by the senior author during the ten years in which she served as medical director of the National Council on Alcoholism and visited treatment facilities of many kinds around the world.

## PATIENT POPULATION

The patients we treat are almost never skid-row alcoholics, and only rarely do we have a patient with an obvious, gross psychopathology other than alcoholism. Most of the patients are white, middle or upper class, and about half are women. Other than housewives, practically all are employed at white collar, management, or professional occupations.

They are higher than the community average in income, education, and intelligence. Their ages range from the early 20s to the 70s, with most in the 30–50 bracket. Nearly all of them have alcoholism of the *gamma* species described by Jellinek (1960), and display symptoms of what Jellinek (1952) called the crucial phase of alcohol addiction.

Since the senior author is known to be a psychiatrist who specializes in the treatment of alcoholics, this reputation undoubtedly encourages certain patients' choice of a physician, and serves to eliminate certain other possible patients.

Many patients are referred by other therapists, some by members of Alcoholics Anonymous and the Al-Anon Family Groups.

About one fifth are sent by their employers. Often a wife or friend makes the initial approach in behalf of the drinker, and many patients are self-referred. Most have had earlier treatment of some kind for alcoholism.

*FIRST INTERVIEW*

When the patient first telephones for an appointment, it is explained that a two-hour initial interview is necessary, and fees are carefully explained on the telephone. Patients unable to afford the fees are occasionally seen if the appointment calendar allows, but otherwise they are referred to other treatment resources for which we have high regard, especially Alcoholics Anonymous and outpatient facilities that specialize in working with alcoholics. We try not to refer to mental health facilities which have not demonstrated special regard for and competence in treating alcoholics.

Of course some patients on first contact need hospitalization for detoxification—a description of which is outside the scope of this paper.[1] Let us say, however, that our experience clearly supports the contentions of so many good physicians who work in this field—namely, that the well-managed alcoholic patient in the modern general hospital is usually one of the most cooperative patients in the hospital, presenting far fewer problems than many other severely ill patients, and that detoxification is easily accomplished with proper medication and good nursing care. Both Mt. Zion Hospital, San Francisco, and Roosevelt Hospital, New York, have demonstrated this using any available bed rather than segregating alcoholics into one special area. One caution: far too often the physician cannot be certain that he knows precisely what drugs in addition to ethanol the patient may have been dosing himself with, so care and close observation are necessary. It should be made certain whenever possible that before the patient is released he is absolutely free of all sedative or tranquilizing drugs for at least twenty-four hours. Patients discharged

[1] For excellent medical guidance on this process, see the A.M.A. *Manual on Alcoholism* (1967) and Block (1965).

still under the influence of these drugs are almost being encouraged to resume their dangerous self-medication with alcohol if not with other psychotropic agents.

In the rare case when prescription of any mood-changing drug is absolutely necessary, the supply should cover only two or three days and the prescription should be non-refillable.

Often in our experience detoxification is easily accomplished at one of the many excellent "rest farms" for alcoholics in some parts of the United States. The best of these convalescent or rehabilitation centers also provide the patient two other valuable pushes toward recovery: a chance to regain good physical health and a prolonged (weeks or months), intensive education about alcoholism and recovery in a pleasant milieu insulated from the patient's former drinking surroundings. The finest of these places are operated as nonprofit foundations in close cooperation with nearby A.A. offices, groups, or members—although of course they are not formally affiliated with A.A. Most have recovered alcoholics on the staff. They are far less costly to the patient than private mental hospitals or psychiatric sanitaria, and have the additional advantage of placing the alcoholic in the company of other recovering alcoholics instead of frightening him by the presence of psychotics and other disturbed people with whom the sick alcoholic cannot identify.[2]

However, whether the patient comes to the doctor's office for his first visit directly from a hospital, one of these rest farms, or his home, he is met in virtually the same way.

In the doctor's waiting room there is always hot water with the makings of a cup of coffee, tea, or broth, and various pamphlets about alcoholism are lying about. The patient is encouraged to bring his beverage with him into the treatment room, where there

[2] There are too many good ones to list them all, but in our area we have seen excellent results from Alina Lodge, Blairstown, N.J.; Chit-Chat Farm, Wernersville, Pa.; Ferguson Hall, Central Valley, N.Y.; High Watch Farm, Kent, Conn.; and Livengrin Foundation, Eddington, Pa. You can check with the nearest A.A. office or affiliate of the National Council on Alcoholism for the names of local good ones, then be sure to spend some time there yourself before referring any patients. Doctors are always welcome guests. And if there is not one near you, help get one started!

are comfortable chairs, ash trays, and cleansing tissue handy. At first the interview is largely allowed to take its own course, with only occasional leading questions, and almost no quick or blunt confrontation of the patient's defenses (the alibi system with which he denies his alcoholism). Instead, the doctor makes friends and gives direct reassurances and support. It may take 45 minutes or so for a patient to get over his anger at the situation. Eventually questions elicit enough specific information for a case history, including past medical history, his childhood, his education, his present family and employment situations, his drinking history, his current drinking behavior, previous therapies, his worries, neurotic or prepsychotic symptoms, his social life and hobbies, his religious leanings if any, and the state of the patient during the interview. (Later a summary of this material is dictated, along with the physician's impression of the patient and plans for treatment, and copies of this are made available to the two co-therapists in the office.)

Usually an effort has been made to have the patient's spouse, or the nearest, most significant, and concerned relative or friend, come to the office with the patient for the first interview. Ideally this person is seen separately, after the patient, and on another occasion if necessary. But it seems helpful to have both patient and spouse present for the last part of the interview, in which the physician explains the illness and details of the treatment. This helps overcome resistance, and replaces despair with hope.

She emphasizes that alcoholism is not a moral weakness, but is a disease, clearly recognized as such by the medical community. This is almost always a relief to the patient, who may have heard it (but hardly dared believe it) or to whom the concept may be totally new (since avoiding such knowledge is one way of denying the illness).

She explains that it does not necessarily mean the patient is mentally ill, or "crazy," [3] and to illustrate she explains the phar-

---

[3] This may seem extraordinarily naïve to the reader, but it pays to remember that very rarely is this patient sophisticated about mental illness. In fact, more often than not he is almost inarticulate with terror that he is "losing his mind." Cheerful, but not unrealistic, assurance that the physi-

macological basis of alcoholism, using Gitlow's (1968) description of the mechanism of alcohol addiction.

Such simple, basic facts about the drug ethanol are almost always completely unknown to the patient, and most patients have even less factual information about the disease alcoholism. They have, instead, a massive structure of misinformation, stereotypes, myths, misunderstandings, and folklore cemented by fear. This bulky mass of emotional misconceptions of course supports the illness and hinders recovery. Therefore it is absolutely necessary at the very first interview to mount a frontal assault on this immense pile of false notions (the attack will have to go on and on), substituting for it a healthy structure of sound, scientific, medically correct information, as far as it is available.

The necessity for absolute abstinence is stressed, and the subject of disulfiram (Antabuse) is introduced. The patient is given a thorough explanation of what the medication does, and is shown that it can be a tremendous aid in the initial stages of recovery (although its use alone is certainly not a "cure" for alcoholism). It reduces the number of decisions that have to be made about drinking to one per day, and it serves to prevent the impulse "to have just one," the innocent-seeming idea which in alcoholics inevitably leads eventually to an episode of intoxication. Thus disulfiram (Antabuse) enables the patient to begin to achieve an alcohol-free period, a prerequisite for all recovery measures to follow.

Provided the physician feels confident that the patient has no alcohol in his bloodstream, the patient is handed his first tablet right on the spot. The dose is generally one pill (0.5 mg) daily for five to ten days, followed then by one-half pill (0.25 mg) a day indefinitely. Further details on the modern dosage, and contraindications, are published elsewhere (Fox, 1967a).

If the patient is obviously suffering from the inaccurately named "alcohol withdrawal syndrome," but hospitalization is not

---

cian sees him as sane, and confidently expects to see him recover, can often elicit visible signs of relief—the beginning of hope, a powerful stimulus to recovery.

indicated, he may also be given in the office a small dose of a mild tranquilizer of the phenothiazine type. Practically never, however, is he given a prescription for tranquilizers or sedatives to be taken under his own supervision. All the experience and studies of which we are aware clearly point to this: the quicker the alcoholic patient is off *all* mood-changing drugs, the better his chances of recovery from alcoholism.

Dangers of cross-addiction and death from overdoses are particularly real for alcoholics, whether or not they have ever been pill takers. Habituating the alcoholic to simply a different form of "oral magic" for dealing with life is a deceptively easy but cruel trap for both the patient and the therapist.[4]

Some physicians who work with alcoholics are afraid that abuse of legitimate mood-changing (sedating, stimulating, tranquilizers) drugs may even now be a national health menace in the United States larger than alcoholism. They may be right. At any rate, we can at least try to prevent alcoholics from unwittingly, with what they believe is medical blessing, slipping into addictions even more dangerous and difficult to treat than alcoholism. Unnecessary dependence on chemicals is a ghastly maladaptation to life.

The terms *alcoholic* and *alcoholism* are rarely used in the early stages of the first interview. "Having a problem with drinking" is more acceptable to most patients, and this helps to sidestep the emotional semantic barriers which block the patient's recognition of his real condition. However, the physician eventually points out the symptoms of alcoholism in the patient's history, and if necessary she administers a question-and-answer test so the patient can see for himself his pathology.

Usually the patient is told that very few additional private treatment sessions will be necessary, but at least one follow-up appointment is made for two or three weeks hence. The patient is also urged to have at least one private session with the psychologist who is co-therapist in the office, and is assured that

---

[4] This does not mean, of course, that the alcoholic must forego medication for ills other than alcoholism, but he must limit himself strictly to the prescribed dosage.

further private sessions with the physician can be arranged whenever necessary.

The physician tells the patient that the next phases of treatment are three kinds of group therapy in the company of other patients: a series of six weekly lecture-discussion meetings (which the spouse should also attend), extensive acquaintance with Alcoholics Anonymous, and eventually participation in psychodrama in the doctor's office.

If the patient has already been to A.A., he is urged to intensify his participation in A.A. meetings. Most patients, however, have not been to A.A. and, because of fear and gross misconceptions of the fellowship, are reluctant to approach it. The physician's strong endorsement of A.A. helps reduce this reluctance. Some mistaken impressions of A.A. (e.g., that it is overwhelmingly religious, that it consists of skid-row derelicts) can be cleared up on the spot, and often the physician simply picks up the telephone in the patient's presence and calls either an A.A. member (usually a former patient) or the local A.A. office. In this way the patient —while motivation to feel better and obey the doctor is still high —can meet an A.A. member on the telephone, and specific arrangements can be made for an A.A. sponsor to take the patient to his first A.A. meeting.

Further ways in which we utilize A.A. in treatment are described below, as are some of the scientific reasons for our high regard for this particular approach to alcoholism.

## WEEKLY LECTURE-DISCUSSION GROUPS

The co-therapist who conducts the lecture-discussion periods is a professional psychologist with special training in alcoholism who happens, also, to be a recovered alcoholic. The physician is usually present, as a participant-observer.

The sessions, held in the doctor's office, consist of a lecture for one hour, beginning at 6 P.M., then an hour for discussion, questions, and answers. The groups are open-ended, with patients joining and leaving at each meeting. Each has a schedule of the lecture topics, and is to attend all six, but he can begin any week.

Attendance ranges from 8 to 18, including a few spouses, for each session.

When patients arrive each one is asked to pin a name tag (first name only) on his chest (we just use index cards and a magic marker), and all patients and therapists use first names. After helping themselves to coffee or tea, patients seat themselves in a semicircle facing the leader and his small blackboard used during the lectures for lists, diagrams, etc.

Although the lecture material is of impeccable medical or scientific content, it is presented in plain, nontechnical language. The didactic approach, relatively objective and impersonal, prevents the patient's feeling too threatened early in his recovery. He need not fear his personal secrets will be publicly revealed before strangers before he is ready to talk openly about himself. By then, he will have begun getting accustomed to new language, other patients, new facts, and new insights about himself and his illness.

We think it is significant that the lecture sessions, while fact-packed, are *not* solemn. They are intentionally made as entertaining and otherwise enjoyable as possible—copying A.A.'s deliberate and unique use of laughter as a therapeutic tool. Almost always patients are enormously relieved to find "therapy" a pleasant experience, not the gloomy, painfully self-searching ordeal they had anticipated. Maybe this is one reason a large proportion of these patients continue to come back faithfully for the sessions.

At the outset it is made clear that the therapists are *not* "against drinking," *per se*. Most patients, understandably, dread hearing from yet more grim-faced "reformers" who frowningly disapprove of their dissolute ways. Most alcoholics, have already experienced their quota of preaching, warning, berating, admonishing, and tearful pleading. To the victim, of course, these feel like rejections of their unworthy selves, and such treatment reinforces their guilt feelings and convictions of hopelessness. Even a physician known to be an occasional imbiber can seem to be scolding or reproving the alcoholic when he speaks of alcoholic beverages in a health context.

While these unpleasant social responses to his drinking may have real value in motivating the alcoholic to seek help, they have no place in professional treatment of the alcoholic, no matter how often the victim may relapse.

Instead, we can offer ourselves as therapists who clearly are not opposed to harmless social drinking, but only to the disease of alcoholism. We are not shocked or horrified by the patient. We are not against the patient, but on his side, against his disease.

This attitude is not unlike A.A. members' striking lack of ambivalence toward alcohol and drinking. Almost uniquely in our culture, many A.A. members do not seem to feel or express any disapproval of alcohol use by those whose drinking is apparently harmless. Because of their own experience, they do not condemn even the alcoholic's behavior; they understand it. It is not drinking they fight—it is the disease. They show almost no concern with the social customs (i.e., drinking) of drinkers who do not have the disease. This is completely different from the old Prohibitionist approach.

Within this attitude framework, then, the following lecture material is presented:

1. ETHYL ALCOHOL, AN ADDICTING DRUG. This lecture introduces the patient to the idea of thinking not of alcoholic beverages, but to their ethanol content—the drug. The manufacture, and some of the legends, of alcoholic beverages are explained, as is the mechanism of alcohol addiction (see Gitlow, 1968).

Also at this session, as at all subsequent ones, patients are urged to attend at least six A.A. meetings soon. It is pointed out that they can go initially as "observers." Reading material about alcohol and alcoholism is discussed, and patients are encouraged to read widely from a list of sound publications, such as those available from the National Council on Alcoholism, the Center of Alcohol Studies at Rutgers University, or Alcoholics Anonymous. In fact, at the close of each session, inexpensive leaflets or pamphlets appropriate to the lecture subject of the day are given to each patient.

2. WHAT THE BODY DOES TO ETHANOL, AND VICE VERSA. This lecture covers the metabolism of alcohol in the body, with emphasis on the disulfiram (Antabuse) reaction. Laboratory and other scientific studies are quoted to explain the effects of alcohol on various body organs and functions, as well as illnesses in addition to alcoholism which frequently accompany alcohol use. Effects of alcohol on the central nervous system are explained in detail, and it is pointed out that these are results of the drug on any living animal, alcoholic or not.

3. ALCOHOLICS DO NOT DRINK. Using this brilliant conceptualization by S. Bacon (1958), this lecture describes drinking customs in various cultures (orthodox Jewry, France, Bali, Italy, nineteenth century Ireland, Chichicastenango, Kenya, Skid Row, etc.) and shows that the alcoholic's ingestion of ethanol violates virtually all the norms of social drinking. Alcoholics use the drug ethanol for its pharmacological effect, and it is harmful to think or speak of their behavior as just excessive drinking.

4. ALCOHOLISM, THE DISEASE: DIMENSIONS, DEFINITIONS, SPECIES, AND SYMPTOMS. Since no laboratory test to detect the presence of alcoholism exists yet, it is acknowledged that our definition of the disease—although it conforms to good medical practice—is essentially functional, or clinical, and somewhat social and residual. Our explanation is essentially that suggested by Mann (1961). Some dimensions of the problem are reviewed. Jellinek's (1960) species are summarized, and the symptomatology described by him (1952) is discussed at length. Special attention is directed to those symptoms which are related to denial, and also to those which are social—that is, those that involve people other than the alcoholic himself. Many of these latter in effect could not exist were it not for people around the alcoholic.

Sometimes there is time to point out that the disease is only one of the problems connected with drinking, and such ballyhooed matters as drinking and driving, young people and drinking, drinking and crime, liquor controls and graft, and Skid Row, are touched upon separately.

Etiology is covered by presentation of a schematic presentation of the illness, as shown in the accompanying diagram.

## ASPECTS OF A CASE OF ALCOHOLISM

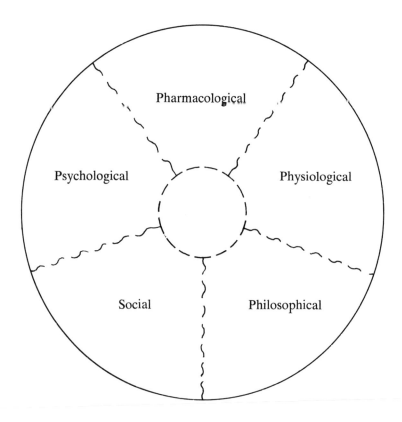

It is pointed out that the relative size, juxtaposition, and interrelationships of the sectors above can vary highly, from case to case—except for the distinguishing part of the illness, the pharmacological (use of the drug). And a case can arise in any or several of the sectors. The sectors are described as components of the illness, or ways in which the alcoholic is sick. However the illness began, it results in disease in at least the five aspects of life shown, and treatment must affect all of them if there is to be a sound recovery.

The void at the center is unnamed. It is described as perhaps the severe lack of self-esteem afflicting so many alcoholics, or perhaps the lack of meaning (see Frankl, 1964)—the absence of any healthy commitment to life. Commitment to the state of intoxication and all other aspects of the alcoholic's sick subculture leaves no room for a more satisfying and positive life impetus.

Pharmacological and social aspects of the illness have already been discussed. The others are covered in the following lectures.

During the last part of this session the patients are urged at last to talk about themselves by discussing the symptoms they have experienced.

5. PHYSIOLOGICAL AND PSYCHOLOGICAL ASPECTS OF ALCOHOLISM. Since somatic illness caused by heavy drinking is discussed in the second lecture, the physiological part of this session is limited to a presentation of some scientific evidence for the possibilities of the hypothesized physical factor X, a biochemical (possibly genetic) vulnerability of any of several kinds to the illness.

Popular psychological theories of the "cause" of alcoholism are discussed as theories, not as truths. Evidence contradicting these theories is shown, with acknowledgment that any of the reputed causative psychological problems could result in a crippling disability for alcoholics or anyone else.

The point is made that pinpointing a psychological origin of alcoholism in the patient's past is of limited value in early stages of recovery. In keeping with good medical practice related to other illnesses, we have to treat alcoholism before getting at its roots—just as surgeons remove infected appendixes without knowing what started the infection, as radiologists treat cancer without understanding its cause, as physicians have to reduce a dangerously high fever before drugs can take effect on the pneumococci which caused it.

Of more importance is the discussion of the psychological problems commonly found current in many alcoholics (perhaps antecedent to the alcoholism, perhaps results of it)—such as feelings of guilt, self-consciousness, depression, lack of self-esteem, impatience, low discomfort tolerance, rage, self-pity, scrupulosity, shyness, fearfulness, and arrogance or overcompliance.

This leads to discussion of these feelings and what to do about them. In addition, of course, discussion at this session as at almost all others permits exchange of experience among the patients about abstinence at drinking parties, use of Antabuse, impressions of Alcoholics Anonymous, etc. An effort is always made to let the group help each patient.

6. THERAPIES FOR ALCOHOLISM. Social responses to alcoholism are reviewed as attempts to "cure" the illness, and several ways in which it has been treated are discussed—aversion reflex, psychoanalysis, hypnosis, and LSD. Most of the lecture, however, is a simplified explanation of the origins and dynamics of Alcoholics Anonymous and a description of what one can expect to encounter at A.A. meetings.

This completes the lecture series.

After completion of the lecture-discussion series of group sessions, patients report to the office once a week for psychodrama, a form of psychotherapy originated by Moreno in 1911 (Moreno, 1959). It has been used in this office since 1958 and the results account for our high regard for this process—*when it is conducted by a well-trained, intuitive therapist*—such as Miss Hannah Weiner, who happens also to be an attractive and admirable human being (qualities which doubtless are no small part of her effectiveness as a psychodramatist). The theory and practice of psychodrama with alcoholic patients are not gone into here, since Miss Weiner has published her own brilliant exposition elsewhere (Weiner, 1967).

This is perhaps the best place to point out that every two months or so we make an additional effort to bring the benefits of Alcoholics Anonymous to all patients. We make special efforts by telephone to round up any patients who have not made a satisfactory affiliation with A.A., and invite them to a special evening session at the office. It is preceded by light refreshments and the tone of the gathering is social. No fee is charged for this session.

We invite to this meeting two members of A.A. (one man, one woman) known to us—often former patients—who have had several years of comfortable sobriety. We select members who are mature enough not to feel threatened or disturbed by the notions of disulfiram (Antabuse) or professional psychotherapy for alcoholics. The A.A.'s are asked not to conduct an A.A. meeting, but to be willing to talk briefly about themselves and answer questions. We leave the patients alone with the members, and the session lasts about an hour and a half.

We know that each such session persuades at least a few patients to take themselves to A.A. At the least, such an encounter also reduces considerably patients' misconceptions of A.A. and reluctance to affiliate with it.

We hold a similar meeting several times a year for the spouses (or any "significant other") of patients, with two members of the Al-Anon Family Groups. In fact, from the very first interview we urge spouses to affiliate with Al-Anon, and get their teen-age youngsters to Alateen. Such a move tends to improve enormously the health of the family, and accomplishes this with breathtaking swiftness—far more quickly and easily than we can do it. That this also changes the human climate around the alcoholic is of great value, of course, often marking the difference between recovery and continued illness for the patient. In one sense, however, that is a secondary consideration. Whether or not the alcoholic gets well, Al-Anon and Alateen specialize in making life much better for his family.

Follow-up of patients is frequently, we are sure, one of the most valuable services we can render them. We get to know most patients well, and really want to know how they are progressing. In the event there has not been any real improvement, we nearly always can suggest one more action of some kind the patient— or we—have not tried . . . one more reason to hope. We have found that a telephone call or brief personal note is truly appreciated, and it practically always results in the patient's resumption of some kind of therapy. We don't care what kind, or where, if it helps.

Hopefully, it is clear by now that the way of treatment bring described here is highly eclectic. We try, too, to avoid a vested interest in seeing the patient recover in "our" way, or to claim credit for recoveries. We borrow freely from all the ways of helping alcoholics we have heard of, and when we learn of promising new or better techniques, we hope to borrow them, too.

Just as alcoholics cannot recover in isolation, physicians alone cannot hope to treat alcoholics successfully. We make extensive use of almost every treatment resource our community offers—especially recovered alcoholics who are members of Alcoholics Anonymous.

It is axiomatic in medical education that one learns about an illness by observing it in patients, and one learns about recovery factors by watching recoveries. We will now discuss how such a process has led to the treatment methods herein described, and some of the scientific (in addition to clinical) evidence supporting our present approach.

## THE BEGINNING OF WISDOM

When the senior author learned she had married into a family in which there was an alcoholic, it was humiliating to find that her medical expertise was unable to stop the inevitable progression of the disease. It was cold comfort to learn that other physicians seemed equally unable to help the many other "drunkards" or "people who drink too much" seen by almost every medical practitioner and psychotherapist.

At about this time (the 1940s), however, three faint mutters of hope were discernible. Alcoholics Anonymous was beginning to be heard of as successful when all else failed; the Center of Alcohol Studies at Yale (now at Rutgers) was beginning its Summer Schools for all persons interested in a scientific approach to alcohol problems; and the National Council on Alcoholism was beginning to arouse the interest and hopes of local citizens, both lay and professional, in the treatment of alcoholism as a health problem.

Now, nearly three decades later, these three and their outgrowths can still be the staunchest allies of any physician puzzled by alcoholism.

### Alcoholics Anonymous

A.A. is now available in nations around the world (Leach et al., 1969), and is listed in practically all North American telephone directories. We urge you to start your understanding of alcoholism by listening to all the A.A. members you can meet, and going to all the A.A. meetings you can find. As a listener, any interested professional person is a royally welcomed guest—but best take with you enough resilience to enable you to laugh at occasional well-earned jibes at "quacks," or "headshrinkers"!

We also find it extremely useful to read all the A.A. books and pamphlets and, by all means, the fellowship's monthly magazine, *The A.A. Grapevine.*

This deep exploration of A.A. is urged upon the physician not only because it can be one of the most encouraging and stimulating experiences any medical person can enjoy, but for other reasons as well:

(a) With its focus on health, not disease, A.A. illustrates and illuminates the recovery process with great cogency. *The physician whose knowledge of alcoholism and A.A. comes only through the sick people in his office gets only a sick, distorted view.*

(b) If you wonder what drinking patients are still trying to tell you, you can find out quickly when you hear their sober counterparts in A.A. describe their own drinking and treatment-seeking days.

It is important to understand that A.A. itself is *not* antimedical, or antipsychiatry, although a few of its louder, newer enthusiasts may sometimes sound so. (The more sophisticated members are usually quieter.) A.A. is *a*medical, quick to disqualify itself in such matters as medical management of acutely intoxicated patients, in handling severe psychopathologies, in furnishing such

social services as financial assistance or provision of food, clothing, and shelter, in research, in public education, and the like.
But more often than not A.A. accomplishes what physicians
alone can almost never do—*prevention* of the drinking episodes.

For the scientist troubled by some of the mystical sounding
jargon popular with some A.A. members, it is helpful to read
professional interpretations of the A.A. program such as those
by Frank (1961), Lewin and Grabbe (1948), Maxwell (1962),
Tiebout (1944, 1961), Trice (1958), and many others.

Large-scale, objective evaluations of the long-term effectiveness of Alcoholics Anonymous published elsewhere (see Bailey
and Leach, 1965; Bill C., 1965; and Edwards *et al.,* 1966),
covering A.A. members in New York, Texas, and London, respectively, are mentioned here only in passing because they
confirm our own impression of the impressive efficiency of A.A.
as a therapeutic modality for alcoholic patients.

The findings of the first two are strikingly similar to those
elicited by A.A. itself in 1968. Because the latter findings are not
otherwise available in the professional literature, we recount them
briefly here.

Surveying 11,355 members who attended 466 A.A. meetings
in the months of June and July (held by approximately 5 percent
of the groups in the United States and Canada), A.A.'s General
Service Office found about one third had been sober more than
five years, one third from one to five years, and one third less
than a year. Twelve percent had been sober ten or more years.

Forty-one percent said they had not had a drink since their
first exposure to A.A. Another 41 percent said it took them 1–5
years to stop.

(Of those who joined A.A. twenty years ago or more, only 12
percent were influenced by doctors. Today, 19 percent say they
were sent to A.A. by physicians. That means the influence of
doctors on A.A. growth has increased more than 50 percent in
the last two decades.[5])

With statistical odds like those, is it any wonder that we fre-

[5] For additional details of this survey and its results, see "Report on
Survey of A.A. Membership," pp. 42–44 in *The A.A. Grapevine,* Vol. 25,
No. 7, December 1968. [*See also* John Norris's article in this volume.—Ed.]

quently feel the finest service a physician can perform for the alcoholic patient is getting him or her into A.A.?

Some patients, of course, continue to deny the applicability of A.A. to their own cases with all the standard ingenuity *any* sick patient can summon to sabotage his own recovery. Alcoholic patients are by no means the only ones who do not follow doctors' orders! In some cases, our patients have already had lengthy exposure to A.A. They need additional help which we try to supply, or find a source which can provide it. Such resources and other developments in the field of alcoholism treatment are the subject of the next and concluding section of this article.

## SOME OTHER TREATMENTS

Other techniques which have been used in treating alcoholics in this office include:

### Psychoanalysis
Conventional depth analysis, although tried for many years, has, as Freud and Jung predicted, rarely been the treatment of choice for alcoholism. Although it may, of course, in the hands of good practitioners be highly beneficial to some alcoholics who need it after they have learned to stay sober.

But it is contraindicated for drinking alcoholics because, among other things, it delays confrontation with the alcohol ingestion itself. Too many alcoholics quite full of insight can die of alcoholism because they are also full of booze.

One patient in this office, himself an eminent psychiatrist, reported he was "up to his neck" in insight after seventeen years of psychoanalytic treatment. But all insight "went out the window" when he took one drink and thus activated his alcohol addiction. Therapy aimed specifically at the ethanol ingestion worked. He subsequently resumed teaching and writing for many years before his death from a cause not related to alcohol.

### Conventional group therapy
Although nondirective or psychoanalytically oriented group therapy, in the hands of therapists knowledgeable about alco-

holism, has proved far superior to individual psychoanalysis in treating alcoholics, it can share many of the handicaps of the latter unless it is specifically adapted to alcoholism. Adjunctive therapy to get at the pharmacological basis of alcoholism is needed.

Some of the reasons ordinary group therapy may often be less effective than A.A. are: (a) the quality of A.A. group interaction among "equals" (i.e., without the presence of an "expert" therapist in a superior role) may be more effective than the doctor-patients tie; (b) conventional group therapy usually involves only one session per week, while A.A. frequently involves the patient three or more evenings weekly (see Bailey and Leach, 1965; Leach, 1969; and Edwards *et al.,* 1966); (c) A.A. attempts to substitute, for the patient's former habits, a total life style completely different—"the A.A. way of life"—while conventional group therapy usually addresses itself only to psychopathology; (d) nondirective therapy teaches the patient no new scientific information about alcohol, but A.A. mounts a massive attack against the alcoholic's ignorance; and (e) conventional therapy deals earnestly with grim matters, while A.A. members are also learning to laugh heartily.

*Hypnosis*
Various claims made for hypnotherapy suggest the possibility that posthypnotic suggestion could help implant in the patient an aversion reflex to ethanol, and that was tried in this office, on both groups and individuals. It did not work, nor do we know of any place it has been consistently successful.

Nevertheless hypnosis can be highly useful for bringing the alcoholic's battered self-esteem up to realistic levels commensurate with his deserts. Removal of despair and feelings of worthlessness can eliminate the paralysis of hopelessness and free the alcoholic to hope, and start building a healthy, happy alcohol-free self.

Some alcoholics can also profit by training in self-hypnosis which they can use in strengthening healthy ego supports and for inducing relaxation and reducing tension.

*LSD*

This drug seems to have raised more questions than it has answered when used with alcoholics. Experience in this office has been reported extensively elsewhere (Fox, 1967b). But some expert clinicians consistently report good results (e.g., Hoffer and Osmond, 1968), and there is no reason to doubt them. What is lacking is indisputable evidence (of the type which could be expected from a double-blind test) that it is clearly the LSD alone that is responsible for such successes. Lacking such proof at present, the possibility of chromosomal damage militates against using LSD with most alcoholics of reproducing age.

In fairness it should be noted that there is also no such evidence of the efficacy of many other widely respected drugs and other treatment tools used throughout the medical world, as Hoffer and Osmond (1968) suggested. Observed clinical results are not always verified by controlled laboratory experiments, but this does not mean a specific treatment should be discarded. The placebo effect and the therapist-patient relationship can validly account for excellent clinical results. Double-blind studies cannot always perfectly control these variables.


## LEADS TO FOLLOW

Many developments in alcoholism treatment are relatively new attempts to put into practice long-available ideas. In the following round-up, limited by space to only a few of these, the young physician in private practice can find many roles for himself. Indeed, almost any brave, humble, and patient citizen can help to put into execution key community facilities for helping solve the alcoholism problems threatening to overwhelm us—provided we realize no one facility, no one therapist, can do the entire job. There is work for all.

ALCOHOLISM INFORMATION CENTERS. Although local affiliate-branches of the National Council on Alcoholism are not established primarily for face-to-face dealing with alcoholics, most of them operate information centers eager to furnish information on alcoholism to anyone, and especially to refer patients to treatment resources. Your local one is a handy encyclopedia that appreciates being used. Their service is free. By all means, join . . . or start one.

NORTH AMERICAN ASSOCIATION OF ALCOHOLISM PROGRAMS. This federation of tax-supported agencies and programs for alcoholics is for professionals only, but its interests are as variegated as are its members' disciplines. Become a member, and go.

ALCOHOL SCHOOLS. The best of these, of course, are modeled after the original held at Yale, now at Rutgers. Most offer brief summer sessions that are shattering, eye-opening, seminal, chastening, liberating, and fruitful experiences. If you have not attended one lately, you need to.

AMERICAN MEDICAL SOCIETY ON ALCOHOLISM. Limited to physicians only at present, this is the newest, longest-needed "club" in the field. Become a member and you share in up-to-date expertise as well as friendship in an otherwise often lonely endeavor.

THE CHRISTOPHER D. SMITHERS FOUNDATION, INC. The first and still virtually the only private foundation whose major interest is alcoholism, the Smithers office is a goldmine of good information. Don't miss any of its excellent publications.

THE GEORGIAN CLINIC. Under the direction of Dr. Vernelle Fox in Atlanta, this is an outstanding example of the multidisciplinary "therapeutic milieu" community. It offers excellent training.

THE B U D SYSTEM. At the Veterans' Hospital in Houston, Texas, alcoholics (and their families) are taught how to recognize when they are Building Up to Drink, and then re-hospitalize themselves for a night or so before the symptom buds flower into a "slip." It is a brilliant follow-up plan.

ALCOHOLISM RESEARCH AND TRAINING, INC. Under Dr. William F. Sears in Albuquerque, New Mexico, this organization has a unique, ingenious, and highly effective plan for utilizing and developing community resources (see Sears, 1967) against alcoholism.

LONG ISLAND COUNCIL ON ALCOHOLISM. This group's work with industries (both management and labor) and its efforts at alcohol education in the public schools make it outstanding. It uses school nurses as case finders, and local judges as motivation-referral agents.

OCCOQUAN (VA.) REHABILITATION CENTER. Forced into existence by the now famous federal court decision in the Easter case, this 425-bed facility for police-case inebriates is an outstanding example of a multidisciplinary rehabilitation center well coordinated with other community efforts.

COMMUNITY COUNCIL OF GREATER NEW YORK. At long last the nation's largest city has taken sensible steps in beginning an attack on alcoholism, thanks to this group. It has a many-faceted research, training, and treatment program, and its efforts to train professionals alone make the effort worthwhile.

DETOXIFICATION CENTERS. In St. Louis, Des Moines, and on New York's Bowery, these short-term treatment centers have already proved amazingly successful. What's more, they save thousands of tax dollars. On the Bowery, some 3,000 patients were treated the first two years. Every day about 100 sober former patients return for disulfiram therapy.

COUNTY COURT OF DENVER, COLORADO. Under Judge William H. Burnett has been developed an inexpensive, simple, and humane probation system—using volunteer laymen and disulfiram for rehabilitating arrested alcoholics. It has cut the court's recidivism rate two thirds.

MUNICIPAL COURTS OF ATLANTA. Working with many other community agencies, this group, too, has evolved a simple warfare against the Revolving Door, with a better than fifty percent success rate. Like Judge Burnett, they have disproved the old notion that an alcoholic has to want help *before* you can help him. Originally forced by the court to accept help, scores of Atlanta derelicts, no longer under legal duress, have *asked permission* to get from their former probation officers daily a dose of disulfiram. They are as surprised as anyone to find themselves sober, employed, and liking it.

INDUSTRIAL PROGRAMS. A few of America's biggest, richest-in-human-resources corporations pioneered at saving problem drinkers—who represent enormous assets—rather than losing them. They, too, found that motivating the alcoholic to seek treatment is the responsibility of those around him, which confirms what Sterne and Pittman (1965) so brilliantly proved: that "he isn't motivated" is the excuse we often use for our own failures.

MARATHONS AND ENCOUNTER THERAPY. For alcoholics of poor ego strength, these like some other therapies may be very harmful unless conducted by highly trained psychotherapists, although of course they can produce results seen nowhere else. However, we particularly recommend that all *therapists* in the field of alcoholism experience some of these sessions, for their *own* benefit. This is based on our own personal participation and the experience of Dr. Donald J. Ottenberg at Eagleville (Pa.) Hospital and Rehabilitation Center, in arranging such therapy for his own staff.

To conquer this tragic illness takes money, of course, but vast reservoirs of money alone will never be enough. It will also require combined medical and psychosocial understanding, plus infinite patience, tolerance, perseverance, imagination, often ingenuity, "faith, hope, love," and a willing spirit among therapists.

If it seems to you, any reader, that our message is contaminated with more than a little of the "Physician, treat thyself" tone, you are right. That's what our experience has led us to conclude, and that is how, in our opinion, all effective treatment of alcoholism must start.

Of our patients in treatment for six months or so, we see easily two thirds on their way to good recoveries. It should be obvious that ours is a simple program that any physician could set up. No medical endeavor is more rewarding.

## REFERENCES

1. American Medical Association, *Manual on Alcoholism*, 1967.
2. Bacon, S. D., "Alcoholics do not drink," *Annals of the American Academy of Political and Social Science*, Vol. 315, 1958, pp. 55–64.
3. Bailey, M. B., and Leach, B., *Alcoholics Anonymous: Pathway to Recovery—A Study of 1,058 Members of the A.A. Fellowship in New York City* (New York: The National Council on Alcoholism, Inc., 1965).
4. Block, M. A., *Alcoholism: Its Facets and Phases* (New York: The John Day Company, 1965).
5. C., Bill, "The growth and effectiveness of Alcoholics Anonymous in a southwestern city," *Quarterly Journal of Studies on Alcohol*, Vol. 26, 1965, pp. 279–284.
6. Edwards, G., et al., "Who goes to Alcoholics Anonymous?" *The Lancet*, August 12, 1966, pp. 382–384.
7. Fox, R., "Disulfiram (Antabuse) as an adjunct in the treatment of alcoholism," in *Alcoholism: Behavioral Research, Therapeutic Approaches*, R. Fox, ed. (New York: Springer Publishing Company, Inc., 1967a).
8. ————, "Is LSD of value in treating alcoholics?" in *The Use of LSD in Psychotherapy and Alcoholism*, H. A. Abramson, ed. (New York: The Bobbs-Merrill Company, Inc., 1967b).
9. Frank, J. D., *Persuasion and Healing: A Comparative Study of Psychotherapy* (Baltimore: The Johns Hopkins Press, 1961).
10. Frankl, V. E., *Man's Search for Meaning* (Boston: Beacon Press, 1959).
11. Gitlow, S. E., "A pharmacological approach to alcoholism," *The A.A. Grapevine*, Vol. 24, No. 5, October 1968, pp. 12–27.

12. Hoffer, A., and Osmond, H., *New Hope for Alcoholics* (New Hyde Park, N.Y.: University Books, 1968).

13. Jellinek, E. M., "Phases of alcohol addiction," *Quarterly Journal of Studies on Alcohol*, Vol. 13, 1952, pp. 673–684.

14. ———, *The Disease Concept of Alcoholism* (New Haven: Hillhouse Press, 1960).

15. Leach, B., et al., "Dimensions of Alcoholics Anonymous, 1935–1965," *The International Journal of the Addictions*, Vol. 15, No. 4, 1969 (in press).

16. Lewin, K., and Grabbe, P., "Conduct, knowledge, and acceptance of new values," in *Resolving Social Conflicts*, G. Lewin, ed. (New York: Harper and Brothers, 1948).

17. Mann, M., *New Primer on Alcoholism* (New York: Holt, Rinehart, and Winston, 1961).

18. Maxwell, M., "Alcoholics Anonymous, an interpretation," in *Society, Culture and Drinking Patterns*, D. J. Pittman and C. R. Snyder, eds. (New York: John Wiley and Sons, Inc., 1962).

19. Moreno, J. L., "Psychodrama," in *American Handbook of Psychiatry*, Vol. II, S. Arieti, ed. (New York: Basic Books, 1959).

20. Sears, W. F., "Community treatment approach for alcoholism, in R. Fox, ed., *op cit.*, 1967a.

21. Sterne, M. W., and Pittman, D. J., "The concept of motivation: a source of institutional and professional blockage in the treatment of alcoholics," *Quarterly Journal of Studies on Alcohol*, Vol. 26, 1965, pp. 41–57.

22. Tiebout, H. M., "Therapeutic mechanisms of Alcoholics Anonymous," *American Journal of Psychiatry*, Vol. 100, 1944, pp. 468–473.

23. ———, "Alcoholics Anonymous—an experiment of nature," *Quarterly Journal of Studies on Alcohol*, Vol. 22, 1961, pp. 52–68.

24. Trice, H. M., "Alcoholics Anonymous," *Annals of the American Academy of Political and Social Science*, Vol. 315, 1958, pp. 108–116.

25. Weiner, H. B., "Psychodramatic treatment of the alcoholic," in R. Fox, ed., *op. cit.*, 1967a.

# The clergyman's role in recovery from alcoholism

## THE REV. JOSEPH L. KELLERMANN

The clergy have always been concerned about alcoholism, but not all have understood the nature of the problem, nor even that they were dealing with a disease and not a sin. Joseph Kellermann, an Episcopal minister, has studied the nature of the disease. As executive director of the Charlotte (North Carolina) Council on Alcoholism, he has put compassion and professional training to work in effective therapy for alcoholics.

The minister has more to offer in preventing alcoholism or helping in recovery than any professional person in the community, provided he learns how to cope with the problem. Since the vast majority of persons who have the illness die without effecting a recovery, we must assume that ministers, along with other professionals, simply have not learned to be effective in this field. Yet the role of the minister provides him with a position of attack on alcoholism which no other person in the community has.

The clergyman as pastor has the traditional privilege of entering the home of the members of his congregation without being invited. The health of people in his parish is his responsibility and obligation. Secondly, the clergyman is usually the first professional person whom the family may approach with problems. In this case, however, if he is hostile toward alcohol and condemns drinking, the family as well as the alcoholic may

avoid him. The key to his role is that with knowledge of alcoholism he may institute a recovery program without having any
conversation or contact whatsoever with the person who, for lack
of a better term, is called an alcoholic. Unilateral treatment of
alcoholism may be effected through a key sober person in the
life of the alcoholic. Not only is it possible, it is actually preferable to begin with the most responsible sober member of the
family in initiating the recovery program. Most recovery programs
fail because everything is concentrated on the alcoholic without
making any real effort to change the very structure of the family
or community in which he attempts to deal with the painful conditions of life by excessive drinking.

In dealing with families, the minister has other advantages. He
prepares men and women for marriage, describing its rights,
duties, and obligations—how a couple should cope with problems when they arise. He baptizes their babies, calls upon them
when sick or bereaved, and has repeated opportunities to establish a counseling relationship with each family in his flock.
Also, in numbers he outranks all other professionals and is therefore more readily available. Despite administrative duties, he
has more time to give to counseling than other professionals.
There is one danger, however. To be effective, the clergyman must
be quarterback of the recovery team and never try to do the
whole job himself.

The clergyman is also the one man who stands before a
cross section of the community each week and speaks of social
and moral responsibility. He may speak about social responsibility
as a public matter from his pulpit, and he may personally and
privately approach any professional person in the community
with a request for services for a member of his flock. Within a
church of normal size a minister could set up a complete recovery
team; for most churches have at least one doctor, nurse, social
worker, and—perhaps most important of all—a member of Al-
Anon and of Alcoholics Anonymous. If none of these services
exists within the parish, they do exist in the community, or near
enough to be within reach.

As quarterback of the recovery program, the minister is in a
position to urge the family and the alcoholic to remain in the

program until recovery is assured. This is usually accomplished over a period of a few years rather than a few weeks or months. Again, the clergyman is in a position to spell out the responsibility of continuing help, especially for the family members. He plays the key role; but, if he is to play it well, he must learn the nature of alcoholism as an illness and as a social disorder. Consciously or unconsciously he is involved with alcoholism. With understanding and knowledge of the illness he may lead the family into an early recovery. Without basic knowledge, he may actually perpetuate the illness. The attitudes and actions of most clergymen handicap the recovery process. There is no other major illness in our country today that professional persons are more ignorant about. It is possible for a clergyman, doctor, lawyer, or social worker to complete his entire education without a single hour of basic instruction on alcohol or alcoholism from a scientific or objective point of view.

## ALCOHOLISM AS DISEASE, NOT DEMON

Most persons want to talk about alcoholism without talking about alcohol. It is as necessary to consider alcohol in relation to alcoholism as it is to consider sugar in relation to diabetes. The use of alcohol by the alcoholic permits the illness to continue its course with multiple consequences, both to the drinker and others. Abstinence is a prerequisite to recovery; but the use of alcohol in our society is widespread without basic social or cultural norms regarding its use. If there is any validity in studies which compare rates of alcoholism in national, ethnic, religious, or cultural groups, we are faced with the fact that there are vast differences in the incidence of alcoholism. The extremely high rate of alcoholism in the United States indicates that we are grossly lacking in a cultural norm and social responsibility related to the use of alcohol. This has two effects. First, it produces a very high rate of alcoholism. Secondly, our own mixed emotions about its use has a profound effect on our attitude and action toward alcoholism. In both areas clergymen have great influence in creating or preserving attitudes.

The following illustration indicates the end result of a hostile attitude toward alcohol. A woman of about sixty years of age remained almost sleepless for two weeks after learning that her son had become an alcoholic. She was referred to the author for counseling. The sleeplessness began when the son phoned from another state and demanded money which the mother felt forced to borrow because the son said he would drive some 200 miles the next day to get it. A week later her daughter-in-law phoned to say that her husband had been drunk for days and was so abusive that she was bringing the three children to live with the mother until he regained sobriety. The mother begged the daughter-in-law not to leave, fearing her son would follow and might be killed while driving drunk. The mother rushed immediately to her son's home in an effort to restore him to sobriety. Failing, she returned to her own husband and her grandchild by her son's first marriage whom she was supporting to prevent her son's imprisonment for nonsupport.

After a long interview about alcoholism the woman suddenly blurted out a question which was the crux of her whole problem, "Do you think my son is going to hell?" When asked why she asked such a question, she replied, "Every preacher who ever stood in the pulpit of our church said that no drunkard can enter the kingdom of heaven. I think I have failed to raise my son right, and he has become a drunkard. I can't sleep at night because I fear I have jeopardized my son's eternal soul."

The emotional conditioning from the pulpit of this church failed to prevent the son's drinking and did not prompt him to seek help when alcoholism appeared. It made the mother totally unprepared to cope with her son's alcoholism and led to her own emotional illness. Her actions helped perpetuate the illness in her son, which in turn made her insomnia more acute.

In any church one may find total abstainers, social drinkers, excessive drinkers, and alcoholics. There are churches with dry pulpits and wet pews. Some denominations take a permissive attitude toward the use of alcohol; others look upon it as the greatest source of evil in our day. This results in an infinite variety of attitudes toward the use of alcohol as it relates to alcoholism. It affects the alcoholic's conception of his own illness, and the attitude of the family and the forces brought to bear by society on the alcoholic and his family. It also affects the entire area of treatment and the approaches to the illness by professional persons and employers. In order to understand the enormous impact the clergy and the church have in this area, one should read Dr. Selden D. Bacon's article, "The Classic Temperance Movement of the U.S.A.: Impact Today on Attitudes, Action and Research." *

This article, when placed beside the development of the care and treatment of the mentally ill in the United States, provides us with an interesting comparison. During a hundred-year period beginning about 1820, the Temperance movement changed to an abstinence movement and then to an antidrinking movement which, combined with other forces, resulted in Prohibition. The thrust of this movement came from the clergy and lay persons with religious motives. The movement taught that alcohol was an evil thing in itself, characterized by the phrase "demon rum."

During this same period, profound changes occurred in the field of mental health. Mentally ill persons held in jails were released and placed in hospitals. No longer were these persons considered possessed of the devil and the sole cure that of the minister or priest. In fact, the medical community began treating mental illness with the respect accorded any other natural phenomenon. Unfortunately, this did not include the alcoholic, who was still jailed, condemned, and classified as a sinner rather than a sick person. During that period in which the doctor took the demonic concept out of mental illness, the clergyman was instilling it in alcohol and those who used it. The influence of this attitude is still alive, although the formal movement has largely disappeared. Its impact is still strong in some branches of the church and unconsciously has strong influence in our whole society.

The clergyman's own attitude is inevitably shaped by the experience and conditioning of his life. When discussing the use of alcohol, clergymen may exhibit more prejudice than knowledge. It is imperative that the clergy understand the disease concept of alcoholism, for the use of alcohol alone does not cause

* Lecture given at Rutgers Summer School of Alcohol Studies, and later published in the *Quarterly Journal of Alcohol Studies*.

alcoholism. If this were true, the alcoholism rate would be ten or fifteen times greater. Repeated, excessive use of alcohol bringing suffering to self, family, and society indicates the existence of alcoholism, not its cause. Effective treatment and rehabilitation begin with an understanding of the illness and acceptance of the alcoholic as a sick person—physically, emotionally, and socially.

The disease concept of alcoholism with repeated drunkenness as a gross symptom enables a clergyman to abandon the idea that alcohol is evil and must be attacked. Sobriety is the goal and may be achieved by abstinence or the temperate use of alcohol. Both positions come within the framework of the Judaeo-Christian ethic. It is unfair to train a child that alcohol is evil and send him into a drinking society armed only with the admonition that it is wrong to drink. It is also very harmful to be permissive toward the use of alcohol without establishing limits and cultural norms. The clergyman in a church which is permissive toward the use of alcohol desperately needs the concept of alcoholism as an illness. Any repetition of drunkenness is the first symptom of alcoholism and a manifestation of mental or social pathology, or both. This knowledge permits the clergyman to promote firm discipline toward excessive drinking without involving sin. Drunkenness is a venial sin, but it is far more effective, especially with younger persons, to approach drunkenness as a gross manifestation of inadequacy and emotional illness instead of as something "bad."

Alcohol is addictive to ten percent or less of the users in our nation. Although the percentage is low compared with heroin, morphine, and other drugs, the total number of alcoholics is about twenty times greater than the number addicted to all other drugs. The antidrinking forces are right in pointing to the tremendous damage done by users of alcohol, but there is no evidence that this position solves the problem. In fact, it adds to the problem by attempting to solve it in a hostile and condemning way. The most basic action the clergy could take in preventing and reducing the incidence of alcoholism by effective recovery is to agree that sobriety is the goal and the norm. Sobriety may be achieved by abstinence or by temperate use of alcohol.

It is impossible to overemphasize the importance of proper moral, social, and cultural attitudes toward the use of alcohol. Families or groups which fanatically oppose any use of alcohol may reduce the number of drinkers, but their attitude often results in increasing the percentage in the group who become alcoholics. On the other hand, permissiveness toward drunkenness increases the incidence of alcoholism, and clergymen who are permissive rarely present the requirements of true temperance for fear of offending their flocks. The result: the United States is a culture with enormous hostility and guilt toward the use of alcohol while being extremely tolerant of excessive use. This ambivalence produces extremely high rates of alcoholism. Nothing could help the families of alcoholics more than an open realignment of clergy and churches by placing the use of alcohol in proper perspective. The use of alcohol produces enormous problems. Understanding alcoholism as a total illness—physical, mental, social, and spiritual—is the common ground on which the antidrinking and overly permissive conflict can be resolved.

There is another benefit for the clergyman who understands alcoholism. He will learn so much about the basic nature of human problems and social relations that it will make him far more effective as a pastor and a preacher.

Accepting the disease concept of alcoholism is a prerequisite to helping as a pastor. Alcohol is not an evil thing which makes the alcoholic a very evil person, nor is alcohol a good thing which the alcoholic is overusing. Alcoholism is a profound and complex illness which destroys the physical, mental, social, and spiritual health of the drinker and has the capacity to destroy the family as well as the alcoholic. The pastor must intervene in a creative fashion or he will have abandoned such families to a tragic fate.

## ALCOHOLISM AS SOCIAL DISORDER

The next basic step in effective pastoral care is understanding alcoholism as a social disorder. The disease concept is only the beginning. The finest medical care, if administered outside a socially constructed framework of recovery, can and usually does make the illness chronic. Persons who are obviously suffering from the illness of alcoholism enter detoxification hospitals on a repeated basis, not just three or four times but, in some instances, twenty-five to one hundred times. The finest medical care does not ensure recovery; in fact, if not administered as part of an overall framework of recovery, it perpetuates the illness.

A simple and direct means of presenting alcoholism as a social disorder is to think of it as a three-act play which might be called a Merry-Go-Round of Denial. It brings on stage the principal characters involved in the illness and the effect of their actions in the overall course of events. The classical medical approach—locate the pathology, give it a proper diagnosis, and treat it—will not work with alcoholism. This method concentrates on treatment of the drinker. Recovery begins when those persons around the alcoholic begin to change their roles.

Alcoholism is a tragic drama played out in three acts with at least four actors involved, although at times one person may play more than one role. Alcoholism cannot appear in isolation, progress in isolation, or sustain itself in isolation. One person cannot become an alcoholic without the help of others. One person drinks in a pathological fashion, others react, and the drinker responds to the action and drinks again. This sets up a merry-go-round of denial and counterdenial, a spiral of social disorder we term alcoholism. To understand the illness we must observe carefully the roles of all those in the drama.

In the first act the alcoholic is the subject and all others the objects of his action. Without attempting to describe the variety of characteristics, we see a few which appear most frequently. He comes from any walk of life. Usually he is a male between the ages of thirty and fifty-five, intelligent, successful in some field, with great self-idealization. Usually he is very sensitive, lonely, and tense. He is also extremely dependent but denies his dependency. This denial mechanism is the key to the drama—a Merry-Go-Round of Denial.

The alcoholic learns from chance or by experimentation that alcohol has profound effects which initially are psychologically beneficial. It dissolves all anxieties, reduces all tensions, removes loneliness, and solves all problems for the time being. If any situation becomes too unpleasant or unbearable, there is the conscious or unconscious knowledge that a few drinks will bring relief instantly. It is his psychological blessing and, regardless of the many curses it brings, alcohol becomes the most important thing in his life because of the enormous, immediate benefits.

In Act One the play opens with the alcoholic asserting his independence in many ways, especially to his family and in particular, his wife or mother. Communication is very difficult and becomes more so as the illness progresses. Conversations become more like one-way streets than exchanges of ideas. Words are the vehicle of denial and cannot be understood apart from the language of alcoholism, a jargon with special meaning in the light of what the alcoholic does or others do in the play. This is why it is so important to see the entire drama.

To observe or converse with the alcoholic alone, to read a clinical evaluation, or to listen to the tales of woe of the family is only a small part of the drama. The title of the play and the key word in the entire illness is *denial* for there is constant contradiction of what is happening and what is being said by all the actors.

At some point in the first act a problem arises creating a "need" for the alcoholic to drink. He does not drink in a normal way. He sneaks or gulps it at a rapid rate and in large amounts, usually concealing from his family the amount he consumes. This is the first aspect of denial. If he were not conscious of overdrinking and not aware of its meaning, he would do it openly. The attempt to conceal excessive drinking is the first symptom of alcoholism. Repeated concealment indicates the tremendous importance of the psychological effects and the inability to stop after one or two drinks.

After a few drinks we witness a profound change in the attitude of most alcoholics. Alcohol gives him a sense of security, well-being, and self-sufficiency. It puts him on top of the world and strengthens his sense of omnipotence. He is now right and others wrong, especially if anyone voices objection to his drinking. He may also exhibit irrationality, irresponsibility, antisocial behavior, and at times, deviate or even criminal behavior—of which driving under the influence is a clear example. If drinking continues long enough the alcoholic creates a crisis, and gets into trouble of some kind. This can be done in an infinite variety of ways, but the movement of the first act follows a basic pattern. A dependent person acts in a very independent fashion, and the consequences of drinking put him in a condition of helplessness or dependence upon others. When he gets into trouble he seems incapable of getting out of it; his primary skill seems to be in getting others to remove or conceal the consequences of his drinking. Alcohol, which initially gave him a very real sense of success, now strips him of his costume of independence, removes the mask of omnipotence, and we see him as a dependent child.

In the second act, three persons come on the scene. The first is one who might be called the Enabler, a guilt-laden Mr. Clean who thinks of himself as a savior of men. His anxiety will not let him endure the predicament of his friend the alcoholic. He sets up a "rescue mission" to save the alcoholic from the immediate crisis and relieve the unbearable tension created by the situation. In reality this person is meeting his own need rather than that of the alcoholic. As a general rule, the Enabler is played by a male outside the family but may at times be a member of the family; and occasionally this role is played by a woman.

Professionally this role is played by clergymen, doctors, lawyers, and social workers, the so-called helping professions. Although some persons working in these professions understand alcoholism, the majority have not had any training or instruction in the nature of the disease and, therefore, play the role of Enabler to perfection. This is natural because the alcoholic turns to these persons with specific needs which are glaring and immediate. Each of these professional groups is trained to meet the needs of individuals and may get caught in the trap of the rescue mission. The doctor, lawyer, and social worker may not respond to the immediate need; but the clergyman may be so thrilled that the alcoholic at long last has turned to him for help that he rushes immediately to his aid, reduces the crisis, and thereby removes the very force which might propel the alcoholic into a recovery program if a different approach were used. Each time the alcoholic is rescued he is denied the chance to learn by correcting his own mistakes; he is conditioned to believe that there will always be a protector who will come to his rescue.

These men, in time, tell the alcoholic they will never again rescue him; but they always have, and the alcoholic believes they always will. Rescue operations are just as compulsive as drinking; and the clergyman, by nature of his training, is more vulnerable to this reaction than any other professional person.

The basic difficulty here is that the clergyman thinks of himself as playing the role of the Good Samaritan, while actually the alcoholic's plight is that of the Prodigal Son. The role of Father of the Prodigal is entirely different and must be played accordingly.

The second character in this act might be called the Victim, the person who gets the job done if the alcoholic is absent or unable to work because of a hangover. He is the employer, the foreman, or supervisor, the commanding officer in military life, or possibly a business partner, professional colleague, or at times an employee. Most men have been at the same job for years and superiors as well as fellow workers are friends who save the job for the alcoholic in much the same way as the Enabler saves the alcoholic from a crisis. When drinking begins to interfere with work performance, repeated overprotection becomes a normal part of the drama. Industrial programs which rehabilitate the alcoholic offer the alcoholic a structured program of recovery while refusing to be victimized. A very high rate of recovery is achieved by industrial programs by the simple reversal of roles in this one primary area of the alcoholic's life. Without such programs the boss and the alcoholic go through the denial process again and again with termination for the alcoholic occurring somewhere in the late thirties or early forties.

The third character in the second act, with whom the clergyman may have far more association, is the wife or mother of the alcoholic. She is the center of the home in which he lives. Most frequently she is the wife, and she has been playing a role longer than the Enabler or Victim because gross symptoms of alcoholism appear in the home several years before they are visible to society. This actor may be called the Provoked One. She is provoked by repeated drinking episodes, but she holds the family together. In turn she controls, coerces, adjusts, never gives up, never lets go, but never forgets. The alcoholic anticipates instant forgiveness from the wife, and she must never fail him. His attitude is one of complete independence (his basic denial mechanism), and she must do exactly what he tells her.

The wife is constantly adjusting to every crisis produced by drinking and compensates for everything that goes wrong within the home and marriage. In addition to the natural role of wife, housekeeper, and, possibly, partial wage earner, she becomes nurse, doctor, and counselor—roles she cannot play without injury to herself and to her husband. Yet everything in our society trains women to play this role. If she did not play it, she would be going against what society thinks her role should be. No matter what the alcoholic does he ends up "at home," for this is where everyone goes when there is no other place to go.

Act Two is now played out in full. The alcoholic in his helpless condition has been rescued, supported on the job, and protected as a member of the family. This reclothes him with a costume of responsibility and freedom; but in effect it has increased his dependency because the consequences of his drinking were removed by others. Others suffered while permitting the alcoholic to avoid the painful consequences of his drinking. This allows drinking to become a very real problem-solving device.

Act Three begins in much the same fashion as Act One but a new dimension has been added. The need for denial has increased and must be immediate, louder, and stronger. The alcoholic denies that he has a drinking problem, denies that anyone helped him, denies that his job or business is in jeopardy, and insists that he is the best or the most skilled in his field. Above all he denies that he has caused his family any problems; in fact, he blames the family for all the fuss, nagging, and trouble. He insists that his wife is crazy, that she needs to see a psychiatrist, and that if it were not for her he would not drink so much. In about two-thirds of the cases the husband accuses his wife of infidelity, knowing all the time it is not true. This is but another vicious denial mechanism: focusing on an imaginary wrong on the part of his wife which, if true, would be far worse than his drinking.

Some alcoholics achieve the same denial by stony silence and absolute refusal to discuss anything related to the drinking episode, or they threaten to get drunk again if previous drinking is mentioned. Others may admit their guilt and worthlessness in such a way as to force the family to reassure them that all is forgiven and they are all right. Others permit the family to rehash every event of the most recent and previous drinking episodes, which are never forgotten by either the alcoholic or the Provoked One. There is never true repentance and forgiveness; therefore, guilt and hostility build up with time and repeated episodes.

Actually, the alcoholic knows the truth which he so vocally denies. He is aware of his drunkenness and resulting failure. His guilt and remorse become acute. Above all, the memory of his utter dependence at the end of the first act is more than humiliating, it is unbearable for one who suffers from a neurosis of omnipotence.

The family adjusts to whatever is the norm when the alcoholic is not drinking. In addition to his denial, others give similar assurances that they will never again act in the same way. The Enabler will never again come to the rescue, the Victim will not tolerate another drinking episode, and the Provoked One assures her husband that she cannot continue to live under these conditions.

This entire verbalization of the situation is in stark contrast to reality. The Enabler, the Victim, and the Provoked One have said this before to no avail. The end result is to increase the alcoholic's sense of guilt and failure, challenge his sense of omnipotence, and add to the reservoir of tension and loneliness. If this psychic pain becomes unbearable, especially with the aid of other members of the cast, there is one and only one certain means of reducing the pain, overcoming the sense of guilt, and achieving a very real sense of worth and value.

If Act Two is played out as described above, it is inevitable that at some point in Act Three the alcoholic will drink again, for this has become the one certain means of relieving pain and achieving a sense of well-being. The hope of immediate comfort far outweighs the memory of the inevitable result. In the back of his mind he hopes that this time he can control his drinking while gaining the maximum benefits as he once did. So the inevitable occurs in Act Three—the alcoholic begins to drink.

When he takes a drink, the play does not come to an end. The audience has the feeling that it is watching a continuous movie rather than a play, for the play has suddenly returned to the first act. If the audience remains seated long enough, all three acts will be played out again in almost identical fashion; and, at the end of Act Three, the alcoholic will drink again. The play continues to run, year after year. The characters get older, but there is little change in the script or the action.

If the first two acts are played as described, Act Three is sure to follow. Act Two is the only act in which the tragic drama of alcoholism can be changed. Act Two is the only one in which recovery can be initiated by persons other than the alcoholic. In Act Two the alcoholic is the recipient of the action and not the initiator of whatever happens. In this act alone there is the real potential to break the tragic cycle of denial.

## THE RECOVERY PROCESS

This simple fact of where recovery begins is the most important thing a clergyman must learn if he is to be effective in helping the alcoholic and his family. In addition to learning the nature of alcoholism it is imperative that the pastor learn to play the proper role and, above all, avoid the role of the Enabler. It is impossible to overstress this point. If the clergyman approaches alcoholism in the role of an Enabler, he not only contributes to perpetuating the illness but restrains the family from taking action which might break the cycle of denial. His attitude and basic philosophy of recovery is far more important than anything he does for the alcoholic. Unless he learns the nature of the drama, he is more likely to harm than help the alcoholic and the family.

There is no one way to learn how to cope with actual cases in a parish. If possible, the pastor should consult the nearest branch of the National Council on Alcoholism for study materials and request help in getting training at the local level through workshops, conferences, and other courses of study. If there is no local council nearby, there is a state alcoholism program of some kind, which may be under the sponsorship of the department of mental health. Special short-term training programs are conducted during the summer months; other courses run for one or two weeks. A year or two later, attending the Summer School of Alcohol Studies at Rutgers would be most beneficial.

For some clergymen alcoholism courses may not be feasible. For those who wish to learn at home, there is a very simple and most effective method. Seek out and attend regularly Al-Anon and Alcoholics Anonymous meetings. Each group has pamphlets and other literature which they will gladly give to the clergyman. Each has published books which may be borrowed for study or ordered for continued study. *Al-Anon Faces Alcoholism* is excellent in helping understand family approaches to alcoholism. *Alcoholics Anonymous,* sometimes called the "Big Book," is still the classic public publication by A.A. The local library should have a copy of the Reverend Howard J. Clinebell's excellent book, *Understanding and Counseling the Alcoholic.* It is a basic text for any pastor. *Alcoholism, a Guide for the Clergy* is a forty-page manual published by the National Council on Alcoholism containing some basic ideas and facts on alcoholism. In addition to this list of three books and one manual there are many excellent textbooks which should be selected according to special needs.

Regardless of background reading, the pastor needs personal contact with alcoholism itself; and there is no better way to gain laboratory experience than attending meetings of Al-Anon and Alcoholics Anonymous. This has a twofold advantage. First, he will learn what alcoholism is. Second, he will establish friendships with persons to whom he can make direct referrals for long-term supportive help. There is one danger in such a program; the clergyman must avoid becoming an alcoholism expert who tries to take on the alcoholism problems of his community unless he is willing to abandon his parish responsibilities, his family, or both. The enormity of the problem is such that a clergyman must limit himself in this area. There should be enough alcoholism in his own church to keep him busy for several years.

Another point should be clarified. In A.A. one hears that an alcoholic cannot be helped until he wants help. For the group this is true. Until the alcoholic comes to the group and participates with sincerity, humility, and regular attendance, A.A. cannot help the person. This must not be taken to mean that an alcoholic cannot be helped until he wants help and therefore we can do nothing until this occurs. The reactions of key persons in the life of the alcoholic determine whether he will receive help in order to recover or is able to engage in a denial process which keeps the merry-go-round going. If we play out the drama in a way that keeps the merry-go-round going, eight or nine out of ten alcoholics will die without effecting a recovery. We cannot demand or force the alcoholic into a recovery program; but, if we (family, professionals, and employer) make sufficient changes in our approach and reactions, there is every reason to anticipate recovery except in a minority of very unusual cases. The role played by key persons in the life of the alcoholic is far more important than all other factors combined. Therefore, these persons initially need knowledge, insight, and understanding before any process of recovery can be anticipated. Only as these persons change is there any real probability that the alcoholic will recover.

Now for the meat of the problem of recovery. Changing our attitudes and approach does not mean that we plan to send all our alcoholics and their families for clinical or inservice treatment and then anticipate that they will follow up with outpatient care and long-term membership in A.A. and Al-Anon. State treatment facilities are geared to treat one to five percent of the alcoholic population. The centers and hospitals are located at some distance from the alcoholic's home and treat the alcoholic in isolation, far from family and others who are so important in the recovery process. Few alcoholics can spare the time and loss of income involved in such a program. Many admitted to such facilities have lost jobs, families, or both, or are committed by the family for relief at home as well as therapy for the patient. Few alcoholics get into such facilities; but, when they do, it should be for detoxification (if necessary) diagnosis, and evaluation. In addition, the nature of the illness should be explained to the alcoholic, and a posthospital program of recovery which includes the family should be instituted. The hospital cannot go beyond the treatment period.

Recovery begins when the alcoholic returns to his home and

the job. By their actions at this point, family and friends force him to return to drinking or support and participate the program of recovery.

Pouring tax money into large state institutions might be interpreted as a corporate escape from the responsibility of becoming involved in the recovery process. Such programs are expensive and ineffectual because they remove the alcoholic from the community in which he has learned to solve his problems by drinking. They administer some type of therapy and return the alcoholic to an unchanged home, job, and community. Under these conditions, most alcoholics relapse. The clergyman who admits a church member into such a facility should first involve the family in their own program of therapy and change. If this happens, it may resolve the alcoholism problem without the need for out-of-town, inpatient care which in itself shows the inadequacy of the local community as a recovery team. Because a church in a very real sense is a community, the clergyman should examine very carefully why the alcoholic should be removed from the interaction of those persons upon whom final recovery so desperately depends. It is always much easier to ship a person to a treatment facility than become involved in his recovery process. It is also a paradox that expensive treatment in a state hospital is easily available for indigent persons while simple, inexpensive forms of local treatment may be totally unavailable.

Looking at the overall picture, a clergyman must face one basic fact. He must lead the family, and ultimately the alcoholic, into a local recovery program and help them stay in the program, or there is little chance that any effort will be more than a series of relapses. As a pastor he does not refer every problem to an expert in counseling but prepares himself to meet the majority of these problems himself. However, in alcoholism a group experience is virtually mandatory in the recovery process. The minister cannot carry the whole family and cannot send the majority of alcoholics for long-term, inpatient treatment. Therefore, he must set up a plan which will suit the needs of each family.

He should have no hesitancy in defining the nature of the problem when he discovers it, whether it be the husband, wife, or adult son or daughter living with a parent. If the alcoholic refuses to begin a program of recovery, then the pastor should explain the nature of the illness to the other primary members of the family and tell them what they may do to lead the alcoholic with their participation into a recovery program. Often what the family is actually doing must be stopped before recovery can occur. Families who believe they have done everything possible to help the alcoholic have in reality perpetuated and contributed to the illness. Here the clergyman must be prepared to break with our present cultural attitude toward alcoholism as it relates to marriage. Not only must he understand the dynamics which perpetuate the illness, he must be prepared to help the family break their part of the cycle without guilt and without fear of censure from family and friends. The clergyman is frequently the only person who can help the family understand that discipline is a part of love and that accepting injustice on a repeated basis destroys love and marriage. If the family is unwilling to break the dependency role and wean the alcoholic from their contribution to alcoholism, he must be prepared to concentrate on the family and spell out in clear, concise terms what changes must be made. He must show them that continuing the present action is destructive.

An alcoholic seeking professional help for the first time revealed that he had "drunk up" his wife and children, his job and home, and was now living with his parents who provided room, board, clothing, and spending money. He stated that he ate three meals a day at his mother's table and resented every bite he placed in his mouth. It was suggested that if he stopped drinking, went to work, and bought his own food, it would taste good. He replied that he knew this better than the counselor but then related what he would do. That afternoon he would go to a beer joint, drink with cronies like himself, and convince himself that the next day he would stop drinking and start looking for a job. He then added the key statement of the interview. "Tomorrow I will do the same thing because I know Mama will have supper on the table at 6:30." Despite his condition of advanced cirrhosis, he continued to drink and died without reaching forty. The family paid for all expenses while he rode the merry-go-round to his untimely death.

A frequent dilemma for the clergyman occurs when the wife decides she cannot continue to live with her alcoholic husband or permit him to continue living in the home because of the destructiveness of the situation. Alcoholism rarely runs its course without some form of separation of husband and wife; and, if not checked in time, it separates the couple by death ten to twenty years before normal life expectancy.

The most basic rule in dealing with matters of separation, as in other aspects involving alcoholism, is to give the couple basic information and let them make their choices. Neither advise separation nor attempt to prevent it, but do try to interpret the meaning of it and help the family understand what is happening if it occurs. Running back to mother one day and home the next is not separation, whether the running be done by the alcoholic or the spouse. Clergymen who browbeat wives into taking husbands back without using this condition as a means of getting the husband into a recovery program make a story in itself; and this is one of the primary acts in which a clergyman becomes the Enabler in the alcoholism crisis. Separation may result in insight and changes on the part of both husband and wife which could not occur without it.

Drinking must stop completely and the alcoholic enter into a genuine recovery program if he is to recover—with or without his wife. If the wife is seeking help for herself and is achieving some degree of emotional maturity, she may decide to give her husband a choice of accepting some type of recovery program as his share of the responsibility in recovery. When this occurs, the clergyman must not barge in and abort the normal interaction of events but use it as a means of motivating the alcoholic to accept the need for help.

Most separations end in reconciliation which fails, not because separation was not beneficial for both parties, but because the terms of reconciliation did not include a recovery program for both parties. Many wives return when the husband is sober and promises continued sobriety but refuses to admit the need for help, without which he cannot remain sober. Sooner or later the husband drinks again and the wife feels her agony of separation was all in vain. Both parties need pastoral care during separation so each understands under what conditions reconciliation may be attempted. The clergyman cannot assure either of what the other will do, but must constantly attempt to interpret to each what is happening and how it fits into the pattern and syndrome of the illness—alcoholism.

It is possible for a wife to offer her husband the alternative of seeking help or consider separation as a choice she must make before her love is completely destroyed. A wife is justified in facing the fact that remaining in an unchanged situation is producing irreparable damage to herself and the children and will destroy the marriage eventually. The wife of an alcoholic is about as normal as any wife and faces separation only as a last resort. A wife who is adequately informed and becomes involved in any reasonable therapy program will rarely be wrong in making choices. This includes considering separation or offering it as an alternative to her husband if he refuses to give up the denial process and accept the help he so desperately needs.

One article cannot spell out all a pastor needs to know in fulfilling his role in helping alcoholics to recovery. Printed materials are readily available and should be obtained from a reliable source, preferably a local or state alcoholism group. If not, the National Council on Alcoholism, 2 Park Avenue, New York, New York 10016, may be contacted directly; but it is far better to reach the nearest program where continued liaison may be maintained. Nothing helps more than becoming actively involved in an existing program such as A.A., Al-Anon, or sitting in with a group engaged in therapy under professional direction. Some treatment centers offer both short-term and long-term inservice training for clergymen.

Perhaps the most basic fact in determining whether or not a clergyman will be successful in helping alcoholics and their families is the ability of the pastor to change himself. The traditional approach of most clergymen today fails not only for lack of understanding of the problem but because the accumulated attitudes and teachings of those who have gone before him. He will have culture and tradition to overcome, whether he be in an anti-drinking or permissive church, for neither type has done much to prevent alcoholism nor help in the recovery process.

In closing, there is one universal barrier in helping the alcoholic or his family—the assumption that there is such a thing as a normal volition, that we all know what it is, and that we possess it. This is of more than clinical importance in pastoral care. The ultimate result of such a presumption separates us from and makes us feel superior to others with human problems, especially the mentally ill, alcoholics, and members of their families who react with emotional distress. The result is that those who so desperately need our help are cut off by the presumption of our assumed normalcy and superiority. In this light, it is we as pastors who fail the alcoholic and the family. The clergy and the churches have failed to give our culture in the United States an attitude toward alcohol and its use which would prevent our extremely high rate of alcoholism.

The role of the minister in the field of alcoholism is multiple. The first is that of changing cultural and social attitudes toward the use of alcohol. Understanding alcoholism as an illness permits the abstaining or permissive clergyman to focus on the real problem while maintaining mutual respect for each other's position as a drinker or a nondrinker.

Second, it is imperative that the clergyman provide information, insight, and understanding of the problem and lead the family and the alcoholic to the sources of help best suited to their needs. As long-term therapy is essential in recovery, he should make every effort to keep all parties in the program, even if it requires years of participation. The most difficult task here is keeping the spouse of the alcoholic in her own program for a sufficient length of time for it to be effective or encouraging her to continue despite the husband's objections or threats, especially if he continues to drink.

Finally, in the field of alcoholism he must not play the role of the Good Samaritan and therefore continue to be an Enabler. His role is to hold out to the family the faith of the father in the parable of the Prodigal Son. This faith permitted the son to choose for himself and to suffer the full consequences of his choice without intervention. Trust and refusal to intervene permitted the son to come to himself. When the son chose to come home in humility the father gave him dignity by treating him as a son. This is the Faith which heals.

# Alcoholism and the work world: prevention in a new light

## HARRISON TRICE, Ph.D.

The work world holds great potential for the treatment of alcoholics, according to Harrison Trice of the School of Industrial Relations at Cornell University. Dr. Trice's first interest in alcoholism began at Ann Arbor, Michigan, when he spent a summer researching the disease. His findings attracted the attention of the group he was studying, Alcoholics Anonymous, and he was invited to become a trustee of the A.A. General Service Board. His work at Cornell has resulted in a revision of many industrial approaches to alcoholism to encompass all the remedial disciplines now available to intervene and treat alcoholics.


## INTRODUCTION

Compared with a decade ago in the United States, the job aspects of alcoholism today receive far more attention. Both government and voluntary programs encourage management and labor to develop policies and programs aimed at treating and preventing this difficult health problem. The number of governmental and private organizations sponsoring such programs has risen significantly in the past ten years, together with major publicity in such publications as *Fortune, Look, Business Week,* and *The Wall Street Journal.* The U.S. Federal government, the largest employer in the country, has begun serious work toward a specific policy and program for its employees who may suffer from the disorder. Various labor unions, despite their understandable fear of such programs as anti-union in character, are showing a willingness to deal openly with the malady.

Despite these advances, the relationship between alcoholism and the job receives relatively little attention in the research literature. The potentials present in the work world to do something truly effective about alcoholism continue to be overshadowed by outmoded efforts centered in social work, and colored by police court obsessions that reflect the "skid-row" image of alcoholism in American society.

This article aims, first, at reviewing in summary form the objective, data-based information available about alcoholism and the job. It also intends to set forth reasons why a much larger proportion of the effort to deal with alcohol pathologies should be devoted toward stimulating management and labor to constructive action. It will then discuss preventive potential in the work world and compare this with other models of prevention.

Problem drinking and alcoholism will be defined in a simple direct manner compatible with the industrial environment, not clinically oriented, nor resting on a medical model of disease. Rather it is behavioral, centering around the major institutions of family and job, in which all persons experience a series of *expectations* that cluster into a *role*. Failure to perform such role expectations constitutes a behavioral deviation. Alcoholism, from the standpoint of the work world, is accepted as repeated disruption of job performance due to the consumption of alcohol which impairs the expected role.

## IMPACT OF ALCOHOLISM ON WORK LIFE

What good reasons are there that the work world should be concerned about alcoholism? Are these reasons more cogent than for other behavioral disorders, such as psychoneuroses and psychoses?

First, the age and sex concentration intensifies alcoholism as a personnel problem. Over and over, studies show alcoholism concentrated in the mature years of the forties and early fifties. Were it spread evenly over the age groups, its impact on work situations would be lessened. As it is, it strikes when productive years are at their zenith, when experience and judgment have matured, but when there is still energy for sustained contributions to their organizations.

Despite much popular clamor to the contrary, it remains chiefly a male disorder, thus affecting the male "breadwinner" category. Discounting the probable increase in female alcoholism in recent years, the change in the sex ratio has not been great enough to alter the basic concentration in the male category, probably still about 5 to 1 in the United States.

Alcoholics experience a high amount of family disruption that produce such simple but frustrating employer problems as garnishments, excessive grievances from agonized wives seeking help, and often divorces. These problems occur rather evenly across all types of industry, and are not concentrated unduly in certain types of occupation, such as bartending or advertising, as is popularly supposed. Alcoholics are more likely to be recognized in lower status occupations, but the distribution apparently remains much the same throughout all types of work.

Although subsequent research may alter this point, employers and unions seem to share a common problem in the drinking employee throughout the whole scale of the industrial complex. This stands in sharp contrast to the concentration of schizophrenia in lowest-class occupations, and the tendency for certain other psychoses to develop among upper-middle-class families. Alcoholism, by contrast, will appear among professional, managerial, and white collar employees in proportions roughly similar to those in blue collar and operative jobs. Industry runs as substantial a risk of losing its greater investment in the managerial and professional persons through alcohol as it does of losing its less valued employees in the lower ranks.

The typical problem drinker continues to work at a full-time job during most of his developing alcoholism, with about 3 percent of a normal work force probably being affected. Among higher status employees, because of their lower visibility, skillful cover-up, and freedom from supervision, this figure should be increased to perhaps 5 percent. In addition, these percentages will fluctuate with age, sex, ethnic makeup, and locality. A small rural plant hiring mostly Italian women in their early twenties will experience a lower percentage; while a company employing mostly Irish males of forty to sixty, and located in a metropolitan complex, could reach 8 or 9 percent.

## SPECIFIC JOB BEHAVIORS

Quality and quantity of work performance decline sharply as alcoholism progresses.[1] One study comparing the work performance of employees who had been diagnosed alcoholic, psychoneurotic, and psychotic showed the alcoholic employee to be the most impaired over a three-year period. Another study indicates that the *manner* in which the work efficiency declined varied with the occupational type. Higher status employees, such as professionals and managers, tended to appear consistently on the job, but performed poorly even though present. Lower status employees, in contrast, engaged in much stay-away absenteeism, but did a substantial day's work when on the job.

Poor work and absenteeism constitute two of the main impacts of the problem drinker on his performance. On-the-job accidents and turnover appear to be less costly for employers. Apart from the general morale effect, which is intangible but quite real, alcoholics have three to four times the off-the-job accident rates of non-alcoholics. There is some evidence to suggest that other behavioral disorders also show high rates, but not in as chronic a pattern, which indicates that the amount of sick pay due to absenteeism is higher for alcoholics than for other emotional disturbances.[2]

Motivated by a sense of duty, professional and managerial level deviant drinkers tend to go to work in spite of the ill effects of deviant drinking, contrasting to the alcoholics in the lower status occupations who tend to stay away from work altogether. The higher level employee seems to rationalize his drinking by proving he can continue to work, although in fact his work suffers, and a form of on-the-job absenteeism occurs as his efficiency declines. He can continue unchallenged for longer periods of time because of his freedom from supervision, which makes the lower level alcoholic more subject to discovery, which in turn leads him to a higher frequency of stay-away absentceism.

On-the-job accidents are not significantly characteristic of the alcoholic employee. Studies of both A.A. members who were exposed to accidents while at work, and of accident records kept by specific companies, deny the popular notion that the alcoholic is accident prone. Five factors seem to account for this finding:

First, the developing alcoholic becomes extra cautious, thereby reducing both his effectiveness and his risk of accident. Second, the extra caution which helps conceal his problem operates especially when his physical condition is at its lowest. Third, when accident risk runs high, the tendency is to resort to absenteeism, which leads to accidents off the job, rather than at work. Fourth, alcoholics work out a routine for controlling the effects of alcohol, which, since most jobs are of repetitious character, again serves to reduce accidents. Finally, the cooperation of fellow workers and supervisors helps to protect a drinker from accident exposure.

According to the available evidence, problem drinkers do not show an unusual turnover rate. Following the same pattern as non-alcoholics, they change jobs frequently in the lower status occupations, but remain relatively longer in professional and managerial positions. The job-hopper stereotype of the alcoholic probably derives from his equation with the skid-row image, which is generally untrue, but more especially false in the high status categories.

Also contrary to popular belief, the supervisor will scldom cover up for the alcoholic, but in fact usually vacillates in his attitude. Self cover-up predominates for the alcoholic, although he is frequently aided by work associates, subordinates, and more occasionally the supervisor. About 20 percent experience little or no cover-up.

Here again occupational status governs, with more help being offered to the higher ranks. Lower status workers often receive no aid from either supervisors or fellow workers. Camouflage efforts in whatever rank are only temporarily successful, with the possible exception of the highest positions, where freedom from visibility and supervision conceals the problem for much of the alcoholism process. In general, cover-up is fragile at best; and the alcoholic moving into the well-developed stages is anything but hidden from his associates, union stewards, or supervisors.

The morale effect of the alcoholic upon these people gives cause for concern to union and management. Fellow workers, picking up part of the alcoholic's work, become disgusted and concerned; and supervisors, faced with unpredictability and accident risk, must allot extra time to the problem. The union shop steward must cope with grievances which are likely to embarrass the union.

When an alcoholic is found in a managerial or professional position, he clearly affects the general morale around him with poor performance in a responsible position; and if lost through alcoholism deprives his organization of a costly investment through training, experience, and special knowledge.

## THE SUPERVISOR ON THE "SEESAW"

The immediate boss of the developing alcoholic is deeply disturbed by the need to work in direct contact with him. As one supervisor reported painfully, "If I had two like him in this group of machinists, I'd apply for early retirement."

Even though we have only two studies of supervisor reaction to the problem drinker, they support this "big headache" conclusion.[3] In one large utility, supervisors were asked to report their experience with alcoholic employees, and at the same time with others who were neurotic and psychotic. Alcoholics were rated clearly the greater problem, including job performance for up to three years previous to the reports.

At the same time that these supervisors were seeing the alcoholics as problems, they were hesitant to take action about them. Such reluctance, although seeming inconsistent, does reflect the general cultural ambivalence about alcohol in America; and the supervisor, even while consistently labeling the alcoholics as deviants, vacillated between "doing something" and "taking it." In contrast, bosses of neurotics and psychotics preferred to act with decision.

A cluster of "blocking" and "pushing" forces play on the alcoholic's supervisor, causing him to seesaw back and forth between utilizing the company medical program and facilities, or "normalizing" the problem by treating it as part of the everyday work of a supervisor.

Among prominent "pushes" was the necessity for closer supervision due to his unpredictability on the job, or his absence from it. Another was the bad effect of the alcoholic on his fellow workers. Finally, the alcoholic did not produce his share of the work, which reflected on the supervisor's record.

Simultaneously, various "blocking" forces were acting against some of these pressures. Normally the supervisor preferred to handle problems himself, rather than send them over to "Personnel" or "Medical," which reflected on his ability to cope, and also often resulted in some form of separation from an employee difficult to replace. Frequently, the supervisor had come up through the ranks with the alcoholic, knew him and his family personally, and preferred to give him a chance to "snap out of it," before taking final action. Finally, the supervisor ran some risk of not being supported "upstairs" in his actions and of getting "mixed up" with the union. Such forces, acting against the pushes, one supervisor called "being torn both ways, but doing nothing."

The desire of the supervisor to handle his own problems finds outlet in the following verbatim statements: "A supervisor should help out and understand his men, rather than turn them over to someone else," and "I do my duty as a boss helping him overcome his problem before turning to formalities." From these it may be seen that the supervisor uses such problems to sustain and enhance his own role, rather than relinquish authority to personnel officers and industrial engineers. Likewise, he communicates only reluctantly across formal lines with staff groups such as "Personnel" and "Medical," tending to keep his problems "among the boys," a sentiment generally shared by his subordinates, who prefer trouble to interference from higher up.

Supervisors seem unwilling to connect poor work performance with deviant drinking when dealing with white collar employees[4] although they do make this connection with lower status workers. This underscores not only the potency of the "skid-row" image, but also indicates that supervisors are less prone to recognize problem drinking among members of their own class. This study concludes[5] also that the supervisor tends to be less tolerant of the white collar drinker than of those of lower status.

## EARLIER RECOGNITION
## OF THE DEVIANT DRINKER

Early recognition of problem drinking could be made by the supervisor, but it is very difficult for him to think in such terms, as he normally wishes to avoid forcing a crisis. Recognition of trouble can be faster on the job than in the home, because of lesser emotional involvement; yet it will still be slow. In any case, early recognition would be of questionable value, due to the risk of premature labeling, and the concurrent danger of establishing a self-fulfilling prophecy.

However, recognition of an alcoholic by the supervisor can be grouped in the following order: First appears the disrupted but normal stage in which deviant behaviors begin to accumulate. Indications such as hand tremors, nervousness, perhaps hangovers, as well as avoidance of bosses and work associates, become evident. Later various types of absenteeism begin, coupled with unusual excuses, lower quality of work, and marked by mood changes and sloppy physical appearance, none of which is severe enough to appear abnormal to the supervisor, but which sets the stage for the next stage of "blocked awareness."

Gradually the supervisor and the shop steward come to realize that the increased deviant behaviors are linked with drinking, although numerous forces "normalize" these behaviors, delaying recognition of an imminent drinking problem.[6] New characteristics are now added to absenteeism and poor work quality, but up to this point the typical response of key people is still toleration.

Although previously the worker had been able to camouflage hangover symptoms, he now begins to show visible signs. His work becomes spasmodic and cyclical, absences increase, as do excuses. In high status occupations, these are less obvious due to the greater freedom at that level, but in lower situations, they are easily seen and eventually connect his behavior with excessive use of alcohol.

## SUPERVISORY TRAINING ABOUT ALCOHOLISM

Realistic training of supervisory personnel and union officers within a supportive company policy provides a means of speeding up the recognition process. Research suggests four training strategies.[7] First, training relevant to the workaday world of the supervisor and shop steward, and hence not exclusively focused on alcoholism, which is obviously not of primary importance in their experience since it affects only 7 or 8 percent of the employees. The training would deal, however, with "problem employees," of which alcoholic employees would be used as examples, since they are admittedly difficult and hence would make good training material. Familiarization with the alcoholic problem would accelerate the ability to recognize an incipient alcoholic.

Second, when such training points out the work problems produced by problem employees, it will act to lower the toleration point of the supervisor, while simultaneously raising the bottom for the alcoholic, and resulting in earlier referral and treatment. Emphasis in training on the supervisory headaches will tend to counteract the factors producing vacillation in the seesaw stage.

Third, trainees should be briefed in advance concerning the emphasis of the training by means of questionnaires and simple tests concerning the subjects to be taught. Having been introduced to the subject, the trainees will then be conditioned to accept training.

Fourth, a number of training techniques should be employed, such as films, lectures, case work, reading. This will make sure that one method or another will meet with success.

## THE WORK WORLD POTENTIAL
## FOR RECOGNITION AND TREATMENT

The work world, despite some barriers, still provides an excellent means for early identification of alcoholism. Compared with the family, or even the professional such as the clergyman or doctor, the work world has decided advantages. Some jobs have low visibility, but a great many are supervised, making drinking behavior obvious. In addition, supervisors, unlike wives and relatives, work under pressure to produce, and are therefore in a less personal relationship to the alcoholic.

Recurrent poor job performance typifies alcoholism in the work world, and such behavior is undesirable, from an unsentimental and practical point of view. Calling a spade a spade, it links poor performance with excessive drinking. The representative of this viewpoint, the supervisor, has the highest readiness to act of any of the people close to the alcoholic; and it is he who must cope with the problems of poor job performance, absenteeism, and perhaps eventually of replacement. He is often on the seesaw, to be sure, but he clearly does have the potential for action.

Potentials for genuine social controls exist in the job situation. Although, at lower-class levels, jobs are not as central in an employee's life as in the middle classes, they remain extremely important as the source of income and also of fringe benefits. The job becomes the key factor in the life of most workers, and in this the alcoholic is no exception. For him, the job is often his last bastion, and so long as it is intact, he sees nothing wrong in his drinking. Consequently, a confrontation for poor job performance may well create a crisis that will open the door for therapy or, earlier, prevent development of the disorder. Only the work world has this potential of constructive confrontation.

An employer should have an explicit policy incorporating the following points: that alcoholism is a health problem; that the company health plan will, without discrimination, include those addicted to the use of alcohol; and that the plan will recognize alcoholism as a unique health disorder which must be confronted with a crisis to effect either prevention or treatment. The policy should call for such confrontation when poor performance occurs. If the condition continues, the drinker should be offered unhesitating support in seeking rehabilitation on condition of cooperation. Finally, if the preliminary steps fail, stringent disciplinary methods should be used, such as curtailment of fringe benefits, layoffs, and finally discharge.

Such action removes the last defense, that of an intact job, and acts as an offset for the emotional rewards of drinking. By realistic sanctions, the confrontation thus reduces the intense value of alcohol to the alcoholic. Policies based on such action produce a high return in rehabilitation.

Management and unions comprise two pivotal institutions in American life which can be more potent in community effort than welfare agencies, medical facilities, or jails in their effect on the alcoholic employee. If they act on the assumption that alcoholism is a treatable disease, and follow through with considered programs, the effect can widely influence the success of constructive programs outside of, as well as within, the work world.

Most alcoholics do belong to the work world, and are more likely to live next door, than on skid row. Thus unions and management, by recognizing their existence in their own world, can counteract the characterization of the alcoholic as a police court inebriate, as, simultaneously, they insure a much higher recovery rate that accrues to those who are treated while still on the job. The strategy is to attack the problem where and when there is a reasonable chance of success, that is, on the job.

## THE UNION AND ITS ALCOHOLIC MEMBER

Union officials participate reluctantly with management in a joint program, for by doing so, they ride on the seesaw. Stewards see cooperation as a potential benefit to both themselves and the alcoholic, for by this means they can obtain realistic help for the afflicted union brother, and at the same time relieve themselves of the burden of carrying the alcoholic. Then, too, cooperation provides a status boost to the union official, since he thus achieves recognition as a co-partner with management. Cooperation achieved in one effort may spread to other union-management relationships, leading to overall understanding and union gains otherwise impossible to attain.

Such increased understanding may also result in a lessening

of the union's militancy in pressing demands for its members, a position which could lead to charges of collusion from the rank and file of the membership, and eventually to the unseating of the union leader involved. Cooperation with management may easily build internal conflicts in the union which would nullify the gains won.

Union leaders agree in theory with the necessity of crisis precipitation to break the alcoholic's hard line of excuses and rationalizations; but if the process leads to loss of job for a union member, the union can be said to have failed in its protection. Yet, unless the threat of final separation remains real, the alcoholic will discount the danger, and the therapy will fail. The union, therefore, by joining management to help cure the alcoholic must risk failing its member.

The reluctance toward cooperation with management goes deeper than the internal political situation that may confront the union. A legal obligation, requiring the union to represent its members, has been established in the National Labor Relations Board hearings and in court cases, and adds another barrier to cooperation. The union brother can demand that his union represent him in opposing a policy of coercion by management, thus forcing a reversal upon a union which has agreed to work with management in constructive therapy.

In examination of these hard realities concerning union cooperation, what can be concluded about union participation? The union can, of course, familiarize itself with, and utilize, the standard community facilities available for the treatment of alcoholism: physicians, clinics, councils, and Alcoholics Anonymous, to name a few which are available in the local telephone books in almost every area. Beyond those, union officials can obtain help from the AFL–CIO community service organization headed by Mr. Leo Perlis, which has considerable information available, and which also can usually recommend local sources of help.

University and community groups frequently conduct information seminars in the handling of alcoholics which can provide guidance to union management, the best known of which are the Addiction Foundation Summer School, held on the campus of Rutgers University; and the Southeastern School of Alcohol

Studies, at the University of Georgia. Unions themselves conduct training programs covering a broad spectrum of health-related problems which have proved effective in training local stewards in the problems of alcoholism.

When management runs a unilateral program, the union can make important contributions, such as early recognition of the alcoholic by the union steward, who can also exert pressure on the member to seek needed treatment. Early recognition of the problem opens many ways in which the alcoholic can be helped by the union before it reaches the stage of company involvement.

The union also can serve as a valuable link in communicating information about a company program to the worker, which, coming from a union source, is more likely to be accepted as believable than if the source were management.

If the drinker has gone beyond the first stages, and nears confrontation with the company for his unsatisfactory work, the union can, in the words of one shop steward "convince the alcoholic that the company really means business, and he had better get down to the clinic regularly." Then, if the alcoholic does accept treatment, the steward is set to provide aid and counsel, to both the alcoholic and his family, helping them through the crisis and back into the work world. Finally, he can persuade fellow workers to welcome the alcoholic back into the old group.

Where the union runs its own alcoholism program, it can perform all the functions that normally would be handled if management were in charge, by enlisting the various community facilities previously mentioned, by setting up an effective training program, and finally by obtaining management cooperation.

Obviously, a unilateral program staged by either management or labor will be less effective than a joint program which they both sponsor. Three steps can be taken to overcome the objections to such a program which were discussed above.

First of all, union participation must be secured during the planning stages. Second, training and education are necessary to stress 1) the broader mental-health aspects of inconsistent and poor performance; 2) the progressive nature of the problem; and 3) the availability of treatment facilities.

Following this, the steward should be closely tied in to the overall program by making him the link between the alcoholic, his family, and his job. He should also act in close touch with higher union officials to maintain clear lines of communication which will simplify necessary dealings with management both at the shop level and in the office. With such safeguards, and with the union handling most of the personal contact with the member, a joint program should prove possible.

## PREVENTIVE POTENTIAL IN THE WORK WORLD COMPARED TO OTHER PREVENTIVE MODELS

In order to demonstrate the superiority of the work place as a setting for preventive and therapeutic action in alcoholism, analysis of the obstacles faced by any approach seems necessary. Then each model (or method) of approach can be studied in relation to the obstacles which it will encounter, and an effective comparison obtained.

Likewise, prevention must be considered in three phases. Primary prevention attacks the forces leading to alcoholism before they have a chance to develop. Secondary prevention attacks the disease early, to prohibit full development. Tertiary prevention provides treatment to slow down the physical and psychological effects of the disease.

Some of the obstacles which confront any model of preventive effort follow below:

FIRST. The difficulty of arriving at a satisfactory definition of alcoholism, a malady which many believe cannot be explained, which tends to make the disease appear unreal to its victims and opponents.

SECOND. Established social values which recognize alcohol as an integral part of everyday life, and which would be difficult, if not impossible to change.

THIRD. The ubiquitous and also the functional nature of alcohol, which has established it firmly in every civilized society, where it acts as tranquilizer, social facilitator, and symbol of sophistication, to mention but a few of its uses.

FOURTH. The American belief in personal and civil privacy, which an alcoholism program inevitably will invade, and which will be resented, especially in early recognition stages.

FIFTH. Premature labeling of an alcoholic as such, which in the early stages of deviant drinking may tend to drive him further into the disease.

SIXTH. Change processes and agents bearing on alcoholism are not yet sufficiently understood. Effective treatments are not always possible which will change the behavior of alcoholics in the tertiary stage, making it possible for them to return to normal roles.

Concerning secondary prevention, how can society reduce (change) the emotionalism about alcohol use? How can it clarify (change) the distinction between acceptable and unacceptable drinking? How can it discourage (change) drinking for its own sake? How can it assist (change) youth to adapt realistically to a drinking society? [8] All of these questions are widely asked, but verified knowledge concerning effective change agents to achieve them is almost nonexistent.

SEVENTH. Preventive schemes are difficult to integrate into the pivotal institutions of society, such as business, the professions, the church, and the family. Preventive efforts cannot remain outside of these central institutions.

With the above realities in mind, specific preventive models, independent of the work world, can be examined for comparison of effectiveness.

*Model 1. Substitution of cultures*
Some subcultures, such as the "Jewish-Italian," consume alcohol regularly and in quantity, but show unusually low rates of alco-

holism. The proposal calls for the incorporation of features of these ethnic groups into American society in the effort to reduce the incidence of alcoholism.

Italian children consider wine a part of each meal, while Jewish children associate wine with religious ceremonies, both of which uses lead to casual acceptance far different from the emotional emphasis on drinking found in the American family.

The idea that children be indoctrinated into a casual and controlled use of alcohol founders on several obstacles. Since a culture is the result of accumulated generations of experience, it cannot easily be grafted onto another of dissimilar background. Even if possible in theory, the necessary change would be to basic American norms by a much less important "foreign" culture, and would hardly earn support from the pivotal institutions of our society.

*Model 2. Substitution of activities*

Assuming that the functions and values satisfied by drinking can be met by other social activities, this effort aims to divert attention into community-directed sports, travel, cultural interests, and recreation. Thus occupied, fewer persons would be exposed to drinking. The positive program would be supplemented with legal prohibitions where necessary.

Alcohol has always been available for those who sought it. Neither diversions nor prohibitions would alter this condition.

*Model 3. Advance conditioning*

This "mental-health" strategy envisions preventive schooling in high risk areas, both for the young and for those exposed to the disease by environment or the vicissitudes of life.

This encounters obstacles four, six, and seven listed above, since it impinges on privacy, assumes ability to change personalities, and relies on key support difficult of winning.

*Model 4. Early identification and control*

Early identification, intervention, and effective treatment are the keys to this method which meet the difficulty of intrusion into private lives upon somewhat insufficient evidence. Favorable response during the early stages is unlikely from the alcoholic, techniques of change are relatively ineffective at this stage, and are often abandoned in favor of "normal" treatment pending further development.

## Model 5. *Training and education*

Altering attitudes about alcohol and alcoholism in the general public is sought here through mass media propaganda, ranging from teaching about the disease in the public schools, to closely focused efforts such as those with work supervisors as discussed above. Among the myriad such efforts, one in the state of Iowa in 1961 attempted to sell the idea by mass media that the alcoholic is "sick," but reported acceptance of the concept by only 14 percent of the adult population.[9] To date no tests have proved that knowledge about alcoholism prevents an alcoholic from progressing further in his disease.

This approach, although popular, suffers from barriers three, six, seven, and to a degree five, the chief deficiency lying in what constitutes genuine change agents. Can educational methods be used to produce deterrents in the drinker? to change ostracism to acceptance? to discourage drinking for its own sake? to clarify the difference between acceptable and unacceptable drinking? The educational effort must also overcome the functional value of alcohol; and must win the cooperation of powerful community institutions.

## Model 6. *Social control*

This strategy seeks to establish sanctions which will define unacceptable drinking behavior at all levels and enforce group opinion on the deviant. It operates with much similarity to the constructive confrontation policy utilized in the job-based approach discussed earlier, in the same early to middle stage of the disease.

Working through an etiological attitude, this approach has more chance of success, as it also makes use of strong social controls by being articulated with the work world of industry and labor and other existing institutions, rather than seeking a complete social overhaul. This model allows intervention into the drinker's private life through the justified route of job impairment. This model does not challenge the functional value of alcohol, but does establish controls for excessive use. It attacks the disease at a relatively early stage, yet does so in a "normalized" atmosphere that does not prematurely label, but which does exert preventive pressure.

The lack of understanding of the change process does constitute a shortcoming for this model, but one which seems gradually to be approaching solution as the spreading use of company programs brings increasing knowledge.

Despite the problems, it seems reasonable to conclude that the greatest preventive possibilities lie in the crisis precipitation strategy growing from natural forces surrounding the job. Unfortunately, this avenue is not yet sufficiently traveled, and is often neglected for less promising ways. The question of why the work world strategy is not more widely exploited lies beyond the purview of this article, but until it is answered, the potentials for a genuine preventive approach via the work world will remain unrealized.

## REFERENCES

1. For evidence on this point see: H. M. Trice, "The Job Behavior of Problem Drinkers" in David Pittman and Charles Snyder (eds.), *Society, Culture and Drinking Patterns* (New York: John Wiley, 1962); Seymour Warkov and Selden Bacon, "Social Correlates of Industrial Problem Drinking," *Quarterly Journal of Studies on Alcohol*, 26, 1965, pp. 58–71; and H. M. Trice, "Reaction of Supervisors to Emotionally Disturbed Employees," *Journal of Occupational Medicine*, 7, 1965, pp. 177–189.

2. Observer and Milton Maxwell, "A Study of Absenteeism, Accidents, and Sickness Payments in Problem Drinkers in One Industry," *Quarterly Journal of Studies on Alcohol*, 20, 1959, pp. 302–308.

3. Trice, 1965, *op. cit.*, and Warkov and Bacon, 1965, *op. cit.*

4. Warkov and Bacon, *op. cit.*

5. *Ibid.*

6. Edwin Lemert, *Human Deviance, Social Problems and Social Control* (Englewood: Prentice Hall, 1967), pp. 18–21.

7. James Belasco and H. M. Trice, *The Assessment of Change in Training and Therapy* (New York: McGraw-Hill, 1969).

8. Thomas F. Plaut, *Alcohol Problems: A Report to the Nation,* Part III (New York: Oxford University Press, 1967).

9. Harold Mulford, "Measuring Public Acceptance of the Alcoholic as a Sick Person," *Quarterly Journal of Studies on Alcohol,* 25, 1964, pp. 314–322.

# The use of pharmacological adjuncts
# in the comprehensive therapy of alcoholics*

*EBBE CURTIS HOFF, Ph.D., M.D.*

Among the many approaches to therapy for alcoholics, the use of selected drugs holds an important place. Dr. Ebbe Hoff discusses treatment in which drugs are used as adjuncts to comprehensive programs. Dr. Hoff is professor of psychiatry and physiology and medical director of the Bureau of Alcohol Studies and Rehabilitation at the Medical College of Virginia. President of the Middle Atlantic Institute on Alcohol Studies, he is also active on the research committee of the North American Association of Alcoholism Programs.

It is now quite clear that alcoholics comprise a mixed group of ill people, suffering from a complex of psychological, social, spiritual, and metabolic disturbances or maladaptations. Although the symptom of the pathological use of alcohol is common to all of them, they also show varied patterns of problem drinking, loss of control, and progressive changes in alcohol tolerance. As more and better research becomes focused on the problems of alcoholics, we are in a better position to explore etiological factors and therapeutic and preventive intervention. It is still, however, a

* This article is a revision of "The Use of Pharmacological Adjuncts in the Psychotherapy of Alcoholics," by Ebbe C. Hoff, M.D., in the *Quarterly Journal of Studies on Alcohol*, Supplement No. 1, pp. 138–150, 1961, published by Rutgers University.

problem for the therapist that he is unable to plan therapy based on a really confident theory of etiology. At present, there is every reason to have confidence in a comprehensive approach to the therapy of the patient and his family in a community setting. This theory of comprehensive treatment goes hand and hand with the use of multidisciplinary teams of therapists and takes into account, also, the essential feature of planned, continuing treatment rather than episodic attempts to handle emergencies only. Whatever else we may conceive alcoholism to be, we know that alcoholics are persons whose drinking is associated with problems, and who have consistently lost control of their alcohol intake, and also characteristically find themselves using alcohol as a psychological drug. That is to say, alcoholics drink as if in an attempt, by their drinking, to handle various emotional and other problems.

In this article, we will first discuss the use of drugs in the treatment of acute intoxication and withdrawal within a hospital setting. Then there will follow a report of studies evaluating pharmacological or metabolic adjuncts in the outpatient therapy of alcoholics. The first of these latter reviews the use of disulfiram (Antabuse) as a measure to enforce motivation for abstinence. The second is a study of adjuncts to correct hypothesized metabolic defects. The third, most detailed, deals with attempts to protect the alcoholic patient against the effects of abnormal autonomic activity generated by presumably disordered cerebral autonomic control mechanisms.

## HOSPITAL SETTING AND
## OUTPATIENT CLINIC TREATMENT

The experiences in this article are based upon the treatment of patients and their families in the facilities of the Bureau of Alcohol Studies and Rehabilitation of the State Health Department of the Commonwealth of Virginia. All the patients were first seen by a member of the therapeutic team in one of the eleven outpatient clinics of the bureau, distributed throughout the state. Most of the patients were introduced into therapy by a period of hospitalization, lasting from one to three weeks, in the specialized service for alcoholics in the Medical Center (Medical College of

Virginia) of Virginia Commonwealth University in Richmond. More than 50 percent of the patients admitted to this hospital facility were sober on admission while others showed intoxication or exhibited alcohol withdrawal symptoms. Relatively few were admitted while deeply intoxicated or exhibiting delirium tremens, hallucinosis, convulsions, or other serious acute manifestations. All patients were on a technically voluntary basis, and were not legally committed. The period of hospitalization was followed by prolonged treatment in the outpatient clinic, usually the one from which the patient originated. There were some selective features, in that only those patients came into therapy who were considered capable of accepting treatment on a voluntary basis. This is not to say that the patients did not, in many cases, respond to certain pressures from family, employers, or themselves.

While the patient was in the hospital, a detailed medical, psychologic, and psychiatric evaluation was carried out, as well as a study by a social worker of the patient and his family, where this seemed indicated. Warm, friendly relations between the staff and patients were part of the therapeutic setting, and both men and women were accepted in the ward. Group therapy in small groups was begun the first day, since most patients were out of bed during the day from the time of admission. Group therapy included psychodrama and film programs, and the objectives of the group therapy program were, first, to give information, second, to stimulate motivation, and third, to encourage group interaction. While in the hospital each patient was seen, if possible, by the physician who was later to follow him or her in the outpatient clinic.

While the patients under study fell into a variety of diagnostic categories requiring specific therapeutic planning, there were certain characteristics which appeared common to nearly all of the patients. The majority, upon admission, suffered from feelings of depression and worthlessness which tended to paralyze effective action. Also, virtually all of the patients were victims of family and community ignorance and misinformation about alcoholism, and tended to have unrealistic ideas about the nature of their own problem and possible means of recovery. An important feature of the initial hospitalization period was to broaden the motivation for rehabilitation and strengthen it by assurance of the therapist's acceptance of them as worthwhile people whose lives are valuable. In general, the primacy of immediate day-to-day abstinence is stressed, as well as the importance of dealing realistically with immediate crises and problems on a daily basis.

In our discussion of pharmacological adjuncts, it should always be kept in mind that drugs are indeed adjuncts and that they are part of a whole plan or program of recovery. The needs for drugs and the discontinuance of drugs are to be decided competently, taking into full account the stage of therapy in which the patient finds himself and the entire picture at the time.

*The use of drugs in the treatment of alcoholics under treatment in hospital for intoxication or withdrawal from alcohol*
In our own hospital service, alcohol ingestion is always discontinued at once. While surreptitious drinking is from time to time discovered on the ward, this practice is very infrequent, not occurring more than once or perhaps twice a year in our service. In general, the patients, themselves, exert sufficient discipline on each other, and the spirit and morale of the service is such that the patients have a sense of loyalty and consideration of one another, making the service a place where alcohol use is regarded as unacceptable. While some "sobering-up centers" still continue the practice of gradual withdrawal of alcohol in the hospital or sanitarium, it is believed that this practice is obsolete, particularly since use of less addicting sedatives or tranquilizers in gradually reducing doses is, on the whole, reasonably satisfactory. We do not use paraldehyde, and, in general, avoid barbiturates. It is customary, as indicated clinically, to rehydrate orally and/or parenterally, but in general, parenteral fluid administration is relatively infrequent. Attention is paid to adequate nutrition, and diets are prescribed individually as indicated. Most patients in the hospital receive high-protein, low-fat diets; and nutritious food is made available in refrigerators for between-meal snacks. As stated, group therapy and individual therapy begin immediately, or as soon as patients are capable of participating in such activities. Family members are brought into the picture as soon

as possible, and there is generally very complete sharing between the primary patient in the ward and members of his family who come in to visit social workers and other professional staff.

Regarding drug therapy at the initial stage, the pharmacological regime depends on the degree of inebriation (best defined by blood–alcohol levels) and the intensity of withdrawal symptoms. Clinical judgment is essential in planning for the use of drugs in any particular acutely intoxicated patient, or alcoholic patient in the throes of withdrawal symptoms. In acute brain syndrome (alcohol intoxication), the patient may present an incoordinative, euphoric phase (usually with a blood–alcohol level around 150 to 250 mg. percent). Such patients may be ataxic, dysarthric, and there may be flushing and dilation of the pupils. Such a patient may be violent, and may engage in other antisocial behavior. It should be stated that there are no reliable clinical methods of accelerating the rate of clearance of alcohol from the blood. Nevertheless, stimulants such as coffee orally and/or caffeine sodium benzoate 0.5 gram (7.5 grains), subcutaneously or intramuscularly, every three hours, may be given as necessary. Sometimes, alternating cold and hot showers may be of value. It is important to help the patient prevent injury to himself and to others, and restraint may be required. Side rails, as required, will help the patient avoid falling out of bed. If a patient is combative, sedatives ought to be administered as necessary: promazine (Sparine) 50 mg. intramuscularly every three hours or chlordiazepoxide (Librium) 50 to 100 mg. intravenously and/or intramuscularly every three hours. Especially with the use of promazine, it is essential to check the blood pressure frequently for hypertension.

If the blood–alcohol level rises to 250 mg. percent or greater, the patient is usually semistuporous or comatose. In such emergencies, parenteral fluids are indicated: 1000 cc. of 10 percent glucose in saline, intravenously, with 2 cc. of Vitamin B complex, 100 mg. of thiamine HCl, and 25 units of regular insulin. Chlordiazepoxide (Librium) 50 mg. may be added to the fluids as required. Such a patient needs constant nursing, and the position of the patient in the bed should be changed frequently, at least, every two hours. The blood pressure, pulse, and respiration should be checked every thirty minutes. If circulatory collapse develops, administer plasma expanders and/or parenteral fluids. Aramine (metaraminol bitartrate) 10 mg. intramuscularly every two hours as necessary may be given or Levophed (levarterenol bitartrate) 4 cc. in 1000 cc. of saline intravenously (maximum thirty drops per minute). Electrocardiograms should be taken and repeated as necessary. If respiratory depression occurs give nikethamide (Coramine) 0.375 gram intramuscularly or subcutaneously every two hours as needed or methylphenidate hydrochloride (Ritalin) 20 mg. intramuscularly every four hours as needed. Dopram (Doxapram) 0.5 to 1.0 mg. per kilogram intravenously may also be used and repeated if necessary every two hours as required. Administration of oxygen by nasal catheter (six liters per minute) or by positive pressure respirator may be necessary and life saving. It is essential to maintain the patient's airway, and a tracheotomy tray should be available.

The immediate complications of acute intoxication may transpire within the first two or three days of cessation of drinking, and some complications may persist as long as a week. No matter how much a patient has consumed, the alcohol is usually all cleared from the blood by 24 hours. Nevertheless, withdrawal symptoms may supervene quite soon and even before all of the alcohol is withdrawn from the blood. Psychomotor agitation (the shakes) is most common. Sedatives and muscular relaxants may be used as needed with a gradual and well-planned reduction in dosage. Chlordiazepoxide (Librium) 25 mg. may be given orally every four hours as necessary or also promazine (Sparine) 50 mg. by mouth every four hours as required. If the patient is unable to retain oral medications, chlordiazepoxide 50 mg. may be given every four hours as required intramuscularly or promazine (Sparine) may be given in 50 mg. doses intramuscularly every four hours as needed.

A typical standard order for a patient suffering from withdrawal might be Vitamin B complex 1 cc. intramuscularly once a day for three days, ascorbic acid 100 mg. by mouth once a day, multivitamin capsules, one by mouth each day, chloral hydrate 1.0 grams by mouth four times a day as required for the first three days, chlordiazepoxide 50 mg. intramuscularly every four hours as required for the first three days, and chlordiazepoxide 25 mg. by mouth every four hours as required after the third day, and Benadryl 50 mg. by mouth at bedtime as required for sleep.

A typical standard order for a patient who was admitted without drinking and not suffering from withdrawal symptoms might be ascorbic acid 100 mg. by mouth each day, one multivitamin capsule each day by mouth, Benadryl 50 mg. at bedtime as required for sleep with the possibility of repetition in three hours if necessary, and chlordiazepoxide 25 mg. by mouth every four hours as required.

DELIRIUM TREMENS. Parenteral sedatives are given as needed. For example, promazine 50 mg. intramuscularly may be given every fours hours and chlordiazepoxide 50 mg. may be administered intramuscularly as required every four hours. The hallucinating patient may also receive chloral hydrate 1.0 gram four times a day. If necessary, parenteral fluids may be given and constant attendance and reassurance is highly desirable. The therapy of hallucinating patients requires an understanding, capable nurse and provision of a room in which there are no disturbing, moving shadows. In our service, we do not usually restrain patients, but we do use side rails. If the symptoms persist it may be necessary to transfer the patient to a closed neuropsychiatric section. Blood pressure, pulse, and respiration should be checked every thirty minutes, and complications should be treated as in semistuporous and comatose phase.

INSOMNIA. The usual bedtime sedative in our service is Benadryl 50 mg. by mouth at bedtime with repetition after three hours if necessary. Under rare circumstances glutethimide (Doriden) 500 mg. orally may be given. We do not usually give chloral hydrate as a nighttime sedation but tend to reserve it for daytime use.

GASTRITIS. A number of patients in the withdrawal state do suffer from gastritis. This may be due to local gastric mucosal irritation or, more rarely, may be a withdrawal symptom of the overactivity of higher cerebral autonomic centers. For the latter cause, appropriate sedatives as have been described may be used. For the local cause, as an antacid, we give cream aluminum hydroxide one half ounce every three hours as required. For antispasmodic action, atropine 0.6 mg. (1/100 grain) may be given subcutaneously every four hours or tincture of belladonna 1 cc. (15 minims) four times a day may be given. A bland diet should be ordered, and if the symptoms persist, an upper gastrointestinal roentgenographic series should be carried out and other diagnostic studies undertaken.

CONVULSIONS. Convulsive seizures usually occur two to three days after the last drink. If the patient on admission gives a history of seizures, we give diphenylhydantoin sodium (Dilantin) 100 mg. orally four times a day. We have found this the drug of choice in these cases. In our service, seizures are extremely rare at the present time and have been so for the last five years or more. On the rare occasion that there is a seizure, we may administer Dilantin intramuscularly 100 mg. immediately, followed by Dilantin by mouth four times a day.

PERIPHERAL NEURITIS AND VITAMIN DEFICIENCY STATES. It is very likely that most alcoholic patients suffer to some extent from a nutritional deficiency including inadequate vitamin intake. Under some circumstances there are specific clinical manifestations of vitamin deficiency. All patients receive a multivitamin capsule by mouth each day and 100 mg. of ascorbic acid orally also each day. This vitamin supplementation persists as long as the patient is in the hospital. Patients who come in either in withdrawal state or with a blood–alcohol level are given an injection intramuscularly of Vitamin B complex 1 cc. for the first three days, and in some cases this is repeated every day that the patient is in the hospital. The regime for signs and symptoms of peripheral neuritis includes Vitamin B complex 1 cc. intramuscularly each day of hospitalization and may also include 1 cc. of $B_{12}$ intramuscularly each day as well. It is our plan to adjust the diet to individual needs.

It should be borne in mind that the drug regime must be adapted to the individual needs and requirements as well as capabilities of each particular patient. The foregoing descriptions of adjunctive drug therapy are, of course, modified as may be required by the individual patient.

When the patient is ready to leave the hospital, the inpatient internist in charge may decide to send the patient out on a particular drug that he may have been adjusted to, while on the ward. As for example, he may continue to use an antidepressant which he has been taking. The use of any such drugs is noted in the summary that is sent to the outpatient clinic physician so that he is fully aware of what the patient has had in the hospital and what he may be continuing to take. As the patient enters the outpatient clinic, his outpatient physician may, of course, decide to modify the drug program.

DRUG REGIMES FOR PATIENTS IN OUTPATIENT THERAPY. All of the patients in our program are encouraged to continue their therapy after leaving the hospital. Usually, as stated, patients attend the outpatient clinic from which they originated and usually with the outpatient physician who was their admitting officer. It is generally suggested to the patient that he continue his outpatient clinic therapy for at least a year. Quite often, contact is also kept with members of the patient's family, and in some cases a husband and wife will continue outpatient treatment together. Also, some patients, in addition to having individual sessions with a physician and/or social worker, will take part in an outpatient group session once a week. By and large, there is no formal "discharge" of a patient. When the time comes that regular, routine visits are considered to be no longer required, the patient is told that this is the case but that if at any time he wishes to ask for help of any sort, he may call and ask for an appointment.

The philosophy and policy of drug-use as an adjunct to the outpatient therapy is that pharmacological agents be used only as required, and that they be discontinued when no longer necessary.

DISULFIRAM. We have used disulfiram (Antabuse) since 1948 and have always given it only to patients who volunteer for it. We have never given disulfiram except as part of a full program of treatment. During the initial years of our service, we started disulfiram in the hospital, and always allowed each patient to experience a disulfiram-alcohol reaction. More recently, we have eliminated the test reaction, but have simply explained what the disulfiram-alcohol reaction is. It has proved to be sufficient. Some times we will initiate disulfiram as a purely outpatient procedure. Our general policy is not to offer disulfiram to patients with serious renal, hepatic, cardiac, pulmonary, or metabolic disfunctions; and we also withhold it from patients with obvious mental deterioration or psychoses. As disulfiram has shown itself to be an excellent therapeutic adjunct, and as the values of taking it usually far outweigh the possible untoward effects of a disulfiram (Antabuse) reaction, our tendency in recent years has been to liberalize the decisions about offering it. In other words, the counterindications do not seem as severe and strict as we previously believed.

Disulfiram has been used for alcoholics in a variety of ways. One method has been to build a kind of "pharmacological fence" around the patient and so to transfer from him to the drug the presumed responsibility for abstinence. Our own experience has been that this is not a desirable procedure. We feel that the alcoholic person can never permanently or consistently delegate to any other person or modality the privilege and the responsibility of his own decision about abstaining. In our own use of disulfiram, we encourage the patient to take one half a tablet of the drug each day (250 mg., or in some cases 125 mg.). The patient is asked to take the disulfiram in the quiet of his own room (say, in the evening) and that he should specifically re-express his own acceptance of the fact that he cannot drink, and that he has chosen to accept another day of abstinence. We believe it is best that the patient take the medication unsupervised, and that he not feel the need to report to a member of his family or, for example, to his employer about this matter. One of the major values of Antabuse taken this way is that the substance serves to reinforce and sustain his own motivation for abstinence, and his own recognition that he is unable to drink safely. Antabuse has a great value in that it relieves the patient from the worry that he may drink impulsively. In general, the Antabuse lasts about three days, and he is thus provided with a kind of "temporal cushion" during which he may handle his need to drink without actually using alcohol.

Antabuse is without effect when taken by itself alone in the above doses, and is a perfectly safe substance. We generally counsel our patients to take Antabuse for at least a year, but assure them that they can continue its use indefinitely without harm.

A lore has developed that the use of Antabuse is a "crutch," and that the sobriety so attained is not as secure or as meaningful as through other procedures. We do not believe this is true, especially when Antabuse is used adjunctively with a full, comprehensive program of recovery and rehabilitation. As will be noted, patients who take Antabuse do significantly better as far as sobriety is concerned than do those who do not take it. The decision to take Antabuse, and the practice of taking it, are substantially correlated with motivational factors of considerable importance. Patients who agree to use Antabuse are often those whose motivation toward sobriety and abstinence is good; and those patients who reject it sometimes do so because they are "hedging" against a feeling that if they have to drink they should have an opportunity.

The disulfiram-alcohol reaction is very well known and need only be briefly described here. In the moderately severe reaction, there is a fall in systolic and diastolic blood pressures of 20 to 60 mm. of mercury and a corresponding rise in the pulse rate to about 120 per minute, usually with a rise in the respiratory rate. The severity of the reaction depends upon the amount of alcohol that has been taken. In our own experience, we have found that it is extremely rare that one of our patients deliberately drinks on top of Antabuse. In a case load of about 1,300 patients at any one time, a deliberate alcohol-Antabuse reaction is reported perhaps once a year. There have been no fatalities. Each of our patients carries a card stating that he is taking Antabuse and describing what the symptoms might be, and stating that he should be taken to a hospital at once. The cardiovascular respiratory changes occur in response to a generalized skin vasodilatation developing within five to ten minutes of ingestion of alcohol. There is usually dyspnea, cough, pounding of the heart, and tingling and numbness of the hands. In some cases there is also dizziness, visual blurring, and pounding frontal headache. We have found that reactions can be successfully controlled by administration of epinephrine in small frequent doses, oxygen, elevation of the foot of the bed and intravenous fluid. If the response is not satisfactory within ten to fifteen minutes, l-Norepinephrine is added to the intravenous fluid. As stated, we have omitted the planned reaction in the hospital, and have permitted the patient simply to discuss the reaction with members of the staff. We have made an analysis of 1,020 patients in our service at the Medical College of Virginia who took disulfiram (Antabuse) and 484 controls.[1] This study revealed that the Antabuse-treated patients constituted a younger group than the controls, the peak of the former being in the 35–39-year age group and that of the controls in the 40–44 age group. It thus seems that in our setting, Antabuse was selected by a younger, presumably healthier, and more highly motivated group and rejected by or denied to older patients presumably with more profound deterioration. Only 55 percent of the control patients benefited from treatment as measured by abstinence criteria; whereas 76 percent of the Antabuse treated patients were improved by the same criteria. The Antabuse group stayed in treatment significantly longer, and only 1 percent broke treatment early and 8 percent cannot be traced. Of the control group 16.7 percent discontinued treatment early—that is to say, they did not continue in the outpatient clinic, and an additional 14.5 percent cannot be traced. In the Antabuse group, 77 percent of the males and 67 percent of the female patients are judged improved. Those in the Antabuse group who were between the ages of 40 and 44 made the best clinical progress. The differences between the Antabuse and the control groups are highly significant, if one compares improved with nonimproved patients. A $t$-test of significance of the difference between the scores of improved patients in the disulfiram group and improved patients in the control group gives a $t$ value of 8.3 and a $p$ of less than 0.01. *The Antabuse patients, therefore, do significantly better than the controls.*

The studies, therefore, reveal that under the conditions of our therapeutic setting, the Antabuse group as a whole has a better record of improvement than the control group. It is of interest that this difference also shows up among patients who established a pattern of sobriety only after one or more drinking relapses.

It was hypothesized that Antabuse is selected by those more highly motivated patients who will continue long-term treatment more faithfully. Additional incentive for continuation of treatment in the outpatient clinic may have been provided by the fact that the Antabuse was dispensed in the clinic itself at the time the patient saw the clinic doctor, and only enough was given of the medication to last him until the next appointment. The motivational hypothesis was evaluated statistically by excluding those patients from both the Antabuse and control groups who broke treatment early and who were lost to contact. In the resulting comparison of 928 disulfiram-treated patients with 333 controls, it was found that 84 percent of the disulfiram group were listed as improved while 80 percent of the controls were so classified, a difference which is not clearly significant. In an earlier study[2] we found that those controls who volunteered for disulfiram, but were denied it, had much better records than those who declined it. Of 69 patients who were denied Antabuse on either physical or psychological grounds, none discontinued treatment early and 62 percent were shown to be improved. Of 152 patients who declined the medication, 31 percent discontinued treatment early and only 44 percent were classified as improved. The group denied Antabuse were apparently, therefore, a more highly motivated group who may have accepted the condition which disqualified them as a challenge to find a new way of life in an abstinent pattern.

*Adjuncts to correct metabolic defects*

MASSIVE POLYVITAMIN SUPPLEMENTATION. This metabolic approach to the treatment of alcoholics stems from studies of Williams[3] who found that rats receiving a marginal diet select high alcohol intake and who has reported cases of alcoholics in whom the compulsion to drink was presumably lost when they were given specific vitamin supplements.

In 1955 Hoff and Forbes[4] reported a study of 100 patients from our clinic which was designed to explore the effects of long-term administration of a polyvitamin formula on the drinking patterns of alcoholics. During their hospital stay the patients received daily oral doses of 100 mg. of ascorbic acid plus 15 cc. of a polyvitamin formula. Each 5-cc. dose of the formula contained 5 mg. of thiamine hydrochloride, 2 mg. of riboflavin, 10 mg. of niacinamide, 10 mg. of panthenol, 2 mg. of pyridoxine hydrochloride, 10 mg. of p-aminobenzoic acid, 500 mg. of choline dihydrochloride, 100 mg. of inositol, 100 mg. of methionine, and 5 mg. of vitamin $B_{12}$. After discharge they were maintained with 10 cc. of the formula plus 100 mg. of ascorbic acid daily for at least a year.

The patient sample comprised all those admitted to the hospital service during a 3-month period. The progress of these patients was compared with that of 100 control patients admitted consecutively during a later 3-month period. All patients in both series were nonpsychotic alcoholics treated on a voluntary basis and subjected to an otherwise identical therapeutic regimen. The patients in the control series received vitamins during the hospitalization period but none subsequently. All the patients were evaluated one, two, and three years after the onset of treatment.

In general, the statistical analysis suggested that the differences in clinical success (i.e., abstinence and family, job, and social adjustment) between the groups could be explained by random variation. It was evident, however, on a clinical basis that patients in the vitamin group felt better and ate better than those in the control group, and subsequent experience with this formula has shown that it is a valuable adjunct in helping outpatients cope with anorexia and excessive fatigue. No patient in any of our series has ever acquired any degree of control over the use of alcohol whether taking vitamins or not.

One problem with any experiment involving administration of drugs or other agents to outpatients is that there is always some doubt as to whether or not the patient took the medication. This can be checked absolutely only by assigning to a member of the family or some other responsible person the task of supervising the administration. As has been implied in the case of disulfiram, such a procedure tends to defeat the underlying principle on which the adjunctive use of the medication is based. It is our impression, however, that disulfiram is taken according to the physician's suggestions more consistently than is a vitamin preparation. Patient acceptance of chlordiazepoxide (to be discussed below) appears to us to be even greater than disulfiram, although the rationale of its use is, of course, different.

As has been said, diet and dietary supplements, including vitamins, are important aspects of inpatient as well as outpatient treatment of alcoholic patients. In our outpatient clinic, we seek to advise patients about good nutrition; and by means of pamphlets and other ways, we give them sound information about the values of correct diet. Vitamins are prescribed to our outpatients as seem necessary, and in some cases patients will receive intramuscular injections of B complex and/or vitamin $B_{12}$ when they visit the clinic. It must be admitted that the exact rationale of dietary therapy for alcoholics is not fully understood; nevertheless, many of these patients do suffer from nutritional deficiencies. It is true that alcohol can be classed as a food in the sense that burning alcohol in the body will produce about 7 calories per gram of alcohol. Its serious limitation as a food lies partly in the fact that it makes energy available at a restricted rate; even worse, it causes intoxication when drunk in excess of its combustion rate in the body.

In the case of alcoholics, alcohol can be taken in such large amounts as to replace other much better foods. Thus the person who drinks, for example, a pint of whiskey each day, will derive 1200 calories from it which may be nearly one half of his daily energy requirement. By thus "drinking" his meals, he is depriving himself of essential vitamins, minerals, and necessary proteins. As a result, he may fall victim of serious nutritional diseases which may harm the nerves, brain, and liver, or other organs. Such nutritional disturbances caused by misuse of alcohol complicate the direct toxic effects of alcohol which may impair, for example, brain and liver function. As a patient becomes abstinent, therefore, it is good policy to supervise his nutrition as a part of the total comprehensive approach to his rehabilitation.

We have recently studied the effects of special protein supplements to the diets of alcoholics undergoing treatment in our hospital unit. These studies, while of a preliminary nature, do show that supplementation may result in weight gain. We feel that metabolic studies of this type should be carried out under conditions in which food intake and excretory function are measured exactly so that the actual role of dietary therapy can be more exactly assessed.

ENZYME DEFICIENCY. It has been suggested that individual genetic differences in enzyme activity may affect alcohol metabolism and conceivably play a part in the etiology of alcoholism.[5] Wilson and Respess[6] found that C57BL/6J mice prefer alcohol to water and show a higher level of liver alcohol dehydrogenase than do C3H control mice. Furthermore, the former animals, under conditions in which an alcohol solution is the only source of liquid, will accept and use greater amounts of alcohol than will the controls. Such studies, while not yet clinically applicable, suggest a promising therapeutic research approach.

Biochemical differences between individual people have been adduced in partial explanation of the etiology of alcoholism. One hypothesis suggests that because of individual high tolerance to alcohol, some people can and do apparently drink more with less hangovers or other difficulties. Such persons, say in their 20s, may drink rather more than other people whose tolerance is less. The high tolerance people may, in some circumstances, discover that these larger amounts of alcohol act for them as a kind of psychological medicine, and that for them, therefore, alcohol does more than for the lower tolerance person. Thus, the high tolerance individual may come to depend more upon alcohol to try to handle situational and personal problems. Eventually, such a person's tolerance may become diminished by some biochemical changes not yet understood, and this person may become, therefore, an alcoholic whose drinking causes him serious symptoms. Such a hypothesis would take account of both biochemical as well as psychological and social factors in the complex causality of, at any rate, certain types of alcoholism.

*Adjuncts to correct hormonal defects*
Many studies support the hypothesis that alcoholism, while not a clear-cut single disease entity, may be causally related in part to

hormonal imbalance. Many alcoholics relate their drinking to feelings of nervousness or tension or depression that may stem from tension. Hoffer and Osmond [7] have suggested that alcoholics and other tense people either may not synthesize enough adreno-chrome or may destroy it too quickly. Alcohol as a tension-dissolving substance may be used as a substitute for this missing adrenochrome. Alcoholics and those with chronic tension states have been found to lose injected adrenochrome from plasma much more quickly than normal subjects. Hoffer and Payza,[8] comparing the adrenochrome levels in the cerebrospinal fluid and in plasma, found that very tense patients had a lower ratio of cere-brospinal fluid adrenochrome to plasma adrenochrome than those who are not tense. Jantz[9] reported that serum from alcoholics metabolized adrenochrome to adrenolutin more quickly than did normal serum. Hoffer and Osmond offer the view that chronically tense people are more likely to become alcoholics than those who are not. Fleetwood [10] has shown that alcoholics have more sym-pathomimetic amines in their red cells and plasma when they are tense than when they are relaxed or have ingested alcohol.

The hypothesis that abnormal tension in alcoholics is based on a physiological peculiarity is potentially useful in treating alco-holics. It can help relieve some of their guilt and self-reproach. Furthermore, the administration of adrenochrome, substitutes for adrenochrome, or substances which aid in its synthesis or delay its breakdown may possibly be beneficial.

At the Medical College of Virginia, preliminary trials with the administration of leuco-adrenochrome (by sublingual absorption in amounts of 15 mg. four times a day) have been effective in abolishing tremor in three tense, tremulous patients all of whom had complained of tremor, especially under emotional stress, most of their lives.

*Protection against autonomic overactivity*

EFFECTS OF CHLORDIAZEPOXIDE AND OF ALCOHOL. Several stud-ies[11-14] have established the existence, both in experimental ani-mals and in man, of cortical and subcortical representation of visceral control. Specifically, stimulation of cortical and other cerebral areas results in alteration of systemic blood pressure, changes in intracardiac dynamics, and modifications of peripheral circulation, as well as functional and vascular changes in the kidneys, gut, and other organs. Acute and chronic changes in pulmonary, coronary, and bone-marrow circulation have been investigated; and it has been shown that higher cerebral stimulation modified activity of epinephrine and norepinephrine as well as salivation. It may be hypothesized that there is an overlapping and integration of visceral and somatic control systems in the brain and that these systems are related to neurological mechanisms of behavior and emotional response. Tension and emotional sensitivity and lability, of whatever origin, may be related at the neurological level to disturbances of these higher cerebral autonomic mechanisms. Neurotropic drugs, therefore, which protect the autonomic system from higher cerebral overresponse to stresses, may be of value as adjuncts in the therapy of alcoholics.

Carroll et al.[15] have studied the action of intravenously administered alcohol and chlordiazepoxide on autonomic responses evoked in cats by threshold stimulation (with controlled parameters) of loci in the limbic lobe, the amygdala, the nucleus of von Bechterew, the hypothalamus, and the mesencephalic reticular formation. Stimulation, through electrodes stereotaxically placed in flaxedilized cats, evoked pressor responses, cardiac arrhythmias (nodal and ventricular extrasystoles and ventricular tachycardia with indications of coronary insufficiency), mydriasis and striking inhibition of the motility of the pyloric sphincter and ileum. Salivation has been elicited from most of these loci as well as retraction of the nictitating membrane. Intravenous administration of chlordiazepoxide in amounts of 10 to 20 mg. per kg. of body weight caused a transient, slight hypotension and bradycardia, whereas intravenous administration of 10-percent ethanol (3 to 15 ml. per kg. leading to blood–alcohol levels of 0.05 to 0.15 mg. per 100 ml.) caused increased pyloric motility with slight to marked alterations in cardiac rhythm. Chlordiazepoxide greatly attenuated the pressor responses from all brain areas studied, whereas alcohol generally exerted weak antipressor effects. Centrally induced cardiac arrhythmias were completely blocked by chlordiazepoxide, but alcohol had no blocking action on these responses except from loci in the limbic lobe. Neither compound showed any activity against centrally evoked salivation, mydriasis, or gastrointestinal inhibition.

Alcohol, as measured by its effects upon centrally induced autonomic responses, appears to be a defective tranquilizing agent. In fact, its central actions on higher brain functions seem to be a complicated combination of excitatory and inhibitory effects. Whereas alcohol is an imperfect attenuator of centrally generated autonomic overactivity, chlordiazepoxide acts effectively to protect the viscera from harmful cerebral autonomic malfunction.

CHLORDIAZEPOXIDE AS A TREATMENT ADJUNCT. Because chlordiazepoxide fulfills criteria of an effective neuropharmacological substance with protective action, as measured by its suppression of cerebrally induced visceral malfunctions, a study was carried out to evaluate its use as an adjunct in the long-term treatment of a group of 100 alcoholics. Fifty patients (40 men, 10 women) received 10 to 25 mg. of chlordiazepoxide orally four times a day both during the hospital stay and after discharge. The first patient in this series was admitted on 1 May 1960 and the last on 10 February 1961. Their ages ranged from 28 to 63. Fifty patients, matched with the chlordiazepoxide patients in age, sex, and time of entry into the hospital, served as controls. The controls received no special placebo; in the hospital they were given capsules of B-complex when the other patients received chlordiazepoxide. All were followed for at least one year. The results of this study can be seen in Table 1. It may be reasonably assumed that Classes IV, NC, and NT represent, for the most part, therapeutic failures.

According to the criteria for degree of abstinence, 72 percent of the chlordiazepoxide-treated patients improved, 10 percent did not, and 18 percent could not be classified. In contrast, 52 percent of the control patients improved, 16 percent did not, 24 percent were lost to contact, and 8 percent discontinued treat-

## Table 1

### COMPARISONS OF DEGREE OF ABSTINENCE AND OF SYMPTOMATIC IMPROVEMENT IN 50 PATIENTS TREATED WITH CHLORDIAZEPOXIDE AND IN 50 CONTROLS (in percentages)

| DEGREE OF ABSTINENCE* | CHLORDIAZEPOXIDE | CONTROLS |
|---|---|---|
| I | 20 | 16 |
| II | 8 | 10 |
| III | 36 | 26 |
| IV | 10 | 16 |
| V | 8 | 0 |
| NC | 18 | 8 |
| NT | 0 | 24 |

| SYMPTOMATIC IMPROVEMENT† | | |
|---|---|---|
| 1 | 22 | 16 |
| 2 | 22 | 18 |
| 3 | 38 | 26 |
| 4 | 14 | 20 |
| 0 | 4 | 20 |

* The criteria for classification were as follows. *I:* Patients reporting total abstinence since the onset of treatment. *II:* Patients abstinent except for one relapse. *III:* Patients not abstinent but showing improvement in wider spacing of drinking episodes, better work records, and happier adjustments in home and community. *IV:* Patients showing no improvement. *V:* Patients placed in the unimproved class in earlier appraisals, who have been continuously abstinent for over 6 months. *NC:* Patients with whom contact was lost. *NT:* Patients who discontinued treatment early through self-discharge or other means.

† The criteria for classification were as follows: *1:* Vast improvement or nearly complete remission of all symptoms. *2:* Decided improvement or partial remission of symptoms. *3:* Slight improvement. *4:* Condition unchanged or worse. *0:* Could not be classified.

ment early. The chlordiazepoxide-treated group shows a significant improvement over the control group (chi square = 4.24; $p < .05$).

According to the less stringent criteria, based on symptomatic improvement, in the lower portion of Table 1, 82 percent of the chlordiazepoxide-treated patients were improved, 14 percent unimproved, and 4 percent unclassified. Of the control patients, 60 percent were improved, 20 percent unimproved, and 20 percent could not be classified. This difference in improvement is also significant (chi square = 5.88; p < .05). It should be noted that in the chlordiazepoxide group, fewer patients withdrew from the series or were unclassifiable than in the control group. There was a higher follow-up rate in the chlordiazepoxide group, and fewer missed appointments.

In no patient in this series was administration of chlordiazepoxide associated with any manifestation of toxicity. A group of 10 of the chlordiazepoxide patients were rehospitalized for special study six months after the onset of therapy. Medical and psychological tests were repeated in these patients but revealed no abnormal changes.

Patients taking chlordiazepoxide showed greater willingness and ability to explore and face personality problems and life situations than did the controls. There was a tendency toward breakdown of alibi systems and a facing of reality. The chlordiazepoxide-treated patients were also more tolerant of job and family problems and better able to handle these situations. They showed less overt tension and slept and ate better. The prior symptoms of some, such as palpitations, epigastric discomfort, pain, and tremulousness, were greatly abated and finally abolished. The chlordiazepoxide-treated patients showed a notable willingness to go beyond relief of immediate tension and overt symptoms and to seek insight.

Since the conclusion of the above study, we have used chlordiazepoxide not only in the hospital service but also in our outpatient clinic. In the clinic we have also used diazepam (Valium). The former we dispense in the clinic and the latter we order by prescription directly to the patient. Our general policy in the use of drugs in the clinic is to limit the amount dispensed or prescribed to the amount that will be required until the next outpatient appointment. Our policy is also to administer any drug only as indicated and as long as the physician believes that the indications persist. Thus, we administer drugs only to patients who are actually attending the clinic and are in active therapy otherwise.

## REFERENCES

1. Ebbe C. Hoff, "The use of disulfiram (Antabuse) in the comprehensive therapy of a group of 1,020 alcoholics," *Connecticut State Medical Journal,* No. 19, 1955, pp. 793–797.
2. Ebbe C. Hoff and C. E. McKeown, "An evaluation of the use of tetraethylthiuram disulfide in the treatment of 560 cases of alcohol addiction," *American Journal of Psychiatry,* Vol. 109, 1953, pp. 670–673.
3. Roger J. Williams, "Alcoholism as a nutritional problem." *Journal of Clinical Nutrition,* Vol. 1, 1952, pp. 32–36.
4. Ebbe C. Hoff and J. C. Forbes, "Some effects of alcohol on metabolic mechanisms, with applications to therapy of alcoholics," in *Origins of Resistance to Toxic Agents,* M. G. Sevag, R. D. Reid, and O. E. Reynolds, eds. (New York: Academic Press, 1955), pp. 184–193.
5. Ebbe C. Hoff, "The etiology of alcoholism," *Quarterly Journal of Studies on Alcohol,* Supplement No. 1, 1961, pp. 57–65.
6. E. C. Wilson and J. C. Respess, "A study of ethanol metabolism in mice which preferentially consume ethanol" (by personal communication).
7. A. Hoffer and H. Osmond, "Concerning an etiological factor in alcoholism. The possible role of adrenochrome metabolism," *Quarterly Journal of Studies on Alcohol,* Vol. 20, 1959, pp. 750–756.
8. A. Hoffer and A. Payza, "Adrenochrome levels in plasma and cerebrospinal fluid" (presented at the annual meeting, American Psychiatric Association, San Francisco: 1958).
9. H. Jantz, "Uber Stoffwechseluntersuchungen bei Alkoholpsychosen, *Zbl. ges. Neurological Psychiatry,* Vol. 137, 1958, pp. 141–142.
10. M. F. Fleetwood, "Biochemical experimental investigations of emotions and chronic alcoholism," in *Etiology of Chronic Alcoholism,* Ohio Diethelm, ed. (Springfield, Ill.: Thomas, 1955), pp. 43–109.
11. Ebbe C. Hoff and H. D. Green, "Cardiovascular reactions in-

duced by electrical stimulation of cerebral cortex," *American Journal of Physiology*, Vol. 117, 1936, pp. 411–422.

12. H. D. Green and Ebbe C. Hoff, "Effects of faradic stimulation of the cerebral cortex on limb and renal volumes in the cat and monkey," *American Journal of Physiology*, Vol. 118, 1937, pp. 641–648.

13. Ebbe C. Hoff, J. F. Kell, Jr., N. Hastings, D. M. Sholes, and E. H. Gray, "Vasomotor, cellular and functional changes produced in kidney by brain stimulation," *Journal of Neurophysiology*, Vol. 14, 1951, pp. 317–332.

14. R. W. Ferguson, B. Folkow, M. G. Mitts, and Ebbe C. Hoff, "Effect of cortical stimulation upon epinephrine activity," *Journal of Neurophysiology*, Vol. 20, 1957, pp. 329–339.

15. M. N. Carroll, Jr., Ebbe C. Hoff, J. F. Kell, Jr., and C. G. Suter, "The effects of ethanol and chlordiazepoxide in altering autonomic responses evoked by isocortical and paleocortical stimulation," *Biochemical Pharmacology*, Vol. 8, 1961, p. 15.

# Jamming the revolving door: new approaches to the public drunkenness offenders

*DAVID J. PITTMAN, Ph.D.*

In this article David J. Pittman brings up to date his famous study with C. W. Gordon of the chronic police-case inebriate. Dr. Pittman is director of the Social Science Institute of Washington University in St. Louis, co-editor of *Society, Culture, and Drinking Patterns,* and editor of *Alcoholism—An Interdisciplinary Approach.* Former president of the North American Association of Alcoholism Programs, he is currently the principal investigator for the U.S. Mental Health Project, "Mental Health Training for Law Enforcement Officers."

## THE PROBLEM

Historically in North America and Europe, public drunkenness has been treated as a criminal offense in almost every legal jurisdiction. Laws exist on national, state, and/or local levels prohibiting public displays of drunkenness. For example, Article 21, paragraph 2, of Poland's "Anti-Alcoholism Act of 10th December, 1959," states:

. . . persons in a state of alcoholic intoxication who by their behavior cause scandal in a public place or working establishment may be taken to the sobering-up center where they shall remain until they recover from the intoxication; such period shall, however, be not longer than 24 hours.[1]

Although disorderliness is a prerequisite under some such laws, the homeless, skid-row inebriates face repeated arrest for disorderly and nondisorderly drunkenness.

Those who are most often arrested are likely to have the most serious drinking problem. A recently completed British study dramatically illustrates this point. In a detailed interview study of 151 men charged with public drunkenness in London, Gath and associates[2] found that the majority (76 percent) had a serious drinking problem and also suffered from extreme social isolation. The researchers firmly established that 50 percent of the men could be classified as being chemically dependent upon alcohol.

Thus, many individuals arrested for public drunkenness are without question alcoholics. Yet treatment for alcoholism is clearly not part of the correctional regimen. The process of arresting inebriates, detaining them for a few hours or a few days, and then rearresting them has been termed by me in an earlier work a "revolving door." Some individuals have been arrested 100 to 200 times and have served 10 to 20 years in jail on short-term sentences. The recidivism rates clearly indicate the futility of the present system in dealing with the underlying sociomedical problems involved. Further, the impact of such arrests—reportedly in excess of two million each year in the United States—is particularly great on the institutions of the criminal justice system. The police, the courts, and the correctional institutions allocate needed manpower and facilities to handle what most people recognize as a public health problem.

Chronic drunkenness offenders are generally excessive drinkers, who may or may not be alcoholics, but whose drinking has involved them in difficulties with the police, the courts, and penal institutions. They are a group for whom the penal sanctions of society have failed and for whom existing community resources have not been utilized. Although some of these men (very seldom women) are alcoholics, others are individuals whose present use of alcohol is preliminary to alcoholism, and others are nonaddicted excessive drinkers who will never become alcoholics.

As yet, research studies which clearly differentiate an alcoholic from a nonalcoholic in the chronic drunkenness offender group are sparse. The most widely accepted definition of alcoholism is one developed by the World Health Organization which states:

> Alcoholics are those excessive drinkers whose dependence upon alcohol has attained such a degree that it shows a noticeable mental disturbance or an interference with their bodily and mental health, their inter-personal relations, and their smooth social and economic functioning; or who show the prodromal signs of such development.[3]

From this definition it is obvious that a history of arrests for public intoxication is indicative of a drinking problem. Repeated arrests for public intoxication are certainly a symptom of the disease of alcoholism. However, as a result of the paucity of scientific research and lack of adequate funds for research and treatment studies on alcoholism, there are few clear-cut answers about this disease.

Over a decade ago, in 1955, when my first study, *Revolving Door,* on this problem was presented in Rochester, New York, I stated:

> A Treatment Center should be created for the reception of the chronic drunkenness offender. This means that they should be removed from the jails and penal institutions as the mentally ill in this country were removed from the jails during the last century. Given the present state of knowledge concerning alcoholism, the time is ripe now for such a change. The present system is not only inefficient in terms of excessive cost of jailing an offender 30, 40, or 50 times, but is a direct negation of this society's humanitarian philosophy toward people who are beset by social, mental, and physical problems.[4]

My position remains the same. Fortunately, as we will be documenting in this article, since 1955 a social movement to humanize the handling of public drunkenness offenders has occurred in Czechoslovakia, Poland, Sweden, Great Britain, Canada, and the United States; however, the task of viewing and managing the chronic inebriate as a sociomedical problem instead of a criminal one is still far from being accomplished in Western society.

## MAGNITUDE OF THE PROBLEM
## IN THE UNITED STATES

The more intense the enforcement of laws, the greater the effect they have on the deviancy. For the public intoxication offender, the enforcement is indeed intense in the United States. In 1967 the FBI reported 1,517,809 arrests for public drunkenness by 4,566 agencies that cover a population of 145,927,000.[5] This figure accounted for approximately 28 percent of the total arrests for all offenses and is almost twice the number of arrests for index crime offenses. If alcohol-related offenses (driving under the influence of alcohol, disorderly conduct, liquor law violations, and vagrancy) were added to this percentage, it would constitute around 49 percent of all reported arrests in the United States in 1967.[6]

The number of police actions involving public intoxication or such legal euphemisms as disorderly conduct, vagrancy, or trespassing, is phenomenal in certain cities. Washington, D.C., in 1965, reported almost 45,000 arrests for public intoxication; St. Louis, Missouri, comparable in size but with different police policies and practices, reported in the same year only 2,445 arrests for drunkenness. Los Angeles reported 100,000 arrests for drunkenness in 1965, and New York City, using disorderly conduct statutes, arrested 50,000.[7]

The approximately two million annual arrests in the United States for public intoxication do not completely represent the involvement of the police with this problem. Police officers in many communities use informal means of handling drunken individuals—in suburban communities they may escort the inebriated individual home, or telephone a taxicab to perform the same function, and in still others they may warn the individual about his behavior and ask his friends to escort him home. In other communities, drunks arrested may be held until sober and released without charge.

Persons arrested and held for prosecution for public drunkenness are almost never represented by counsel and almost always found guilty. In 1967 reports to the FBI from 2,486 cities representing a population of 71,828,000 showed that 87.2 percent of all persons charged with public drunkenness were found guilty.[8] This suggests that the chronic drunkenness offender frequently finds himself incarcerated. Indeed, there is strong evidence that chronic inebriates constitute one of the largest groupings of individuals incarcerated in short-term correctional institutions.

Given two million arrests for public drunkenness in the United States, the cost for handling each case involving police, court, and correctional time can be estimated at $50 per arrest. Admittedly, some cases are disposed of without court or correctional action, but maintaining a person in a county or city jail is extremely expensive. A minimal annual expenditure of $100 million for the handling of chronic drunkenness offenders is a conservative national estimate. And this heavy cost provides no expenditure of funds for treatment or prevention. It is a high cost for maintaining a system which is an abysmal failure in rehabilitating alcoholics.

## COURT DECISIONS IN THE UNITED STATES

In 1967, the Supreme Court of the United States was asked to rule, in *Powell v. Texas,* on the constitutionality of the use of a public intoxication statute in cases involving chronic alcoholics. It was the contention of medical, legal, and other professional groups supporting Powell that chronic alcoholism was a positive defense to the charge of public intoxication, and that these individuals should not be incarcerated but should receive medical and social treatment. In June 1968, the Supreme Court, in a narrow five-to-four decision, held that a chronic alcoholic could be convicted under a state law against public drunkenness. The majority decision was by four members of the Court who joined in one opinion and by a fifth Justice whose opinion agreed with the result reached by them but took a narrower position in doing so. It is expected that other test cases of the public drunkenness statute will be brought to the attention of the Supreme Court in the future.

Prior to the 1968 Supreme Court decision, two legal decisions in 1966 affecting public intoxication offenders were rendered. First, the U.S. Court of Appeals for the Fourth Circuit in Richmond, on January 22, 1966, found in favor of the appellant, Joe B. Driver of North Carolina, who had been arrested more than 200 times for public intoxication. Judge Bryan stated:

> The upshot of our decision is that the State cannot stamp an unpretending alcoholic as a criminal if his drunken display is involuntary as the result of disease. However, nothing we have said precludes detention of him for treatment and rehabilitation so long as he is not marked a criminal.

On March 31, 1966, the United States Court of Appeals for the District of Columbia ruled unanimously in favor of the appellant, DeWitt Easter. The decision of the judges was that "chronic alcoholism is a defense to a charge of public intoxication, and therefore is not a crime in violation of Section 25-128(a) of our Code . . ."

## THE PRESIDENT'S COMMISSION

The President's Commission on Law Enforcement and Administration of Justice, commonly known as the Crime Commission, was appointed by former President Johnson in 1965 to study the crime problem; it made its report in 1967. One chapter of the Commission's report dealing with drunkenness made significant recommendations concerning this problem which we would hope to see enacted into law by states and municipalities. The Commission recommended: [9]

> 1. Drunkenness should not in itself be a criminal offense. Disorderly and other criminal conduct accompanied by drunkenness should remain punishable as separate crimes. The recommendation requires the development of adequate civil detoxification procedures.
> 2. Communities should establish detoxification units as part of comprehensive treatment programs.
> 3. Communities should coordinate and extend aftercare resources, including supportive residential housing.

4. Research by private and governmental agencies into alcoholism, the problems of alcoholics, and methods of treatment should be expanded.

Under the fourth recommendation the Commission stated: "Consideration should be given to providing further legislation on the Federal level for the promotion of the necessary coordinated treatment programs."

The Crime Commission's recommendation that drunkenness in itself should no longer be a crime is a major breakthrough in establishing a redefinition of the chronic drunkenness offender as a sick instead of criminal individual. The seeds of the concept of alcoholism as an illness were sown over the last 25 years in Europe and the United States and have gradually grown to the point of the widespread acceptance of alcoholism as a disease on both continents.

## INNOVATIONS IN HANDLING PUBLIC INTOXICANTS

Bold approaches to handling the problem of public drunkenness within a sociomedical context first occurred interestingly enough in Eastern Europe—namely, Czechoslovakia and Poland—with the establishment of "sobering-up stations" or detoxification centers. These stations instead of jails were used to process drunkenness cases.

Sobering-up stations have become an integral part of the network of alcoholism services in Poland and Czechoslovakia. For example, in Warsaw any person found drunk on the street or lying in a doorway is taken by the police to the sobering-up station. The Warsaw station is a 150-bed facility on the grounds of the State Sanatorium for Mental Disorders, and is one of the 22 such sobering-up stations in the country established under the Anti-Alcoholism Act of 1959 to handle "drunk-on-street" cases. The Warsaw facility in 1967 had approximately 25,000 admissions; thus the public drunkenness offender in Poland is originally handled in a sociomedical facility instead of a jail.

Basically, the Warsaw sobering-up station routine for an intoxication case is as follows: The intoxicated person is registered by a clerk at the station, undressed, examined by a physician or intern, given a shot of vitamins or other medication, given a shower, and put to bed for eight to 24 hours. These stations provide for treatment of acute alcoholism and early case detection of alcoholics.

In Czechoslovakia, patients from the sobering-up station are referred to lectures on alcoholism and its effects (called "Sunday Schools" since the lectures are held on Sunday). Generally when the individual appears a second or third time at the sobering-up station, a full-scale medical and social evaluation begins and a plan for therapeutic intervention is worked out, involving voluntary approaches at first. If the patient does not proceed with voluntary treatment, then compulsory treatment is begun.

The first detoxification center to open in North America for persons detained by the police for public intoxication was in St. Louis in November 1966, sponsored by that city's Metropolitan Police Department in cooperation with St. Mary's Infirmary and the Social Science Institute, Washington University, under a grant from the Office of Law Enforcement Assistance of the U.S. Department of Justice, supplemented by local and state funds.

The elements for social change in St. Louis were found in the emphasis the city's power structure—government, police, civic leaders, and social agencies—placed on the rehabilitation of the alcoholics. Much educational work with these groups and the area's mass media had prepared the community to accept the idea that public drunkenness offenders were sick individuals who needed sociomedical care instead of a fine or jail term. For example, in 1962 and 1963 many key St. Louis personnel visited the Alcoholism Treatment and Referral Demonstration Project (D. J. Pittman, principal investigator) at the Malcolm Bliss Alcoholism Treatment and Research Center and held many informal conferences with staff members.[10]

As a result of these conferences and further studies, the St. Louis Board of Police Commissioners in 1963 instituted a major policy change in reference to intoxicated persons on the street. The St. Louis Metropolitan Police Department made it mandatory for all individuals "picked up" from St. Louis streets to be taken to the emergency rooms of one of the two city hospitals for physical examination. This meant that routine physical evaluation was provided all alcoholics processed by the police; if these individuals were in need of medical care, they were to be hospitalized instead of being jailed. If medical care were deemed unnecessary, the intoxicated person was "held until sober"—not more than twenty hours—and released to the community.

St. Louis was one of the few American cities in which this innovation in the handling of the public intoxication case occurred. It squarely placed the locus of responsibility for the alcoholic in the treatment sphere and was in keeping with modern practices toward the publicly intoxicated person in a number of European countries. However, the Board of Police Commissioners was dissatisfied that large numbers of alcoholics were not admitted to the hospitals for medical care. At times more than 90 percent of the "examined" public intoxicants were returned by the physicians to the police for processing.

Thus, the Metropolitan Police Department of St. Louis was one of the few agencies to apply for a grant for the operation of a detoxification center when such centers became eligible for support under the Law Enforcement Assistance Act of 1965. The Detoxification and Diagnostic Evaluation Center in St. Louis (originally at St. Mary's Infirmary, and in December 1968 permanently transferred to the St. Louis State Hospital) is a 30-bed unit with 24-hour medical and nursing coverage, a total of 40 full- and part-time employees, and an annual budget of approximately $325,000. The goals of the center are:

1. To remove chronic inebriates to a sociomedical locus of responsibility which will markedly reduce police processing.

2. To remove chronic inebriates from the city courts and jails.

3. To provide sociomedical treatment for them.

4. To begin their rehabilitation.

5. To refer them to an agency for further rehabilitation, with the goal that they will return to society as productive persons.

This Detoxification Center is the first systematic attempt in North America to provide treatment for the alcoholic at the moment the police intervene in the process. The center works as follows:

1. A police officer brings the "intoxicated" person to the reception room.

2. Center personnel complete a medical examination of the patient.

3. The patient is showered, given clean clothing, and assigned a bed.

4. Special nursing care and diets are provided.

5. Therapeutic activities—films, group meetings, discussions, and lectures—are provided.

6. Each patient is counseled individually.

7. The patient, when necessary, is referred to other social, health, and governmental services for further help.

8. The average length of stay is seven to ten days.

The St. Louis Center in the first two and a half years of its operation has become a model for the United States. A follow-up evaluation study conducted by the Social Science Institute[11] of 200 patients who were treated at the center showed results which far surpassed our expectations. Approximately 20 percent of the chronic inebriates were abstinent when reinterviewed in the community three months after discharge from the center, 56 percent were gainfully employed, and 31 percent had shown marked improvement in their drinking patterns. Table 1, based on Weber's study, shows how the patients fared in the areas evaluated.

The tabulated results were achieved with a group that had been considered helpless and hopeless by most observers. But we must always remember that no group is ever hopeless unless our expectations define it as such.

Given the success of the Detoxification Center in St. Louis, the public was extremely receptive to legal changes in the public intoxication ordinance. In Missouri, public drunkenness is governed by local laws; in October 1967, the St. Louis Board of Aldermen unanimously passed a new ordinance governing public intoxication without any court pressure being needed. It was

Table 1

EVALUATION OF 200 PATIENTS FOLLOWED-UP
THREE MONTHS AFTER DISCHARGE FROM THE
ST. LOUIS DETOXIFICATION AND DIAGNOSTIC
EVALUATION CENTER

|  | PERCENTAGES | | | |
|  | Markedly Improved | Remained Same | Deteriorated | Unable to Rate |
|---|---|---|---|---|
| Drinking | 51 | 46 | 3 | 0 |
| Employment | 25 | 66 | 5 | 4 |
| Income | 16 | 72 | 8 | 4 |
| Health | 56 | 35 | 9 | 0 |
| Housing | 14 | 83 | 3 | 0 |

sponsored by then Alderman Joseph Roddy, who had been active in creating a more enlightened community climate for rehabilitating alcoholics in Missouri. The essence of St. Louis' new ordinance is that chronic alcoholism is a positive defense to a charge of public intoxication. However, few cases of public intoxication involving chronic alcoholics find their way to the municipal court anymore, as they are given medical and social treatment at the Detoxification Center.

Further support for innovations in handling public drunkenness cases in Missouri occurred during a special budget session of the State Legislature in early 1968. Acting on an appropriation request of the Missouri Alcoholism Program of the State Division of Mental Diseases, submitted by Governor Warren E. Hearnes, the Legislature appropriated $650,000 for alcoholism treatment and control activities for the fiscal year 1968–1969. Of special note is the fact that $150,000 of these funds were allocated for the partial support of detoxification centers in the state's major urban areas of St. Louis, Kansas City, and Springfield. Furthermore, the Governor's Advisory Council on Alcoholism in Missouri has established as one of its high priority items the creation of emergency care facilities for public alcoholics throughout the state.

These innovations in the care for chronic drunkenness offenders in St. Louis and in Missouri are indicative of changes occurring throughout the United States. As examples, the North Carolina General Assembly in 1967 and that of Maryland in 1968 revised their public intoxication statutes to provide that chronic alcoholism was a disease and thereby a positive defense to the charge of public intoxication. We can expect other states and municipalities, at a quickening pace, to revise and liberalize their public intoxication statutes.

The provision of adequate emergency care facilities for public alcoholics is now accelerating both in the United States and Europe. In New York City the Vera Institute of Justice established in 1967 a demonstration alcoholism treatment project known as the Manhattan Bowery Project [12] for skid-row indigent individuals. The operation is composed of three parts: (1) a street rescue team, composed of a civilian medical person and a plainclothes policeman, who attempt to persuade the indigent drunkenness cases to voluntarily enter the treatment facility; (2) a detoxification center to provide emergency medical care for approximately five days; and (3) placement or referral to an aftercare facility. As has been the case with the St. Louis Center, the Bowery Project has found that these chronic alcoholics have been extremely responsive to treatment, and some are beginning to show progress in coping with their chronic debilitating disease of alcoholism. Similar results are being shown by the detoxification centers in Des Moines, Iowa, Washington, D.C., and Denver.

In 1963 the Swedish Parliament ordered the creation of a governmental commission to study the "criminalization of drunkenness and the methods of care and treatment of acutely intoxicated persons." [13] As did Pittman and Gordon in their study, *Revolving Door,* the Swedish commission rejected the traditional policy in their country of arresting and punishing the acutely intoxicated individual. Following the lead of Poland and Czechoslovakia, the Swedish commission recommended that special medical stations or detoxification centers be established in the major cities of the country. The commission tested the practicability of the detoxification centers in the two cities and stated, "The detoxification clinic concept is not only fully workable but it also creates entirely new premises for an active and effective sociomedical treatment of drunks."

It should also be noted that the British government has proposed that the public intoxication offender be removed from the criminal process, and that he be treated as a medical and social welfare case.

## CONCLUSION

But the tragedy is that implementation of new medical and social philosophy in reference to alcoholism with new programs has been so difficult to obtain, and that individuals are still being jailed for exhibiting the symptoms of chronic alcoholism, repeated public intoxication.

However, as this article demonstrates, major advances in handling the problem of chronic drunkenness offenders are taking place in Poland and Czechoslovakia, in St. Louis and Missouri, in New York City, and in Sweden. These advances, based on legislative action and the creation of detoxification facilities and supportive social welfare services, demonstrate what governmental agencies can accomplish when they are willing to take action on this major sociomedical problem. The ultimate goal of all governmental bodies in reference to this problem area should be the complete removal of chronic alcoholics, whose only offense is public intoxication, from the jail cells and drunk tanks of the world to sociomedical treatment facilities.

## REFERENCES

1. Poland, "The Anti-Alcoholism Act of 10th December 1959," p. 11.
2. Denis Gath, et al., "The Drunk in Court: Survey of Drunkenness Offenders from Two London Courts," *British Medical Journal*, Vol. 4, pp. 808–811, December 28, 1968.
3. "Expert Committee on Mental Health, Alcoholism Subcommittee,

Second Report," World Health Organization technical report series, No. 48, August 1952.

4. David J. Pittman and C. Wayne Gordon, *Revolving Door: A Study of the Chronic Police Case Inebriate* (New Brunswick, N.J.: Rutgers Center of Alcohol Studies, 1958), pp. 141–142.

5. FBI, *Uniform Crime Reports*, 1967.

6. *Ibid.*

7. Arthur and Norma Due Woodstone, "Death of a Skid," New York Sunday *Herald Tribune* Magazine, April 3, 1966, p. 17.

8. FBI, *Uniform Crime Reports*, 1967.

9. President's Commission on Law Enforcement and Administration of Justice, *The Challenge of Crime in a Free Society* (Washington, D.C.: Government Printing Office, 1967), pp. 236–237.

10. David J. Pittman, "The Open Door: Sociology in an Alcoholism Treatment Facility," in *Alcoholism*, David J. Pittman, ed. (New York: Harper and Row, 1967), pp. 131–141.

11. James Weber, "The St. Louis Detoxification and Diagnostic Evaluation Center" (St. Louis: Social Science Institute, Washington University, 1968 [mimeo.]).

12. Robert Morgan and Charles Goldfarb, "Report on the Manhattan Bowery Project," January 31, 1968 (mimeo.).

13. This section on Sweden is derived from Ministry of Justice, Stockholm, "Detoxification Instead of Fines," *Särtryck ur Sou*, 1968, p. 55, and conversations with the Honorable Daniel Wiklund, M.P., a member of the Governmental Commission.

# Assessment and treatment
# of youthful drug users

## BY DAVID J. MYERSON, M.D.

Knowledge of the clinical problems of drug addiction and possibilities for recovery comes only through hard work and deep devotion. Dr. David Myerson's article is based on a five-year study of youthful drug users treated at the Boston State Hospital Drug Addiction Rehabilitation Center, where he was clinical director. Few studies of the drug problem have covered a comparable period under controlled conditions. This work has particular importance in a period of increasing drug dependence. Dr. Myerson is presently director of Worcester (Mass.) State Hospital.

This article focuses on techniques of both evaluation and treatment developed from five years' experience with youthful drug-addicted or drug-dependent people at the Drug Addiction Rehabilitation Center at the Boston State Hospital, Boston, Massachusetts. This center consists of a 17-bed inpatient service with adjoining outpatient facilities. The same treatment personnel are actively engaged in both inpatient and outpatient treatment so that there is no loss of continuity in the long-term therapy with the patients. During these five years the clinic has evaluated about 1200 drug users, almost all young people, 400 of whom were accepted for the treatment program. While in the initial evaluation these patients reveal many similarities derived from the psychiatric interview, they eventually present important differences in terms of potential assets and liabilities for improvement. It is our contention that the choice of treatment and prognosis should be based on the determination of the differences rather than the similarities.

Accordingly, the treatment program presents gradually increasing stressful situations in terms of psychotherapy leading to self-awareness, work and educational responsibilities, and freedom from outer restraints. Through observations of each person's individual response to these varying stressful situations, the treatment staff is able to conceptualize the differences among the patients and choose the modality of treatment that is best suited for each individual's capacities.

Initially, these patients usually demonstrate the following symptom complex: They tolerate poorly any psychic pain, especially loss, rage, depression, and anxiety. They avoid any exposure to situations that might cause psychic pain, such as the competitive aspects of school, work, and sex. They use denial, isolation, and projection as a first line of defense when faced with psychic pain. At the same time, they engage in secretive and vigorous seeking of pharmacological relief and gratification, in place of any psychic pain. For those physically addicted, abstinence itself can precipitate a painful syndrome, which further lowers their tolerance to psychic pain. Moreover, even after a long period of abstinence the addict who experiences any strong emotion may suffer the abstinence syndrome, much like a conditioned response, and may return to drug taking for relief. These patients become intellectually peroccupied with attempts to justify and rationalize the use of drugs as well as to insist on their "right" to seek and procure drugs. As a result, they create continuous conflict between themselves and, at first their parents, later, the police or other authorities. The ensuing conflict causes true persecution which serves two purposes: First, as with any persecuted group, the persecution gives a sense of identity to those people who are otherwise riddled with feelings of failure, loss, and social limitations. Second, the persecution masks their internal problems to such an extent that neither the persecuted nor the persecutors recognize the importance of these internal problems except through the use of such vague and meaningless terms as "sickness" or "disease."

By and large, in this country, the persecutions have become harsh and the numbers of the persecuted have risen. The persecutors seemingly are content to persecute through raids, arrests, and imprisonment. Judging from the endless discussions of their battles with the police, the persecuted savor the harassment and use it to avoid facing inner psychic pain.

This symptom complex is sometimes referred to as "acting out character disorder." The term, however, as used to label this drug-taking pattern is not diagnostic. Rather, it represents a special mode of adaptation used to cope with their inner emotional problems. Thus, the narcissistic youngster who suffers a profound sense of failure and is terrified of the competitive demands of school finds relief from his depression by this mode of behavior. The impulse-ridden, overaggressive boy may be able to contain his violence only through the use of drugs and the activities involved in obtaining drugs and the resultant persecution. The schizophrenic individual may prevent a complete psychotic withdrawal by identifying and allying himself with a tolerant, mystical, and noncompetitive group of drug takers. The adolescent who runs from a dangerous oedipal complex may not only find relief through drug taking, but find revenge through the resultant humiliation of his parents. Then there is the overt homosexual who tries to mask the strength of his homosexual drives by the de-sexualizing effects of the drugs.

These brief vignettes reveal the variations in the psychopathology that may underly the similar overt clinical picture. It is under the stress of the treatment program that these problems ultimately are revealed.

## TREATMENT PROGRAM

The treatment program begins with a test of motivation. Each patient is required to make three weekly visits to the outpatient department. Here, in a group, they meet various members of the treatment staff and are greeted with a didactic lecture in which the rules and regulations of the program are explained. Basically, however, the purpose is to test the patient's response to a situation in which his immediate needs are not satisfied. Those people who come for a free supply of methadone, for exploitive purposes, for a magical, effortless cure are disappointed and do not return. Those who complete these three visits are accepted into the outpatient service and then, if necessary, into the inpatient service. A patient may have to wait as long as two months from the first visit to the time of admission to the inpatient service. By and large, the ones who obtain an inpatient bed easily attach little value to it and tend to be more exploitive.

The first treatment problem after admission is that of withdrawal, which usually lasts for two to three weeks depending on the severity and type of addiction. From the beginning, the patient is exposed to both individual and group therapy programs. In both, the therapist confronts the individual with his rationalization and encourages him to face and to deal with his present emotional conflicts. The emphasis is more on the immediate problem than on the past. We try at all times to deal with the many crises and conflicts that arise on the ward as treatment situations. For this group, this continual confrontation with emotional reactions is stressful and a great deal of support is needed from the staff members and the other patients. The hope is that, instead of seeking relief from his painful emotional conflict by secretive drug taking or flight, the patient will increase his endurance through verbalization of his feelings.

In addition, the patient is exposed to work and educational programs. At first these programs are carried out within the confines of the hospital; later, when the patient is ready, within the community. Thus we gradually apply increasing psychological awareness, freedom, and responsibility, dependent on each patient's native ability and capacity to mature and to cope with the responsibilities of everyday life.

It is of the utmost importance to note that the ward is never locked. Therefore, at all times, each patient is faced with two sets of choices which only he can make: 1) to stay or to leave, 2) to take drugs or not to take drugs. Rehabilitation and treatment of these patients occur under the continual stress of having to make these choices as they learn to endure increasing tension resulting from work or school pressures and emotional self-awareness. After a month or two of exposure to this kind of program in which stress is gradually increased, we have an accurate appraisal of the individual's strength. Final choice of the different treatment modalities then depends on this assessment, be it individual or group psychotherapy, methadone maintenance or even incarceration.

It is difficult to categorize the results of this treatment program. On the whole the patients exhibit a spectrum, varying from people who are barely able to survive to those who show almost complete recovery. There is no question, however, that the patients as a group fit into the lower end of the spectrum in terms of degree of recoverability.

## TYPES OF PATIENTS

In general they fall into three categories: First, those patients who need sustenance and demonstrate such fragile egos that they are not capable of tolerating any kind of stress without drug taking or flight. Although they are not able to identify with the goals of the treatment program, they are willing to be sustained through their many visits to the clinic. They demonstrate dependency to an extraordinary degree. We frequently prescribe methadone to these people, not for the purposes of social readjustment but really for the purposes of keeping them alive. When they become ill or injured, one of our responsibilities is to advise physicians in other hospitals how to treat them on the ward. We try to cooperate with the many social service agencies that are involved with them and their families.

The second group is able to identify with the goals of the treatment staff but is not able to fulfill these goals without pharmacological help. They are able to go to school, work, and fulfill their family responsibilities only as long as they are supplied with methadone. These people present a serious problem in long-term management. Pragmatically, they show improvement, but the problem of how long to maintain them on methadone has not been answered. We have been able to encourage only a few to give up methadone and continue. their social improvement. By and large, in order to hold their improvement, it seems that these people are going to need methadone for many years to come; but none of us has had enough experience to know whether this is a true prognostic picture.

The third group includes those people who are able to identify with the goals of treatment and show sufficient inner strength to maintain these goals. They need no methadone to continue along in their social recovery. These patients not only identify with the staff but frequently they become part of it. We have learned that they make excellent treatment personnel. First, they demonstrate to the young drug takers that their situation is not hopeless and that it is possible to reverse their drug-taking tendencies. Second, they are often competent in breaking through the rationalizations that many of the drug takers characteristically use. Third, since they have at one time been drug takers but now have become part of the treatment group, they help bridge the gap between the treatment group and the drug takers.

In summary, we have demonstrated that there is considerable variation among the young drug takers in their ability to withstand frustrations, learn to cope with their emotional feelings, and show a social recovery. Some patients are so crippled that the goals of treatment are essentially to sustain life and to protect them and their families from disease or social abandonment. Yet once involved in this therapeutic relationship, others give up chronic drug use, mature, and develop enough work skills to become self-sufficient citizens. The considerable variation in the capacity to mature among the many drug users indicates that the stereotype, characterized by such terms as "drug fiends" or "junkies," is based on prejudice and ignorance. Even the term "drug addict" is a poor one because it implies a single conception of these people. It is better to recognize that numbers of people respond to their life's situations, especially during adolescence, through drug use. Many are indeed crippled in a psychological sense, with gross limitations in their ability to mature. Certainly we have demonstrated that, given an environment that through stress encourages growth over a period of time, even years, some patients are able to control their addictive needs and progress to a point where they can cope with their problems as responsible adults. The range is so wide that it is highly unlikely that any one treatment approach or facility can treat all addicted patients.

Some are so criminalistic that incarceration is needed; others are psychotic; and still others demonstrate that their drug problem was a regressive one and in an open treatment situation they can mature. Finally, some need various kinds of institutional protection all their lives. Each clinic, institution, or self-help group must recognize these variations and be willing and able to develop techniques to assess the patients referred to them and select those who fit into their particular style of operation.

## THE DEVELOPMENT OF THE THERAPEUTIC COMMUNITY

Our program, with its educational and rehabilitative goals tempered by the realistic appraisal of the patients' capacities, did not develop without serious and painful stresses among the staff members. From the beginning of the program, we were aware that the nursing staff would play a crucial part in the success or failure of the inpatient service. We emphasize the fact that we have had no strict physical security measures designed to control the patients' behavior. Even the nalorphine test and chemical examinations of the urine have only limited value for controlling the patients on a day-to-day basis so that the burden of control has fallen chiefly on the nurse-patient relationship. The problems encountered in the training of the nursing staff, therefore, offer the best opportunity to describe the development of our present therapeutic orientation.

Before we opened the center, we visited several institutions which had established treatment programs for this group. In contrast to our unit, each institution relied on physical means of control so that the role of the nurses and physicians was really secondary to that of the guards or other security means. We questioned how a situation in which the choices of both the patients and the treatment staff were surrendered to the physical means of security could encourage individual growth. If an institution depends on physical security for control, then it is basically a jail even if called a hospital. While we were aware that some drug users need incarceration at different times in their lives, we wanted to know whether they could contain themselves and mature in an open ward setting in which the relationships among staff and patients rather than security played the important role.

Even though with our limited experience we expected difficulties, we were not prepared for the intensity of the anxiety produced by working day and night with the drug users. Between the problems of an inexperienced staff with few guidelines for treatment and an exploiting, impulse-ridden but often ingratiating group of patients, it was not surprising that at first crises and conflicts were an almost daily occurrence.

To meet these crises, we inaugurated formal weekly conferences in which all the nurses who could attend would share their experiences and exchange their feelings about the patients, themselves, or any problems they care to discuss with the psychologist as the group leader. Although there was considerable informal exchange of ideas and feelings between the nursing staff and the clinical director, these group meetings seemed a practical and valuable teaching step.

The reaction to this innovation was explosive. Some of the nurses felt it was a direct insult to their professional integrity to have as a supervisor a psychologist rather than someone from the medical or nursing profession. These nurses sabotaged the meetings through deliberate absenteeism and the establishment of rival meetings which they directed themselves. The opponents of the meetings were reinforced by several key nurses in other sections of the hospital so that this resistance became a "cause celebre," fortunately short lived, among many of the hospital personnel.

Nevertheless, the psychologist persisted. It soon became evident that the causes of the resistance went deeper than professional pride. Truly, the nurses' resistance centered about the revelation of their anxieties resulting from the merciless assaults upon their emotions. The drug-using patients are quick to perceive the narcissistic involvements, masochism, sadism, rivalries, sexual anxieties, or depressive features among the various staff members. The patients did not hesitate to exploit these emotional problems to gain special privileges to break the usual rules, or, most frequently, to convert the professional therapeutic relationship into a highly personal one in which the patient was not expected to change. To reveal their specific anxieties to their peers was more than some of the nurses could endure, and they had to leave.

Gradually, over a three-year period, the atmosphere of these meetings changed. The resistance due to professional pride melted. Those who could not endure the personal revelations in these meetings either left the unit or were assigned to more impersonal duties. The nurses who remained acknowledged the value of these meetings and became full participants in the work with their patients. They learned that no one, no matter what his professional rank, was exempt from emotional flaws which were inevitably revealed to both the patients and staff in the closely knit ward. They learned that the difference between the problems of the staff members and those of the patients was a matter of degree. All of us are people who suffer from anxieties, but the staff members tend to deal with them through more mature mechanisms; whereas the patients respond impulsively by drug taking.

When we were able to remove the artificial barriers separating the professionals and patients, we recognized that there was no "right" or "wrong" way in treating a drug user. As he worked with the drug users over a long period of time, each doctor, nurse, social worker, or attendant developed his own style of relating to patients, based upon his personality, values, and experience. As in all relationships, his character revealed certain strengths as well as weaknesses. In this prolonged therapeutic relationship, it became the function of the groups to encourage the therapist's strengths and to be alert for demonstrations of his weaknesses in his relationship to the patients.

Certain therapists, for example, tend to respond consistently by "giving" to their patient's helplessness. This response can be of great value to the depressed patient, but the groups must be prepared to point out to the therapist times when he is being exploited or when his kindness leads to favoritism and acts to the detriment of the rest of the ward. On the other hand, there are some therapists who are strict and consistently fair. They set well-defined limits which they explain to their patients. Any transgression of these limits means a punishment; adherence to them means a reward. Certain impulsive patients respond with relief to this well-defined approach, but the group has to supervise this limit setting to prevent it from becoming rigid and doctrinaire. These therapists must be helped to recognize that the kinds of limits they set should vary considerably from one patient to another, depending on the assessment of impulsivity, motivation, age, and ethnic background.

Thus from a ragged, inexperienced group, riddled with the worst kind of professionalism, we have a cohesive unit that recognizes and respects individual differences among both the staff and the patients. There is a feeling of freedom to exchange ideas, often critical, but with the intent of encouraging growth ot not only the patients but also the staff members. This freedom is our concept of a therapeutic community.

## COMMUNITY RELATIONSHIPS

Many other agencies are deeply involved in the care and control of the addicted people and their families. Our therapists are in daily contact with welfare agencies, child guidance clinics, vocational training centers, antipoverty programs, the legislature, and, above all, law enforcement agencies. Our participation with these diverse agencies, with their different traditions, administrations, and community responsibilities, is vital since a failure to work with them would restrict our ability to help our addicted patients.

Our efforts have helped some agencies to change their attitude toward the drug users. The vocational training centers, for example, deliberately avoided addicts until recent federal policy changes coupled with our pledge of cooperation permitted them to become some of the most cooperative and useful community resources.

Because the attitudes of school authorities are in a state of flux about the drug user, their responses to our requests for school placement are unpredictable. Until recently school administrators viewed the drug-using student as a contaminant to be eliminated quickly from the school system. Now many administrators are at least in a state of doubt. They have recognized that the elimination of the student user from school perpetuates the problem of the user's poor preparation for life. At the same time, the administrators run educational programs rather than social service agencies.

Furthermore, they face pressure from anxious parents who fear for their children's safety. Recently some schools have offered a panel of speakers to discuss with the parents, teachers, and students various aspects of the drug problem. While these panels have only a limited value, they are a beginning. With further effort, we hope to aid the schools in the development of realistic educational programs designed to meet the varied abilities of the different drug users.

Of all the agencies, however, the police and the courts are the most deeply involved. When we began our unit, we had to learn the hierarchy of those officials within the judicial system who cope with drug users. There are the officers from the Federal Food and Drug Administration who deal with users of non-narcotic but dangerous drugs and from the Federal Bureau of Narcotics who focus on crimes associated with narcotic users. Also, there are officers from the Massachusetts State Pure Food and Drug Administration, from the narcotic squad of the State Police, and from the Vice Squad of Boston. Finally, each district in Boston and the outlying areas has, as a rule, a detective who is assigned to the control of drug takers.

The District, Superior, Federal, and, most recently, Juvenile Courts also influence the lives of many drug users. We have noticed that sentences vary considerably from court to court.

It is difficult to predict who is going to be committed to a correctional institution, placed on probation, released, or committed to us. In general, our impression is that the court officials do make a genuine effort to distinguish between the passive, self-destructive users and those who are more aggressively involved in criminal activities, and to adjudicate accordingly.

Finally, we recognized the importance of the probation and parole officers who supervise the addicted men under the jurisdiction of the court or parole board. Some of these officers deal intimately with the addicts over a long period of time; their problems often are similar to ours.

Clearly, it would be unlikely for all these people to have similar attitudes toward the drug users. Indeed, their reactions often resemble those of our staff members. That is, some officers, responding to the drug users' helplessness, use their power to incarcerate only with great reluctance and as a last resort. Others find it difficult to tolerate the defiance of the users, advocate a punitive restrictive approach, and view our tolerant therapeutic approach with grave misgivings.

Several courts, however, welcomed the opening of the unit and from the beginning referred us many drug users. These referrals eventually created some serious problems which warrant description along with our attempts to solve them.

One district court, plagued by increasing numbers of young men arrested on drug charges, referred to us a group of these youngsters for treatment and rehabilitation. The judges and probation officers tended to view the users as sick people who needed medical help. Eager to please this particularly friendly court, we accepted as many of their referrals as we possibly could and without prior screening. Since they came into the ward directly from the courts, our first contact with them was after admission. Many of these patients were difficult to control and had to be discharged from the ward.

With the hope that the legal supply of methadone would keep these young men away from illegal activities, we prescribed this drug to some of them after discharge. This technique did help a few pursue rehabilitative goals, but others from this court misused the whole therapeutic procedure. They not only used the ward experience to avoid jail, but, if prescribed methadone, sold it or added it to other drugs. Even when successfully maintained, some continued their involvement in illegal activities.

The court officers responded with frustration and disappointment. They had overestimated our therapeutic abilities, and we fed into this overestimation by our continual acceptance with no screening of their referrals. Then, when disappointed, they referred their drug users to other—more physically secure—institutions.

We overcame this problem by the establishment, together with the courts, of a selective screening process. Either we see their referral as an outpatient for evaluation or we accept him on the ward for a 10-day or 35-day observation period. In a few weeks, we usually have a reasonably accurate impression about a patient's ability to respond favorably in our open ward.

The court itself acknowledged its responsibility and assigned a special probation officer to supervise the drug users under its jurisdiction. This officer set up group treatment sessions, evaluated the addicts' families, and supervised their rehabilitative efforts. He visited us and soon recognized our limits and assets. As a result, when he referred a drug user, we were able to communicate directly with him and discuss the problems of management that might arise in our inpatient or outpatient program.

Obviously, we can work better with carefully screened and supervised patients than with poorly motivated and manipulating drug users. Our solution depended on the court's participation with us in the care of the drug users and the recognition of both agencies that there are some users who need strict control and others who are ready for rehabilitation. Above all, we would emphasize the value of a friendly relationship and immediate communication between this particular court officer and ourselves.

Another successful working relationship evolved with the parole board. This agency assigned to a single officer the duty of visiting the center frequently and keeping in close touch with the parolees who are also our patients. We have been able to work out an agreement with the patient and the parole officer. With the patient's understanding and consent we discuss freely with the officer his parolee's progress or regression in treatment. In turn, the officer has been willing to avoid one-sided decisions to return a parolee to prison. This agreement is not official but based on understanding and the desire to help the parolee as much as possible. Several parolees have had to be returned to jail, but the decision was made when both the parole officer and the therapist realized that the parolee was badly out of control and needed incarceration.

It is important to emphasize our chief conclusion, that the successful relationship between nonmedical agencies and ourselves is dependent on an understanding of each other's problems, limitations, and assets, and, most important, on a personal trust between members of agencies working together at a clinical level.

## A FIRST APPRAISAL OF THE RESULTS

From July 1964 to June 1967, of the 499 patients who were referred to us for aid, we accepted 197, or nearly 40 percent, for the inpatient program. With a minimum time of six months for follow-up, we classified these patients as follows: 77 patients or 39 percent were included in group 0; 45 patients, or 23 percent, were included in group 1; 30 patients or 16 percent were included in group 2; and 43 patients or 22 percent were included in group 3.

GROUP 0 (39 percent) includes those addicts who never became involved in a long-term relationship with their therapists or anyone connected with the rehabilitation unit. Many of this group did not agree with our work goals or did not see the use of any involvement with us other than for withdrawal. Others were too aggressive or exploitative for the therapist to treat. A few revealed such incapacitating psychotic problems that transfer to other sections of the Boston State Hospital became necessary.

We do not have an accurate appraisal of the outcome of this group. While many have done badly, a few turned to various self-help groups and consider themselves successfully rehabilitated. In addition, we know of two patients who, presumably without any further help after withdrawal, have shown considerable social improvement.

GROUP 1 (23 percent) includes those patients who are involved in long-term relationships with either therapists or with various staff members, but have not been able or willing to renounce drugs. We aid in their existence but have accomplished little rehabilitation. They turn to us with their medical, marital, work, or housing problems. We refer them to other hospitals for their medical, surgical, and obstetrical emergencies; and we help the doctors with the ward management of these patients. We frequently try to interpret their behavior to the courts and arrange for as reasonable and nonpunitive disposition as possible.

GROUP 2 (16 percent) includes those patients who are involved in long-term relationships with us, are able to give up the drug way of life for periods of time, but remain quite dependent upon us, as well as upon their families or welfare agencies. Many of these patients are women who are attempting to manage fatherless households. The men of this group are so dependent that they are supported by their families or wives, but they have at least given up most of their drug taking.

GROUP 3 (22 percent) includes those patients who form a long-term relationship with us, are able to give up the drug way of life, and over the years have returned to work, developed new work skills, or completed their education. We include in this group women who are able to care for their children or run their households with or without help from their husbands. Occasionally, some of these patients might revert to drug taking. If they turned to us quickly for help or controlled themselves, they were still classified in this group.

*Clinical examples*

GROUP 3. Frank was 22 at the time of referral. Since he already had a lengthy record for crimes associated with drug taking, his probation officers warned him that the slightest infraction would mean a long prison sentence.

He began to take drugs at 14, first the codeine cough preparations and later the narcotics including heroin when available. He considered himself addicted when 17, and experienced withdrawal illness many times. He nearly died from one overdose but was rescued by friends, one of whom did die from an overdose. This experience caused Frank considerable guilt and acted as a deterrent to his enjoyment of drug taking.

He was not an introspective person. He seemed totally unable to relate his drug taking and his emotional reactions. His explanations were the epitome of simplicity: drugs were available and he enjoyed them.

He described his childhood only in factual terms and could not say whether it was happy or unhappy. From his description, it appeared that his father was preoccupied with the unsuccessful struggles to earn a living and to give up his excessive drinking. His mother worked and evidently gave up her role as housewife and mother many years ago. All we know for certain is that neither parent ever visited him or called any member of the staff.

Frank's adjustment to the ward was good. He performed his tasks well, cooperated with the staff, and even held some of the younger patients in check, but he was detached. It was not that he avoided people, for he was lively enough and could respond vigorously and appropriately if pushed around; but it was important to him not to show any feeling of affection or dependency.

Despite a high intelligence, he refused to go to school and chose to work when he was deemed ready for outside activities. He worked industriously for a month. Then he was arrested for forging a prescription for morphine. He thus spoiled his last chance, returned to his referring court, and received a prison sentence for a maximum of five years.

His therapist visited him monthly at the prison. For some time Frank carried on a deception. During each visit for the first six months, the patient described to the therapist, with pleasure, how his father had visited him and how they were trying to be close to each other to live a new and happier life. Shortly after Christmas, however, the therapist noted a change in Frank. Previously, he had been clean and industrious, but he became slovenly and irritable and dropped out of the prison school program. His therapist regarded this change as a depressive reaction to his situation at Christmas time. Frank then confessed that he had been lying about his father's visits, that his father had not visited him and had made no effort to communicate with him, despite Frank's rather unusual first step of writing several letters to his father.

Frank's reserve broke down. He described how much the therapist's visits meant to him, especially as he felt so badly rejected by his parents. Gradually, Frank's spirits began to improve, at least to a point where he returned to prison school. It became evident that his aloofness had been a defensive character trait to protect himself from the hurts of disappointing parents.

After 14 months of imprisonment, he was granted a parole on condition that he return to the center. This time, when he returned to the ward, he was willing to continue his education. He was accepted at a technical school which he completed with honors in six months. Then he received an apprenticeship to a newspaper firm. Over the subsequent period of time, now three years since our first contact with him, he has developed into a highly skilled technician. He has moved off the ward and lives as a bachelor in an apartment near the hospital. During all this time, Frank has maintained a useful and friendly relationship with his staff therapist and parole officer. From our observations, he has remained drug free and has done well. When under pressure, he tends to regress to drinking, irritability, and even paranoid-like outbursts of rage. On these occasions, his therapist confronts him with his regressive behavior and demands to know the events or problem that led to his emotional reaction. He recovers quickly so that, at present, these outbursts do not represent a major problem.

Frank has made considerable progress and seems to be able to control the violence and disturbing behavior of his earlier days. He remains a vulnerable person who tends to act aggressively when depressed. He still needs the relationship with the therapist. Although it is a parole requirement that he visit his therapist, it is obvious that he enjoys his visits. In fact, he spends some of his spare time helping out on the ward and visiting his favorite staff members.

GROUP 2. Mary was 25 when she came to us on the advice of her parole officer. Raised under gross emotional deprivation, she had shown early signs of developmental behavior problems. She had been a truant and runaway. The many charges of "stubborn child" indicated the inability of foster parents to cope with her except through punitive means. She began her drug taking at 15, and was soon addicted to heroin. Her arrests had continued, and she was incarcerated twice at the Massachusetts Correctional Institution for Women at Framingham.

When she was 18, she married another addict, bore one child, but soon lost both husband and child. Her husband was killed in a gun battle and her child was turned over to the care of the Division of Child Guardianship. Despite her imprisonments and drug taking, she managed to see her child occasionally. This child became of special significance to her, and she volunteered for hospitalization to gain the care of her child. As soon as withdrawal symptoms subsided, she requested the care of her child. We explained to her that she still had to show that she could control herself in the community before assuming this responsibility. She was angry at what she considered a rebuff, but with the encouragement of the therapist and the other patients, she did not run away.

She continued on the inpatient program for three months, during which time she attempted to work as an aide, first in the geriatric ward of this hospital, later in another hospital. Her capacity for work was limited. She complained of physical pains and found it hard to adjust to the authority of the nurses. She used heroin sporadically and then re-addicted herself. Again she was withdrawn and placed on a daily dose of 20 mg. of methadone which sustained her for over one year. She insisted that we accept her work limitations and allow her to accept financial help from welfare.

By this time, Mary was willing to proceed slowly. Together with a social worker from the Division of Child Guardianship, we worked out a plan for weekly visits with her child provided that if she remained drug free (except for methadone) for a year, she could assume full-time care of her daughter. At first, the girl, now 13, was pleased with her mother's visits. But then she began to bombard her mother with accusations. "How come she did not love her only child enough to care for her all these years?" Mary withered under her child's attacks and seriously thought of returning to drugs. She began to avoid her daughter.

The situation became alarming, for the girl reacted by truancy, stealing, and fighting in her foster home. The therapist forced the issue by confronting Mary with her evasion and then demanded to know if she were going to cope with her child or run away.

Mary summoned up her courage and told her daughter the

truth; that she was addicted, had been imprisoned, and now was trying to improve so she could take care of her daughter. The situation improved in the sense that the girl's behavior became more subdued, but she still was furious at her mother's prolonged absence. Mary learned that she could cope with her child's problems although she needed considerable support and advice from the various social workers involved.

After Mary remained drug free for a year, she assumed full-time care for her daughter. She still depends on the community for Welfare Aid and on us for medical and psychiatric help. She works only sporadically. In the past several years, she made one brief return to drugs but was easily withdrawn and returned to her present way of life. Most of the time, she functions well as a conscientious and sensitive mother determined to help her child through adolescence.

We have tried to work with other community agencies to extend aid to the drug users rather than to reject or punish them. Our hope is that all members of our community will recognize the complex nature of the drug-taking problem and respond with less frustration. When this happens, we believe that there will be an abatement of the traditionally harsh and punitive response toward these people and we will learn to live and deal with their problem more intelligently and constructively.

# A response to the drug age

## H. DAVID ARCHIBALD

Under David Archibald's guidance the Addiction Research Foundation of Canada has established an international reputation. Dr. Archibald has been president of the North American Association of Alcoholism Programs, and has held high positions in both the International Council on Alcohol and Addictions and the Committee on Drug Dependence for WHO. He writes with authority on the growing problems of the drug age.

One of the important dialogues—national and international—on public policy is a debate on how to respond adequately to the problems of public health that are the consequences of the drug age. In recent years, there has been an enormous development of the drug industry, much of it to the benefit of mankind. One major result, however, among many others, has been the proliferation of drugs and compounds that affect the central nervous system. Drugs, including alcohol, are now used widely to promote relaxation, stimulation, sleep, energy, to change mood, to "expand the mind," to produce new and indescribable experiences, and to enable one to opt out of society completely. There is an increasing tendency to subscribe to the premise—whether implicit or explicit—that life cannot be lived or enjoyed without some form of "chemical comfort."

The drugs used and abused vary from country to country, and even between groups and subcultures within the same country. In Canada and the United States, the main drug of abuse is alcohol; however, the use of other drugs both legal and illegal has increased tremendously over the last few years. Similarly in Chile and France, the abuse of alcohol is still the most common problem. However, in Singapore, opium smoking and heroin use are common and there is little abuse of alcohol. In some countries of Africa and Asia, the production of beverage alcohol has increased remarkably over the past few years, sometimes up to tenfold; and sporadic tribal or village ceremonial drinking has in many instances been replaced by more regular drinking in bars. The impact of a drug substance on this rapidly changing society is considerable. In India, opium and cannabis are used extensively although this consumption is now declining somewhat. In Hong Kong and Thailand, heroin is tending to supersede opium and morphine as the chief drug of abuse. Problems of opium and hashish abuse are widespread in Egypt. Khat is widely used in the countries on the east and west coasts of the Red Sea. Cannabis is used in most countries of the African continent. Coca leaf and cocaine are extensively used in Peru and Bolivia, and cannabis in Brazil.

The absence of a constant, universal shape to the problem makes it difficult to provide any universal answer to the question of how to respond adequately to drug use and abuse, in a way that will ensure that the public health problems are reduced to the "irreducible minimum."

There are, however, a few principles that legislators, policy makers, and health officials should consider. Questions of definition, conceptual framework, epidemiological patterns, relationships, and nonrelationships between the drug substances used and abused and other matters are among the overall considerations.

In 1965, the World Health Organization reclassified alcoholism as "drug dependence—alcohol type." Similarly, drug addiction was reclassified as "drug dependence" followed by the name of whatever drug was being abused. Hence, morphine addiction became "drug dependence—morphine type," cannabis addiction became "drug dependence—cannabis type."

By introducing the "common denominator" dependence, the debate as to whether or not any particular drug substance is or is not addictive becomes somewhat irrelevant. Even though a substance may not produce any physical dependence, its use by some persons in some ways may still involve psychological dependence.

Drug dependence, as defined by the World Health Organization Committee, is "a state of psychic or physical dependence, or both, on a drug, arising in a person following administration of that drug on a periodic or continuous basis." [1] It is noted further that the characteristics of such a state will vary with the agent involved, hence the need to designate the type of dependence by the modifying phrases—of morphine type—of alcohol type—of cannabis type, and so on.

It is important to emphasize that drug dependence relates to an individual and by itself carries no connotation of damage to public health; the latter must be assessed separately.

For example, the majority of the population of North America —at least 70 percent—are able to use alcohol—a potent psychoactive agent—in moderation, with relatively little risk to health. A minority, but nevertheless a very substantial number of individuals, use large quantities of alcohol on a daily basis with consequent damage to their own health, to their families, and to surrounding communities.

In the Province of Ontario, Canada, with a total population of approximately 8,000,000 people, 250,000 individuals consume the equivalent of 8 ounces of whiskey or more per day. Approximately 125,000 of these individuals are alcoholics in the traditional clinical sense of that term.

In contrast, a small minority of the population use morphine-like substances, and the majority of this minority develop quite rapidly a high degree of dependence—both physical and psychological—with very considerable damage to their health and to society generally.

Barbiturates, amphetamines, tranquilizers, and hallucinogens are now being used in increasing quantities and by an increasing number of people in many countries including Canada and the United States. A variety of relatively new drug-dependence phenomena are now developing. The risk to public health has not yet been adequately assessed and depends on circumstances which change from drug to drug and from culture to culture. The World Health Organization Expert Committee has stated that:

> If a drug abuse or dependence is likely to be, or is known to be, only sporadic or infrequent in the population, if there is little danger of its spread to others, and if its adverse effects are likely to be, or are known to be, limited to the individual user, there is no public health problem. Such forms of abuse may be prevented or managed by adequate information and appropriate medical care. On the other hand, if the drug dependence is associated with behavioural or other responses that adversely affect the user's interpersonal relations or cause adverse physical, social or economic consequences to others as well as to himself, and if the problem is actually widespread in the population or has a significant potential for becoming widespread, then a public health problem does exist. Society must then, among other things, take the responsibility for determining whether or not the drug in question should be controlled.[2]

One conceptual approach to the problems of drug dependence is via the public health communicable disease model in which are involved three factors: (a) the agent—in this case some drug, filling the role that in some other illnesses is played by bacteria or viruses; (b) the host—the individual persons in whom the use or abuse of a particular chemical involves a dependence; (c) the environment—the social, economic, legal, and cultural situation in which the first two factors are interacting.

With dependence on a substance like alcohol, whose use is subject to a very few legal or social restrictions, each case involves a long history of excessive intake. Alcohol (which is the "agent" in public health terms) is being overused by the individual person (the "host") within a particular set of social circumstances (the "environment"). The environment includes the prevailing attitudes and customs of the community toward drinking and toward other "chemical escape routes," particularly the level of alcohol consumption beyond which a particular society begins to regard such use as abuse.

With dependence on those drugs whose use is subject to prohibitive legal restraint, the "environment" is very different from that surrounding alcohol use. The user of prohibited drugs is alienating himself from society's mainstream; however, he frequently obtains support from some subculture. Conceivably such a subculture may grow to the point where its influence begins to modify society to some extent.

## FOUR APPROACHES

While the agent, host, and environment concept describes the targets for public health efforts, the methods of reaching these targets need to be spelled out somewhat differently. A comprehensive program directed toward the reduction and prevention of alcohol and drug problems requires four interrelated approaches:

1. Research
2. Education
3. Legislation
4. Treatment of the drug dependent person

Legislation by itself is not an effective answer to the problem, nor is education alone, nor is treatment. While none of these approaches will suffice separately, their combined application seems promising to the agent of infection (the drug substance) to the host (the drug-dependent person) and to the environment in which the transaction between the agent and the host takes place. For example, the kind and extent of legal control of a given drug must be related to the nature of use and abuse, the degree of its acceptance in a community, and the type and degree of hazard to public health. Sound decisions on legal control measures can be taken only if reliable and comprehensive data are available from the research section of the program. Research, for instance, into the attitudes toward drugs, their patterns of use and abuse, and the changes in such attitudes and patterns over time, provides important data concerning possible increases in prevalence of drug dependence and related abuse and the potential for epidemic spread. In addition, material essential for the development of legislative, educational, and therapeutic strategies must be derived from research. Of great importance also is scientific evaluation of possible consequences of changes in various control measures.

Similarly, education programs have a direct bearing on community attitudes toward legislative control and therapeutic programs on the one hand, and the decisions taken by individuals respecting their use of drug substances on the other hand. The content of educational programs must be factual and credible. The educational material must be presented in a form that is comprehensible, credible, and meaningful to the audience. The educational program should rest heavily on data derived from research and clinical experience.

Numerous other examples could be stated to illustrate the major conclusion, namely, that all program parameters—research, education, legislation, and treatment—are necessary in their own right and must be interrelated to provide a comprehensive approach to the problems of alcohol and drug dependence

Until recently much of the worldwide effort against dependence on drugs has been concentrated on legal control of the agents of dependence. With narcotic substances, this approach was directed toward control of international "trade and traffic." With alcohol, the most notable legal approach of recent years was prohibition as practiced in the United States, in Finland, and in modified forms in other countries, such as Sweden and India. It was reasoned that if the "infectious agent"—the drugs of abuse—could be sufficiently well controlled or eradicated, then problems of drug dependence and other damage to society would be prevented. This approach, using only one element of the public health model, has not provided the answer to the problem. Here, too little attention was paid to the problems of the drug user (the host) or to the environmental factors in which the agent and the host were interacting.

## MAJOR PROBLEMS

In attempting to broaden a program so as to include all four approaches, a number of basic problems emerge. Specialists working in any one section of the program, that is, the legislative section, educational section, treatment section, have a tendency to believe that their approach to the problem provides the basic answer rather than simply one part of the answer. For example, traditionally there has been little communication between legal control authorities and those concerned with public health. Some representatives of the control group still believe implicitly that the only way to solve problems of drug dependence is to rigorously control the production and sale of the various drug substances. On the other hand, some health people believe that the only way to solve the problem is to concentrate on drug dependence as an illness of the individual and society, and approach it with a vigorous program of preventive education and a wide range of treatment services. The need for much more communication between the legal and health authorities, to promote greater understanding and appreciation of their relative roles and contribution, is a fundamental problem needing much attention.

Another major area of debate is whether or not the problems of alcohol dependence and dependence on other drug substances can be combined within one comprehensive program. Some hold strongly to the view that they should be dealt with as separate programs; others hold equally strong views that they should be combined. The matters are of direct concern not only to the professional community but also to those responsible for establishing governmental policies. The allocation of public funds, of professional personnel, and of scientific resources, and perhaps in the long run the overall progress and success in controlling and preventing problems of alcohol and drug dependence hinge on the kinds of decisions governments and other bodies make on this major policy issue.

As one of the first organizations to officially combine programs related to the use of both alcohol and drugs, the Addiction Research Foundation of Ontario has accumulated some experience which may have some bearing on the debate.

For the first fourteen years, major attention of the foundation was devoted to developing programs of research, treatment, and education in the field of alcohol dependence. In 1963, the legislation governing the activities of the foundation was amended to extend all sections of the program of the foundation to all drugs liable to produce dependence—alcohol, barbiturates, amphetamines, hallucinogens, and narcotics.

Many questions had to be considered carefully before making this major change in policy. We recognized the vast difference between educating a society that accepts alcohol as a legitimate beverage and a society that rejects alcohol in favor of some other drug. We were also concerned that by integrating educational approaches we would be liable either to oversimplify or to complicate the educational methods and message to the point of confusion. In treatment, we recognized that there were many similarities in the therapeutic approach to patients dependent on such substances as alcohol or barbiturates but great differences between these and patients dependent on narcotics. We recognized further that a combined approach would perhaps be most useful to research programs and to some aspects of the treatment program, but it would be less applicable to consideration of control measures since at least in our culture the instruments of legal control for alcohol are vastly different from the instruments available for the control of narcotics.

In the final analysis, it was the experience that we had had in the field of alcoholism that led to our policy decision to extend our program to include all drugs of dependence. The interest and practice of our staff had constantly reached into the area of other drug dependencies for comparisons as research was conducted into the etiology and other facets of alcoholism. In our clinical and research work we found that drugs were often used in combination by the same individual—barbiturates with alcohol, for example, and that transfers from one drug of dependence to another also occurred frequently. Consequently many of the studies we were doing relating to alcohol dependence were also applicable to other drug use.

The World Health Organization Expert Committee lists three general patterns of drug transfer and combined use which are substantiated by our own experience: the first is a shift from one drug to another in the same group with a particular type of dependence, say from opium to morphine to heroin; the second is a switch among closely related types, such as between barbiturates and alcohol; the third is a switch from one dependence type to another of substantially different kind, as between barbiturates (depressants) and amphetamines (stimulants).[3]

We also found many drug takers, including many dependent on alcohol, who were using sedatives and stimulants at the same time. Currently, in both Canada and the United States, reports are appearing of the use in sequence of quite different drugs, such as barbiturates for a limited period, alcohol for a few days, followed by amphetamines, marihuana, LSD, and so on.

A note of caution should be inserted. Although our clinical section is responsible for handling patients using various kinds of drugs, it does not follow that all patients are handled in the same unit by the same methods. For example, a special clinical team and special facilities had to be established for patients dependent on narcotics. We found that the person dependent on heroin or morphine did not mix well with alcohol dependent patients or other drug groups. Moreover the treatment methods used for the narcotic patient are quite different from methods applied to alcoholics.

Dr. Dale Cameron has stressed the same point.[4] He notes that there is a vast difference between treating all drug-dependent persons in a single ward or in a single hospital or outpatient setting and having several different but closely coordinated treatment sources that may serve different patients according to their drug dependence, underlying psychopathology, social background, and legal status. He notes: "It is the commonality of 'escape through drugs,' that is, the utilization of drugs as a 'crutch,' that prompts us to consider integration of programs for all drug dependent persons." He concludes that it makes sense that if a patient who has been treated by one team for alcoholism returns for abusing other drugs, the same team should maintain his treatment.

Our experience in Ontario over the past ten years with "the combined approach to alcohol and other drugs" has strengthened our conviction that the policy of integrating alcoholism and other drug-dependency studies and services within one umbrella organization is a sound one.

What then are the directions which should be taken by comprehensive programs intended to cope with alcoholism and drug dependence within a state or community?

The first essential is, of course, to define the nature and extent of the problem as accurately as possible. Simply to label it as a public health problem is not enough: the basic need is to have specific and valid answers to such questions as:

> How many people, of what age, from what sections of society, are using what kinds of drugs, in what form and amount and how often?
>
> What kind and amount of damage, if any, occurs as a consequence of drug use to the health of individuals and to the health of the community?

These are the questions that epidemiological research must answer in order to place program planning on a solid basis of fact. They call for what might be called "community-oriented" research, as distinct from research moving toward an understanding of the nature of the individual disorder of dependence on chemicals.

Along the latter lines of research, our findings in Ontario support the hypothesis that acquired physical dependence, in the neurocellular sense at least, is reversible, but that psychic dependence is not yet as fully understood. Psychic dependence therefore becomes a priority area for research. Within this area are two important components, on the one hand to elaborate and test motivational factors and psychological learning theories, and on the other hand to pursue a clearer understanding of the social factors which provide much of the environment in which dependence on a substance develops and is maintained. In all of these areas there is much to be learned from cross comparison of phenomena related to different drugs and to different societies.

Educational programs, which ideally should be anchored to research findings, are called upon to inform and guide in areas where scientific information is still very sketchy. The conscientious educator evolves his methods by trial and error; he knows he is experimenting, but is he conducting his experiments in such a way that their outcome can ever be known? It is vital that he should do so and that he should enlist the support and guidance of research-minded people so that his educational experiments can in fact produce knowledge about educational process.

Close liaison between educators and researchers is also vital in order to preserve the credibility of the educator in dealing with subjects on which there is much controversy and quite a few self-appointed experts.

Legislation should not be limited to providing mechanisms for controlling or prohibiting distribution of the drug agent. It should also provide for educational and therapeutic services. It may well be that some of the future legislation governing nonmedical use of drugs might in some countries evolve along lines similar to legislation governing alcohol use in other countries. Certainly legislation, to play its part at all effectively, must have widespread public assent and support, and that may have to be preceded by education designed to sell the public health value of what is proposed.

Treatment services, like educational activities, proceed by trial and error and must in the process attempt to provide effective research opportunities which can help the therapist discern what works and what does not. In addition, the training of therapists, both lay and professional, requires actual experience in work with those in the field concerned; hence nearly all therapeutic or treatment services need to budget for and carry on a good deal of professional or semiprofessional training.

It is also important that those engaged in treatment define their treatment goals in terms that are meaningful to the society in which they work, and meaningful also to those in the subculture from which they expect to draw their patients. The ritual of describing a form of behavior as a disease, illness, sickness, disorder, disability, or crime does not make it so. To some individuals, their use of alcohol or drugs is none of these things. Our labels must realistically take into account how their application will affect those to whom they are applied.

## REFERENCES

1. Nathan B. Eddy *et al.,* "Drug Dependence: Its Significance and Characteristics," *Bulletin WHO,* 1965.
2. WHO Expert Committee on Drug Dependence, Sixteenth Report, Technical Report Series, No. 407.
3. "Services for the Prevention and Treatment of Dependence on Alcohol and Other Drugs," Fourteenth Report of the World Health Organization Committee on Mental Health, World Health Organization technical report series, No. 363, Geneva, 1967.
4. D. C. Cameron, "Integration of Alcoholism and Other Addiction Programs," *International Journal of Addictions,* Vol. 1, 1966, pp. 5–8.

# Part Three

# New Dimensions

# Alcoholism and drug dependence— under one umbrella?

## M. M. GLATT

Can treatment programs for alcoholism and drug addiction be combined, or should the problems be attacked separately? The question is analyzed in depth here by Dr. Max Glatt, lecturer and consultant psychiatrist to a number of British hospitals. Dr. Glatt is honorary editor of *The British Journal of Addictions* and associate editor of *Alcoholism* Zagreb/Lausanne. He is a consultant to WHO committees on alcoholism and drug dependence and to the Scientific Board of the International Council on Alcoholism and Addictions.

## HISTORICAL INTRODUCTION

At the 28th International Congress held in 1968 in Washington, the plenary session on the last day was partly given over to a panel discussion of what was termed an "unresolved" question—the interrelationship between alcoholism and drug dependence. This question—whether to combine or not—has been hotly debated over the past few years. The annual Institute on the Prevention and Treatment of Alcoholism had for years occasionally also touched on the problems of drugs other than alcohol, but not until the 12th Institute held in Prague in 1966 was a whole session given over to the problem of drug dependence,[1] and a paper read on the theme "alcoholism and drug dependence: resemblances and dissimilarities."[2] When, two years earlier, the International Council on Alcohol and Alcoholism had decided to set up an International Scientific and Professional Board, a section on drug dependence was included. In 1965 a preliminary informal meeting of experts brought together by the World Health Organization recommended to the W.H.O. the convening of an Expert Committee to consider both the problems of alcoholism and dependence on other drugs, and in fact a 1966 W.H.O. Expert Meeting had as its theme "Services for Prevention and Treatment of Dependence on Alcohol and Other Drugs." [3] At a national level, in a few countries examples already existed of organizations whose programs included both alcoholism and drug dependence. Thus in Great Britain the Society for the Study of Inebriety (founded in 1884) had in 1923 added to the name of its official journal, *The British Journal of Inebriety,* the subheading "Alcoholism and Drug Addiction," before becoming, in 1946, "The Society for the Study of Addiction (to Alcohol and Other Drugs)," and its journal, *The British Journal of Addiction (to Alcohol and Other Drugs).* More recently a similar development took place in Canada; the Alcoholism Research Foundation in Ontario, established in 1949, and publishing its journal *Alcoholism,* changed its name in 1961 to "The Alcoholism and Drug Addiction Research Foundation," and the journal's name to *Addictions.*

However, the feeling that alcoholism and drug dependence are basically similar problems which should be "combined," or at least coordinated, under one large "umbrella" was by no means unanimous. For example, many members of Alcoholics Anonymous (especially those whose alcoholism had arisen mainly on a sociogenic, as different from a psychological, basis) do not regard themselves as fundamentally suffering from the same affliction as "dope fiends"; and clearly from the sociological aspect the fact that in Western culture alcohol is legal and freely available, its use encouraged by society and sanctioned by tradition, is quite different from drugs which in Western society can only be obtained as a rule by prescription. In order to provide a forum for the discussion of the problem, the International Council on Alcohol and Alcoholism in 1967 convened in Amsterdam a meeting of international authorities, and the debate also continued in the columns of the scientific journals, some condemning the "rush to combine" (Pittman),[4] others stating that such combination offered many advantages (Popham et al.).[5] As mentioned above, the question was also discussed at the 28th International Congress, but as it turned out, in practice quite a few American and other organizations had by then started the combination or coordination process, and the International Council decided in Washington to alter its name to that of "International Council on Alcohol and Addictions." Whereas in 1968 the 28th Congress dealt officially with alcoholism only, and was followed a few days later by an international meeting on drug dependence in Quebec, the next (29th) International Congress will deal officially both with alcoholism and dependence on other drugs.

In the following an attempt will be made briefly but systematically to review the problem of similarities and dissimilarities between alcoholism and dependence on other drugs, and the advisability or otherwise of a combined approach.

## CAUSATION [2,3,6]

Although the etiology of alcoholism and drug dependence is not fully understood, a number of factors working in close interaction with each other are clearly involved. Among them the pharmacological nature of the drug, the makeup of the personality, and the individual's surroundings are analogous to the infectious diseases—agent, host, environment.

### 1. The agent: the pharmacological nature of the drug

The point that alcohol is no longer used medicinally excludes it, in the view of some observers, from the list of drugs.[7] However, the facts that alcohol (like cannabis) is no longer used as a medicine, that it also constitutes a (not complete) foodstuff, that it commonly is taken as a social beverage as well as in religious rituals (however, opium and cannabis, too, have been taken in India in association with social rituals and religious belief); that in Western culture taking alcohol is regarded as more "respectable" than that of "drugs"—all this does not contradict the finding that not only do alcoholics employ alcohol as a "drug" habitually and compulsively, but so also do many heavy and occasionally also predominantly "social" drinkers, from time to time.

There are of course many different definitions as to what constitutes a "drug." For the pharmacologists, in the view of C. R. B. Joyce,[8] "a drug is any chemical which is introduced into a living organism and which leads to physiological effects . . . which can be detected by objective means"; and he emphasized that "drugs are not only substances used for therapeutic reasons: many kinds of alcohol, opium, 'purple hearts,' cocaine and the fantasticants beloved by Aldous Huxley, are all drugs for none of which, in my view, are there any therapeutic indications whatsoever."

While not everybody will necessarily agree completely with these sentiments, it is certainly true that following in particular the increased abuse by youngsters of opiates such as heroin, of amphetamines (such as the amphetamine-barbiturate combination known in England as "purple hearts"), of LSD (and cannabis), responsible medical opinion has swung more and more to the view that their medical use—if at all justified—should be limited to a few strictly defined indications. As regards cannabis, the World Health Organization at present finds no medical indication for its use.

In the past, alcohol shared with ancient drugs, such as the opiates and cannabis, the role and the task of helping the pain-ridden and unhappy man to a less painful and more enjoyable way of living. Possibly its main therapeutic use—alongside the opiates—was as "an analgesic and surgical anaesthetic before the introduction of ether."[9] As late as 1873 doctors were gravely warned by a medical journal that if they were rashly to attempt to treat disease without alcohol they might lay themselves open to a conviction for manslaughter.[10] Some former uses of alcohol have now been taken over by more modern drugs, such as sedatives, hypnotics, tranquilizers, and stimulants (and indeed some modern drug abusers employ many of them—including alcohol —as substitutes for each other when for some reason they are unable to get hold of the drug of their primary choice). Because of its socially high standing and its widespread social acceptance,

Jellinek calls alcohol "a domesticated drug";[11] however, often among some Western nations sedatives, hypnotics, and tranquilizers too are nowadays swallowed without clear medical indications.

The relative position of alcohol in regard to (other) dependence-producing drugs has been repeatedly studied by Expert Committees of the World Health Organization. A 1952 committee[12] divided drugs into three classes, on the basis of the user's psychological makeup and the pharmacological property of the drug.

With the first group of drugs, the pharmacological nature of the drug is paramount, the user's individual reactions no more than an adjunct; and sooner or later "addiction" (i.e., physical dependence) will develop in practically every user of the drug.

In a second category of drugs, their pharmacological nature plays no more than a subsidiary role, the drug user's psychological makeup being decisive; such drugs never produce "addiction" or an irresistible need for the drug, but lead to "habituation" (psychological or emotional dependence) in vulnerable personalities.

Finally, with a third group of drugs, their pharmacological action is intermediate in kind and degree between the "addiction-producing" and "habit-forming" drugs; their pharmacological role is significant but the predominant factor is the mental makeup; "addiction" may develop in psychologically vulnerable personalities.

Five years later another W.H.O. Expert Committee[13] tried to differentiate more clearly between "habituation" and "addiction" (an attempt more recently, in 1964,[14] was superseded by a recommendation to employ the term "dependence" in place of both "addiction" and "habituation"). Alcohol could not be clearly fitted into the groups of either "addiction-producing" or "habit-forming" drugs. From the latter it differs because, unlike them, alcohol used to excess may create grave social damage and produce "compulsive craving." On the other hand, as compared to the "addiction-producing" substances (such as the opiates):

(a) Tolerance increase in the case of alcohol amounts to no more than perhaps 3 to 4 times the original "inherent" tolerance

—namely, much less than the 25- to 100-fold rise in the case of morphine.

(b) Incidence of "addiction" in alcohol users is only a small fraction, in contrast to the nearly 100 percent occurrence in heroin users and 70 percent of morphine users.

(c) Whereas it takes morphine users no more than 3 to 4 weeks of usage of therapeutic doses to develop "addiction," a similar development in drinkers necessitates 3 to 20 years of excessive alcohol consumption. A severe physical abstinence syndrome—though of a different symptomatology from its much more common counterpart in opiate addiction—can also occur in a minority of very heavy drinkers.

Other differences between alcohol and the opiates were found to exist in the different attitudes of society to alcohol and the opiates, and the much less satisfactory therapeutic results in morphine addicts as compared to alcoholics.

Therefore, two W.H.O. Expert Committees in 1954[15] and 1955[16] concluded that *alcohol was a drug* with "a pharmacological action intermediate in kind and degree between addiction-producing and habit-forming drugs, so that compulsive craving and dependence can develop in those individuals whose makeup leads them to seek and find an escape in alcohol," personal makeup being the determining factor, but the pharmacological action also being significant. The 1955 W.H.O. Committee felt that, despite the existence of "so many clinical and biochemical analogies between alcoholism and opiate addiction," both in medical practice and in the medicosocial or legislative measure one had to make a clear distinction between them.

Unlike the Central Nervous System stimulants (such as the amphetamines, phenmetrazine, and cocaine) and the hallucinogens (such as LSD and cannabis), the CNS depressant alcohol, like the opiates and other CNS depressant drugs, can produce physical dependence. There exists a close functional relationship between alcohol and the barbiturates, illustrated by resemblance of the abstinence syndrome (epileptiform convulsions, delirium tremens) on sudden cessation of heavy alcohol and barbiturate intake respectively (incidentally, the danger of abstinence convulsions is still widely unknown and overlooked in both conditions). Many alcoholics—the "psychogenic" type probably, rather than the "occupational"—also habitually take other drugs to excess (mainly barbiturates) either while still drinking or while attempting to give up alcohol; and one important cause of death of alcoholics is from accidental (as in a state of "automatism") or intentional overdosage with barbiturates.[17]

Whether alcohol and the barbiturates taken together are merely additive or potentiating is as yet undecided; according to the pharmacologist, D. R. Laurence, "all cerebral depressants (hypnotics, tranquillizers, anti-epileptics, antihistamines) can either potentiate or at least synergize with alcohol," a risk which he regards as highly dangerous mainly in heavy drinkers, but which one might feel is also important in the case of car drivers with ordinary dosage.

Alcoholics with their acquired increased tolerance to alcohol are also ". . . relatively tolerant to some other cerebral depressant drugs (hydrocarbon anaesthetics and barbiturates)," but "no significant acquired cross-tolerance (exists) with the morphine group of drugs." Certain experiments carried out by Goldberg[18] showed that administration of certain popular tranquilizers, such as chlorpromazine, meprobamate, and chlordiazepoxide) reduced the amount of alcohol required to produce uncoordination.

The 1964 W.H.O. Expert Committee, when suggesting the use of the term "drug dependence" ("a state arising from repeated administration of a drug on a periodic or continuous basis"), recommended specification in each case of the particular type of drug dependence—such as dependence of the morphine type, cocaine type, etc. More recently, drug dependence of the alcohol type—not surprisingly in view of our previous discussion—was bracketed by Eddy et al. (1965)[19] with that of the barbiturate type. According to these authors, the intensity of the alcohol abstinence syndrome probably varies with the duration and amount of alcohol intake.

The mortality in the case of a severe alcohol abstinence syndrome is stated by them as averaging 8 percent; the fact that this figure is much higher than any seen by the present author in England may reflect the influence of local or regional drinking habits and other sociocultural factors.

The midway position occupied by alcoholism in relationship to other forms of drug dependence holds good in many aspects:

PSYCHOLOGICAL DEPENDENCE. In alcoholics psychological dependence varies in intensity, but it may sometimes be as severe as in the case of the barbiturates, though less strong than with the opiates, cocaine, and amphetamine-barbiturate mixtures; psychological dependence (as different from physical "addiction") may also occur with cannabis[20] and LSD, though in most individuals it may not be very marked. The question of cannabis dependence is often hotly debated, most cannabis users usually insisting that they can take the drug or leave it whenever they want to; but as with the alcoholic they usually prefer to make their point by taking it rather than leaving it, unless or until they find a stronger drug; and as cannabis is widely available the necessity for the user to give it up may not often arise.

PHYSICAL DEPENDENCE. As described above, physical dependence occurs with alcohol in a minority of users only, and usually after many years of very heavy drinking; with opiates, after using therapeutic doses for a few weeks; with barbiturates, after doses of only slightly above therapeutic levels, often after a few months only. On the other hand, alcohol- and barbiturate-abstinence syndromes may constitute a greater threat to life than does opiate withdrawal. In treatment, barbiturates should be tapered off gradually, whereas alcohol is usually stopped suddenly, though precautionary measures may be indicated against the occurrence of convulsions and D.T.'s; "cold turkey" in the case of the opiates should be avoided.

TOLERANCE. The irregular, incomplete tolerance increase in the case of alcohol and the barbiturates is much less marked than with the opiates. Tolerance increases slowly and markedly with the amphetamines, but not with cocaine. With LSD, tolerance may develop and disappear rapidly. Tolerance is usually said not to occur with cannabis; however, the present writer has come across quite a number of regular cannabis users who stated that after having "smoked" reefers for a certain time they failed to get the former "high" or "satisfaction" from it, and because of this began to search for more potent drugs.[21]

SOCIOECONOMIC COMPLICATIONS: HARM TO THE INDIVIDUAL. The alcoholic, preoccupied with drinking to the neglect, and often virtual exclusion, of eating and of his personal hygiene, may suffer from undernutrition with the resultant "diseases of chronic alcoholism" (although more recently alcohol itself has once more been said to produce liver damage),[22] of intercurrent infections, of chronic intoxication in the final "bender" stage, of accidents at home, at work, and on the road, of suicide, etc. Similar preoccupations with the drug may cause neglect, undernutrition, and infection in the opiate user (infections following unsterile injections being not uncommon in the young heroin, methylamphetamine, and the cocaine addict). Preoccupation with the drug leads to neglect of food and personal hygiene in the barbiturate addict who, like the longstanding alcoholic, may finally reach a state of chronic intoxication—its picture resembling that of chronic alcoholism with features such as ataxia, dysrhythmia, confusion. Anorexia—though for quite different reasons than in the alcoholic—and insomnia are common in amphetamine "addicts," who may also develop toxic psychoses, resembling the picture of paranoid schizophrenia); psychotic episodes may also occur in alcoholics and barbiturate addicts, as well as LSD and more rarely in cannabis users. The question of the effect of cannabis on mental functioning is not yet clear, but at any rate preoccupation with the drug in the growing-up youngster is liable to interfere with emotional growth as he loses the opportunity to learn from having to face up to and cope with the challenge arising out of day-to-day obstacles.

SOCIOECONOMIC COMPLICATIONS: HARM TO SOCIETY. Alcoholism leads to marked economic loss (absenteeism, interference with work performance, costs arising from society's obligation to maintain the alcoholic in hospitals or jails, to look after his dependents etc.). The alcoholic's relationships at home, at work, and in social intercourse are seriously disturbed, and his increasing dependence on alcohol may involve him in accidents and antisocial activities. Driving in an alcohol-impaired state is an exceedingly common and early feature in alcoholism. Similar effects resulting in disturbed relationships with others and increasing isolation, economic loss, and involvement in antisocial activities are seen in the other types of drug dependence, as in opiate addiction (e.g., in the recent British scene the young heroin-cocaine addict withdraws from ordinary society, gets involved with a group of other addicts within a "subculture," gives up work, lives on National Assistance, and makes money by selling his surplus of drugs to adolescent "newcomers"). Similarly, the young abuser of amphetamines may be inclined to give up work and to peddle drugs, and through his psychomotor impairment, coupled with his reckless attitude, he may get involved in accidents. Alcohol thus shares with other drugs risks to the individual arising out of his constant preoccupation with his drug to the exclusion of other vital interests, and risks due directly to the effects of the drug, and damage caused to society. Through their vastly greater numbers, alcoholics are responsible for much greater social damage than addicts to other drugs.

*2. The host:* the influence of the personality makeup

As yet no conclusive evidence regarding the etiological role of a physical makeup in alcoholism and drug dependence appears to have been put forward (this does not exclude the possibility that some such evidence may yet come to light, at least regarding certain types of alcohol and drug dependence). On the other hand, the importance of the *psychological* makeup in the causation of alcoholism and drug dependence is generally recognized. No definite conclusions can be drawn about the features of the prealcoholic or preaddictive personality from a study of the individual after he has become an addict. The search for a uniform preaddictive or prealcoholic personality has proved negative, and the so-called "alcoholic personality" is nowadays regarded to be the result rather than the cause of excessive drinking.

Many features in the established alcoholic and drug addict may have arisen during the course, and as a consequence, of prolonged alcohol and drug abuse, with its ethical and emotional deterioration, the social ostracism and pressure, and the abuser's reaction toward it, and with the addict's increasing need to have his drug at any price, and in the face of what he—often rightly— regards as a hostile and nonunderstanding environment. All these reactions may in time bring about a deceptive feature of a uniform personality. On the other hand, a number of personality traits are often found in future alcoholics and drug abusers, such as emotional immaturity, a desire to escape from reality, a low frustration tolerance, a low capacity to endure tension, etc. There seems nothing specific about such characteristics, and whether the individual with a low frustration tolerance "escapes" into excessive drinking, drug abuse, or other forms of gratification, relief or deviant behavior may be largely determined by environmental factors and opportunity, such as the availability of a special escape route within easy reach at a time when the individual is under strain and stress.

In Western culture alcohol naturally may be a favorite choice —especially for males—since alone among dependence-producing drugs (apart from nicotine) it is freely available without medical prescription, and its use sanctioned by tradition and culture. Under similar situations of stress the African and Asian living in a Mohammedan country may be tempted to seek solace in cannabis (although generally outlawed by legislation) rather than in alcohol, which is forbidden by his religion. The number of cannabis users in Africa and Asia is estimated to run into many millions.

The often reported finding that alcoholism and other forms of drug dependence frequently occur in the same individual, either at the same time or following each other, seems to confirm the impression that there is no specific predisposition—inborn or acquired—to develop alcoholism. For example, more than 25 percent of our alcoholic patients had at some time or other in the past also taken other drugs to excess, most commonly barbiturates, but also nonbarbiturate sedatives and tranquilizers (such as meprobamate), or stimulants, such as amphetamines and phenmetrazine. Again, after "successful" treatment of their alcoholism, many individuals in a desperate struggle to stay sober, may become dependent on substitute drugs, in particular those sold without prescription over the counter and marketed as being "nonaddictive." For vulnerable personalities, including many alcoholics, practically all sedative or stimulant drugs may carry a dependency risk.

Three interacting factors named as being important in the personality of the potential addicts and in the development of drug dependence[23] seem to be of equal importance in alcoholism: degree of emotional and physical discomfort, the individual's ability to endure such discomfort, and the strength, character, and directional internal controls of behavior (i.e., conscience and ego-control). Dependence may develop when discomfort is not well tolerated and when the internal controls are inadequate or misdirected.

In contrast to the high incidence of barbiturate abuse among our alcoholic patients, previous, simultaneous, or later addiction to opiates among them was very rare, a finding also remarked upon by some other observers (although in the United States their abuse by the same individual seems to be less uncommon). To a certain extent this seems to be in line with Wikler's hypothesis,[24] according to which all dependence-producing drugs reduce pain and have a (direct or indirect) hypnotic effect. Moreover, they screen from consciousness matters which may cause unhappiness: alcohol (with its anaesthetic effect on higher brain levels) by letting loose aggression and by stimulating sex urges (though reducing performance); opiates, on the other hand (affecting primarily the lower brain levels) by weakening the aggressive and sexual drives. Thus, confronted with the choice between alcohol and opiates, the individual in need of a discharge of aggressive emotion may turn to alcohol, whereas the man who feels more at ease when his aggressive feelings have been quieted down may choose opiates. Seen in cultural perspectives it has been argued that competitive Western culture, with its stress on manliness, approves of alcohol and condemns opium (and cannabis), whereas the more placid Eastern culture condemns aggression and therefore accepts opium rather than alcohol. It is interesting that many modern young drug abusers look down on and condemn the (middle-aged) alcohol consumer as being noisy and aggressive, contrasting alcohol unfavorably with hashish which allows them to be "high" while remaining quiet and peaceful.

Psychoanalysts often see alcoholism and drug dependence as phenomena resulting from "oral fixation." However, the common view nowadays is that both alcoholics and drug addicts are people with many different kinds of personality structure. Two fairly different, though sometimes overlapping, preaddictive personality types seen nowadays among alcohol and drug abusers are, on the one hand, the (frequently middle-aged) individual suffering from emotional discomfort and trying to relieve it by drugs such as alcohol, barbiturates, opiates, etc.; on the other hand, the (often younger) person dissatisfied or bored with the meaninglessness of day-by-day existence, searching for "kicks," for a "high" and a "buzz" ("like hanging on the edge of a cliff," as one youngster expressed it), or for consciousness expansion. This second group may prefer—if they have a choice between alcohol and drugs— stimulants (amphetamines, cocaine) and, if possible, intravenous "fixing" (with its more rapid and more intense effect—"flash"); or to the hallucinogens. By and large, generalizing widely and not quite accurately, younger and more psychopathic individuals may predominate among the second group (intellectuals and the artistically minded may search for "mind-expanding" psychedelic drugs), and the more neurotic and middle-aged among the first group may turn to alcohol and barbiturates. At any rate, other factors being equal, emotionally unstable, immature, and insecure individuals run a greater risk of gradually proceeding from "relief" drinking or drug taking to alcoholism or drug dependence than more stable and mature people; and a large random sample of alcoholics and drug addicts will contain a relatively higher proportion of neurotics and psychopaths than the general population. However, even so-called "normal" personalities, with no more than their fair share of personality disturbances, may, under excessive stress or under unfavorable environmental or occupational circumstances, develop alcoholism or drug dependence (e.g., publicans and "professional" drug addicts, respectively). Similarly, nowadays basically "normal" students, for fear of being "odd-man-out" and living in a subculture where drugs are "in," may embark on the "smoking" of cannabis reefers.

THE POSSIBLE ROLE OF GENETIC FACTORS. The question of a specific inheritance of alcoholism is not generally accepted—as different, possibly, from a vague concept of a constitutionally low capacity of the Central Nervous System to tolerate frustration. However certain observers in various countries feel that their recent research results illustrate the possible importance of genetic factors at least in certain cases. For example, J. Mardones (Chile),[25] a pioneer in this type of research, points to the wide individual fluctuations not only of the normal "physiological appetency" but also of the "pharmacological appetency" (i.e., drinking for the effect of alcohol) and the "pathological appetency" (characteristic of the "loss of control" and "inability to abstain" drinker), and also of the susceptibility to medical complications. These fluctuations may originate from genetic or environmental factors. He argues that, since in the case of alcohol, the environmental factors (accessibility to alcohol, and cultural rules concerning alcohol use) act on everybody, and yet there exist important individual fluctuations, genetic factors must exist which would influence the progress from one step of the evolution of dependence to the next one. He quotes three examples where genetic influences have been demonstrated:

1. The genetic origin of individual fluctuations in alcohol preference of rats preferring alcohol solutions to water—such fluctuations probably being related to the "physiological appetency" for alcohol.

2. The existence of an atypical alcohol dehydrogenase of a six times higher activity than the typical one (von Wartburg).[26]

3. The discovery of a significant correlation between color blindness, liver cirrhosis, and alcoholism.[27]

Mardones claims that these three main facts, showing the presence of genetic factors in relation to alcoholism, encourage further studies in order to establish whether or not they interfere in the step-by-step development of alcohol dependence. As regards other forms of drug dependence, such as morphine- or barbiturate-type dependence, the transition between excessive drug use and physical dependence is less influenced by individual fluctuations than in alcoholism, but nevertheless, in his view, the influence of genetic factors here, too, cannot be definitely excluded, which could possibly be shown by studies in populations where the abuse of the drug concerned is widespread.

Other investigators interested in this problem include Camps and Dodd, who found a higher incidence among alcoholics of individuals not secreting in their saliva ABH blood-group substances than among the random (normal) population. In their view the apparent association between nonsecretion of ABH substances and alcoholism may be fortuitous, but might, on the other hand, illustrate the possibility of a "genetically determined predisposition to the disease of alcoholism."

Finally, a number of Finnish authors have recently investigated the question of the relative importance of environmental and hereditary factors by means of twin studies.[28] An influence of inheritance was found to exist for the practices of normal drinking, heavy drinking, abstinence, and for lack of control in the young; whereas no such influence was detected regarding social consequences of drinking, including arrests, and the presence of addictive symptoms (including the lack of control in the young). However, the authors themselves are careful to point out the difference in Finnish drinking habits to those of other societies, and to the many uncertainties besetting the results of twin studies. One must also remember that twenty years ago, in an American study, Roe[29] found no evidence of hereditary influences on the development of alcoholism. Thus, the question of the importance of inherited factors in the development of addictions seems still very obscure.

## 3. The environment

Previous examples have illustrated the fact that, apart from personality stability, opportunity and drug availability often play an important role in the genesis of alcohol or drug dependence. The bartender, his wife, the waiter, the journalist, the executive moving in an environment where business is often transacted in establishments which serve beverage alcohol, are all tempted to imbibe frequently and heavily; the doctor, pharmacist, chemist, the nurse, all have access to drugs almost as easily as the rest of the population to alcohol; and moving in a subculture in which the smoking of cannabis, or the LSD "trip," or the "mainlining" of heroin or methylamphetamine are generally accepted, the youngster who wants to "belong" may easily drift into doing likewise.

In all such cases alcohol and drug abuse cannot just be ascribed in the main to greater personality vulnerability. Similarly, the proportionately higher representation among alcoholics the world over and throughout history of men as compared with women can hardly be explained by the greater emotional stability of the female sex or by its lesser exposure to strain and stress. In the latter example, too, it seems more plausible to attribute the numerically less strong representations of women among alcoholics at least partly to an environmental factor, i.e., the greater social taboo against female heavy drinking as contrasted with the acceptance or even encouragement of such drinking behavior among men. Under similar circumstances, therefore, the woman in need of emotional relief may feel tempted to turn to barbiturates, more easily carried in the handbag than the gin bottle, and less easily detected because of the absence of the treacherous smell of alcohol on the breath. Under similar conditions her husband may escape to the bottle.[30]

It is also of interest to mention here another example of environmental influence in the choice of drug abuse—local fashion. The habitual excessive use of analgesics in this country seems to be rare, but it is a common form of drug abuse in Switzerland, so that the Swiss woman (for example, the one working in industry) may take to analgesics under similar conditions where the British housewife may abuse barbiturates. The importance of sociocultural factors is often illustrated by quoting the rarity of alcoholism among Jews, despite the virtual absence of Jewish teetotalers; and by the tendency for alcohol abuse to increase among Jewish students the more they are removed from religious orthodoxy.

The influence of economic conditions is reflected in countries such as France, with her very high alcoholism rates, her enormous wine production, and the existence of powerful vested interests; and throughout the Western world the former "poverty and misery alcoholism" (depicted one and two centuries ago by Hogarth and Cruikshank, respectively) have nowadays been replaced by "affluence alcoholism" and with the "Geltung's alkoholismus" (status symbol).

The importance on rates of alcohol abuse of another environmental factor, legislation, may be seen in the reduction of drunkenness convictions, of deaths from liver cirrhosis, etc., following the restrictive legislation subsequent to the work of the Liquor Control Commission in the United Kingdom during the First World War, and in the changes of drinking behavior during the time of Prohibition in the United States.

In the field of drug dependence some examples of the influence of environmental factors have been given above. Another example can be seen in the emergence of the recent heroin-cocaine epidemic among English youngsters. At a time of affluence, even unskilled, uneducated youngsters were able to get highly paid jobs immediately on leaving school. Having too much money in their pockets, without any idea of how to use their leisure time constructively, they were attracted by curiosity and the search for "kicks" to the abuse of drugs, and they could easily afford to pay either private doctors or the black market price of (then) £1 per 60 mg. (1 gr.) of heroin or cocaine. However, compared to the widespread cannabis habit, the number of youngsters abusing heroin in the United Kingdom has not increased beyond a few thousand—and the latter group, by and large, may contain the emotionally more disturbed segment of the youth population, reflecting in this instance once more the importance of the "host" factor in the addiction problem.

Reference has already been made above to the emergence over the past few years in England of young addicts' subcultures, with their own values, attitudes, ideals, standards of behavior, use of slang, etc. In the case of American Skid Row alcoholics (and in the surgical spirit drinkers of large cities in the United Kingdom) the homeless, outcasts, drifters, etc., have found a "niche" and a way of living totally at variance with the standards of society at large; the coexistence of heavy drinking customs and of repeated arrests for intoxication is said to bind these "chronic drunkenness offenders" to the Skid Row way of life and to group membership. Similarly, the participation of the English young drug abusers in forbidden activities ("smoking" of hashish reefers, "mainlining" of illegally obtained heroin, the "pushing" of drugs, the sharing of the excitement, including the risk of being caught, appearing in court, and being sent to prison) may help in forming and cementing group cohesion, and at the same time lead to increasing alienation from society-approved values, such as steady work, maintenance of family ties, acquisition of higher education and vocational skills, etc.

Beyond their influence on the genesis of alcohol and drug dependence, sociocultural attitudes may also have a bearing on the predominance of certain types of alcoholics or drug addicts, and on prognosis. In countries or occupational groups, for example, where heavy drinking is widely accepted, even the emotionally fairly stable and relatively "normal" individual may habitually drink to excess and thus expose himself to the risk of becoming an "alcoholic." On the other hand, where heavy drinking is "taboo" and frowned upon, in the main the emotionally unstable may drink to excess (Jellinek's "acceptance-vulnerability" hypothesis). The prognosis for the average (mainly "sociogenic") alcoholic in the first group, therefore, will be considerably better than in the second (predominantly "psychogenic") group, provided something could be done about the environmental influences. Similarly, in Western culture, where drinking is widely accepted, but the illicit consumption of dependence-producing drugs largely frowned upon, the "average" alcoholic may be expected to have had originally a less unstable personality than the average drug addict, and his prognosis may therefore be expected to be correspondingly better; and similar considerations may apply when the personalities of the hypothetical "average" male and female alcoholics are compared. Again, the personalities of Eastern narcotic addicts (e.g., of Chinese opium addicts as described in Singapore)[31] where, by and large, opium use is less frowned upon than in Western culture, may be less disturbed than that of the English narcotic addicts. However, prognosis, too, depends not only on personality makeup (the "host") and social stability, but on the possibility of manipulation of the environment, such as improvement of domestic unhappiness and the alleviation of economic distress and of loneliness in the female or elderly alcoholic, or in the overcoming of boredom and the removal from his asocial subculture in the case of the drug-using youngster.

## DEVELOPMENT OF ADDICTION

The development of alcohol addiction has been well described by Jellinek,[32] and, by and large, there are many similarities here between alcoholism and drug dependence, although in the latter the pace is much faster, particularly in opiate addiction. Cannabis, too, is largely taken in the company of others; but the aim of the reefer smoker, unlike the social drinker, is probably always to achieve a state of "high," of intoxication, which is not the aim of the social drinker. From social drinking, the future alcoholic proceeds to relief drinking, just as the drug taker may look to his drug to rid him of emotional discomfort or pain (or, on the other hand, to achieve a supernormal "high" state). In other cases, excessive drinking may have originated not in the search for emotional satisfaction or relief, but in continual occupational temptation such as experienced with bartenders, in the case of alcoholism; and doctors and nurses in the case of drugs. The greater the degree of emotional pain or distress, the more often the drinker or drug taker's search for relief or for enhancement of pleasure is "rewarded" by obtaining the required result, the greater becomes the hold of the drug on the individual and his tendency to repeat the experience. Increasing tolerance necessitates increasingly higher doses with most types of drug dependence, and a state of psychic dependence develops, in which the alcoholic or drug-dependent individual continually (or periodically) yearns and searches for satisfaction and gratification by consuming "his" drug. Progressive psychological dependence leads to increasing preoccupation with alcohol or the drug concerned, with neglect of obligations toward family, employer, and society, and of personal care, increasing alienation from society and possibly involvement in antisocial activities. Neglect of nutrition or toxic effects of the drug may lead to mental or physical complications. Self-respect dwindles away, and there may be serious behavioral changes in the direction of irresponsibility, so that even erstwhile respectable and ordinary people with a high moral and ethical code of behavior come to behave as if they were irresponsible "psychopaths."

Similar to the way in which, after some time, beer drinkers no longer feel satisfied with beer and turn to the more potent wines or spirits, so cannabis or amphetamine takers may, in order to find a better "high," be tempted, especially when moving in a subculture using "hard drugs," to try opiates, or the hashish smoker searching for greater "awareness" may move on from cannabis to LSD. One essential difference between alcohol and certain drugs is in the possible "progress" of the drug abuser from initial oral use to hypodermic and later intravenous injection (though the drinker, too, may achieve a more rapid and intense effect by gulping his drink). On the other hand, with progressive impoverishment, similar to the gradual decline in the quality of drink, in the man from whisky to cider and surgical spirits, in the woman from gin to cheap wine, so the poor Chinese opium addict in Singapore may have to make-do with "Dross," the residue obtained after the first smoking of opium.

Alcohol and other CNS depressant drugs may also induce a state of physical dependence. Psychological and physical withdrawal symptoms may in time become important reasons for continuing or resuming the consumption of alcohol or "other drugs" respectively. In the case of both alcohol and narcotic addicts, physical dependence—an adaptive state becoming apparent (as a rule) by physical disturbances when the drug or alcohol intake is suddenly discontinued or greatly reduced—may become an important factor in continuing alcohol and drug abuse. For example, a conditioning process (unpleasant withdrawal symptoms in the past having been relieved by further drug consumption) may contribute to a relapse,[33] although it is the psychological (and social) rather than the physical dependence which seems to be the most important reason in inducing relapse after alcohol or drugs have been completely withdrawn.

At any rate, with progressive dependence, the drinker and drug taker become more and more preoccupied with them, to the exclusion of other activities, with progressive lowering of ethical, moral, occupational, and social standards, and with harm ensuing both for the individual and for society, as already sketched above. The degree and extent of the individual's regression will depend on factors inherent in the "host," "environment," and "agent." Thus, the more "integrated" and stable the drinker's or drug taker's original personality makeup, the more "resistance" he may be able to muster to stem the tide of the downward process, and this will be easier for him when he is still anchored in a helpful, understanding family, or has the stabilizing influence of an interesting job and helpful employers. The pace of his downward process will also be affected by the pharmacological nature of "his" drug and its ability to erode the individual's psychological and physical functioning. For example, the final step in the alcoholic addiction process is the "chronic phase," with its prolonged periods of intoxication. Many alcoholics never reach this stage, to some extent because the psychopathological destructive process was not strong enough to destroy all their original "resistance"; on the other hand, predominantly psychopathic personalities may reach this chronic phase relatively quickly, as illustrated by the rapidity of the downward process in many drinkers who became alcoholics at a very youthful age.

## SOCIAL COMPLICATIONS

As already discussed, apart from the often disastrous effect of alcohol and drug taking on the individual (producing heightened morbidity and mortality rates), the harm caused to society may often be considerable.

### 1. Antisocial activities and crime[34]
Many alcoholics and drug abusers are, during the latter course of their career, driven to criminal activities in order to be able to satisfy their overpowering hunger or thirst for "their" drug. Prohibition of alcohol and drugs of addiction in a given community can usually not be expected to eliminate these problems completely, as the "addicts" will try to get their drug by illegal means if they cannot obtain them legitimately (a possibility or likelihood which, of course, must be kept in mind in any attempt

at legal controls). However, in both alcoholics and drug addicts it is important to distinguish between, on the one hand, the basically antisocial personality, whose excessive drinking or drug taking is merely an aspect of a deep-seated and severe personality disturbance, and whose criminal career may have begun long before his heavy drinking or drug abuse, and, on the other hand, the alcohol or drug addict who turned to criminal activities only after years of alcohol or drug abuse. The great majority of alcoholics probably never turn to crime, despite their personality deterioration following long-standing heavy drinking—and of those who do, many do so only after years of heavy drinking. From the point of view of management, need for close long-term supervision and support, prognosis, etc., there is a great difference between the much more difficult "alcoholic or drug dependent criminal" and the "criminal alcoholic or drug addict," the latter presenting a much more hopeful therapeutic proposition.

Incidentally, alcoholism and drug dependence release aggression directed not only against others, but often also against oneself. In view of strong self-destructive tendencies (described by K. Menninger in his book *Man Against Himself*)[35] it is not surprising that suicidal acts are common in alcoholics and drug addicts, not only as exhibitionistic acts or as "cries for help," but not uncommonly as acts which end fatally. Accidental fatal overdosage of drugs, such as barbiturates, is another real risk in alcoholics as well as in drug addicts.

## 2. Traffic accidents

In recent years it has been shown that alcoholics contribute much more than their fair share to traffic accidents—in particular to more serious ones. Even fairly low amounts of alcohol have been shown to affect judgment and driving performance. In theory tranquilizers and stimulant drugs could be expected to do likewise, although so far the evidence has been scanty,[36] and further research is urgently needed. In our own experience, many youngsters regularly taking drugs such as cannabis or amphetamines have told us of risks taken by reckless and irresponsible driving in a drug-affected state, which they would never have dreamed of taking in a drug-free state. By their additive or possibly potentiating effects, a combination of even moderate amounts of alcohol and other drugs may produce a considerable hazard on the road.

### 3. Industry

Whereas the association of crime and alcoholism has often been greatly exaggerated, the incidence of alcoholism in industry and its influence on industrial production has usually been played down.[37] However, many investigations have clearly indicated that alcoholism, by impairing judgment, skill, and concentration and by being responsible for much absenteeism and industrial accidents, etc., presents a grave, though often overlooked, problem in industry.[38] In this respect dependence on drugs other than alcohol can probably be expected to present industry with a proportionately lesser and somewhat different problem. Alcoholism in the main affects the middle-aged, often highly trained, and experienced man, who would be at the height of his productivity at the time; whereas drug dependence nowadays (apart from barbiturate addiction) occurs generally in the very young, who have not yet been trained for an occupation. However, as drug abuse often starts so early in life, industry is robbed of many potentially valuable recruits, and in countries where drug abuse is widespread, the influence of drug dependence (other than alcoholism) on industrial production may also be considerable. In the United Kingdom, the proportion of middle-aged therapeutic and professional drug addicts in recent years has greatly decreased.

### 4. Financial cost to the community

Dependence on alcohol and other drugs produces a vast amount of human misery and waste of human lives, but beyond that the economic loss to the community must not be forgotten. This includes such items as the upkeep of the unemployed or sick alcoholic or drug addict and his dependents, his maintenance in hospitals or prisons, the professional staff needed to look after them, the lessening of industrial efficiency, the cost of accidents, etc.

## 5. *Family*

The disastrous effect which alcoholism often exercises at home is well known, the unpredictable behavior of the alcoholic leading to marital disharmony and an unhealthy, often bitter, home atmosphere, so that by the time the alcoholic is brought into the treatment situation, his wife, too, is often in an anxious state which may itself require attention. A parent's alcoholism may often also have far-reaching effects on the personality development of his children, neurotic symptoms, behavior disorders, delinquency, and alcoholism in later life (in our experience, a history of the father's alcoholism is not very uncommon in the case of young drug abusers). In the case of young drug abusers of the age groups affected, it will be in the main the drug addict's parents who may suffer emotionally, and only relatively rarely wives or children (except in the case of the middle-aged barbiturate addicts). On the other hand, home circumstances—initial marital disharmony, unhappiness in the parental home, etc.—may often have contributed to the development of alcoholism and drug dependence. At any rate, both these conditions therefore are often symptomatic of, and leading to, family disruption, and their management is not complete without including other family members into the treatment situation.

## TYPES OF ALCOHOLISM AND DRUG DEPENDENCE

Just as there is no such person as "the" alcoholic—the prealcoholic personalities differ from each other a great deal, people become alcoholics for a great variety of reasons, and Jellinek recommends talking of "alcoholisms" rather than of "alcoholism"—so there is also no such person as "the" typical addict. Among drug abusers there are many different types of personality who, for a great variety of reasons under widely different circumstances, take drugs of varying effect and composition.

Many attempts have been made to define alcoholism, all meeting with some criticism, but Jellinek's classification of the "alcoholisms" into various types has been widely accepted. How far is this classification applicable for other forms of drug dependence?

## 1. Alpha alcoholism

Alpha alcoholism is ". . . a purely psychological continual dependence or reliance upon the effect of alcohol to relieve bodily or emotional pain." Such "undisciplined" drinking is symptomatic of the ". . . pathological conditions which it relieves." In the same way, many forms of drug abuse and drug dependence start as symptoms of underlying bodily or emotional discomfort: barbiturates initially taken to relieve insomnia or tension, amphetamines in order to overcome depression, opiates taken to alleviate pain. To a certain extent drugs taken by youngsters because they are dissatisfied, bored, feeling despondent or hopeless, could also be counted as examples of alpha drug abuse and drug dependence.

## 2. Beta alcoholism

In this condition ". . . such alcoholic complications as polyneuropathy, gastritis and cirrhosis of the liver may occur, without either physical or psychological dependence upon alcohol"—heavy drinking in such instances being caused by ". . . customs of a certain social group in conjunction with poor nutritional habits," and leading to impaired nutritional state and family budget, lowered productivity, earlier death, etc. There are many similar examples of drug abuse—in the absence (at least initially) of psychological or physical dependence—for example, if arising out of one's belonging to a certain subculture or out of prevalent national habits, such habitual (sociogenic) drug abuse may lead to "complications." For example, youngsters injecting themselves intravenously with such drugs as heroin, cocaine, or methylamphetamine may develop septic complications or serum jaundice; even before becoming psychologically or physically dependent, regular amphetamine abuse may lead to undernutrition and loss of weight (and sleep); regular cannabis abuse may interfere with the "smoker's" working habits, etc.—all this often produced initially largely at a stage of "social dependence" on the customs of the drug taker's friends and social circle. Similarly, in certain South American and African regions the widespread customary use of cocaine and khat respectively among the poor may affect the family budget and lead to undernutrition.

3. *Gamma alcoholism* (*"loss of control"*)     } the "addictive"
4. *Delta alcoholism* (*"inability to abstain"*)   } types of
alcoholism

According to Jellinek, these are the only types which are "addictions" or "diseases" in the strict pharmacological sense, "since it is the adaptation of cell metabolism and acquired tissue tolerance and the (physical) withdrawal symptoms which bring about 'craving' and loss of control or inability to abstain." Jellinek himself believed that "anomalous forms of the ingestion of narcotics and alcohol, such as drinking with loss of control and physical dependence, are caused by physiopathological processes and constitute diseases." Physical dependence, as evident from the occurrence of a physical abstinence syndrome, also occurs in dependence on barbiturates and at least a number of other nonbarbiturate hypnotics, and on meprobamate; all these would constitute "addictions" like the gamma and delta forms of alcoholism. Whether in fact a biochemical factor underlies the gamma alcoholic's "loss of control" has not yet been proven; in practice, addicts to drugs other than alcohol—like the "loss of control" alcoholic—cannot be certain of being able to discontinue taking the drug on a given occasion having once started it. However, in many aspects the behavior of many drug addicts more closely resembles that of the delta alcoholic, as they often cannot or will not start a day without taking their drug, and as they then throughout the day intermittently keep "topping up"; narcotic addicts often live "from one fix to another," and, similar to the minor physical withdrawal symptoms of the delta alcoholic, to some extent the occurrence of abstinence symptoms may often be the reason for the narcotic addict's continual repetition of his drug taking throughout the twenty-four hours.

5. *Epsilon alcoholism* (*periodic*)

The nature of periodic alcoholism is often obscure. Likewise, in some addicts drug abuse only occurs from time to time, and may be associated not only with the abuser's state of mind or emotional and physical health, but also with environmental factors, such as drug availability, of conflicting outside influences and pressures exercised on the one hand by the young drug abuser's peers and, on the other hand, by his parents, etc. Recurrent depression is probably not a very common cause of "periodic alcoholism," but depression, as well as states of tension and anxiety, could easily cause recurrent abuse of drugs such as amphetamines or barbiturates, perhaps mainly among middle-aged women.

## TREATMENT

A number of principles hold good almost equally for the treatment of all forms, of drug dependence, including alcoholism.

### 1. The need for early diagnosis and early treatment

In all forms of drug dependence there is more hope for a successful outcome if patients could come into the treatment situation earlier than is often the case at present. Insofar as the unfortunate gaps in the education and training of the future doctor and the general public interfere with medical and general recognition of these conditions as illnesses requiring urgent medical attention, they hinder the task of early diagnosis. Formerly it was often held that alcoholics could not really make a serious attempt until they had reached the "rock bottom." One knows nowadays that there is no need for such people to sink to a state where they have lost home, health, and happiness, and that they can have the subjective experience of reaching their "individual rock bottom" at a much earlier phase. It should therefore be the task to try to "motivate" alcoholics and drug abusers toward treatment in the relatively early stages. This is the more important as nowadays drug abuse so often afflicts the young, and there is also some evidence that alcoholism is progressively becoming more common among younger people than in former years.[39] Early diagnosis and treatment are important in order to forestall the development of harmful (and sometimes irreversible) mental, physical, and social complications, before the onset of definite psychological, physical, or social dependence (which bind the abuser more firmly to his drug), and before social dependence on his subculture has anchored him too firmly to its often pernicious habits, and has alienated him completely from the standards and attitudes of society at large. Early diagnosis of course is of utmost importance from the aspect of prevention; in the case of drug dependence, for example, it diminishes the likelihood—at least in the case of British addicts, most of whom at some time or other also sell drugs—of yet another ·addict-pusher emerging who, in order to enable him to buy further supplies for himself, might "turn on" newcomers to drug use.

## 2. The need for long-term treatment and after-care

From the time of first seeing the alcoholic or drug-dependent patient, one has to remember that sobering-up the drunk or getting the addict off his drug in itself does not constitute adequate "treatment." These are no more than first-aid measures, and when "treatment" stops short at this stage, all that has usually been achieved is to put the patient physically into a better state of health so that he could reembark on his drug abuse. Getting such people off their drugs or alcohol is in general not a difficult task; the real difficulties are encountered in helping such patients to maintain their newly gained freedom from drink or drugs. From the beginning the therapist's aim should be directed toward long-term treatment and rehabilitation, so that finally there should be—if at all possible—a state of contented sobriety and freedom from drug abuse. In the case of young drug abusers, hospital treatment has practically no chance of ultimate success if after this phase of therapy has finished, the addict is virtually forced to drift back to his former drug-taking friends and to his old haunts and subculture. In fact, success or the failure of any therapeutic program largely rests on whether or not adequate provision is made for after-care and rehabilitation, the necessity for which cannot be overstressed.

## 3. The need for a multidisciplinary approach and teamwork

As all forms of drug dependence are multifactorial in origin, clearly one single form of treatment will not be invariably the best for each and every patient. Physical, psychological, and social treatments will be needed to a major or lesser degree in every case, and therefore various processional disciplines will have to contribute their share. There is thus a need for a well-co-ordinated and integrated, multi- and interdisciplinary approach, including the help of voluntary agencies. The medical practitioner, social worker, nurse, clergyman, probation officer, local authority (with its welfare workers, etc.), the patient's family, his employer, organizations of recovered alcoholics and drug addicts—they all will have to contribute their share. Each must be aware of the role of other members of the therapeutic team within the comprehensive approach and be prepared if necessary to refer the patient to another team member when indicated—not in order to shift the task, but to share it.

### 4. The importance of the therapist's attitude

In alcoholism quite a number of different therapeutic approaches have occasionally yielded satisfactory results in the hands of various therapists. Although such treatments may have certain principles in common, it would seem that often the basic attitude of the therapist may be more decisive as regards success or failure than the type of therapy he employs; and to some extent the same may hold good for other forms of drug dependence. It is not enough that the therapist be well informed about alcoholism and drug dependence. Acquiring such information nowadays unfortunately is more a matter of private enterprise and interest on the part of the therapist, rather than—as it should be—the responsibility of the medical and professional schools. What may be even more important is that he have emotionally accepted the alcoholic or the drug addict as a sick person, and avoid a moralistic, condemning, and rejecting attitude. Such negative attitudes would serve only to reinforce the addict's own feelings of guilt, isolation, hopelessness, and helplessness, and of inevitable gloom and doom—all feelings which would constitute reasons for further and more intensified alcohol or drug use. Clearly this means that the professional therapist would have to be far ahead of the thinking and feeling of his own social environment about such problems. Many professional therapists with such patients have been helped to gain this all-important emotional attitude toward alcoholics and drug addicts after watching from the sidelines the recovery of a patient, for whom they themselves had held out little hope, in the face of daunting odds which to an outsider may often have seemed insuperable.

### 5. Phases of treatment

Treatment and rehabilitation of alcohol and drug dependence pass through a number of overlapping phases. The first step—drug withdrawal—may be sudden and complete (as in the case of the stimulating drugs, cannabis, LSD, and, as a rule, alcohol) or gradual, decreasing the dosage (as with the barbiturates, the nonbarbiturate "addictive" hypnotics and tranquilizers, and the opiates). In the case of the latter, drug withdrawal is often carried out by means of temporary substitution by another, less "addictive" drug (physeptone). Withdrawal is accompanied by physical building-up, adequate nutrition and hydration, etc. After preliminary diagnostic evaluation of the causative factors which have been at work in the individual patient's case, treatment is carried out by means of a combination of physical, psychological, and social methods which seem to be best suited in his particular case. All the time the principle should be stressed that the patient should look at himself not as a merely passive recipient of miraculous treatment given to him by the doctor, but as an active collaborator in a common task, to which he himself has to make the most important contribution. He then enters the often long drawn-out final phase of the rehabilitation process—carried out in the community itself—during which he has to learn to cope with internal and external problems and difficulties without falling back on his old-time crutches, alcohol or other dependence-producing drugs. Long-range plans for rehabilitation and often long-continued support are absolutely essential, but are still, unfortunately, the most neglected part of the therapeutic and rehabilitation program.

ACUTE PHASE. The patient's state of malnutrition, dehydration, tension, agitation, insomnia, and depression may require drug and supportive therapy, for example, vitamins, extra fluids, tranquilizers, nonbarbiturate hypnotics and antidepressants. In order to avoid the risk of development of dependence on hypnotics they should be employed sparingly and discontinued as soon as feasible. During the acute phase there will be many opportunities to lay the foundations of a constructive relationship with the patient; this should be used to motivate him to carry on with treatment even if he begins to feel quite well physically and—in the sheltered hospital atmosphere, with its freedom from stress.

LONG-TERM THERAPY. The long-term physical therapeutic methods employed in alcoholism are aversion treatments and the use of alcohol-sensitizing drugs. Aversion methods have also been tried occasionally with other forms of drug dependence—for example, the late J. Y. Dent,[40] the main protagonist of the alcohol-apomorphine treatment for alcoholism in England, also suggested using this method for addiction to other drugs, but this technique has not found wide application. There is no drug therapy available in dependence on other drugs quite comparable to the deterrent and alcohol-sensitizing disulfiram and citrated calcium carbimide treatments in alcoholism, and in group sessions drug addicts often complain bitterly of this. To a certain extent the use of the long-acting opiate antagonist cyclazocine[41] and of the maintenance methadone (physeptone) treatment [42] for opiate addicts could be loosely compared to the alcohol-sensitizing techniques, as in both methods the addict fails to derive satisfaction and relief from his drinking or drug taking, respectively, as long as he is taking "therapeutic" drugs prescribed for him. There may also be a certain similar beneficial long-term effect. In the past, indulgence in drink or drugs "rewarded" the individual by regularly bringing him relief or gratification; conditioning brought about in this way (in Wikler's view) is an important element in precipitating relapses in the drug-free addict. When on a maintenance dose of disulfiram, methadone, or cyclazocine no such "rewarding" relief follows the taking of drink or drugs (in its place there may indeed be a very unpleasant reaction). In this way, such drugs may in time lead to a deconditioning.

In alcoholism as in drug dependence, physical therapies are generally seen as no more than valuable adjuncts to the fundamental psychological and social treatment methods, enabling these other techniques to be used in an alcohol and drug-free state, so that addicts become more amenable and more responsive to other therapeutic approaches. Many alcoholics and probably the very great majority of drug addicts (the young ones rather than the middle-aged professional and therapeutic addicts) require an intensive process of reeducation and emotional reorientation, after having acquired some insight into the nature of their personality problems which have contributed toward their turning to excessive drinking and drug taking in the first place.

In general there seems little hope to "get through" to the alcoholic and drug dependent patient until he has been sobered up and detoxicated. Moreover, so many difficulties are often encountered in the psychotherapy that—as Schulte[43] expressed it—it is no surprise that Freud almost totally avoided the subject of psychotherapy in drug addicts. Yet much can be achieved by a patient, tolerant, yet firm therapist using a comprehensive program, at the core of which would be a brief psychotherapeutic —combined with social—approach.[44] The alcoholic and drug addict should not be left in the vacuum created by merely removing their drugs from them. Addicts use alcohol or drugs because their present personality malfunctioning requires it. In order to learn to live happily and usefully, they need a change of attitudes and outlook, new goals, ambitions, and satisfactions, so that they no longer require alcohol or drugs. They have to come to appreciate that there is something in the world worth giving up drugs for.

Among psychological methods, both individual and group psychotherapy have been widely employed in alcoholics and drug addicts. Group methods have been found of great value in alcoholics, not only because of the lack of therapists, but also (or mainly in the present author's view) as it meets their need for resocialization, helps them to overcome their feelings of ostracism and isolation, and gives them an opportunity to identify and to find a feeling of "belonging" among a group of people with the same affliction, similar underlying problems, similar experiences, etc.[45] In principle similar factors should also make group therapy a valuable tool in the treatment of drug addicts, despite certain risks and snags—a view supported by experiences such as those of Synanon and Daytop Lodge in the United States, and to a certain extent by our own observations with the community treatment of addicts in hospitals, and with group therapy with addicts in prison.

Despite certain exceptions, it would seem that the self-help organizations in the case of drug addicts have been less successful than Alcoholics Anonymous. This must to a certain extent be related to the greater emotional maturity of (the often older) alcoholics than (the younger) addicts; and whereas A.A. functions well despite (or because of) the absence of professional therapists, one might feel that it is vitally necessary for professional workers to cooperate in attempts by addicts to form their own self-help groups. Again, it is not enough to have just well-meaning "do-gooders" involved in such tasks; despite the best intentions, such people, with their sentimental outlook, may often do more harm than good, although under professional guidance their cooperation may often be very helpful. Even with professional supervision, groups of addicts are usually more difficult and "sticky" than those of alcoholics. Moreover, even in hospitals there may be the risk of "infection"—youngsters learning about new drugs, etc. Because of administrative factors (lack of accommodations) we have over many years treated alcoholics and addicts in the same wards, and occasionally in the same groups.[46] Middle-aged barbiturate and amphetamine "addicts" were found to fit well into therapeutic communities and groups formed largely by alcoholics, but young drug abusers and "addicts" (such as those dependent on amphetamines, cannabis, heroin, and cocaine) much less so. By and large, there seemed to be greater functional "proximity" between the middle-aged addicts to the "soft" drugs and alcoholics, than between such middle-aged addicts and young drug addicts; middle-aged barbiturate and amphetamine abusers usually preferring to participate in the alcoholic groups rather than in those where young narcotic addicts were numerically preponderant. In latter years we have therefore run separate group sessions for young addicts and for alcoholics, although so far (because of lack of accommodation) they still live in the same wards.

There exists, in our experience, a danger that in groups formed exclusively by young addicts, the ideals, ideas, and the often asocial attitudes and activities of the subculture to which these youngsters belonged in the past might continue even while in the hospital. For this reason the placing of such young addicts in a heterogeneous group (i.e., one not formed exclusively by drug addicts) may offer certain advantages. Young drug addicts often look down on the "inferior" drug alcohol (cannabis-smoking youngsters often condemn alcohol as stupefying and aggression-producing, comparing it unfavorably with their own "hash" or "weed," with its alleged perception-enhancing property and peace-conducive atmosphere). Many difficulties are bound to arise when young drug addicts with their tendency to "act out" live together with middle-aged alcoholics who do not fully appreciate the "blessings" of pop music blaring out noisily all day long from the record player. Nevertheless, many young drug addicts admit that they receive a great deal of help from the older, more experienced, more mature, usually better educated, and often highly skilled alcoholic co-patients. In fact, certain alcoholics take much interest, and show a great deal of empathy for the problems of the young drug takers. It is the generally held view that the combined approach toward alcoholics and drug addicts should not go so far as to treat them actually in the same ward. By and large, the present author agrees with this view. However, middle-aged barbiturate and amphetamine addicts are probably better treated alongside alcoholics than with young narcotic addicts; and those alcoholics willing to assist in the task of helping young drug addicts can often be employed with great benefit by the professional therapist. For that reason, we intend shortly to open a separate addicts' ward in the same hospital as the alcoholics ward, and hope to enlist the assistance of "volunteer" alcoholic patients in running the addicts' ward. Clearly, this is one of many fields in which further planned research with different therapeutic approaches is urgently required. At any rate, in different cultures, with different social attitudes toward alcoholics and addicts, with their different "images," with different legal provisions, there is opportunity and need for a wide variety of carefully planned and observed research projects into the available therapeutic and rehabilitation programs.

In many ways the most important and most difficult treatment phase is the rehabilitation period. Hospital follow-up facilities, such as outpatient clinics, and close support by social workers should be provided, as well as half-way houses catering specially to such patients. As far as possible, treatment and rehabilitation facilities should be closely integrated, facilitating easy transfer from one to the other where indicated, as in the case of a threatened relapse.[47] It is in the rehabilitation period that organizations of recovered alcoholics and addicts (see above) should prove particularly helpful. Clearly not all addicts, and only a certain proportion of alcoholics, require hospitalization; and at any rate the hospital can be regarded as no more than one link in a comprehensive, integrated chain of therapeutic and rehabilitation facilities. The less the stigma, and the better the professional and lay education in this field in the future, the more important are those facilities likely to become, which are directly situated within the community. There will also always be a necessity for inpatient accommodation. The old argument—"inpatient or outpatient facilities"—seems, therefore, to be no more than an academic discussion, as there will always be a need for both, working in close collaboration with each other.

Often a decisive role during the after-care period is the attitude of the alcoholic or drug addict's family, which may often make all the difference between ultimate success or failure. All forms of drug dependence are family illnesses. The drug user's behavior has been determined to a large extent by family factors —its tensions, cohesion or lack of it, the patient's attitude to his wife, children, parents, etc., and vice versa. In turn, his own often unpredictable behavior during his drinking or drug-taking career cannot but have important consequences on the emotional state of the members of his family who, by the time he himself comes for treatment, may often require help almost as much as he does. Treatment of such a patient is therefore not complete without including his family in the treatment situation; they, too, should learn to accept the illness concept of alcohol and drug dependence which will assist them greatly to understand the otherwise often inexplicable behavior of their addicted relative, and make it easier for them to help him. Relatives' groups run by a member of the therapeutic team may be very helpful in this connection, as are the self-help groups, such as Al-Anon, formed by alcoholics' relatives and friends.

## 6. The question of compulsory treatment

The prevalent opinion, at least in the United Kingdom, is that treatment of alcoholics and drug addicts can be successful only when they present themselves for treatment voluntarily. It is often held that the liberty of the subject should be the overriding consideration. Yet it cannot be honestly held that the "practicing" alcoholic or drug addict is really at liberty to decide on the best course to follow, seeing that he is held in a powerful grip by his drug dependence; with his mind befuddled by the effects of the drug often he can see no further than searching desperately for the best ways and means to obtain his next drink or "fix." As matters stand at the present many addicts are allowed to proceed with their alcohol or drug abuse, despite the obvious dangers and high mortality.

As long as young drug addicts are able to obtain their drugs quite legitimately (as is the case at present with the British Treatment Centres) it must be very difficult for them to make a voluntary decision to enter a hospital for withdrawal treatment, and to stick it out there at the first sign of abstinence symptoms. Clearly, voluntary treatment is preferable and should be aimed at wherever possible. However, in certain cases, the initially lacking motivation of alcohol and drug dependent patients can be induced, even when admitted under compulsion, once such a patient is no longer under the influence of his drug, and is free from withdrawal symptoms—and, in particular, when he is treated in a therapeutic community alongside other, well-motivated, patients suffering from the same affliction. This has been our experience with alcoholics, and more recently in the case of some compulsorily admitted young drug addicts; whereas voluntarily admitted young drug abusers as a rule discharged themselves after a few days, before regaining their ability to think rationally.

"While receiving drugs at the Treatment Centre it was a complete waste of our own and the doctor's time to go along and discuss our son's case . . . he just went on taking the drugs and going downhill" was the comment of the parents of a 19-year-old drug addict. "It was his good luck when he was finally caught, and the Court put him in hospital on a Condition of Residence . . . it gave him a chance which he would never have sought voluntarily."

Imprisonment is no treatment for alcoholics and drug addicts. They are sick people, and should be treated as such, and not as criminals to be sent to prison. All the same, a certain proportion of drug addicts and alcoholics will, for some reason or other connected with their drug dependence, land in prison. The time spent there need not necessarily be wasted, but could offer an opportunity for starting a rehabilitation program.

Group sessions in prison with selected alcoholics and drug addicts, in our experience, are quite practicable; and it is often possible to enlist their active cooperation, seeing that at the time they are not under the influence of their drug. In such cases it is—even more than with hospital-treated alcoholics and addicts—necessary to provide a planned, long-term, after-care program, including the provision of special hostels. The question of whether, and when, compulsory treatment may be indicated and helpful is another example of the need for well-planned and controlled research. At any rate, whereas in the case of alcoholics in a hospital an open-ward arrangement with a completely permissive atmosphere, and a large measure of patients' own administration and government, is probably the best course to follow, in the case of the much more immature and irresponsible young addicts, a "closed" ward arrangement may often be more helpful, at least in the intial stage of their hospitalization. Those who do well can then be "promoted" into an "open" ward. This illustrates again the advisability of treating alcoholics and young addicts in different wards (see above).

At any rate, it is useless seriously to consider the extensive use of compulsive measures until a sufficient number of suitable special facilities are available to look after these patients. It must also be stressed that compulsion in such cases would only

mean admission without the patient's consent—within the ward
the atmosphere should be as "permissive" and therapeutic as
possible.

## REHABILITATION GOALS AND PROGNOSIS

The ultimate goal one may hope to achieve with alcoholics and
drug addicts will vary a great deal since one cannot hope to go
beyond the individual patient's potential. Naturally, the aim
should be total sobriety and abstinence from drugs, but "improved interpersonal relations, working patterns, and satisfactions in living" are other important goals of rehabilitation programs. Depending on the personality potential one has often to
be contented with a much more modest and realistic result. In
individuals with a fairly good personality, and a history of socio-
occupational and domestic stability, goals may be set fairly high,
and prognosis would seem fair. This group would include many
(in particular middle-aged) alcoholics, professional and therapeutic addicts, individuals who took to alcohol or drug abuse
after exposure to extraordinary strain and stress (e.g., bereave-
ment), or where alcohol or drug abuse was common and widely
accepted, either by society at large or by the "subculture" in
which the individual may temporarily have found himself (as a
student, for example). On the other hand, goals and hopes cannot be set very high in the case of those alcoholics and addicts
whose alcohol and drug abuse was in the main a consequence of
personality disturbance, e.g., many young alcoholics and drug
addicts, inadequate and emotionally very unstable, highly neurotic, and psychopathic individuals, "alcoholic or drug-dependent
criminals," the mentally subnormal, and the basically psychotic
drinkers and drug abusers.

In this second group, however, care has to be taken not to
confuse personality changes, superimposed during the course of
the addict's "career," with the preaddictive personality which is
the decisive factor as to prognosis. By and large, in Western
culture, because of the acceptance of heavy drinking by wide
segments of the population, the hypothetical "average" alcoholic
may be expected to be a less "abnormal" type of personality than

the "average" drug addict. Therefore his prognosis in general can be expected to be better. However, there is no such person as "the" addict, just as there are many types of alcoholics. Many different personalities take drugs of different composition and widely varying pharmacological effects for a great variety of reasons, in different ways, under different conditions, and for a varying length of time. Thus, the techniques, settings, goals, and chances for rehabilitation must also vary a great deal. At any rate, the outlook for the rehabilitation of drug addicts is much better than could be expected if one were to think only of the emotionally disturbed young narcotic addict. Among the latter —as we have seen—mortality is very high, but provided they are able to "hang on," some of them may in fact be able to "mature out" of their addiction—a process described by Winick[48] in order to explain the finding that heroin addiction is much commoner in the young than in older people.

One explanatory hypothesis he puts forward is that of a self-limiting of the addictive process. It is of some interest in this connection to compare this with the concept of alcoholism as a self-limiting disease, recently described by Drew,[49] who points out that alcoholism tends to disappear with increasing age; and though he agrees that ". . . morbidity and mortality may account for a large part," he thinks that "a significant proportion of this disappearance is probably due to spontaneous recovery." In fact, when taking a patient's history, one not infrequently encounters the remark that the patient's own father had been in his younger days a heavy drinker, but had given it up when getting on in years.

On the other hand, alcoholism in the elderly may be less uncommon than generally assumed.[50] At any rate, not everybody would agree with Drew's conclusion that "if alcoholism is a problem of young adulthood and middle-age . . . regardless of whether mortality or spontaneous recovery is the primary factor in reducing the incidence of alcoholism with increasing age . . . ," a therapeutic program as carried out in Scandinavia seems appropriate, in which ". . . attempts to accelerate recovery from the phase of excessive drinking take a very secondary place compared with the efforts to reduce the complications encountered. . . ." In Drew's view, the Scandinavian approach to the treatment of alcoholism consists in ". . . offer[ing] medical care for the acute alcoholic episodes and encourag[ing] social acceptance of the alcoholic himself . . . ," providing "prolonged protective custodial care" when such measures fail or are inadequate. The same type of argument could of course be put forward in the case of drug addicts. However, one might feel that merely treating alcoholics and drug addicts during their acute episodes and merely trying to reduce complications till they may reach the stage of "maturing out" and "spontaneous recovery" may mean for many of them abandoning them to a very unsatisfactory way of life punctuated by many distressing and often life-threatening relapses—not to speak of the effect of such behavior on their families. Surely attempts should be made to help them to recover long before the onset of "spontaneous recovery" toward the latter years of their life. At any rate, the possibilities of "maturing out" and of "spontaneous recovery" in alcoholics and drug addicts in middle-age or later life constitute further examples of areas where research is urgently necessary.

Whether or not a certain proportion of alcoholics or drug addicts will in later life grow out of their drug dependence, it is essential to look at these conditions as relapsing illnesses. Resumption of alcohol or drug taking should, therefore, not be regarded as a personal affront to the therapist, but rather as a challenge to resume and to redouble one's efforts. A great many alcoholics—probably the very large majority of those who finally recover—have done so only after a number of relapses. Thus, the members of the therapeutic and rehabilitation team must possess a full understanding of the condition, endless patience, and a high frustration tolerance; and while keeping free from a punitive outlook, they should not fall into the trap of an all-forgiving sentimentalism. The ambivalent alcoholic and addict, with his need and craving for drugs, will be quick to recognize this and be tempted to manipulate it toward obtaining means for his immediate gratification—which in the long run may run counter to the goal of achieving his optimum degree of mental and physical health.

## THE NEED FOR TOTAL ABSTINENCE?

Although, clearly, total abstinence from addictive drugs is not the only goal, most therapists would probably rank it foremost. The validity of the concept of total abstinence as the only worthwhile goal has recently been challenged in several quarters, and certainly—as already stated—the patients' personal adjustments, satisfactory interpersonal relationships at home and in society, satisfying occupations, etc., ought to be aimed at. Likewise, in the case of alcoholics the aim should be that of a contented state of sobriety. As a general rule it is probably fair to say that the chances to find happiness and successful adjustment are much greater in the alcoholic or drug addict who has managed to give up his drinking or drug taking.

It must be very difficult to decide at what stage, and in what patient, one should give up the hope and the effort to motivate them toward complete abstinence, and be satisfied with less ambitious aims, such as moderate drinking without too many bouts, or "maintenance therapy" in the case of drug addicts. A number of studies have found a small proportion of alcoholics who have learned to drink in moderation or "normally." Further research into this important question is necessary—and to what extent such "nibbling" can be called "normal" drinking and is satisfying to the drinker in the long run is as yet open to question. At any rate, the possibility that there may be a few alcoholics who may become moderate drinkers does not alter the fact that they must be regarded as exceptions (until, possibly, further research indicates in which type of alcoholic, and under what conditions, this may be possible). At present the only realistic therapeutic goal in alcoholism must remain total abstinence. Similarly, care has to be taken in the case of opiate addicts to differentiate between the older, more mature, professional, therapeutic addict (who might possibly be able to function to a certain extent not too unhappily as a "stabilized addict") in whom "maintenance" therapy without the risk of spreading drug taking to newcomers may be perhaps a legitimate procedure; and, on the other hand, the typical young, emotionally unstable, drug abuser on the current British drug scene.

The latter may have used drugs for a short time only (and all too often no attempt has been made to find out whether he really needs any drugs at all)—his mortality rate has been found to be twenty times as high as that of the nonaddicted youngster, and he often "pushes" drugs, thus "infecting" newcomers. These young drug abusers claim as a rule that they are not yet "ready" to give up drugs, and clamor for "maintenance doses"; but one might question whether it is fair to them or to society to consent (or to condemn them) to a possibly life-long state of drug dependence, without first evaluating how genuine is their need for drugs, and whether they are indeed unable to function without them.

The necessity to determine valid rehabilitation goals relative to "personal functioning and social productivity," and the problem of how to discover those for whom total abstinence must remain an unrealistic goal, is one of the most important subjects for further research. At present there would seem to be a need to experiment with various forms of rehabilitation projects and goals, under carefully planned and observed conditions, depending to a certain extent on the different legal provisions in the various countries.

## PREVENTION

In view of the large and rising numbers of sufferers involved, alcoholism and drug dependence constitute important public health hazards requiring urgent attention. Treatment of the established alcoholic can be expected to be successful in perhaps 50–70 percent; of the drug addict in a much lesser proportion. The task of prophylaxis is, thus, of vital importance.

### 1. Control and legislative measures
In the past the approach to alcoholism and drug addiction consisted in deprivation and punishment; prohibiting or restricting the sale of drinks, limiting opening hours of public houses, punishing the drunk, imprisoning him and the drug abuser. However,

complete prohibition of alcohol not only failed to solve the problem, but created new ones in addition. Punishment does not deter the alcoholic or drug addict from repeating over and over again his self-destructive behavior, which often seems almost designed to invite punitive measures.

To what extent is it possible to eliminate or to diminish the influence of the causative "agent"? In the United Kingdom, restrictive legislation applied intensively during the First World War proved of great value in diminishing cases of drunkenness, deaths from liver cirrhosis, etc. The British, for so many years suffering from widespread drunkenness, became in a matter of a few years a relatively sober nation. Legislation out of step with widely accepted public sentiment may be expected to arouse bitter hostility. In Western culture alcohol use is widely accepted; public opinion is strongly antagonistic to the idea of prohibiting drinking merely because a minority may come to grief; and notions of helping alcoholics who are drinking themselves to death, by compulsorily placing them into hospitals, arouse strong objections in the name of protection of the liberty of the subject.

On the other hand, there is strong public support in favor of outlawing the use of other intoxicants and CNS-affecting drugs, and of harsher penalties for those using them. Smokers of cannabis reefers are incensed about the different standards society adopts toward alcohol and cannabis, which they regard as less harmful than alcohol. However, in Western culture, society, by and large, has learned to come to terms and to live with alcohol, despite the undoubted presence of so many casualties—whereas cannabis in the West is still a relatively new drug. At any rate, the fact that so many middle-aged (and in the past few years apparently also an increasing number of youngsters) chose to risk health and life by alcohol and tobacco is in itself no good reason to enable youngsters to do likewise by adding a third potential poison to the list. Moreover, whereas the majority of alcohol abusers have reached a more mature age, in the West cannabis is attractive in the main to the very immature young, and this may contribute to its risks (just as alcohol abuse is more dangerous in the case of the young).

The glamor of the forbidden certainly attracts some youngsters, but, on the other hand, freeing cannabis from restrictions would probably greatly encourage "smoking" among those people so far deterred from doing so because of its illegality; and with the vastly increased numbers of users, also the absolute number of those coming to grief is likely to be much higher. There is no evidence that legislation of cannabis will reduce the number of heavy drinkers. Thus, the question is not "alcohol or cannabis?" but whether society can take the risk of sanctioning, in addition to alcohol, yet another drug which is undoubtedly dangerous for a minority, even if, like alcohol, the majority can take it with impunity.

There seems little doubt that, as in the case of alcohol, a policy based only on prohibition, harsh laws, and dealing with the drug addicts as criminals—as carried out in the United States—has failed to make inroads into the numbers of drug addicts. The punitive approach in the United States prevents the addict from obtaining his drugs legally; the addict is therefore driven into the arms of peddlers, and has to commit crimes in order to obtain the money to pay for his drugs. Treated by the law as criminals, drug addicts may be forced into a criminal subculture, with which in time they come to identify themselves.

The different (permissive) policy adopted in the United Kingdom toward the addict was held by some, in the past, to explain the relative absence of a narcotic problem in Britain. (Whereas other observers regarded as most important the difference of "public image" of the drug addict in the two countries, i.e., of a criminal in the United States, a sick man in the United Kingdom.) It was argued that the permissive "British System" prevented the emergence of a drug problem because addicts could obtain their drugs from their doctor; they therefore did not have to buy them illegally. There was thus no demand for a black market, and no need for the addict to commit crimes and to become part of an antisocial subculture. However, despite—or because of—the legal availability of drugs in the (over-)permissive British System, a narcotic problem has also sprung up during the past decade in Great Britain.

The fact that easy availability of alcohol or drugs is an important factor has been illustrated already in the foregoing, i.e., in the disproportionately high number among drug addicts of doctors, nurses, and other professional workers with easy access to drugs, and of bar tenders and their wives among alcoholics. The beneficial effects of a reduction of availability was seen—as mentioned above—in the improvement of public drunkenness figures, following the measures taken in 1915 by the Liquor Control Board of limiting the number of opening hours of public houses to no more than 5½ hours per day, in place of the former 20 hours; and of higher taxation. The effect of the latter has also been reflected in very recent years in the changeover in Czechoslovakia from spirit to beer drinking, following the relatively much higher taxing of spirits than of beer.[51] That a change from the drinking of more highly concentrated spirits in favor of the weaker alcoholic drinks may be of some prophylactic value is a notion often put forward, as, twenty-five years ago by Y. Henderson in the plea for "Dilution." [52] The influence of price (relative to income), as influenced by taxation policy, on drunkenness and alcoholism is to a certain extent illustrated in the relative preference of the English middle classes for spirits, and of the English working classes for beer. "Loss of control" alcoholism seems more common among the spirit-drinking middle classes, and "inability to abstain" alcoholism is possibly more frequent among beer-drinking working classes. Thus, availability (as affected to some degree by taxation) may also exercise some influence even on the type of alcoholism. As shown by Canadian investigators, what is important is not the absolute price of drinks, but the price in relation to income. The influence of the latter factor is reflected in the gradual changeover from drinking spirits to cider and finally surgical spirits, among impoverished male alcoholics, and from gin to cheap wine among females.

The state (apart from its taxation policy) and the medical profession could diminish availability of drugs by a number of measures. Steps taken by the state include strict control of the distribution, manufacture, sale, and importation of existing drugs; and restriction of the sale of new drugs. It would certainly seem preferable to restrict access to new drugs immediately, rather than to wait until evidence of their risks have come to light, because sooner or later practically any substance with depressing or stimulating effects on the CNS will be found to lead to dependence, at least in emotionally vulnerable personalities (the only exceptions from this rule, so far, seem to be the phenothiazine tranquilizers).

The "glamor of the forbidden," the excitement of risking being caught, etc., may attract certain immature and asocial personalities but, by and large, restricting easy access and availability seems a much more important factor in reducing abuse. To mention but one example: the author saw quite a number of cases of dependence on methypentynol nearly fifteen years ago when its sale was unrestricted, but not a single case after it had been made subject to restrictions. Likewise, the popular barbiturate-amphetamine cycle (taking the hypnotic in the evening, the "pep pill" in the morning), very popular in the early 1950s, was replaced (after restrictions were put on amphetamines) for a while by the carbromal-phenmetrazine cycle, until the latter drugs, too, were made subject to similar restrictions.

However, total control of all possible intoxicating or dependence-producing drugs by law is not possible, and other measures (education, parental example, etc.) have possibly an even more important part to play. The medical profession should be taught more about the dependence-producing properties of psychotropic drugs, and should exercise restraint in prescribing them. It seems highly questionable that the enormous amounts of hypnotics and tranquilizers prescribed today are really medically necessary, but confronted with the urgent demands coming from patients who have read all about the miraculous effects of new wonder drugs, and having a crowded waiting room, the practitioner may often not have time to discuss the patient's emotional problems at length, and may find it easier to write out yet another prescription.

Legal steps taken against alcoholics and drug addicts falling foul of the law all too often consist in fines or imprisonment, measures which by themselves have no preventive or therapeutic value. An alternative program—the referral of such offenders to specialized medical facilities for a period of observation and assessment permitting proper diagnosis, followed where indicated by treatment and rehabilitation measures—would serve to rehabilitate at least a certain proportion and would assist other offenders to a somewhat lesser extent. Such a program would certainly be indicated for those "criminal alcoholics and addicts" whose antisocial behavior was a secondary consequence of their long-standing state of alcohol or drug dependence, and whose basic personality structure may be a fairly stable one. But also for the basically antisocial "alcoholic and drug-dependent criminal," whose alcohol and drug abuse and dependence are superimposed upon marked personality defects and whose offenses necessitate imprisonment, treatment for alcoholism or drug dependence may often be required before any attempt at resocialization can have any chance for even partial success.

For such offenders the establishment of therapeutic community set-ups with group therapy facilities, within prison, would certainly seem indicated, since it is a forlorn hope that just keeping the alcoholic or drug addict away from drink or drugs will help to "bring him to his senses."

While punishment of the alcoholic and drug addict by itself is inhuman and useless, the punishment of the illicit drug peddler, by its deterrent effect, assists in controlling supplies, and is thus part of a prophylactic policy.

In summary, while legislative measures are absolutely essential in the task of preventing alcoholism and drug dependence, by themselves they cannot solve the whole problem. As Halbach put it, ". . . no restriction, however severe, on production, distribution, and administration of dangerous drugs can entirely solve the problem of prevention. Or, in epidemiological language, preventive measures should not be limited to the agent, they should also deal with the host and the environment, thus aiming at the underlying causes of the addiction." [53]

## 2. Influencing social attitudes

In the long run, preventive public health measures aimed at influencing and changing the attitudes of the lay and professional public toward alcoholics and drug addicts—if successful—could perhaps be expected to be much more effective than legislative measures. But they are also much more difficult to plan and carry out; their effectiveness may also show itself only many years later, and may be difficult to evaluate. Certainly this is another example for the need for research to accompany and measure the effects of such educational programs. In the foregoing account frequent references have been made to the influence of social attitudes; e.g., when speaking of the public images of the alcoholic and the drug addict, varying from country to country, the high and low alcoholism rates among the French and Jews respectively, and the relative incidence of alcoholism and barbiturate dependence in men and women. (Incidentally, the finding that the ratio of female to male alcoholics in England—perhaps one woman to every three males—is probably higher than in any other country, may possibly also reflect—apart from economic factors—changing social attitudes.)

Social acceptance or rejection of heavy drinking and drug taking may have a bearing even on symptomatology. The French alcoholic, living in a country where heavy drinking is widespread, is free from the severe guilt feelings that plague the Anglo-American alcoholic, who knows that his drinking habits are severely frowned upon. Feeling rejected, the latter may react bitterly to his condemnation by society; and his guilt and isolation feelings may in turn become further motivations for more intensified drinking. The stage at which such sufferers (and their families) seek help is strongly influenced by social attitudes. Where there is a severe stigma attached to the diagnosis of alcoholism or drug dependence, sufferers may prefer to remain underground, undiagnosed and untreated, and families will prefer to conceal the "skeleton in their cupboard." Moreover, it is only under the clamor of a well-informed, enlightened public and professional opinion that governments—faced with many other competing demands from other pressing social and other problems—will establish a sufficient number of specialized therapeutic and rehabilitation facilities.

Public and professional education is required in order to make an impact on social attitudes. Public education has to start at school. There would seem to be one important difference in that respect between alcohol and drug education—whereas at school there should be education *on* alcohol, rather than *against* alcohol (although not everyone would agree with the recent frequently heard proposition that school education on alcohol should mean teaching drinking in moderation), education as regards drugs would have to emphasize strongly the dangers of all forms of illicit drug taking. But all such education in school should remain objective. Likewise, education of all other sections of the lay public should be factual and objective, rather than moralistic, although ethical considerations obviously enter into these problems. Professional education in these fields—so far very neglected —would also have to start early, e.g., in the medical schools. Early education of the medical student would help the future doctor to accept alcoholism and drug dependence emotionally as genuine illnesses, to be on the lookout for them and diagnose and treat them early. The knowledge that such people are regarded by the medical profession as sick will in time help the lay public to do likewise.

In recent years much progress has been made toward an acceptance of the "disease concept" of alcoholism by the professional and lay public. No such advance has as yet been made as regards attitudes toward other forms of drug dependence. Looking at drug addicts as "dope fiends" merely anchors them more strongly in their subculture, their criminal behavior, and their dependence on drugs, as the only available means of finding temporary (but rapid) relief. One might hope that one important beneficial consequence of a "combined approach" toward alcoholism and drug dependence might consist in greater acceptance of the concept of the drug addict as a sick person. This, in time, might also assist in altering the attitude of the addict toward himself and his disability, and encourage him to find his way back to society.

### 3. Earlier diagnosis and earlier treatment

All too often nowadays alcoholics and drug abusers present themselves in a relatively late phase of their affliction. More understanding professional and public attitudes, by reducing the stigma, would encourage earlier consultation of the doctor, enabling earlier diagnosis and treatment. Although saving the "casualties" is not in itself a very effective method of prevention, early treatment would often help in forestalling the further downward progression with its risks of irreversible mental or physical changes, of emotional harm to family, etc.; and in the case of addict-pushers it would diminish the risk of these "foci of infection" turning-on newcomers to the use of dangerous drugs.

## 4. Mental hygiene measures and improvement of socioeconomic conditions

Psychological and socioeconomic factors play an important role in the development of many cases of alcoholism and drug dependence. Children brought up in unhappy homes by "inadequate" parents or under economically hopeless circumstances cannot be expected to grow up into emotionally secure adults. Maladjusted psychoneurotic and psychopathic individuals form a more vulnerable group than more mature, secure, stable, adequate types of personality. Thus, the application of the principles of sound mental hygiene in childhood, and the improvement of general social and economic conditions, should contribute toward decreasing the risks of emotional and social insecurity, and indirectly diminish the need of insecure personalities to escape to drink or drugs in the search for relief and oblivion.

## 5. Research

In alcoholism as well as in dependence on other drugs, fact-finding research is needed to answer many unresolved fundamental questions. Lack of factual knowledge is often reflected in confused attitudes and contradictory statements made by "experts." A good example is the flood of contradictory medical pronouncements on the dangers or otherwise of smoking cannabis reefers. In the absence of factual knowledge emotional bias can reign supreme, and emotionally biased hypotheses are often mistaken for facts.

Some areas in which research is needed have already been indicated. On the basis of a careful review H. Kalant [54] concluded that ". . . from the point of view of research, alcoholism cannot reasonably be separated from other forms of drug dependence," and he goes on to say that ". . . indeed, answers to basic questions about the nature of dependence phenomena can come only from a systematic comparison of the behavioural and biological effects, acute as well as chronic, of all types of drugs which give rise to problems of dependence. . . ."

## POLICY AND ADMINISTRATION

The first major organization to put into practice the "combined approach" to alcoholism and drug dependence was the Addiction Research Foundation of Ontario. Having originally started its work in the field of alcoholism only, about ten years later the legislation governing the work of the foundation was amended to include all forms of drug dependence. As H. D. Archibald, the Executive Director of the Foundation, pointed out ". . . this policy of integration, or extension, was the result of our experience and our practice . . . our practice preceded the development of an official policy—and subsequently amendment of our legislation." [55] In the Ontario clinics, which were originally organized primarily for alcoholics, many patients were seen suffering from "double addiction." (We had the same experience in the early 1950s in our Alcoholic Unit at Warlingham Park Hospital.) Because of the frequent abuse of alcohol and other drugs by the same person, Archibald thinks it ". . . logical to accept responsibility for treatment of patients with problems of dependence on any chemical, whether alcohol, amphetamine, or narcotic," but he stresses that the Ontario foundation had found it necessary "to formulate a special clinical team and provide special facilities for the narcotic addict" since heroin and morphine addicts did not mix well with other patient groups. Archibald quotes D. Cameron as also being in favor of integration of programs for all drug-dependent persons, but as pointing out that "there is a vast difference between treating all drug dependent persons in a single ward or in a single hospital or outpatient setting, and having several different, closely coordinated treatment sources that may serve different patients according to their drug dependence, underlying psychopathology, social background and legal status." By and large, our own experiences tend to support this view.

Other points made by Archibald in favor of an integrated agency are that its clinicians would be more knowledgeable and judicious in the use of such treatment methods as psychoactive drugs; that in research better comparisons are likely to be made when carried out on a variety of drugs used by different persons, "with the differences possibly providing aetiological clues" and the possibility of achieving a perspective which one might find otherwise difficult to obtain; that bringing all forms of drug dependence within the scope of one agency encourages a broader approach to the patient; that the intercommunication of specialists leads to ". . . economical and fruitful productivity." Incidentally, it is an interesting finding that in countries where new drug problems emerged, it was often the professional worker concerned with alcoholics who also started to work with the addicts to other drugs. Archibald concluded that the experience of the Ontario foundation ". . . endorses the concept of integrating the alcoholism and other drug dependency services within one establishment," and that in any case the undoubted differences existing between alcoholism and other forms of drug dependence ". . . can give us fruitful leads in planning educational, therapeutic and research activities."

## CONCLUSIONS

No doubt there are dissimilarities between alcoholism and drug dependence. In particular, there is the fundamental difference that alcohol is legally available and its use in Western culture hallowed by tradition and encouraged in social intercourse, whereas drugs as a rule are available on prescription only. This difference must have repercussions on the type of person who may become dependent, on prognosis, on educational and control measures, etc. On the other hand, there are a great many similarities, and for many reasons an integrated, comprehensive approach would seem very promising as regards treatment, rehabilitation, research, etc. Clearly, the degree of integration would have to depend on local and regional circumstances, and in general the "combined approach" philosophy does not mean that alcoholics and heroin addicts should actually be treated in the same ward. But in many aspects it would seem that there are greater similarities between alcoholics and, say, barbiturate addicts, than between the latter and heroin addicts; and just as there are many various types of "alcoholisms" and alcoholics, so there are also great differences between the various forms of drug dependence and between "drug addicts." In recent years alcoholics have been recognized more and more as sick people in need of understanding and professional help; and by adopting a comprehensive, integrated approach it may confidently be hoped that in time the public image of the drug addict will improve likewise, with favorable repercussions in the field of treatment, rehabilitation, and prevention. A great deal of work has been carried out in recent years in regard to alcoholism, and one may hope that much of its findings and results could—with certain modifications—be applied successfully to cases of dependence on other drugs.

## REFERENCES

1. *Selected Papers, 12th International Institute of Preventive Treatment of Alcoholism,* Vol. 1 (Prague: International Council on Alcohol and Alcoholism, 1966), pp. 39–80.
2. M. M. Glatt, *ibid.,* p. 39.
3. "Services for the Prevention and Treatment of Dependence on Alcohol and Other Drugs," 14th Report, World Health Organization Expert Committee on Mental Health, WHO technical reports series, 1967, No. 363.
4. D. J. Pittman, *British Journal of Addictions,* 1967, Vol. 22, p. 337.
5. R. E. Popham, et al., *ibid.,* 1968, Vol. 63, p. 25.
6. M. M. Glatt, *WHO Chronicle,* 1967, Vol. 21, p. 293.
7. M. Retterstol and A. Sund, *Drug Addiction and Habituation* (Oslo: Universitatsforlaget, 1965).
8. C. R. B. Joyce, in *New Horizons in Psychology,* B. M. Foss, ed. (London: Penguin Books, 1966), p. 271.

9. D. R. Laurence, *Clinical Pharmacology*, 3rd ed. (London: Churchill, 1966).

10. M. M. Glatt, *British Journal of Addictions*, 1958, Vol. 55, p. 51.

11. E. M. Jellinek, *The Disease Concept of Alcoholism* (New Haven: Hillhouse Press, 1960).

12. WHO Expert Committee on Addiction-Producing Drugs, WHO technical report series, 1952, No. 57, p. 9.

13. ———, *ibid.*, 1957, No. 116, p. 9.

14. ———, *ibid.*, 1964, No. 273, p. 9.

15. ———, *ibid.*, 1954, No. 84, p. 10.

16. ———, *ibid.*, 1955, No. 94, p. 10.

17. M. M. Glatt, *United Nations Bulletin of Narcotics*, 1962, No. 14, p. 20.

18. L. Goldberg, in *Alcohol and Road Traffic*, Proceedings of the Third International Conference in London, 1962 (London: British Medical Association, 1963).

19. N. B. Eddy, H. Halbach, H. Isbell, H. M. Seevers, et al., *Bulletin of the World Health Organization*, 1965, Vol. 32, p. 721.

20. M. M. Glatt, D. J. Pittman, D. G. Gillespie, and D. R. Hills, *The Drug Scene in Great Britain* (London: Edward Arnold, publishers, 1967).

21. M. M. Glatt, *British Journal of Addictions*, 1969, Vol. 64, p. 109.

22. E. Rubin and C. S. Lieber, Proceedings of the 28th International Congress on Alcohol and Alcoholism (Abstracts), Washington, D.C.: 1968, p. 43.

23. J. D. Reichard, *American Journal of Psychiatry*, 1947, Vol. 103, p. 721.

24. A. Wikler, *Psychiatric Quarterly*, 1952, Vol. 26, p. 70.

25. J. Mardones, Paper read at the 28th International Congress on Alcohol and Alcoholism, Washington, D.C.: 1968.

26. J. P. von Wartburg, Paper read at the 28th International Congress on Alcohol and Alcoholism, Washington, D.C.: 1968.

27. R. Cruz-Coke and A. Varela, *Lancet*, No. 1, p. 1348.

28. J. Partanen, K. Brunn, and T. Markkanen, *Inheritance of Drinking Behaviour* (Helsinki: The Finnish Foundation for Alcohol Studies, 1966).

29. A. Roe, in *Alcohol, Science, and Society* (New Haven: 1945), p. 115.

30. M. M. Glatt, *British Journal of Addictions,* 1955, Vol. 52, p. 55.
31. ———, and Leong Hon Koon, *Psychiatric Quarterly,* 1961, Vol. 35, p. 1.
32. E. M. Jellinek, in WHO Expert Committee on Mental Health, Alcoholism Subcommittee, Second Report, WHO technical report series, 1952, No. 48, p. 26.
33. A Wikler, in *Narcotics,* D. M. Wilner and G. G. Kassebaum, eds. (New York: McGraw-Hill, 1965).
34. M. M. Glatt, *British Journal of Addictions,* 1967, Vol. 62, p. 35.
35. K. A. Menninger, *Man Against Himself* (New York: Harcourt, Brace, and World, 1938).
36. J. D. Havard, *Practitioner,* 1962, Vol. 188, p. 498.
37. "A Managing Director," *British Journal of Addictions,* 1957, Vol. 54, p. 5.
38. M. M. Glatt and D. J. Hills, *British Journal of Addictions,* 1965, Vol. 61, p. 71.
39. L. Brill and J. H. Jaffee, *British Journal of Addictions,* 1967, Vol. 62, p. 375.
40. J. Y. Dent, *Anxiety and Its Treatment* (London: Skeffington, 1955).
41. M. M. Glatt, International Symposium on Drug Addiction, Quebec: 1968.
42. ———, *British Journal of Addictions,* 1958, Vol. 54, p. 133.
43. W. Schulte, Dtsch. Med. Wschr., 1963, Vol. 89, p. 223.
44. D. B. Louria, *The Drug Scene* (New York: McGraw-Hill, 1968).
45. H. R. George and M. M. Glatt, *British Journal of Addictions,* 1967, Vol. 62, p. 147.
46. M. M. Glatt, in *New Aspects of Mental Health Services,* Freeman-McFarlane, ed. (London: Pergamon, 1967).
47. "Treatment and Care of Drug Addicts," WHO Study Group, *Bulletin of Narcotics,* 1957, Vol. 9, p. 36.
48. C. Winik, *United Nations Bulletin of Narcotics,* 1962, No. 14, p. 1.
49. L. R. Drew, *Quarterly Journal of Studies on Alcohol,* 1968, Vol. 29, p. 956.
50. A. Rosen and M. M. Glatt, Paper read at the 28th International Congress on Alcohol and Alcoholism, Washington: 1968.
51. J. Skala, personal communication, 1969.

52. Y. Henderson, *Plea for Dilution.*
53. H. Halbach, *British Journal of Addictions,* 1959, Vol. 56, p. 27.
54. H. Kalant, Paper read at the 28th International Congress on Alcohol and Alcoholism, Washington: 1968.
55. H. D. Archibald, Paper read at the 28th International Congress on Alcohol and Alcoholism, Washington: 1968.

# Predisposition to alcoholism

JORGE MARDONES, M.D.

If a physical predisposition to alcoholism can be proved, a new path for scientific research will be opened. The research that Dr. Jorge Mardones has pursued for twenty-five years could be of inestimable value in understanding and controlling alcoholism. Dr. Mardones is director and co-founder with Dr. Jellinek of the Institute for Research on Alcoholism. His University of Chile posts include chairman of the Institute of Pharmacology and director of the Center for Biological Publications. He is also an active member of the WHO Expert Committee on Drug Addiction, and the Scientific Group of the International Council on Alcohol and Addictions.

## INTRODUCTION

Many who have studied alcoholism agree about the existence of certain individual predispositions to the disease. It seems evident that only some of the individuals who are in similar situations regarding accessibility to alcoholic beverages, cultural rules governing their use, and stress situations favoring the use of alcohol as a drug become excessive drinkers. And the signs considered characteristic of alcohol-type dependence appear in only some of them. Nevertheless, knowledge about the nature of this predisposition is rather scarce. This article is an attempt to systematize the study of such predisposition.

The importance of early recognition of individuals who appear to be predisposed to alcoholism is obvious. As a matter of fact,

preventive measures are more efficient when they can be restricted to predisposed individuals. This would be possible if the
recognition of what, in epidemiologic language, is called the vulnerable groups, were feasible. On the other hand, the knowledge
of the nature of a predisposition would give a useful basis for the
correction of the determining factors and would eventually be useful for either the prevention of alcoholism or the treatment of
patients.

## DIFFERENT FORMS OF APPETITE
## FOR ALCOHOL

Drug dependence generally originates in the autoadministration
of a drug which is the expression of the desire for feeling its
effect. In the particular case of ethanol, it is essential to point out
that this substance is not only a drug but also a substrate supply-
ing biologically profitable energy, although its absorption and
metabolic pathways are partially different from those of other
nutriments. Consequently, it is permissible to think a priori that
the appetite for alcohol may correspond to the appetite for sugar,
starch, proteins, or fat.

Recently Varela[1] has reported that it is possible to recognize
different forms of appetite for alcohol. It is pertinent to discuss
this assertion here, since each of these forms of appetite may be
a factor of the predisposition to alcoholism. Varela describes
physiological, pharmacological, and pathological appetites for
alcohol. Physiological appetite is the desire to drink alcoholic
beverages without wishing to feel the effects of ethanol on the
central nervous system. He calls pharmacological appetite the
desire to feel the drug effects of ethanol in various degrees,
ranging from a slight euphoria to the mental alienation of inebriety. Finally, pathological appetite is considered the abnormal
desire to drink alcoholic beverages which can be observed in
individuals who have been excessive drinkers for relatively long
periods. It is expressed in two behavioral signs of alcoholism,
namely: "inability to stop" after indulging in drinking a certain
amount of alcoholic beverages (the gamma alcoholism of Jellinek)[2] or "inability to abstain," peculiar to inveterate drinkers,

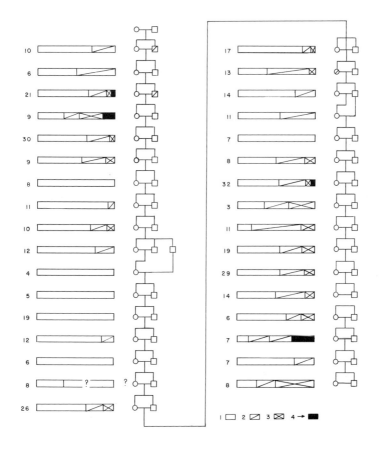

Fig. 1. Pedigree of the rats of the "nondrinker" strain. The figures
close to the bars represent the number of siblings. Key: voluntary
alcohol intake in ml per 100 g body weight and day: $1 = < 0.20$;
$2 = 0.20 - 0.39$; $3 = 0.40 - 0.59$; $4 - = > 0.59$.

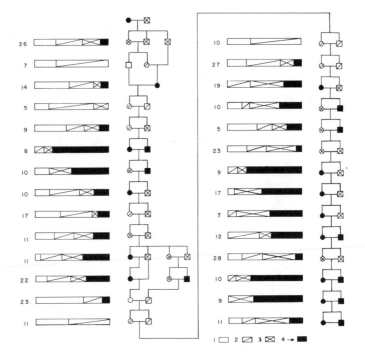

Fig. 2. Pedigree of the rats of the "drinker" strain. The figures and key are the same as in Fig. 1.

who may maintain themselves under the influence of alcohol driven by the need to alleviate slight withdrawal symptoms (the delta alcoholism of Jellinek).[2]

## Individual fluctuations of physiological appetite

Probably physiological appetite has its equivalent in the voluntary intake of ethanol observed in experimental animals when they are offered a free choice between water and ethanol solutions as drinking fluids. Generally speaking, these animals do not exhibit overt signs of intoxication, and the amount they drink is limited and distributed throughout the day.

In the case of rats, Richter and Campbell[3] reported in 1940 that rats are able to recognize alcohol in solutions as weak as 1.8 percent and that they prefer alcohol solutions of five percent to water, while the opposite occurs with alcohol solutions of higher concentrations. We have been working on this problem since 1942[4] and have been able to observe that the total daily alcohol intake is about the same when the offered ethanol solutions ranked from 5 to 20 percent. Furthermore, we showed that the daily alcohol intake increased when the diet was deficient in some vitamins.[5] In 1948, the importance of individual fluctuations in daily intake of ethanol came to our attention,[6] and we started a selection of rats by inbreeding, which allowed us to demonstrate the genetic origin of the appetite for alcohol in this species.[7,8] Figures 1 and 2 show the pedigree of our two strains: A "nondrinker" and B "drinker." As can be seen, no matter how high the number of inbred generations, we have not been able to obtain a "pure line," since "drinker" rats are observed in the "nondrinker" strain and vice versa. This failure can be explained, assuming that at least two genes play an independent role in the determinism of alcohol appetite, giving several genotypes of "drinker" as well as "nondrinker" rats. This idea is in agreement with the composition of our colonies of both strains.[9]

For the purpose of this article, it is sufficient to point out that these results demonstrate that voluntary alcohol intake in rats is genetically determined.

It has been shown that in mice, also, the appetite for alcohol is genetically determined. It is well known that there are many strains of mice maintained for numerous generations of inbreeding. MacClearn and Rodgers[10] have reported that some strains of mice can be ordered according to the amount of their voluntary alcohol intake, the C57BL/Crgl strain being at the highest level and the BALB/cCrgl strain, at the lowest one.

The genetic differences observed among rats and mice should be related to different metabolic patterns. Few metabolic differences between "drinker" and "nondrinker" strains have been reported until now. But the results open a way to study the predisposition in relation to an increase of physiological appetite for alcohol. Thus the subject deserves to be analyzed here.

The results of our experiments performed in rats from the "nondrinker" and "drinker" strains receiving ethanol labeled with $14_C$ in carbons one or two, have shown that the rate of recovering the activity in expired $CO_2$ was not different among rats of both strains.[11,12] Furthermore, no difference between either strain was observed in the oxidation rate to $CO_2$ of the two carbons of acetate, the three carbons of pyruvate, and the one carbon of butyrate.[12] Concerning the oxidation of glucose, we have found that a group of males of the "drinker" strain who received an overload of glucose, labeled with $14_C$ in the carbon one, exhibited an oxidation rate $CO_2$ significantly higher than did a group of males of the "nondrinker" strain.[13] This result is in agreement with the fact that the rate of oxidation of the carbon one of gluconate appeared higher in the rats of both sexes belonging to the "drinker" strain than in those of the "nondrinker" one.[14] This is an evidence that at least some of the "drinker" genotypes have more active enzymatic systems of the oxidative pathway of glucose—also called pentose way—than that of the "nondrinker" ones. It is necessary to point out that the main enzymes of this pathway require NADP as coenzyme, while alcohol dehydrogenase utilizes NAD; as if rats more capable of obtaining energy from glucose through pathways not disturbed by simultaneous oxidation of ethanol exhibited higher appetite for alcohol. When a tracer dose of gluconate labeled with $14_C$ in carbon one was given simultaneously with a high dose of ethanol (1.55 mg. per kg. body weight) the activity recovered in $CO_2$ was significantly higher in rats of both sexes and strains than in controls without ethanol, but the strains' difference was veiled.[15] Research directed to study the activity of some enzymes of this metabolic pathway is now going on in order to recognize the exact place of the metabolic difference between strains.

Another metabolic difference between rats of the "drinker" and "nondrinker" strains was found in the lipid content of the liver of males fed without alcohol: the liver of the males of the "drinker" strain exhibited a significantly higher content of fat than those of the "nondrinker" one, while no difference was found in females.[16]

Concerning mice, it has been reported [17] that the liver of those belonging to the strains C57BL/Crgl (which showed higher appetite for alcohol) exhibited a somewhat higher alcohol dehydrogenase activity than those of the strains BALB/cCrgl (which showed less appetite for alcohol). It has been observed also that the sleeping time after a fixed dose of ethanol was longer in mice of the latter strain than in those of the former,[18] while no difference in ethanol found in the brain 40, 100, and 140 minutes after ethanol administration was registered.[19] Recently[20] a difference has been reported between the same strains concerning the metabolism of acetaldehyde, which is the first step of the oxidation of ethanol.

In humans, the physiological appetite is clearly observed in individuals who prefer wine to any other drink as a beverage used with meals, without looking for the effect of ethanol on the central nervous system. This is also shown in individuals who prefer to mitigate thirst with beer, even of a very low alcohol content, than with any other beverage. Little is known about the distribution of this appetite among human populations. It is important not to confuse the absence of physiological appetite with total abstinence, because there is a high number of abstemious people who feel a strong appetite for alcohol; and many individuals without physiological appetite who are not abstemious.

## Individual variations of pharmacological appetite

When a person drinks alcohol in such amounts that the function of his central nervous system is disturbed, he experiences changes in his perception both of himself and of the exterior world. These changes are pleasant for some individuals and indifferent or even disagreeable to others. In general, human beings, as well as animals, like to repeat pleasant experiences. Thus, even when first experiences of the effects of ethanol originate in physiological appetite or social pressure, they may bring about the repeated desire for feeling the effects of the drug, i.e., they can awaken a pharmacological appetite.

For some individuals, only slight effects of alcohol on the central nervous system, inducing merely changes of mood, are pleasant; while the most intense effects leading to the blurring of consciousness are rather unpleasant. Other individuals prefer the blurring of consciousness accompanying inebriation.

It is a task for psychological and psychiatric exploration to determine whether a pharmacological appetite does exist in each individual; and in positive cases, to determine its degree and whether or not it is a predisposing factor to alcoholism. On the other hand, these explorations would allow one to recognize the motivations and characteristics of the pharmacological appetite in each patient, information which is very useful for prevention during the first stages, and eventually for the treatment of alcoholism.

It is more difficult to recognize the influence of organic factors in the psychological field than in the case of physiological appetite, since it is not easy to obtain equivalent psychological patterns in experimental animals; and the research of this aspect in humans is filled with all kind of difficulties.

*Individual variations in pathological appetite*

Surveys performed in population samples have shown that the number of excessive drinkers widely exceeds that of alcoholics. On the other hand, everyday observation shows that there are many individuals who remain for long periods—even for life—excessive drinkers without exhibiting the signs of gamma or delta alcoholism. Furthermore, in an important proportion of alcoholics the clinical record reveals that the duration of the period of excessive drinking, before the appearance of behavioral signs of alcoholism, varies widely. While in some individuals this is rather short—one or two years or even less—in others it lasts ten years or more. These facts indicate the presence of individual variations

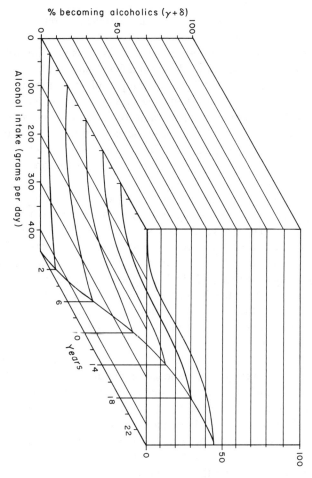

*Fig. 3. Schematic representation of the relationship of appearance of alcoholism with daily intake of alcohol and duration of drinking habit.*

concerning the susceptibility to pathological appetite, i.e., that there are individuals specially predisposed to become alcoholics while others appear rather refractory.

Figure 3 is a schematic representation of the variations of susceptibility to alcoholism in relation to the amount of daily intake of alcohol and of the duration of this habit. The position of the curves is merely an estimate, and are designed to represent only the tendencies of the relations.

This figure shows the well-known fact that it is very improbable that an individual who daily drinks small amounts of alcohol (e.g., less than 100 grams) would develop a pathological appetite, even after many years of this habit. However, in those individuals drinking higher amounts of alcohol (e.g., 300 or more grams daily) the risk of becoming alcoholic is very high, even during the first years of this habit. The diagram also shows there are excessive drinkers who do not develop a pathological appetite, even after many years of this behavior.

It is pertinent to discuss here whether susceptibility toward developing a pathological appetite may be a genetic trait. The observation that among alcoholics, as well as among their non-alcoholic female relatives, the proportion of individuals suffering from color blindness is significantly higher than in control groups, strongly suggests that pathological appetite may be influenced by a factor located in the X chromosome. In 1964 Cruz-Coke[21] reported that in the course of a study on the correlation between some marked chromosomes and arterial hypertension in the population of patients admitted to the J. J. Aguirre Hospital of Santiago, Chile, he found that the only significant correlation he observed was between liver cirrhosis and color blindness. Later on, Cruz-Coke and Varela[22] reported a significant correlation between alcoholism and color blindness. The principal disturbance of color vision they observed in both cases was classified as "undetermined" since it was mainly expressed in failures in the Plate 3 of the Hardy-Rand-Ritter test. A more accurate study was performed later on, using the 100-hue test of Farnsworth and Munsell. In that study we observed[23] that the most prevalent defect appeared in the spectral zones related with the vision of the blue-yellow (tritanopia and tetarohedral), and not in the red-green zone (protan and deutan as it is observed in the classical Daltonism). It was also possible to demonstrate that the same disturbance appeared with equivalent frequency among nonalcoholic first-degree female relatives of alcoholics, a fact which allows one to eliminate the possibility that color blindness could be secondary to the abuse of alcohol. The results of this study are summarized in Table I. We are now continuing this study with the aim of

### Table I
### FARNSWORTH-MUNSELL TEST

| | LINE | PROTAN | DEUTAN | TRITAN | TETARTAN |
|---|---|---|---|---|---|
| **MALES** | | | | | |
| Alcoholics | 1 | 48–17 | 46–19 | 41–24 | 32–33 |
| Controls | 2 | 46–7 | 46–7 | 48–5 | 48–5 |
| Relatives of alcoholics | 3 | 17–1 | 17–1 | 15–3 | 15–3 |
| **FEMALES** | | | | | |
| Relatives of alcoholics | 4 | 19–4 | 20–3 | 13–10 | 16–7 |
| Controls | 5 | 43–1 | 43–1 | 42–2 | 42–2 |
| $\chi_Y^2$ (1 v 2) | | 2.27 | 1.79 | 10.46† | 20.99‡ |
| $\chi_Y^2$ (2 v 3) | | 0.005 | 0.65 | 0.16 | 0.16 |
| $\chi_Y^2$ (1 v 4) | | 0.31 | 1.59 | 0.09 | 2.07 |
| $\chi_Y^2$ (4 v 5) | | 3.02 | 1.47 | 13.00‡ | 6.62† |

Distribution of mean of errors in the different spectral zones of the Farnsworth-Munsell test observed in groups of alcoholics, their first degree relatives and controls. The figures in each column represent the number of cases where the mean of error per capita was $\leq 1.5$ and $> 1.5$ respectively. $\chi^2$ represent the values of chi square with the correction of Yates (from Varela et al.).[23]

† = $P < 0.01$
‡ = $P < 0.001$

establishing whether color blindness is related to a factor influencing the development of pathological appetite or to other stages of the predisposition to alcoholism.

We have seen above that the problem of relating physiological appetite with enzymatic activities is very difficult, even in experimental animals which can be crossed at will, and where the study of enzymatic activities of their organs is not difficult. Thus, it is obvious that the study of the correlation between enzymatic activities, color blindness, and pathological appetite for alcohol is much more difficult in human beings. The goal of this study should be the finding of a sign of the metabolic disturbance eventually responsible for the development of pathological appetite. At present, the positive correlation between alcoholism and dyschromasia should be considered only as a mere indication that the eventual genetic factor is located in the X chromosome; but there are no reasons to think that dyschromasia and pathological appetite for alcohol should be different expressions of the same metabolic disturbance.

### Predisposition to organic complication of alcohol abuse

It is well known that not every excessive drinker (including gamma and delta alcoholics) develop organic complications. Since the most common complication of alcohol abuse is liver cirrhosis, it is pertinent to limit the discussion to this disease.

Figure 4 is a diagram—submitted to me under the same limitations as Figure 3—which was prepared with the aim of orientation only. It shows that the incidence of fatty liver and cirrhosis are related to both the amount of daily alcohol intake and the duration of the drinking habit.

Those who have had the opportunity of examining alcoholics admitted to hospitals because of their alcoholism, and not because of their medical complications, have been able to observe that not all of them exhibited organic disturbances, even when their drinking habits appeared to be rather strong. In Chile, Ugarte et al.[24] have found that in 25 percent of the alcoholics admitted to the hospital because of their alcoholism, liver biopsy observed under optical microscope was not different from normal; that a proportion of 60 percent exhibited fatty liver at admission; and that only 12 percent showed liver cirrhosis. Lieber and Spritz[25] have reported that patients who exhibited fatty liver at admission, and whose lesions disappeared after some days of hospital care, when subjected for 12 days to a balanced diet with a supplement of $180 \pm 200$ grams of alcohol per day showed fatty liver again.

Ugarte et al.[26] have reported that alcoholic patients, whose biopsy did not show fatty liver at admission, when subjected for 10 days to an alcohol-supplemented diet equivalent to that em-

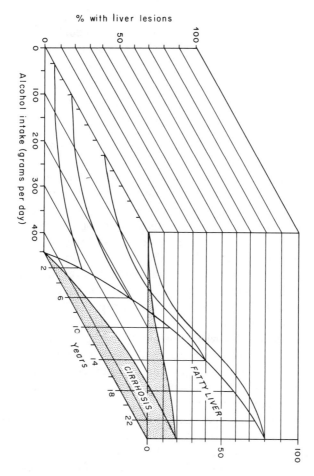

*Fig. 4. Schematic representation of the relationship of appearance of fatty liver or liver cirrhosis with daily alcohol intake and duration of drinking habit.*

ployed by Lieber, the biopsy at the end of this period remained without observable lesions of fatty liver. According to these results, the absence of lesions of fatty liver at admission appears not to be the consequence of a smaller daily intake of alcohol than that declared by the patient, but rather to a certain stubbornness to suffer this liver disturbance.

These facts show that differences in individual susceptibility to liver damage induced by ethanol may exist. Undoubtedly the possibility of recognizing this susceptibility and its mechanism deserves further studies.

## OTHER FACTORS THAT MAY INFLUENCE PREDISPOSITION TO ALCOHOLISM

J. P. von Wartburg et al.[27] demonstrated the presence in human livers of an atypical dehydrogenase with an in vitro activity six times as high as the typical one. They found [28] that the frequency of this atypical enzyme is about 17 percent in Switzerland while in England it is only about 4 percent. Ugarte et al.[29] in Chile, following the method proposed by von Wartburg, found this atypical enzyme in about 29 percent of liver biopsies. Obviously these figures have been obtained from samples not sufficiently stratified to permit a generalization to cover the total population of the mentioned countries; but they do indicate that there are important differences between human populations concerning the presence of this enzyme.

These studies—for which von Wartburg received the 1968 Jellinek Award—are rather recent, and thus very little is yet known concerning the relations of this enzyme with the oxidation rate of ethanol in vivo and its disappearance from the blood, and with the dose-effect relationship.

In unpublished studies, Ugarte et al.[29] were unable to find significant differences in the distribution of this enzyme among alcoholic patients with and without liver lesions.

Undoubtedly, the study of the distribution of this enzyme among alcoholic and nonalcoholic persons seems to be a very interesting part of the study of individual susceptibility to alcoholism.

## SUMMARY

Summarizing, it can be said that individual differences concerning susceptibility to alcoholism and to its organic complications have been recognized, and that some knowledge which may orient the research on the origin and nature of these fluctuations has been obtained.

First, the presence of a so-called "physiological appetite" for alcohol which is determined genetically has been demonstrated in experimental animals. This fact has opened the way to the exploration of enzymatic and metabolic differences which may originate this appetite. The problem is now in the genetic and biochemical field.

The study of the origin and mechanism of individual fluctuations concerning "pharmacological appetite" for alcohol is undoubtedly the task of psychologists and psychiatrists.

It seems that research concerning individual fluctuations in "pathological appetite" for alcohol has also entered the fields of genetics and biochemistry, since some facts strongly suggest that a genetic factor located in the X chromosome plays a role.

Last but not least, it seems to be a task for biochemists and geneticists to study the origin and mechanism of the susceptibility to suffer organic alterations as a consequence of alcohol abuse. Scientists, together with pharmacologists, have the task of establishing the eventual role of atypical alcohol dehydrogenase in the dose-effect relationship of ethanol as well as in predisposition to alcoholism.

All these tasks are rather appealing not only because of the importance they have on prevention and treatment of alcoholism; but specially because of the general implications they have on the knowledge of genetic and biochemical influences on human behavior.

## REFERENCES

1. A. Varela, "Papel de la personalidad en el abuso del alcohol" in *Simposio Internacional sobre Alcohol y Alcoholismo,* ed. J. Mardones y A. Varela.—*Arch. Biol. Med. Exper. Supl. No. 3,* 1969, pp. 144–149.

2. E. M. Jellinek, "The Disease Concept of Alcoholism." Highland Park, N.J.: Hillhouse Press, 1960.

3. C. P. Richter and K. M. Campbell, *Science,* Vol. 91, 1940, p. 507.

4. J. Mardones and E. Onfray, *Rev. Chilena High. y Med. Prev.,* Vol. 4, 1942, p. 293.

5. ———, *Quart. J. Stud. Alcohol,* Vol. 12, 1951, p. 563.

6. ———, A. Hederra, and N. Segovia, *Bol. Soc. Biol. Santiago,* Vol. 5, 1948, p. 27.

7. ———, N. Segovia, and A. Hederra, *Quart. J. Stud. Alcohol,* Vol. 14, 1953, p. 1.

8. ———, *Intern. Rev. Neurobiol.,* Vol. 2, 1960, p. 141.

9. N. Segovia-Riquelme, A. Hederra, M. Anex, O. Barnier, I. Figuerola, I. Campos-Hoppe, N. Jara, and J. Mardones, "Factores nutrimentales y genéticos que influyen sobre la apetencia de alcohol," in *Simposio Internacional sobre Alcohol y Alcoholismo,* ed. J. Mardones y A. Varela. *Arch. Biol. Med. Exper. Supl. No. 3,* 1969, pp. 89–96.

10. G. E. MacClearn and D. A. Rodgers, *Quart. J. Stud. Alcohol,* Vol. 20, 1959, p. 691.

11. N. Segovia-Riquelme, J. J. Vitale, D. M. Hegsted, and J. Mardones, *J. Biol. Chem.,* Vol. 223, 1956, p. 399.

12. N. Segovia-Riquelme, I. Campos, W. Solodkowska, G. González, and J. Mardones, *J. Biol. Chem.,* Vol. 237, 1962, p. 2038.

13. ———, I. Figuerola-Camps, I. Campos-Hoppe, N. Jara, E. Negrete, and J. Mardones, *Arch. Biol. Med. Exper.,* Vol. 2, 1965, p. 74.

14. ———, I. Campos, W. Solodkowska, I. Figuerola-Camps, and J. Mardones, *Med. Exper.,* Vol. 11, 1964, p. 185.

15. I. Figuerola-Camps, N. Segovia-Riquelme, I. Campos, and J.

Mardones, VI Congreso de la Asociación Latino Americana de Ciencias Fisiológicas, Viña del Mar, Chile, *Resúmenes de comunicaciones libres,* p. 140, 1964.

16. W. Solodkowska, R. Alvarado-Andrade, E. Muñoz, and J. Mardones (to be published).

17. E. L. Bennet and M. Herbert, *Univ. California, Radiat. Lab. Quart. Rep.,* Vol. 14, 1966, p. 9208.

18. G. E. MacClearn, *Proc. Int. Conf. Alc. Road Traffic,* Vol. 3, 1962.

19. R. Karihana, P. R. Brown, G. E. MacClearn, and I. R. Taleshaw, *Science,* Vol. 154, 1966, p. 1574.

20. J. R. Sheppard, R. Albersheim, and G. E. MacClearn, *Proc. of XXVIII Int. Congr. Alcohol Alcoholism,* Vol. 1 (abstracts), 1968, p. 110.

21. R. Cruz-Coke, *Lancet,* Vol. 2, 1964, p. 1064.

22. ———— and A. Varela, *Lancet,* Vol. 1, 1966, p. 1348.

23. A. Varela, L. Rivera, J. Mardones, and R. Cruz-Coke, *Brit. J. Addiction* (in press).

24. G. Ugarte, I. Insunza, e H. Iturriaga, "Some effect of ethanol in normal and pathological liver," in *Progress Liver Disease* 3 (in press).

25. C. L. Lieber and M. Spritz, *J. Clin. Invest.,* Vol. 45, 1966, p. 1400.

26. G. Ugarte, H. Iturriaga, I. Insunza, *Proc. XXVIII Int. Congr. Alcohol Alcoholism,* Vol. 1 (abstracts), 1968, p. 14.

27. J. P. von Warthurg, J. Papenberg, and H. Aebi, *Canad. J. Biochem.,* Vol. 43, 1965, p. 889.

28. ———— and P. M. Schürch, *Ann. New York Acad. Sc.,* Vol. 151, 1968, p. 936.

29. G. Ugarte, M. E. Pino, and H. Altschiller (in press).

# Issues and trends

## ELIZABETH D. WHITNEY

Can alcohol and drug addictions be treated under one umbrella? Recognized scientists and authorities around the world have debated this issue, and some, such as Max Glatt, David Archibald, David Myerson, and others, have come up with an affirmative answer. Among the voluntary rehabilitation organizations, Dederich, the director of Synanon, says that all problems can be treated under one roof, provided the motivation and the atmosphere are right for the patient.

Today the trend is toward integration of clinical services for many types of patients. Perhaps alcoholics and drug addicts, because of the nature of their physical and mental withdrawal reactions, might preferably be treated in separate wards, although in the same hospital; but they could be cared for by the same groups of trained professionals.

One reason for combining the treatment of similar illnesses in a single unit is pragmatic. Trainees are scarce, and it is more efficient to train them in a number of similar diseases than to allow them to specialize on one which may, in fact, overlap others in many characteristics. While the diseases are not identical, mental, physical, and emotional similarities do exist, and professionals familiar with one type of addiction can readily understand and learn to treat others. For example, withdrawal from heroin is more drastic than withdrawal from acute alcoholism; yet, even though treatment differs, and the behavior of the patient varies (see the article by Dr. Myerson, pp. 277–295), it is usually necessary to isolate either type of patient in progressive stages of his illness, whether it be alcoholism or heroin addiction.

Members of Alcoholics Anonymous find combining alcoholism and drug treatment difficult. The drinker has been involved in nothing illegal; the drug taker has been breaking the law. The dissimilarity erects a barrier between the two types; but paths converge far more often than they separate in the treatment of various addictions, so that a concentration of facilities and a multiple use of personnel would appear more economical and more effective.

Since the current trend in the hospitalization of both alcoholics and drug addicts is to treat the withdrawal and acute phases as quickly as possible and to establish the patients on ambulatory, outpatient programs, group therapy for screened mixed groups could no doubt be arranged for separate days, with A.A. groups perhaps scheduled in the evenings, and club groups for professional guidance of the more severe alcoholic cases and the drug addicts arranged for the daytime. Upon discharge from the hospital, patients could be motivated to return for long-term therapy, or referred to community groups for further help.

What should become the function of voluntary agencies? For the past twenty-five years in the United States, and for a longer period in other countries, such as the Netherlands, a broad combination of activities on alcoholism has been performed by voluntary agencies. Mainly this had occurred because public agencies had not been prepared to take over the responsibilities built up by private initiative; and because the magnitude of the work was not sufficient to warrant governmental take-over.

Now, however, with worldwide recognition of the problems of alcoholism and drug dependence, the demand for adequate education, treatment, and rehabilitation has suddenly magnified to the point where it can no longer be handled by private institutions. The voluntary groups have thus accomplished well the preliminary objective of publicizing the problem. Now they must hand over the routine work to public agencies better equipped to cope with the volume, and move on to other areas, particularly education and research, which can be better handled by independent entrepreneurs than by government bureaus.

The question of whether the time is yet ripe for the counseling and rehabilitative functions to be taken over by governmental agencies has been widely discussed. It appears to be the consensus of the National Council on Alcoholism and many of its affiliates that professionally trained personnel, working in an official state setting, would be preferable for all phases of treatment of alcoholism and drug dependence, thus effecting a clean-cut transfer of responsibility. This would free the voluntary agencies to concentrate on studies, research, and education, where their particular abilities could be more effectively put to work. In all events, the fresh, creative approach that stems from independent thinking, beyond the influence of government control, must be continued; and to do so implies the continuing vigorous existence of voluntary agencies.

Professionals and interested civilians alike are aware that the mechanics of the treatment of alcoholism and drug addictions have now grown too large and too complicated for private handling, that these matters are now recognized as aspects of public health, becoming the responsibility of the government. The knowing private citizen is concerned that under impersonal state control treatment may become routine and lose the personal touch so valuable to genuine recovery. Dr. Kjolstad, citing the experience of Norway in his article in this volume (see pages 41–65), points out that not until the state program was decentralized by shifting the authority back to small community units did it become effective. It has become axiomatic that close personal relations constitute a necessity for any permanent rehabilitation.

Divided authority has been successfully practiced in the Netherlands, where a state program of treatment is in effect, but new methodology is developed under private auspices. After a supervised trial period, the state agrees to accept (or reject) the new, thus providing a happy cooperation of interests.

A major question arises as to who should foot the bill. Treatment costs for all ills are rising, and, with the complexities of alcohol and drug addiction, cost increases here are above average, far too high for private funding. The only answer must then be public recognition of these responsibilities, and the assumption of the financial burden as part of the public health program. Private sources should still support research and education, but they are no longer either willing or able to bear the burden of treatment. As has been the case in the past, private charity has sponsored and developed vast campaigns to attack tuberculosis, cancer, heart disease, dystrophy, mental health, and many others. It has started to do so for alcoholism and drug addiction, an undertaking which should be continued and expanded by private interests for the public good.

Education, too, can benefit vastly from concentrated private efforts to expand and improve teaching and research in the addiction field. Training programs must be substantially enlarged, and refresher courses offered. Every factor influencing the life of an alcoholic or a drug dependent—his family, his minister, his doctor, his employer—all must be brought to understand the relation each has to rehabilitation, which in itself becomes a major job of education to be accomplished.

In this period of transition straight thinking will require careful discrimination between the areas of public and private endeavor, between research and practical reality, between local practice and international procedure. Yet contact must not be lost in any of these areas, since broad understanding is vital in world health problems. If we can keep the channels of communication open between the active elements in the field of alcohol and drug dependence, the battle will be sooner won. To this purpose these dialogues are written and this book is dedicated.

# *Appendix*

*For further information on alcohol and drug dependence*

For information concerning national and international schools of alcohol studies write to:

North American Association of Alcoholism Programs
Suite 615, 1130 Seventeenth Street, N.W.
Washington, D.C. 20015

Other sources of information in the United States:

Alcoholics Anonymous
A.A. World Service, Inc.
Box 459, Grand Central Station
New York, N.Y. 10007

Al-Anon Family Group Headquarters
P.O. Box 182, Madison Square Station
New York, N.Y. 10010
(For relatives and associates of alcoholics)

Alateen
P.O. Box 182, Madison Square Station
New York, N.Y. 10010
(For teenagers with an alcoholic relative)

The National Council on Alcoholism, Inc.
2 Park Avenue
New York, N.Y. 10016

The Christopher D. Smithers Foundation, Inc.
41 East 57th Street
New York, N.Y. 10022

Rutgers Center of Alcohol Studies
Rutgers, The State University
New Brunswick, N.J. 08900

United States Department of Health,
    Education, and Welfare
Division on Alcoholism and Narcotics
Washington, D.C.

North American Association of Alcoholism Programs
1130 Seventeenth Street, N.W.
Washington, D.C. 20036 (recently added drug services)

Worldwide information may be obtained from:
        The International Council on Alcohol and Addictions
        Case Postale 140, 1001
        Lausanne, Switzerland

        World Health Organization
        Division on Drug Addiction
        Geneva, Switzerland

# Index

*A.A. Grapevine:* 155, 162, 168, 189

ABH blood-group: 325

Absenteeism: 224

Abstinence: 201; and chlordiaze-poxide, 258–260; inability to abstain, 336; total, 351–352

Accidents. *See* Driving; Home accidents; Industrial accidents; Traffic safety

Action: in the U.S., 139–140

Act 120 of 1962 Concerning the Struggle against Alcoholism, Czechoslovakia: excerpts from, 96–100

Addiction: and habituation, 315–316; development of, 329–331

Addiction Research Institute, Australia: 86

Addiction Research Unit, Maudsley Hospital, London: 17

*Addictions:* 312

"Affluence alcoholism": 327

AFL-CIO: 232

Africa: 5, 297

Age and alcoholism: 15, 349

*Aggiornamente Sociali:* 126

Akron, Ohio: 157, 158

*Al-Anon Faces Alcoholism:* 213

Al-Anon Family Groups: 174, 187, 200, 213, 346

Alateen: 187

Alcohol: as social problem, 9–13; and drugs, comprehensive approach to, 16–17; as a drug, 56, 315–316; schools, 194; rate of addictiveness, 204; social attitudes toward use of, 205; clear-

ing from blood, 244–245; different forms of appetite for, 368–378; physiological appetite for, 369–373; pharmacological appetite for, 373–374; pathological appetite for, 374–378; predisposition to organic complication from abuse of, 378–379; studies, international schools of, 389

Alcoholic(s): defined, 52; percentage of population, 91; psychoses in Italy, 128; treatment by private doctors, 173–197; earlier recognition of, 228

Alcoholics Anonymous: 141, 150, 151, 155–172, 174, 180, 182, 187, 188, 189–191, 200, 213, 343; in Norway, 51; in Australia, 68–69; defined, 155; history of, 157–159; twelve steps, 159–160; twelve traditions, 160–161; meetings and organization, 161–164; how it works, 165–167; effectiveness of, 167–172; and drug users, 312, 385

*Alcoholics Anonymous:* 168, 213

"Alcoholics Anonymous in Your Community": 163

Alcoholism: early approaches to, 2–3; new approaches to, 3–4; and existing services, 5; in France, 20–40; in Scandinavia, 41–65; defined, 52, 265; in Australia, 66–89; in Czechoslovakia, 90–115; in Italy, 116–133; in the U.S., 134–145; as disease, 183–185, 201–205; physiological and psychological aspects of, 185–186; and clergymen, 199–220; as social disorder, 205–212; and work, 221–238; and work supervisor, 229; and unions, 231–234; use of drugs for, 240–260; and environment, 299–300; and drug dependence, combined programs, 302–306, 311–363; causation, 313–329; and Jews, 326; types of, 334–337; "addictive" types of, 336; treatment, 337–348; and age, 349; predisposition to, 367–381; sources of information in U.S., 389–390; sources of worldwide information, 390

*Alcoholism:* 312

*Alcoholism, a Guide for the Clergy:* 213

Alcoholism and Drug Addiction Research Foundation, Ontario, Canada: 17, 86, 302, 312, 361

Alcoholism Information Centers: 193–194

Alcoholism Research and Training, Inc.: 194–195

Alexander, Jack: 164

Alpha alcoholism: 335

American Medical Association: 148, 151

American Medical Society on Alcoholism: 194

Amphetamines: 298, 314, 316, 330, 332

Analgesics: 326

Antabuse. *See* Disulfiram (Antabuse)

Antoniotti, Ferdinando: 125

Apolinarska clinic: 101–106

Apolinarska regimen (A-regimen): 103–106, 107, 108–109

Appetite for alcohol: forms of, 368–378

Aramine: 245

Archibald, David: 384

Archibald, H. D.: 361–362

Asia: 297

Atlanta. Municipal Courts: 195–196

Attitude(s): importance of therapist's, 339–340; of family, 345–346; influencing social, 357–359

Australia: 66–89, 148

Availability: reduction of, 355

Aversion treatment: 64, 103, 341

Aviation: 10–11

Bacon, Dr. Selden D.: 203

Bacon, S.: 183

Barbiturates: 243, 298, 318, 319

Beer: in Czechoslovakia, 92–93

Belgium: 17

Benadryl: 246

Beta alcoholism: 335

Blood-alcohol concentration: 10, 28, 81, 244

Bolivia: 297

Bonfiglio, Giovanni: 121, 126

Boston State Hospital: 150, 277

Brazil: 297

Breathalyser: 81

*British Journal of Addiction:* 312

*British Journal of Inebrity:* 312

British Medical Council on Alcoholism: 14

British Treatment Centres: 346

Bryan, Judge: 268

BUD system: 194

Building trades: 14

Bulgaria: 15

Bulletin Hebdomadaire de Statistique: 118

Burnett, Judge William H.: 195

*Business Week:* 221

Calciumcarbamide: 64

Cameron, Dr. Dale: 304, 361

Campbell, K. M.: 369

Canada: 15, 18, 119, 148, 265, 296, 304, 312, 355

Cannabis: 297, 314, 318, 319, 321, 327, 329, 332; legalizing, 353–354

Carroll, M. N., Jr.: 257

Catholic Church: 135

Causation: of alcoholism and drug dependence: 313–329

Central Nervous System: stimulants, 316; depressant drugs, 330

Central Office Against Addiction Dangers, Federal Republic of Germany: 17

Character disorder: and drug use, 279

Chile: 18, 297, 378

Chloral hydrate: 245

Chlordiazepoxide (Librium): 244, 245, 256–259

Christopher D. Smithers Foundation: 194

Cirrhosis of the liver: 25, 30, 119, 128–129, 378–379

Citrated Calcium Carbimide: 341

"The Classic Temperance Movement of the U.S.A. . . .": 203

*Classified Abstract Archive of Alcohol Literature:* 140, 144–145

Clergymen: 6, 199–220; own attitudes, 203–204; as Enabler, 208; and recovery process, 212–220; background reading for, 213; and family, 215–218

Clinebell, Rev. Howard J.: 213

Cocaine: 297, 316, 318, 327

Coca leaf: 297

"Cold turkey": 318

Community Council of Greater New York: 195

Comparative monthly statistics of death from alcoholism and cirrhosis of the liver, France: 38

Comparisons of degree of abstinence and of symptomatic improvement in 50 patients treated with chlordiazepoxide. . . . : 259

Consumption: in Italy, 127; daily in small quantities, 129

Control, loss of: 52, 55, 336

Convulsions: 247

Cooperation: national and interdisciplinary, 17–19

"Cooperation But Not Affiliation"; 163

Corsini, Mario: quoted, 125

Costs: financial, to the community, 333; of treatment, 386–387

Council of Europe: 18

Courts: and drug users, 287

Crime: 331–332

Crime Commission. *See* President's Commission on Law Enforcement and Administration of Justice

Cruz-Coke, R.: 376

Cyclazocine: 341

Czechoslovakia: 90–115, 265, 274, 275; prison programs, 9; 1962 legislation quoted, 96–100; treatment in, 100–111; sobering-up stations, 109–111, 269–270

Daytop Lodge: 343

Deaths due to alcoholism and cirrhosis of the liver, France: 36

Dederich, Chuck: 150–151, 384

Dehydrogenase: 380

Delirium tremens: 246

Delta alcoholism: 336

Denial mechanism: 206

Denmark. *See* Scandinavia

Dent, J. Y.: 341

Denver: 274; County Court, 195

Des Moines, Iowa: 274

Detoxification: 175–176; Centers, 195

Detoxification and Diagnostic Evaluation Center, St. Louis: 270–273

Diagnosis: need for early, 337–338, 359–360

Diazepam (Valium): 260
Diet: 243, 254
Diphenylhydantoin sodium (Dilantin): 247
Disease concept: legal acceptance of, 7–9
Disulfiram (Antabuse): 64, 178, 183, 186, 241, 248–252, 341; -alcohol reaction described, 250–251
Doctors: 6; and alcoholism in Italy, 130–131; private, and treatment of alcoholics, 173–197
Dopram (Doxapram): 245
Drew, L. R.: 349, 350
Driver, Joe B.: 268
Driving: in Great Britain, 11; in France, 27–29; in Scandinavia, 47. See also Traffic safety
Drug dependence: defined by WHO, 297–298; approaches to, 300–301; and legal control of drugs, 301; major problems, 301–306; and alcoholism, combined programs, 311–363; causation, 313–329; and personality, 320–323; and genetic factors, 324–325; and environment, 325–329; and crime, 331–332; and harm to society, 331–334; and traffic accidents, 332–333; and types of alcoholism, 334–337; treatment, 337–348
Drug(s): and alcoholism, comprehensive approach to, 16–17, 302–306; use of for alcoholism, 64, 240–260; abuse, 77; and volunteer agencies, 150; pharmacological nature of, 313–317; defined, 314; 3 classes of, 315; legislation, 352–357
Drug users: youthful, 277–295; and character disorders, 279; treatment program, 279–281; types of, 281–283; development of

therapeutic community, 283–286; and nurses, 284; community relationships, 286–289; self-help groups, 343–344
Drunkenness: public, 8, 263–275; as sin, 204

Easter, DeWitt: 268
Economic conditions: 326–327
Eddy, N. B.: 317
Education: 13–16, 301, 305–306, 358–359, 387; different philosophies of, 13–14; in France, 29–32; in Scandinavia, 47–49; in Australia, 82–84
Egypt: 297
Employers: 5
Encounter therapy: 196
England: 380; environment and drug dependence, 327–328
Environment: 299–300, 325–329
Enzyme deficiency: 255
Enzymes: 380
Epsilon alcoholism (periodic): 336–337
Ethyl alcohol: 182
Ethanol: 178, 183, 368
Europe, Eastern: 8
Evaluation of 200 patients followed-up three months after discharge from the St. Louis Detoxification and Diagnostic Evaluation Center: 273

Families: 200, 209, 223, 334; and clergymen, 215–218; attitude of, 345–346
Farnsworth-Munsell test: 377
Fascism: 117
Federal Bureau of Narcotics: 287
Federal Food and Drug Administration: 287
Finland: 13, 18, 91, 301. See also Scandinavia
Fleetwood, M. F.: 256

Forbes, J. C.: 253

*Fortune:* 221

Foundation for Research and Treatment of Alcoholism and Drug Dependence of New South Wales, Australia (FRATADD): 17, 66, 69–73, 74–75, 76, 81, 86

Foundation for Research and Treatment of Alcoholism of Australia (FRATA): 74

Fox, Dr. Vernelle: 150, 194

Fractionalization: in U.S., 140–143

France: 4, 5, 12, 14, 15, 119, 124, 297, 326; struggle against alcoholism, 20–40; economic aspects of alcoholism in, 20–22; declared production of wine, 21; social aspects of alcohol, 22–24; total consumption of wine, 23; total consumption of pure alcohol contained in all types of alcoholic drinks, 24; Special Comittee for the Study and Publicity of Alcoholism, 25–26; legislative and procedural measures, 26–29; publicity and educational action in, 29–32; awareness of anti-alcohol campaigns, 32–34; consumption of alcoholic beverages, 39, 127

Frankl, Viktor: 166

French State Railways: 6

Freud, Sigmund: 342

Gamma alcoholism: 336

Gastritis: 246–247

"Geltung's alkoholismus": 327

Genetic: factors and alcoholism and drug dependence, 324–325; differences and appetite for alcohol, 372

Georgia, University of, Southeastern School of Alcohol Studies: 232–233

Georgian Clinic, Atlanta: 150, 194

Germany: 13, 17

Giacomo, Umberto De: 120

Gitlow, S. E.: 178

Glatt, Max: 384

Glutethimide (Doriden): 246

Goldberg, L.: 317

Gordon, C. Wayne: 274

Government: and treatment, 151

Great Britain: 4, 148, 265, 275; and drinking driver, 11; licensing, 13; Society for the Study of Inebriety, 312; control of drugs, 354

Greater Boston Council on Alcoholism: 148

Group therapy: 61–63, 104, 180, 191–192, 242, 243, 280, 342, 385

"Habituation": 315–316

Halbach, H.: 357

Half-way houses: 345

Hallucinogens: 298, 316. *See also* Cannabis; LSD

Hamburg: 29

Hearnes, Gov. Warren E.: 273

Henderson, Y.: 355

Heroin: 297, 314, 327

Herron, Sir Leslie: 77

Hewlett, Augustus H.: 149

Hoff, Dr. Ebbe: 150, 252

Hoffer, A.: 256

Holland. *See* Netherlands

Home accidents: 12

Hong Kong: 297

Hormonal defects: 255–256

Hospitals: 385; in Italy, 121–122; treatment in, 241; and use of drugs to treat alcoholics, 243–246

House Subcommittee on Health Appropriations: 148–149

Hudson, Sir William: 81

Hughes, Harold E.: 149

Hungary: 15, 18

Huxley, Aldous: 314
Hypnosis: 63, 192

India: 297, 301
Individual, harm to: and alcoholism and drug dependence, 319
Industrial: accidents, 12, 225; programs, 196, 209; production, 333
Insomnia: 246
Institute on the Prevention and Treatment of Alcoholism: 311
Insurance: sickness and alcoholism, 7; companies in Norway, 51
*International Bibliography of Alcohol Studies:* 140, 145
International Congress Against Alcoholism, 14th, 1913: 117
International Congress on Alcohol and Drug Addictions, 28th, 1968: ix, 1, 171, 311, 313
International Congress on Alcoholism and Drug Dependence, 29th: 66, 78, 82, 313; and social and behavioral sciences, 84–85; results of, 85–89
International Council on Alcohol and Addictions: 8, 18, 66, 76
International Council on Alcohol and Alcoholics, 1967: 312–313
International Council on Alcohol and Alcoholism: 311–312
International Institute on the Prevention and Treatment of Alcoholism, 14th, 1968, Milan: 132–133
Italian Automobile Club: 126, 131
Italian Institute of Social Medicine, 125
Italian League for Mental Hygiene and Prophylaxis: 124
Italian Society for the Study of Problems of Alcohol and Alcoholism (SISPAA): 132
Italy: 4, 15, 116–133

Jantz, H.: 256
Jellinek, E. M.: 17, 24, 52, 92, 103, 146, 147, 174, 183, 315, 328, 329, 334, 336
Jellinek Award: 380
Jews: and alcoholism, 326
Joyce, C. R. B.: 314

Kalant, H.: 360
Karolinska Institute, Sweden: 86
Kentucky State Hospital: 149
Khat: 297
Kjolstad, Dr.: 386

Langton Clinic: 70, 73, 74, 79
Laurence, D. R.: 317
League of Arab States: 18
League of Nations: 3
Lecture-Discussion groups: 180–186
Legislation: 7–9, 300, 327, 352–357; in France, 26–29; in Czechoslovakia, 96–100
LeGo, Dr.: 24
Leuco-adrenochrome: 256
Levophed: 245
*Liberty* magazine: 158, 164
Lieber, C. L.: 378
*Life* magazine: 151
Liquor Control Commission, United Kingdom: 327
Liver. *See* Cirrhosis of the liver
Loneliness: 329
Long Island Council of Alcoholism: 195
*Look:* 221
Los Angeles: 266
LSD: 193, 314, 318, 319, 330

MacClearn, G. E.: 372
*Man Against Himself:* 332
Mann, M.: 183
Mann, Mrs. Marty: 147
Marathons: 196
Marchiafava, Senator: 117

Mardones, J.: 324
Marine transport: 11
Markey, Morris: 158, 164
Maryland: 274
Massachusetts State Pure Food and Drug Administration: 287
Massignan, Luigi: quoted, 130
May, Dr.: 24, 35
Medical College of Virginia: 150
Menninger, K.: 332
Mental: isolation, 58–59; illness, 120, 203
Merry-Go-Round of Denial: 206
Metabolic: defects, 252–255; differences and appetite for alcohol, 372–373
Methadone: 281, 288, 341
Methylphenidate hydrochloride (Ritalin): 245
Meyer, Dr. G. R.: 83
Milan: 132
Ministers. See Clergymen
Minogue, Dr. Silvester: 68
Missouri: 273, 275
"Mjod": 41–42
Moreno, J. L., 186
Morphine: 298
Mortality: and alcohol abstinence, 317
Mother. See Families
Motivation: for treatment, 5–7; for drinking, 56
Multidisciplinary approach in treatment: 338–339
Myerson, Dr. David: 150, 384

NAACP: 149
Narcotics: 301, 304
National Alcoholism Center: 140
National Council on Alcoholism: 147, 151, 164, 182, 188, 212, 218, 386
National Federation of Consultation Bureaus . . . , Belgium: 17

National income: percentage spent on alcohol, 95
National Labor Relations Board: 232
Netherlands: 18, 91, 118, 384, 386
Neuritis: 247–248
Neurotic reactions: patterns of, 58–60
New York City: 266, 275; Vera Institute of Justice, 274
Nikethamide (Coramine): 245
North American Association of Alcoholism Programs: 17, 148, 151, 164, 194
North Carolina: 274
Norway: 18, 386; treatment in, 49–54. See also Scandinavia
Nurses: and drug users, 284
Nutritional problem: alcoholism as, 14

Occoquan (Va.) Rehabilitation Center: 195
Occupations: 328, 329
Office for the Prevention and Treatment of Alcoholism and Drug Addiction, Quebec, Canada: 17
Ontario, Canada: 298
Opiates: 316, 318
Opium: 297, 328, 330
O'Quin, Sally: 151
"Oral fixation": 323
Organic complications: from alcohol abuse, 378–379
Osmond, H.: 256
Ottenberg, Dr. Donald J.: 196
Outpatient therapy: drugs for alcoholics in, 248–252
Overactivity, autonomic: 256–258
Oxford Group, Akron: 157

Paraldehyde: 243
Parents: and drug users, 287
Parole boards: and drug users, 289

Pathological appetite for alcohol: 374–378

Payza, A.: 256

Pedigree of the rats of the "non-drinker strain": 369

Pedigree of the rats of the "drinker" strain: 370

Perico, Giacomo: quoted, 126

Periodic alcoholism: 336–337

Perlis, Leo: 232

Persecutions: of drug users, 279

Personality: and alcoholism and drug dependence, 320–323

Peru: 297

Pharmacological appetite for alcohol: 373–374

Pharmacologists: drug defined by, 314

Phenmetrazine: 316

Physical dependence: 305, 318, 330, 336

Physicians. *See* Doctors

Physiological appetite for alcohol: 369–373

Pittman, David J.: 274, 313

Poland: 8, 18, 91, 265, 274, 275; Anti-Alcoholism Act, 1959, quoted, 263; sobering-up stations, 269– 270

Police: and drug users, 287

Popham, R. E.: 313

Population: percentage that are alcoholics, 91

*Powell v. Texas:* 267

Prague: 101–106; sobering up stations, 109–111, 114

President's Commission on Law Enforcement and Administration of Justice: recommendations on drunkenness, 268–269

Prevention: 13–16, 353–362; in Scandinavia, 47–49; in Italy, 123–125; and work world, 234–238; mental hygiene measures, 360

Prices: 355; in Scandinavia, 44; in Czechoslovakia, 92–93, 94

Prisons: treatment in, 9, 106–107, 347, 356

Prohibition: 135, 327

Promazine (Sparine): 244, 245

Protein supplements: 254

Protestant Churches: 135, 138

Psychic: pain, 278; dependence, 305

Psychoanalysis: 63–64, 191

Psychodrama: 107, 180, 186, 242

Psychological dependence: 318

Psychoses, alcoholic: 122–123

Psychotherapy: 58, 60, 342

Public health: and drug dependence, 299

Public intoxicants. *See* Drunkenness, public

Publicity: in France, 29–34

Punishment of addicts: 356–357

"Purple hearts": 314

*Quarterly Journal of Studies on Alcohol:* 147

Railroads: 10

Recognition: in U.S., 138–139; and the work world, 229–231

Rehabilitation: 345; goals and prognosis, 348–350. *See also* Treatment

Research: 229, 360–361; need for, 87–88; in U.S., 139–140

Respess, J. C.: 255

Rest farms: 176

*Revolving Door:* 265, 274

Richter, C. B.: 369

Rockefeller, John D., Jr.: 159

Roddy, Joseph: 273

Rodgers, D. A.: 372

Roe, A.: 325

Rum Rebellion: 67

Rush, Benjamin: 156

Rutgers: Center for Alcohol Studies, 124, 146, 147, 151, 164,

182, 188, 213; Addiction Foundation Summer School, 232

St. Louis: 266, 275; and public drunkenness, 270–273
Sales restrictions: 356; in Scandinavia, 48
*The Saturday Evening Post:* 164
Sauvy, Alfred: 29
Scandinavia: 14, 17; alcoholism in, 41–65; prices of alcohol, 44; consumption rates, 45; drinking patterns in, 44–47
Schematic representation of the relationship of appearance of alcoholism with daily intake of alcohol and duration of drinking habit: 375
Schematic representation of the relationship of appearance of fatty liver or liver cirrhosis with daily alcohol intake and duration of drinking habit: 379
Schools: and drug users, 286–287
Schulte, W.: 342
Schumann, Maurice: 29
Sears, Dr. William F.: 194
Sedatives: 244
Separations, family: 217–218
Seppilli: 121
"The Seriousness of Alcoholism in Italy": 126
"Services for the Prevention and Treatment of Dependence on Alcohol and Other Drugs": 16
Sharfenberger: 129
Shatwell, K. O.: 77
Silkworth, Dr. William D.: 157
Singapore: 297
Sobering-up stations: 8, 109–111, 269–270
Social: drinking, 9, 329; problem, alcohol as, 9–13, 205–212; isolation, 58; attitudes, influencing, 357–359

Society, harm to: and alcoholism and drug dependence, 319–320, 331–334
Socioeconomic: complications of alcoholism and drug dependence, 319–320; conditions, improvement of, 360
South Africa: 148
Soviet Union: 4, 13
Space travel: 11
Spain: 4, 15
Spritz, M.: 378
Stress: and drug use, 281
Supervisor: and the alcoholic, 226–228, 229
Sweden: 14, 91, 124, 265, 274, 275, 301. *See also* Scandinavia
Switzerland: 14, 118, 326, 380
Synanon: 150–151, 343, 384

Teachers: in France, 35
Temperance Movement: in U.S., 134–136, 203
Thailand: 297
Therapist: importance of attitude of, 339–340
Therapy: 57–58, 60–63, 186, 341–346. *See also* Group therapy
Thimann: 103
Tolerance: 318–319
Total number of deaths and commitments to psychiatric hospitals from 1946 to 1967, France: 37
Towns Hospital, N.Y.: 149, 157
Traffic safety: 10–11, 126, 332–333; in France, 34; in Australia, 81–82. *See also* Driving
Tranquilizers: 179, 298, 317, 332
Treatment: motivation for, 5–7; compulsory, 7, 346–348; in Scandinavia, 49–65; in Czechoslovakia, 100–111; by private doctors, 173–197; and clergymen, 212–220; and the work world,

229–231; clinic, 240–260; of alcoholism by use of drugs, 240–260; of drug users, 279–295; of alcoholism and drug dependence combined, 306, 337–348, 384; need for early, 337–338; need for long-term, 338; phases of, 340–346; costs, 386–387
Turmoil in U.S.: 143–144

Ugarte, G.: 378, 380
*Understanding and Counseling the Alcoholic:* 213
Unions: and alcoholics, 231–234
United Kingdom: and compulsory treatment, 346–348
United Nations: 118; Commission on Human Rights, 8; Narcotics Commission, 17
United States: 18, 91, 119, 128, 134–145, 296, 301, 304, 385; prison programs, 9; prohibition, 13, 327; Temperance Movement, 134–136; limbo period, 1925–1943, 136–137; last 25 years, 137–140; fractionalization in, 140–143; turmoil in, 143–144; voluntary agencies in, 146–151; and public drunkenness offender, 266–275; sources of information on alcoholism, 389–390
U.S. Federal Government: and employee alcoholism, 221–222
U.S. Supreme Court: and public drunkenness laws, 267–268

Varela, A.: 368, 376
Vera Institute of Justice: 274
Virginia. Bureau of Alcohol Studies and Rehabilitation: 241
Vitamin: deficiency, 247–248; supplementation, 252–255
Voluntary: agencies, 146–151, 385; treatment, 346

*The Wall Street Journal:* 221

Warlingham Park Hospital: 361
Wartburg, J. P. von: 380
Washington, D. C.: 266, 274
Weiner, Hannah: 186
Wife of alcoholic: 209, 334; and separation, 217–218
Wikler, A.: 322, 341
Williams, Roger J.: 252
Wilson, E. C.: 255
Wine: production of in France, 21; consumption of in France, 23; and cirrhosis of the liver, 129
Winick, C.: 349
Withdrawal: 340; from alcohol, use of drugs for, 243–246; from drugs, 280
Women: 112, 128, 171, 326; in France, 34–35
Work: and alcoholism, 221–238; impact of alcoholism on, 222–224; behavior at and alcoholism, 224–226; supervisor and the alcoholic, 226–228; and treatment, 229–231; and prevention, 234–238
World Health Organization (WHO): 3, 5, 6, 12, 18; definition of alcoholism, 265; classification of drug dependence, 297–298
World Health Organization. Expert Committee on Mental Health: 16, 88; and public health and drugs, 299; patterns of drug transfer, 303–304; 1966 meeting, 312; 3 groups of drugs, 315

Yale School of Alcohol Studies: 146. *See also* Rutgers Center for Alcohol Studies
Youth: 171; and alcohol, 15; in France, 34; in Czechoslovakia, 112–113; as drug users, 277–295

Zola, Emile: 121